Phenomenal Sydney

Phenomenal Sydney
Anglicans in a Time of Change, 1945–2013

Marcia Cameron

Foreword by Glenn Davies

WIPF & STOCK · Eugene, Oregon

PHENOMENAL SYDNEY
Anglicans in a Time of Change, 1945–2013

Copyright © 2016 Marcia Cameron. All rights reserved. Except for brief quotations in critical publications or reviews, no part of this book may be reproduced in any manner without prior written permission from the publisher. Write: Permissions, Wipf and Stock Publishers, 199 W. 8th Ave., Suite 3, Eugene, OR 97401.

Wipf & Stock
An Imprint of Wipf and Stock Publishers
199 W. 8th Ave., Suite 3
Eugene, OR 97401

www.wipfandstock.com

PAPERBACK ISBN: 978-1-4982-8931-3
HARDCOVER ISBN: 978-1-4982-8933-7
EBOOK ISBN: 978-1-4982-8932-0

Manufactured in the U.S.A.

To Ewen Donald Cameron,
Assistant Bishop of Sydney 1975–1993,
who gave me the idea for this book.

Contents

Foreword by Glenn Davies | ix
Acknowledgments | xi
Abbreviations | xiii

Prologue | 1
1 A Unique Brand of Anglicanism | 3
2 Laborers of the Right Kind 1788–1945 | 12
3 The Greatest Gift to Evangelical Anglicanism 1945–1950 | 36
4 Loyal Sons of the Reformation 1950–1958 | 53
5 The Last of the Englishmen: The Gough Years 1959–1966 | 78
6 One of our Own at Last: Marcus L. Loane 1966–1982 | 108
7 Sound and Fury 1982–1992 | 142
8 The Cost of Relationship 1993–2001 | 179
9 The Jensen Ascendancy 2001–2013 | 225
Phenomenon | 261

Interviews, Emails, and Letters Listed | 265
Appendix | 267
Bibliography | 277
Index | 287

Foreword

UNDERSTANDING THE DIOCESE OF Sydney has always been a challenge for outsiders, and indeed for some insiders as well. Firmly grounded on the Reformation principles of *sola scriptura, sola fide,* and *sola gratia* (by Scripture alone, by faith alone, and by grace alone), the Anglican Church in the Diocese of Sydney has, since its formation, sought to proclaim the gospel of our Lord Jesus Christ with clarity, conviction, and confidence in the teaching of the Bible as the revealed word of God. This was certainly the desire of the first chaplain to the colony of New South Wales, the Reverend Richard Johnson, and it has on the whole characterized the Diocese of the Sydney since its genesis in the late eighteenth century.

Dr. Marcia Cameron has provided us with an insider's view, in contrast to numerous publications from outsiders whose desire to criticize the diocese more often than not stems from a lack of appreciation of the character of the diocese as an expression of Reformed Anglicanism in the tradition of Archbishop Thomas Cranmer. However, Dr. Cameron's history of the Diocese of Sydney is nonetheless a critical evaluation. While she clearly expounds the theological commitments that shape the diocese as a whole, she is also able to expose some of its flaws, in particular, the flaws of its leaders. This is always a perilous task for an author, as such candor will inevitably invite criticism. However, Dr. Cameron has stood her ground and thus exposed some secrets of the diocese that others would prefer to have been kept secret.

While Dr. Cameron's book provides an overview of the Diocese under the leadership of its first five bishops or Archbishops, the focus of her attention is the period following World War II, and the episcopates of Howard Mowll through to Peter Jensen. Viewing the history of the Diocese through the lens of its next six leaders provides Dr. Cameron with an opportunity for exploring the way in which each of these leaders has contributed to the growth and development of the diocese, and strengthened its distinctiveness within the Anglican Church of Australia. Controversy is not avoided, whether it be relationships with the national church in the adoption of its constitution or the ordination of women, or indeed within the diocese, where strains and tensions invariably arise.

However, readers will find in Dr. Cameron's work a robust and informative analysis of the Diocese of Sydney which will assist in understanding the complexity and simplicity of the diocese, with all its flaws and all its strengths.

Glenn N. Davies

Archbishop of Sydney

Acknowledgments

The gestation time for *Phenomenal Sydney* has been almost a decade—five times longer than that of the proverbial elephant. This has given me the opportunity to ruminate and reflect on an amazing Australian diocese. Over the years I have been indebted to many people. Kim Robinson, Julie Olsten, and Erin Mollenhauer with the rest of the library team at Moore College Library; Louise Trott at the Sydney Anglican Diocesan Archives; the staff of Lambeth Palace Archives in London; and Joanne Burgess at the General Synod Archives have all been unfailingly patient and helpful. Megan Chippendale, Mysie Harper, Danusia Cameron, Donald Cameron, Peter Jensen, Glenn Davies, Paul Barnett, and Neil Cameron have each read the MS and given invaluable critiques. Ramon Williams very generously supplied the excellent photos taken during his time as diocesan photographer, of some key leaders. Helga de Jersey allowed me the use of her splendid beach house so that I had time to write. Many, many people were interviewed and each person gave me stimulating insights. It was like looking into a vast treasure house of experience, enigma, and wisdom. My thanks to the team at Wipf & Stock who have brought this long labor to birth.

My husband Neil has been an unfailing support and encouragement, and I am deeply grateful for such a partnership.

My hope is that this book will enable those who read it to gain new understanding of the phenomenon that, under God, is the Diocese of Sydney.

Marcia Cameron

August 2016

Abbreviations

AAPB	*An Australian Prayer Book*
ACC	Australian Council of Churches
ACR	*Australian Church Record*
ACT	Australian College of Theology
ACA	Anglican Church of Australia
ACL	Anglican Church League
ADB	*Australian Dictionary of Biography*
ADEB	*Australian Dictionary of Evangelical Biography*
ACR	*Australian Church Record*
AFES	Australian Fellowship of Evangelical Students
AIO	Anglican Information Office
AMiA	Anglican Mission in America
ARCIC	Anglican Roman Catholic International Commission
AUQA	Australian Universities Quality Agency
BCA	Bush Church Aid Society
CMS	Church Missionary Society
CEBS	Church of England Boys' Society
CENEF	Church of England National Emergency Fund
CESA	Church of England in South Africa
CMS	Church Missionary Society
CPSA	Church of the Province in South Africa
CSSM	Children's Special Service Mission

DEB	Diocesan Executive Board
ECUSA	Episcopal Church in the USA
HMS	Home Mission Society
IVF	Intervarsity Fellowship
IVP	Intervarsity Press
KYC	Katoomba Youth Convention
MHC	Marcia Helen Cameron
MOW	Movement for the Ordination of Women
NCLS	National Church Life Survey
NEAC	National Evangelical Anglican Congress
NSW	New South Wales
OAC	Open Air Campaigners
PCEU	Protestant Church of England Union
PTC	Preliminary Theological Certificate
REPA	Reformed Evangelical Protestant Association
SCEGS	Sydney Church of England Grammar School 'Shore'
SCEGGS	Sydney Church of England Girls' Grammar School
SDM	*Sydney Diocesan Magazine*
SSM	Society of the Sacred Mission
SU	Scripture Union
WCC	World Council of Churches

Prologue

AN ACUTE DILEMMA FOR a Christian historian writing about the behavior of human beings is the balance between truth and love. When is a person so far removed from the present age that everything about him (or her) can be said? Or is there always a duty to the dead, however far removed from us in time, to respect their privacy? On the one hand, if I were to speak and write publicly what I know about some contemporaries' behavior, I might be classed as unkind, destructive, or gossiping. If I wrote the same kind of things (which were true) about a Christian of 2,000 years ago, I would not be open to the same charges.

What is the difference between a recent event and one which is years into the past in terms of confidentiality? How long is secrecy necessary, and why? Does each decade or century change the requirements for discretion? For example, would King David's affair with Bathsheba have been kept secret by his contemporaries for a time? And for how long? In terms of the damage to other people caught up in a man or woman's sinful behavior, it is understandable that some secrecy is kind.

What is the historian's duty in examining and recounting the events of the past? Is the sin of the past always to be hidden? If not, where does the boundary lie?

Some of this history of the Diocese of Sydney is not the whole story, for the sake of charity and peace. Some confidential information has been given on the basis that it will stay confidential. This means that some of the real causes and effects remain hidden, despite their potency. This means that some men and women may be painted in cleaner, brighter colours than they deserve.

The biblical authors were honest about sin when it occurred: King David's adultery, Noah's drunkenness, Abraham's lies, Adam and Eve's rebelliousness. There can be plenty of reasons to keep some information confidential—for a start, what would be the purpose of making some information public? And how is love worked out, both towards the main player and towards those his or her actions have hurt? Is it possible to balance truth with love?

Perhaps there is no such thing as honest recent history, for these reasons. And when it is possible to write frankly, too much may have been lost, so the past is distorted by chunks of truth alongside chasms of ignorance.

Writing too close to the present also brings the problem of emotion, not recollected in tranquility, but in heat and bias.

Chapter 1

A Unique Brand of Anglicanism

THERE IS A PHENOMENON in Australia. It is a phenomenon of growth, of good news, of hope, of adherence to Reformation theology, and most of all, to a belief in the authority of the Bible. The phenomenon is the evangelical Diocese of Sydney, which is growing whereas some other dioceses are wondering how long they may survive; it is indigenizing Anglicanism in Australia, and in the process, forging a new identity for Australian Anglicanism.

The Diocese of Sydney is hated, loved, admired, and feared. It has more in common with evangelicals in whatever denomination than with many contemporary expressions of Anglicanism. It is often criticized as no longer Anglican, but at its heart is an adherence to classic Anglicanism, namely the principles enshrined in Cranmer's *Book of Common Prayer* and the *Thirty-nine Articles of Religion*. This diocese has continued to stand out from the other non-evangelical dioceses in Australia as a light on a hill, a beacon in the darkness. Its steady growth under God's hand, and its search for a contemporary identity in taking the gospel of Christ to Australians, and nurturing them to maturity, is the story of this book.

The Anglican Diocese of Sydney is regarded as a phenomenon, both within Australia and in the entire Anglican Communion.[1] For example,

---

1. Avis, *The Identity of Anglicanism*, 69; Carnley, *Reflections in Glass*, 16; Fletcher, *The Place of Anglicanism in Australia*, 14, 114–15; Frame, *A House Divided*, 15; Frame, *Anglicans in Australia*, 75; Frame and Treloar, *Agendas for Australian Anglicanism*, 27; Giles, *Jesus and the Father*, 25; Kaye, *An Introduction to World Anglicanism*, 81–82, 39, 168–74; Lawton, "Australian Anglican Theology," 184; Kaye, *A Church without Walls*, 32; McGillion, *The Chosen Ones*, vii–xii; Piggin, "Sydney Anglicanism," 184–93; Porter, *The New Puritans*, 150; Porter, *Sydney Anglicans*; Ward, *History of Global Anglicanism*, 13, 254–86; Thompson, *Religion in Australia*, 117.

In Australia, the word "Anglican" replaced "Church of England" sometime after 1 January 1962. In this history of the Diocese of Sydney the word "Anglican" is used

Peter Carnley, a former Primate of the Anglican Church of Australia and no friend to Sydney, queried whether the Diocese was Anglican at all, and wrote "sometimes one has the sense that the Sydney website is regularly consulted by those who imagine they are logging on to *the most extreme and idiosyncratic Anglican position*" [my italics]. Kevin Ward, in *History of Global Anglicanism*, makes a number of statements about the unique position of Sydney within the Anglican Communion. He states that Sydney is "probably unique in the Anglican Communion in the dogmatic clarity with which it holds its clear and narrowly-defined version of Reformed Anglicanism." Tom Frame refers simply to "Sydney's unique brand of Evangelicalism" and Sydney historian Brian Fletcher has written, "Not only was the Bible the sole repository of revealed truth, but . . . Sydney alone possessed the key to that truth."[2]

In addition, the Diocese is the subject of much contemporary criticism, aired by a number of books published in recent years. These include Muriel Porter's *The New Puritans: The Rise of Fundamentalism in the Anglican Church*, and, more recently, *Sydney Anglicans and the Threat to World Anglicanism*—the latter book's title leaving no room for ambiguity. Muriel Porter is a Melbourne Anglican, whereas Chris McGillion, author of *The Chosen Ones: The Politics of Salvation in the Anglican Church,* is a Sydney journalist fascinated by the Diocese, but certainly not an Anglican. While his book purports to be about the wider Anglican Church, in reality it focuses on the Diocese of Sydney in the 1990s and affirms the view that Sydney is very unusual in its brand of Anglicanism. He states that Sydney "represents one of the extremes of the great diversity of the Anglican Church worldwide."[3]

The criticisms levelled at the Diocese have been oft repeated in publications and in interviews conducted for this book. They are held with a high degree of strong emotion. For example, Muriel Porter acknowledged unashamedly that her approach is not objective but polemical.[4]

Criticisms include Sydney's resistance to the ordination of women to the priesthood, promotion of Lay Presidency (a lay person celebrating Holy Communion), lack of emphasis on the sacraments, a blurring of the line between laity and clergy, almost total abandonment of prayer book use[5] by

throughout.

2. Carnley, *Reflections in Glass*, 16, 87; Ward *History of Global Anglicanism*, 314; Frame, *Anglicans in Australia*, 83; and Fletcher, "Memory and the Shaping of Australian Anglicanism," 27.

3. Bouma in McGillion, *The Chosen Ones*, vii, xix.

4. Porter, *The New Puritans*, 6.

5. There are three recognized prayer books in the Anglican Church of Australia: the 1662 *Book of Common Prayer (BCP), An Australian Prayer Book (AAPB)* 1978, and

many rectors of parishes who claim to live by the principles of the *Book of Common Prayer (BCP)* and the Thirty-Nine Articles, lack of emphasis on ceremonial dress and architecture, "church planting" in other rectors' parishes and in other dioceses, and the stand taken against practicing homosexuality. Underneath all the charges lie the facts that the Diocese is very wealthy (even after its $160,000,000 loss in 2008), and that, against a backdrop of general decline in the number of Anglicans in Australia, Sydney Anglicans are growing in numbers. This provokes envy, resentment, and fear.[6]

Sydney is also said to be *arrogant*. Its wealth, its size, and its claim to be biblically orthodox seem to be the chief causes. An anecdote from a Baptist illustrates this perfectly.

> I also came to learn very slowly, and much later, about the "Sydney Anglican" thing. I had come to many of my own conclusions about it all long before I heard other people pontificate about it, and I have to say that everyone at that first Team meeting apart from me were Sydney Anglicans—St Barnabas, St Matthias, students or teachers at Moore College—and I am so glad I got to know them as people and formed my own ideas long before I knew there was a label, or a style etc. I always felt a bit different, but never excluded.
>
> One of the best lines I remember from a discussion one night was about some ecumenical event that was being speculated about. We were all laughing loud about how the charismatics would be over there, speaking in tongues and raising their hands, and the Uniting Church types would be in another corner, signing people up to Amnesty International and fighting for the poor, and the Catholics would be somewhere else running Bingo but also reaching people we were scared of, and the Baptists (my denomination) would be singing daggy 1970s choruses and dressing terribly. Someone in the group said: "What will we (the Sydney Anglicans) be doing?" Quickly someone quipped back: "Sitting round in a group being right."[7]

I am writing this history as one formed by and grateful to the people of the Diocese of Sydney. But, as any child appraising her parents, I am not uncritical. In this book I am setting out to examine the history of this unusual Diocese, and will focus on the period since World War II to seek to explain us to ourselves, and to explain us to those outside who watch in admiration

---

A Prayer Book for Australia (APBA) 1995. In addition, Sydney Diocese has published *Sunday Services*, 2001, and *Common Prayer*, 2011.

   6. Boyd, "Geared to High Heaven."

   7. Email to MHC from "a Baptist from a Sydney suburb" March 2012.

or fear or even hate. How did the Diocese of Sydney acquire its present identity? And how has it changed over the years? One characteristic of Sydney Diocese is that, despite a widespread perception, it is far from monochrome.

Why is Sydney Diocese the way it is, and what drives it? Taken as a whole, the following characteristics describe Sydney but each characteristic is not necessarily unique to Sydney.

First and foremost is a very serious commitment to the centrality of God's Word, the Bible. It is pre-eminently authoritative for the individual Christian and for the Christian congregations which meet as God's community. Accordingly, verbal communication, especially through the sermon, but also through the liturgy and print media, are of prime importance. Non-verbal symbols and ritual are suspect because their meaning is ambiguous. The commitment to the Scriptures comes straight from Reformed theology and it is hardly surprising that Sydney Anglicans have been labeled the new Puritans. A mark of the commitment to the authority of Scripture is daily bible reading. Archbishop Peter Watson, formerly Archbishop of Melbourne, has commented,

> I was asked as the new archbishop to take a bible study. I had an idea who would be there so I prepared a study, and took my Bible along, and I can't remember another person in the room with a Bible. I came home . . . and said "This is weird!" You might say that's purely cosmetic, but is it? That just would not happen in Sydney. Everybody would have at least a New Testament, and some would even have a Greek New Testament, but everybody would have a Bible. I thought, if I were asked to do this again, I'd print out the passage and hand it around. But these consisted of the leading clergy of the diocese, of whom 75% were evangelicals![8]

---

8. Archbishop Peter Watson interview with MHC 28.20.2008.

Archbishop Peter Watson, wearing a mitre

Because of the scriptural injunction in places like Matthew 28:19, the great commission of Jesus to "Go and make disciples of all nations, baptizing them in the name of the Father and of the Son and of the Holy Spirit, and teaching them to obey everything I have commanded you," there is an urgency about evangelism. For Sydney Anglicans this means explaining the saving gospel of Jesus: his death and his rising, to bring men and women to God. And then to instruct them in the Scriptures so that they may live lives obedient to God. This kind of focus on evangelism and sermons can seem very narrow-minded and lacking aesthetic sensitivity, to those who observe.

It is an exclusive faith, in that, according to Jesus' words in John 14:6, there is only one way to God: by faith in Jesus Christ and in no other. It is an inclusive faith because all who want to come to God through Christ, are invited.[9]

Second, it is a militant faith, because it has faced, and continues to face, many kinds of challenges and opposition. John McIntosh notes five major challenges demanding a response from Evangelicals at the beginning of the twentieth century.[10] These were:

1. The rise of a new concept of God and of revelation. According to the Anglo-Catholic Edward Pusey, unbelief was the parent, not the offspring of skepticism. The new scholarship's underlying assumptions

---

9. Matthew 11:28–30.
10. McIntosh, "Anglican Evangelicalism in Sydney," 33–111.

included ongoing human moral autonomy and intellectual progress, and the methodological need to exclude the supernatural.

2. The nature and understanding of the Bible in the light of new historical criticism and the new natural sciences. While the Cambridge triumvirate of BF Westcott, JB Lightfoot and FJA Hort, and George Salmon at Trinity College Dublin, rescued New Testament scholarship from German biblical criticism, there was no one to do that for the Old Testament. Darwin's theory of natural selection contrasted with God's purposeful action in creation. Purpose in human life, as well as at creation, had become a question rather than an assumption.

3. The rejection of the church doctrine of atonement. For example, in 1889, *Lux Mundi* rejected the penal substitutionary view (that Christ's death paid the penalty for our sins), stating "the punishment of the innocent instead of the guilty is unjust."[11]

4. The rise of materialism. In theological and philosophical terms, this term represented the idea that all life, even consciousness itself, found its origin in the matter of which the world consisted. It flowed out of Darwinism and essentially it was a form of atheism.

5. The Tractarian or Anglo-Catholic movement was in-house for Anglicans. While the movement began as an attempt to inculcate more holiness in worship, by looking back to pre-Reformation practices, and by focusing on the Eucharist, the movement fell prey to the theological liberalism of the latter part of the nineteenth century.[12] Anglo-Catholics taught that they were not merely a party within the Church of England; they were the fullest expression of Anglicanism and their aim was to catholicize the Church of England. After World War I, renewed in confidence and energy, they appeared to be a formidable opponent to Evangelicals.[13]

Challenges came in a new form with the dechristianization or secularization of Australia in the 1960s. It swept through this nation like a tsunami. It was the same in Britain and New Zealand, and to some extent, the USA. The resulting moral metamorphosis was revealed in the steep decline in church attendance, the rise of co-habitation in place of marriage, the rise

---

11. Lyttleton, "The Atonement," 309.

12. See for example, Ramsey, *From Gore to Temple*, 5–7, 278; McIntosh, "Anglican Evangelicalism in Sydney," 43–44, 53, 189; Bebbington, *Evangelicalism in Modern Britain*, 200–201.

13. Frappell "1933 and All That," 136; and Frame, "Recapturing the Vision Splendid," 146–47.

of divorce and re-marriage, homosexuality and sexual licence, the growing recourse to birth control and abortion, and irresistible social pressures for government liberalization for restrictions on drinking, Sunday closing and recreation.[14] The Sydney Diocese sought to meet these challenges and tried new ways to connect with a society which now bypassed the church. Hence the experiments with music, language, style, and location of worship. Sydney is now routinely criticized for being non-Anglican in discarding such things as robes and prayer books, organ and choir music, but this experimentation and flexibility is integral to the Diocese's primary commitment to evangelism.

Third, Sydney Diocese's focus upon equipping its clergy well academically and with a good grounding in biblical theology makes sense in the light of the challenges faced and its identity as a scion of the Reformation. Moore College, the diocesan theological college, has enormous influence as the thermostat of the Diocese.

Fourth, that Sydney Diocese is not "Anglican" foremost in its identity is hardly surprising, when one considers the liberal theology of some of many prominent Anglican leaders. While *BCP* and the *Thirty-Nine Articles* contained therein were "Reformed," Anglican leaders did not necessarily consider themselves bound by them. Their love of "tradition," their sacramentalism, their ritualism and their doctrine of the church (for example, that baptism conferred salvation) undercut Reformed doctrine. The consecration of a bishop in a non-evangelical diocese provides a picture of non-evangelical Anglicanism. The non-evangelical bishop is likely to be given a number of things at his or her consecration: a cross, a ring, a crozier, a cope and a Bible. An evangelical bishop is given a Bible and nothing else. The gift of the Bible alone is in accordance with the instructions laid out in the 1662 *Book of Common Prayer*.[15]

There are further differences, which mark Sydney Diocese out as distinctive. Whereas the bishop is a powerful leader in non-evangelical dioceses, and the governance is from the center, in Sydney the parishes are the key. It is in the parishes that the evangelism and teaching and discipling takes place, and the bishop, if he earns the respect of rectors and laypeople, has an advisory role. He has little real power. In an interview with Archbishop Harry Goodhew, I was asked "What is meant by the term, 'the Diocese?'" He went on to say, "I think the Diocese has meant for me primarily, the parishes—the people and those who minister to them."[16] Archbishop Peter

---

14. Callum Brown, *The Death of Christian Britain*, 190.
15. Archbishop Peter Jensen interview with MHC 16.7.2014.
16. Archbishop Harry Goodhew interview with MHC 15.2.2010.

Jensen stated: "In my view, an archbishop doesn't have much power: he has influence. He may motivate. He shouldn't use too much of the power he's got anyway. I was always cautious trying not to overuse power."[17]

To the irritation (and worse) of some General Synod delegates from other Australian dioceses, Sydney strongly resists centralism, for much the same reason as centralism is resisted within the Diocese. Just as the parishes are the powerhouses of the Sydney Diocese, so the dioceses are, or should be, the locus of energy and action in The Anglican Church of Australia. Not top-down but grass roots, up.

Empowering the parishes has also in time empowered the laity: men and women have been equipped and encouraged to involve themselves in what Sydney people call "ministry:" scripture teaching, running youth groups and Bible studies and ESL initiatives and helping in the church services too: leading, praying, reading the Scriptures and also preaching. Many attend Moore College and many enroll for its external theology courses.

An aspect of the Diocese, which is relatively unknown, is its concern for social justice. Perhaps the focus on evangelism and mission has masked this, but the Home Mission Society later called Anglicare, the Anglican Retirement Villages and the Archbishop's Appeal Fund are some of the big agencies that care for the old, the sick, the poor and the needy. Hammondcare, an independent welfare agency, has also received huge support from Sydney Anglicans.

In the drive to bring the treasures of the Gospel of Christ to the "lost sheep," youth work has been a strategy predating the period under review (1945–2013) in this book. It has included camps, missions where the gospel is the main focus, and scripture teaching in schools. Whereas "mission" can be a vague term when used by non-Evangelicals, and can mean a variety of ways to get people into church, to Evangelicals mission is primarily about gospel proclamation.

Many observers would point to Sydney Diocese's official position rejecting the ordination of women to the priesthood as its most salient characteristic. The foregoing indicates that this aspect of the Sydney Diocese, though its most famous and contentious, is only one characteristic (and one that is hotly debated by Sydney Anglicans) of what is a robust and growing company of the saints.

Many of the current criticisms of Sydney Anglicanism are levelled at the Diocese by those who are resistant to radical change of a particular kind: in particular changes to the way we worship and changes in the way

---

17. Archbishop Peter Jensen interview with MHC 16.7.2014. Others would disagree. The Rev. John Cornish has commented that Archbishop Jensen "Was very directive." Note to MHC December 2015.

the timeless truths of the Scriptures can be effectively communicated to contemporary Australia. These changes made by the Diocese embody an attempt to indigenize Anglicanism in Australia and have led to measurable growth and new hope for its future. But the theology has not changed. It remains essentially the theology of the *Book of Common Prayer* of 1662. This resistance to theological change is of huge significance.

Chapter 2

Laborers of the Right Kind 1788–1945

Jane Barker's letters are a good vantage point from which to view Evangelicalism in Sydney in the second half of the Nineteenth Century. She was the wife of the evangelical Bishop of Sydney, Frederic Barker. Her letters reveal the thoughts and piety of an Anglican Evangelical who arrived there in 1855. She wrote home regularly to her sister in England but only the letters of the first couple of years survive. Jane expressed a longing for spiritual life to quicken there: what was needed was no less than a "revival" among the "dry bones" in Sydney. Her commitment to the authority of the Scriptures and to private and corporate prayer was such that she wanted the people of Sydney to be "ever drinking at the pure fountain" of God's Word and "obtaining strength at His footstool." She believed that only the influence of the Holy Spirit could "put life into the skeleton form of outward observance, that surrounds us." The clergy she met on arrival mostly disappointed her and among them there were only a few Evangelicals. But evangelical clergy were "laborers of the right kind" and were essential if there were to be spiritual revival and growth in the church. The primary task of such laborers would be to remind people of God and his Day of Judgement.

Anglican Evangelicals like the Barkers found much more in common with the Dissenters than with fellow Anglicans who were of a different churchmanship. The common enemies of both evangelical Anglicans and Dissenters were "Popery and Infidelity." For instance, Frederic Barker would have nothing to do with the University and its Principal, the Rev. John Woolley, an Anglican clergyman, whose Broad Church faith shifted over the years toward Deism. Barker's dislike of Woolley, almost certainly on theological grounds, was cordially reciprocated.[1]

Opposition from High Churchmen, "Puseyites" and "Tractarians" caused the Bishop much stress—Jane Barker thought of troublesome clergy as nuisances like "mosquitoes." Barker's founding of Moore College in 1856 at Liverpool marked a high point of hostility when the appointment of the Rev. William Hodgson, an Evangelical, as the foundation Principal, aroused the opposition of the tractarian local clergyman, Charles Priddle. It was an age of sectarian battles. In the same way that Barker would have nothing to do with the Anglican Principal of the University, he kept "quietly aloof" from the Roman Catholic Archbishop, JB Polding.[2]

Strong-minded and single-minded, Jane Barker's words ring true as typical of the evangelical language and mindset of her day. The emphasis upon a personal faith in Jesus Christ is a striking characteristic of her thinking, and that continues as a mark of conservative Evangelicalism to this day. While this defines many other Christians, peculiar to Evangelicals is what has been termed the Bebbington Quadrilateral. This comprises biblicism (a reliance on the Bible as the ultimate religious authority), conversionism (a stress on the new birth), activism (an energetic, personal approach to religious duties and social involvement), and crucicentrism (a focus on Christ's redeeming work as the heart of essential Christianity).[3] While this definition may be too simple to accommodate nuances in the very wide spectrum of meaning now represented by the term "evangelical," it suits the Barker's kind of evangelical faith very well, and also, I think, that of the majority of Sydney Evangelicals in the 21st century. It is a religion of the heart: of personal conviction lived out in vital response to God's work of grace in redemption. As a result, conversion is critical, because it is a change of heart. DW Bebbington has written: "It [conversion] marked the boundary between a Christian and a pagan."[4] It has been well said that "Evangelicalism lives or dies, on evangelism."[5*]

The presence of evangelical Anglicans in Sydney from the very beginning can be traced to the activity of Evangelicals in London. It was the strategic brilliance of William Wilberforce, leader of the Clapham Sect and close friend of the Prime Minister William Pitt, who saw the Botany Bay

---

1. Cable "John Woolley," 436.

2. Barker, "Journal 1855–1856," 219–48.

3. Noll, Bebbington, and Rawlyk, *Evangelicalism*, 6; Larsen, *Biographical Dictionary of Evangelicals*, 1; Ward, "The Making of an Evangelical" 309, notes "insuperable difficulties" with this definition and with the dating of Evangelicalism.

4. Bebbington, *Evangelicalism in Modern Britain*, 5.

5. Kuan, "Evangelical Continuity in the Anglican Diocese of Melbourne," 9.

scheme as a base for evangelizing the South Seas. His associates put forward the name of the Rev. Richard Johnson for the work of chaplain to the colony.[6]

Johnson stayed in the colony until 1800, establishing the colony's first school in 1798. His letters reveal many discouragements, including active opposition to his ministry by Major Grose of the New South Wales Corps. Despite privations, he was committed to remaining in the colony, writing, "I am persuaded that I am where God aims and intends me to be, and till I see my way home more clearly . . . I think it my duty to abide where I am." Johnson was deeply concerned for the souls of his Sydney flock while also distressed at the physical condition of convicts upon their arrival and the treatment they received subsequently. But such was the indifference to his ministry in Sydney, particularly in the early days, that he confessed "I dread Sunday."[7]

Governors Hunter and Bligh made life much easier for Johnson. Hunter supported his work and Bligh, it seems, might well have been an Evangelical, since he sought out Evangelicals for his associates. The Rev. Samuel Marsden, also an Evangelical, and arrived as chaplain in the colony in 1794. He worked there and in New Zealand for nearly 45 years. Two other evangelical clergy arrived in the first decade of the 19th century: William Cowper and Robert Cartwright. They were "firm and undemonstrative Evangelicals, [who] stiffened the chaplaincy and saved its credibility."[8] They were also men with a heart for social welfare.[9]

The first Archdeacon of Sydney, Thomas Hobbes Scott, was appointed in 1824. A bankrupt wine merchant, and brother-in-law to Commissioner JT Bigge, he was a good administrator but not liked by his clergy. He resigned after four troubled years. William Grant Broughton succeeded him, arriving in 1829. He remained in Sydney till 1853. A well-born, scholarly High Churchman, Broughton became the first and only Bishop of Australia in 1836. This was also the year in which the Church Act, which effectively ensured that Anglicans had no greater privileges than other denominations, was passed.[10]

At the same time, Evangelicalism was growing respectable. According to Ken Cable,

---

6. Yarwood, "Samuel Marsden," 250.

7. Murray, *Australian Christian Life*, 17.

8. Ibid., 18, 34–35; Judd and Cable, *Sydney Anglicans*, 6.

9. Cable, "William Cowper," 79–80; Braga, "William Macquarie Cowper," 80–81; Cable, "Robert Cartwright," 211–12.

10. Judd and Cable, *Sydney Anglicans*, 26.

In England it was no longer the radical critic of the Church. It had triumphed in its mission to abolish slavery in the Empire; its overseas missions were flourishing; it was becoming the conscience of the powerful middle classes. The Evangelical wing of the Church was becoming the ally of the State. For Cowper, in the pulpit of St Phillip's at Sydney, the Church should co-operate as closely as possible with the State, whatever the implications of the Church Act.[11]

The Church Act financed the expansion of the denominations and, in particular the Anglicans, by paying clergy stipends and granting finance for church buildings. As a result, Broughton's clergy numbers grew substantially with some emigrating from England and others being ordained by Broughton locally. According to Cable they were "a substantial, if oddly assorted clerical force." By the time Broughton's successor arrived, there were 52 clergymen.[12]

In 1847, with the creation of three new dioceses and their bishops—Melbourne, Newcastle and Adelaide—Broughton became Bishop of Sydney. Of the new bishops, the academic Charles Perry of Melbourne was the sole Evangelical.

In Broughton's remaining years as Bishop of Sydney, the inner ring of clergy became firmly High Church, although evangelical clergy were still in parishes further afield. He attempted to establish a theological college, "Lyndhurst," and five men were ordained after attending it. It closed by 1849, partly because of the opposition aroused by its "Puseyite teaching."[13] The establishment of an Anglo-Catholic theological college in Sydney and its subsequent failure are very significant indeed. Had it succeeded, it would have trained clergy in the Tractarian or Anglo-Catholic tradition and Sydney Diocese would not have been the evangelical diocese that it is today. While Evangelicals and Anglo-Catholics shared much in common initially, the rise of liberal theology and its weakening of a commitment to biblical authority, meant a parting of the ways by the second half of the 19th century.[14] Some

---

11. Ibid. 6, Parsons, "Thomas Alison Scott," 430–33

12 Judd and Cable, *Sydney Anglicans*, 36.

13. Cameron, "Aspects of Anglican Theological Education in Australia," 47–53.

"High Church" refers to the party or movement within the Anglican Church which stressed continuity with Catholic Christendom, the authority of bishops, and the importance of sacraments, rituals, and ceremonies.

"Puseyites" were followers of Edward Bouverie Pusey who was an English churchman, and for more than fifty years Regius Professor of Hebrew at Christ Church, Oxford. He was one of the leaders of the Oxford (or Tractarian) Movement.

14. McIntosh, "Anglican Evangelicalism in Sydney," 105. McIntosh states that before the publication of *Lux Mundi* in 1889 there were great areas of agreement between

of the extremes reached by the turn of the century in England included: sacrifice of the Mass, elevation and reservation of the sacrament, extreme unction, the doctrine of purgatory, prayers for the dead, invocation of saints, and the whole body of Tridentine doctrine. Some ritualists encouraged fasting before Communion and even auricular confession.[15]

Frederic Barker arrived in Sydney in 1855. An Evangelical, his tenure has been the longest of the Bishops of Sydney: 28 years in all. When he arrived, despite the fact that the tractarian movement was only two decades old, most of the city clergy were High Churchmen and unsympathetic to his Evangelicalism.[16] During his long episcopate, Barker established a strong evangelical presence in Sydney. Since his time, while there have been fluctuations in the churchmanship of Sydney's leaders, Barker laid such a foundation that Sydney Evangelicals look to him as the architect of Sydney Evangelicalism. In his long episcopate Barker held strong convictions with unquestionable authority, but was moderate, effective and properly Anglican.[17] Two important strategies for creating an evangelical diocese were the appointment, where possible, of evangelical clergy and the establishment of a clergy training college. This, of course, had also been Broughton's strategy, but with a different kind of churchmanship.

It was clear to Barker on his arrival that he would need more clergy. The Gold Rushes had imposed new and heavy demands for more men, and many clergy were ready for retirement. The Society for the Promotion of the Gospel (SPG) had been a source of funding clergy stipends for Broughton, but its High Church orientation meant that Barker could not expect it to be favourably disposed to him. He managed to recruit "excellent young men," according to Jane Barker, within a year of his arrival. There were some disappointments, but over the years a steady stream of evangelical clergy answered his call.

Within two months of setting foot in Sydney he was making arrangements to set up a theological college to train local men. Moore College opened in 1856 at Liverpool, with an old friend, the Rev. William Hodgson, as foundation Principal. Hodgson stayed there until 1867. The College did not begin to train sufficient men for Sydney's needs for another 50 years,

---

Tractarians and Evangelicals

15. McIntosh, "Anglican Evangelicalism in Sydney," 66. "Tridentine" is the adjective from "Trent," referring to the Council of Trent which met between 1545 and 1563 to define the doctrine of the Roman Catholic Church. "Auricular confession" refers to confession to a priest. It is a 13th century dogma from the Council of Trent made canonically binding in the Roman Catholic Church in the year 1215.

16. McIntosh, "Anglican Evangelicalism in Sydney," 63.

17. Judd and Cable, *Sydney Anglicans*, 73.

but it was very important from the beginning in setting a standard for the clergy. Arrivals from England and Ireland were to be measured by it. No other Anglican theological college was established in Australia until 1878, the year that Trinity College at Melbourne University began training ordinands. Until then Moore College trained men for Melbourne; Goulburn, Ballarat and Bathurst, and North Queensland also sent their men there. It was the center of evangelical studies for Eastern Australia.[18]

The first few Principals of Moore College were "a dull lot," according to Cable. Hodgson himself gave good practical training but was an unremarkable clergyman in England. His successors were the Rev. Robert Lethbridge-King (1868-74) who came reluctantly, the Rev. Lukyn Williams (1878-84) who was very young and whose scholarship was as yet unripe, the Rev. Thomas Ernest Hill (1885-1888) under whom the College numbers dropped and the College actually closed, and the Rev. Bernard Schleicher (1891-1897) who was dying of tuberculosis when he was appointed. The evangelical character of the College was maintained under Hodgson's successors, King and Williams; but not under Hill and Schleicher who were High Church.[19] Moore College moved from Liverpool to its present site in Newtown in 1891.

Barker was always a keen supporter of Moore College. He had arrived in Sydney to find something of a vacuum and Cable notes,

> He proceeded to fill it with his evangelical faith—amid a wide degree of approval. [When he left] in the estimation of his clergy, Barker had so interwoven the existence of the Diocese with the existence of the evangelical ethos that the two could never be separated. It was Barker's memorial that their belief was to be well founded.

By 1881 the number of clergy had grown to 127 men—more than double the number when he arrived.[20]

A very tall man (6 feet 5 ½ inches tall), Barker set his stamp on education, on diocesan organization, social welfare and non-denominational societal work. According to Grant Maple, he and his wife Jane "viewed Sydney as a short-term missionary assignment," and were "appalled at the lifeless outward observance of Christianity" they found on their arrival in blatantly materialist Sydney of the gold-rush decade. Education

---

18. Cameron, "Aspects of Anglican Theological Education," 60.

19. KJ Cable conversation with MHC 30.4.1997; DWB Robinson interview with MHC 23.5.1997; Cable, "Robert Lethbridge King," 200–201, and Dickey, "Williams," 407.

20. Judd and Cable, *Sydney Anglicans*, 121; Murray, *Australian Christian Life*, 54.

was a priority throughout his tenure. The year after his arrival in Sydney he founded Moore College and that same year (1856) his wife Jane established a school for the daughters of clergy, St Catherine's School at Waverley, the first Anglican school for girls in the colony. Again in 1856 Barker established the Church of England Training School for teachers, and the position of Inspector of Anglican Schools. Barker's vision for diocesan schools was that they be nurseries for evangelism and instruction in Christian living. Barker also greatly valued the work of Sunday schools, and between 1867 and 1880 there was dramatic growth with the number of attendances trebling.[21]

He seized the opportunities created by the dual system of education (that is, of church and state), created in 1848, and by 1861 there were 107 Anglican schools in the Diocese. When in 1866 the Public Schools Act abolished the dual system and brought all state-aided schools under the control of the Council of Education, Barker secured the legal right of clergy to enter the schools to provide special religious instruction.[22] This right was continued in the Public Instruction Act of 1880, and is still effective in NSW state schools today.

In his recent Master's thesis on the Public Instruction Act of 1880, Riley Warren has written:

> These remarkable efforts of Bishop Barker for the spiritual welfare of the colony's children are still in evidence today. Davis [in his essay on Barker] shows Barker and his Church's hand behind the changes. It is no doubt to these achievements that Piggin refers [in *Spirit of a Nation*] when he claimed they were Evangelicalism's greatest achievements in social engineering. While Barker's efforts were pivotal in these concessions, Spaull shows he had an ally in [Sir Henry] Parkes, who declared that he would never give up a system of general religious instruction in the schools because he did not believe that any people would become a great nation without a profound faith, which was essential to the higher qualities of humanity and the performance of the higher duties of citizenship.[23]
>
> In 1856 Barker founded the Sydney Church Society, one of his first initiatives and of prime concern to him. He sedulously nursed it through its early years. Its focus was mission: to

---

21. Maple, "Frederic Barker," 23–26. "Piggin" refers to Stuart Piggin, author of *Spirit of a Nation*.

22. Ibid.

23. Warren, "Instructing Them in 'the things of God,'" 12–13, quoting Davis, "Bishop Barker and the Decline of the Denominational System," 145–46; Smith and Spaull, *History of Education in New South Wales 1788–1925*, 172; Piggin, *Spirit of a Nation*, 33.

bring the gospel to the people of the colony by establishing new churches. The Church Society was set up to provide funds for building new churches and for clergy stipends. It later became the Home Mission Society, and more recently, Anglicare. It had a number of spin-offs: while it was reasonably effective in redistributing the resources of the Diocese, it proved very effective in helping organize the laity for their eventual participation in church government.[24]

Barker did not restrict himself to Anglican organisations, nor to purely church activities. He became involved with the British and Foreign Bible Society within a month of his arrival in Sydney—a contrast with Bishop Broughton's aloofness—and he was elected vice-patron of the NSW Auxiliary. He supported and led community welfare: the work of the Sydney City Mission, founded in 1862 and the Home Visiting and Relief Society formed in the same year, for those in parlous circumstances. He and his clergy were leaders in aiding the victims of the 1864 flooding of the Hawkesbury and Shoalhaven rivers, and again in the drought of 1869.

Barker's legacy to the Sydney Diocese was immense. It was due, at least in part, to his long tenure (over a quarter of a century), his indefatigable drive and effective strategies to establish evangelical faith in his diocese, and also his ability to choose suitable men for key positions, in particular the principals of Moore College. In the ensuing years of less effective episcopal leadership, key clergy and laymen carried the torch he had lit.

While the evangelical character of Sydney Diocese waned somewhat at certain periods following Barker's death, in essence the evangelical stamp he gave the Diocese has endured to the present. By contrast, the evangelical Archbishop Charles Perry of Melbourne did not implement Barker's stringent policy of importing only evangelical clergy. Nor did his diocese have an evangelical theological college. Ridley College Melbourne was established long after Perry's episcopate, in 1910. The result, for Melbourne, was a mixture of different kinds of churchmanship.

Barker's successor Bishop Alfred Barry (1884-1889), headmaster and academic, was quintessentially an educator. He is not easy to pigeonhole in terms of his churchmanship. In his youth he had sympathies with both Evangelicals and Tractarians. He was a Broad Churchman, having little interest in the trappings of episcopacy or sacrament, and is best described as a "liberal-minded academic." He did not like controversy among Anglicans

---

24. Judd and Cable, *Sydney Anglicans,* 95; Maple, "Frederic Barker," 23–26.

and was not a Party man. Sydney Evangelicals regarded him as "not one of us."[25]

At the beginning of his episcopate he supported wholehearted "promotion of education in all its grades and forms."[26] He stated that the Church's role was to influence society, saying it should "strive any way and every way, so far as we might rightly do so, to make the education of the country a Christian education." This was in 1884, in his first Synod charge. But his enthusiasm for religious instruction in public schools waned after the first two years, as did his support for Sunday schools.[27]

While Barker eschewed the University, Barry was elected a Fellow of the University Senate. The University of Sydney, established in 1850, during Broughton's episcopate, was a secular university, owing to WC Wentworth's strong influence and his abhorrence of sectarian strife. This had consequences for the Anglican Diocese of Sydney. First, it dealt the death-knell to Broughton's theological college "Lyndhurst," a college which he had dreamed would become Sydney's university. Second, it meant that a college to teach theology would need to be established separately. Third, St Paul's College, while established as the Anglican college adjoining the University, was a residential college only, since all teaching was to be given at the University. In these ways Sydney University was markedly different from most of its English and Irish counterparts.[28] Barry's vision for St Paul's College, which bore no fruit, was to establish a close link with both the University and with Moore College. (The latter moved to the edge of the University campus in 1891, but this was after Barry had resigned from the See of Sydney).

In the five years of his short episcopate, he moved, as his Synod charges reveal, away from supporting the sterling work of religious instruction which reached some 18,500 Anglican children in 1885. Instead he focused on the work of the Anglican Church's Day Schools, which reached only 2,000 children. Sunday schools were not one of his priorities either. He did not mention them in his 1885 Charge, despite the fact that they catered for 19,000 children.

Warren concludes his analysis of Barry's educational focus with these words:

---

25. Judd and Cable, *Sydney Anglicans*, 125, 127–28; Barry is not listed in the *ADEB*.
26. Warren, "Instructing them in 'the things of God,'" 42.
27. Ibid., 43–45, 54, 69, 70–71.
28. Cameron, "Aspects of Anglican Theological Education," 53; Judd and Cable, *Sydney Anglicans*, 59–60; Turney, Bygott and Chippendale, *Australia's First*, 15–20, 29–40.

The *Proceedings* [of the Sydney Synod] reveal time and again that Barry showed only passing interest in the education of those he considered lower or working class—that is, the majority of the children in his flock. "Influence," "prestige," "power," "privilege," "leadership," "high social standing," "men of higher culture," "children above the working classes," "of the middle and upper class"—such words and phrases, used by Barry, indicate an élitist stance. Barry's commitment to the higher levels of society, in which he held a prime position, appears to be a strong motivator for his push to establish Grammar schools into the Diocese . . . He wanted to recreate the Great Public Schools of England in Australia: the English Church assisting the creation of Greater Britain.[29]

Barry's lasting memorial was Anglican education—the schools he established and those he successfully revived. Five flourishing Sydney Anglican schools owe much to Barry. He ensured that The King's School (established in 1831) became responsible to the Sydney Synod in 1885 and he appointed a new, reforming headmaster. The result was that enrollments had doubled by 1888. He established St Andrew's Cathedral Choir School in 1885, gave strong support to St Catherine's School at Waverley, the Clergy Daughters School established by Jane Barker (1856), foreshadowed the founding of SCEGGS Darlinghurst (which opened in 1895) and as his last official act before leaving Sydney, formally opened "Shore," Sydney Church of England Grammar School (SCEGS), in May 1889. Against these achievements must be balanced his neglect of religious instruction in schools, and of Sunday schools, where by far the greatest number of Anglican children were to be found. In addition, it was he who brought out TE Hill, a High Churchman, to be the new Principal of Moore College in 1885. As we have seen, under Hill the College declined. There were only three students enrolled by the time of Hill's last term in 1888. The College then closed down, reopening in 1891 with a new Principal.[30]

Barry's successor William Saumarez Smith (1890-1909) became the first Bishop of Sydney to be designated Archbishop.[31] Formerly Principal of St Aidan's College Birkenhead, he was an Evangelical, a quiet, scholarly man of deep personal piety. He was not a strong leader and his episcopate was a difficult one. It began badly, with a dispute over his election. The two other nominees for the position were both Evangelicals, an indication of

---

29. Warren, "Instructing them in 'the things of God,'" 71-2.

30 Loane, *A Centenary History of Moore College*, 69-71, 91.

31. This happened in 1897 when the General Synod resolved that all metropolitans be given the title "Archbishop."

the strength of Evangelicals in Sydney by 1890. The election procedure was bungled by the bishops' chairman, the ageing Mesac Thomas of Goulburn, with the result that the non-evangelical bishops, in particular Kennion of Adelaide, feared that the election procedure would foist on them an unsuitable Primate. The controversy soured relations between dioceses for years.[32] Aware that there was a strong probability that Sydney would withdraw from the rest of the Australian Church unless Smith was appointed, the bishops had no choice but to concur in Smith's election. From Sydney's point of view, a number of dioceses which had begun as Evangelical, had already become Anglo-Catholic or liberal in their theology, so an Evangelical bishop was vital for the continuity of the Evangelical tradition in Sydney.[33] It was vitally important for Sydney to be tough-minded: otherwise it too would lose its evangelical character.

In addition, Sydney Diocese was becoming more politicised, with the growth of the power of the synod. As a legislative body its members were pushed into party positions, each trying to ensure that its views triumphed over the others. The most powerful of the parties to emerge was the PCEU (Protestant Church of England Union), founded by Mervyn Archdall. Led by the clergy, its platform was to prevent any expression of Anglo-Catholic practice. Anglo-Catholicism was, in Evangelicals' eyes, the greatest threat they faced. Since the infiltration of liberal and pre-Reformation doctrine into Anglo-Catholicism, the latter seemed to pose a real threat to the gospel, with its sacerdotalism, its focus on the Eucharist, its pre-Reformation rituals and its unbiblical dogma such as Purgatory and prayers for the dead.

Of great moment in Sydney's spiritual life was the Grubb mission in 1891. George C Grubb, an evangelist from the Church of Ireland, came as missioner to the colonies as a direct result of the Keswick Convention. The very popular Keswick placed much emphasis upon experience of the Holy Spirit and on personal holiness. The Grubb mission (in Victoria as well as Sydney) revived evangelical commitment and confidence and a number of future Sydney leaders were converted during its meetings: notably EP Field who later founded the OAC (Open Air Campaigners), RBS Hammond and HS Begbie, both prominent Sydney clergy.[34] The Grubb mission also led to the formation of the Sydney Clerical Prayer Union. This was centered on

32. Robinson, "The Origins of the Anglican Church League," 141–42, *Lucas* 21 & 22; Judd and Cable, *Sydney Anglicans*, 140–1; Treloar, "William Saumarez Smith." 346.

33. This was a continuing trend in the Anglican Church in Australia. Such dioceses were, for example: Bendigo, Gippsland, Bathurst and Goulburn. The bishop had the power to change the churchmanship of his diocese chiefly by the clergy he appointed and the training they received.

34. RBS Hammond originally came from Victoria.

Moore College, which was the springboard for much evangelical activity, including Reformation rallies.

Moore College gained a new Principal in 1897: the Rev. Nathaniel Jones. His tenure at the College was enormously significant for the future of the Diocese of Sydney, although it was relatively short: he died at the early age of 50. An Evangelical, Jones' influence was great because he built Moore College into a significant theological college, and under him 104 men were trained and ordained for Sydney. After this, Moore College trained most of the clergy working in the Diocese of Sydney.

His many speaking and leadership engagements were with Protestant Christians, not just Anglicans. This has continued to be a characteristic of Sydney Evangelicals, and Jones' own position has probably been influential in the formation of a Sydney Diocesan concept that being Anglican is of only relative importance.[35] Jones' men—the students who passed through his hands in the first decade of the twentieth century—came into their own as diocesan leaders in the 1930s, at the beginning of Howard Mowll's episcopate. It is through their influence that we see Jones' very significant contribution to Sydney Diocesan identity. Such men were AL Wade, SH Denman, PJ Bidwell, SJ Kirkby, ES Langford-Smith, DJ Knox and RB Robinson. Third, his involvement with the Keswick holiness movement, which had its epicenter at Moore College, tied a particular kind of evangelical expression to Moore College. Jones' emphasis on personal holiness, according to J McIntosh in his recent PhD thesis, was not insular and inward-focused, as has been previously thought. Instead, "the premillennial Keswick holiness preacher by no means discouraged Christian participation and exercise of influence in society."[36]

Archbishop Smith died in 1909 and Jones in 1911. Following their deaths the years up to the mid 1930s were a hiatus in the evangelical leadership of Sydney. None of the three most influential leaders during this time was a robust Evangelical: neither Archbishop Wright, nor Moore College Principal DJ Davies nor AE Talbot, Dean of the Cathedral.

John Charles Wright (1909-1933) had been in the forefront of the Evangelical Renewal Movement in England, Archdeacon of Manchester and a member of the evangelical Simeon Trust before his appointment to

---

35. For example, Archbishop Marcus Loane's statement, "I am a Christian; I am a Protestant; I am an Anglican. It is of far greater significance to be the first rather than the second, or to be the second rather than the third." *Sydney Year Book* 1981, 224.

36. McIntosh, "Anglican Evangelicalism in Sydney," 279, 277–294; Cameron, "Moore College under Nathaniel Jones," 96–117; Cameron, "Aspects of Anglican Theological Education," 182; Lawton, *The Better Time to Be,* 34 and 43; Yarwood-Lamb, "Out of All Proportion," 98–101.

the See of Sydney. Those who supported his appointment hoped he would be a moderating influence, and he was favoured over Nathaniel Jones' good friend Griffith Thomas, whom it was thought might be too extreme and too narrow in his brand of Evangelicalism. It was hoped that Wright would work well with the other Australian bishops and that Sydney, being the senior metropolitan diocese, might thereby retain the Primacy.[37] McIntosh has thrown further light on JC Wright's background. As Archbishop-elect of Sydney, in 1907 he was the first Chairman of the Group Brotherhood, later named the "Anglican Evangelical Group Movement." McIntosh has stated:

> Only later did its leaders . . . define the (liberal) principles of their position, which probably never had strict boundaries . . .
> When John Charles Wright became Archbishop of Sydney (1909) he called two early "Brothers," David John Davies and Edward Albert Talbot, to be Principal of Moore College (1911) and Dean of St Andrew's Cathedral (1912) respectively. These three men self-consciously brought to Sydney—its diocese, theological college, and cathedral—their liberal broadening of the evangelical spectrum.[38]

Wright was convinced that Anglicans were poorer without variety, and offered positions to a range of churchmen. Hence his appointment of Davies and Talbot, both of whom were regarded by Sydney Evangelicals as disturbingly liberal in their theological outlook.[39] Sydney Evangelicals' misgivings about Davies's and Talbot's liberal theology were well-placed, especially as both were active and influential for almost a quarter of a century. Despite his connection with the Group Brotherhood, Wright was not regarded with the same suspicion because he enforced canon law, thereby giving Tractarians no quarter.

Wright for the most part exercised a non-directive leadership, which in time gave opportunities for the exercise of power elsewhere. But shortly after his arrival he provoked a major row with St James' Sydney, the congregation in central Sydney's oldest church building and formerly the principal church in the colony. The row erupted over the appointment of a new rector. Wright, a constitutionalist above all else—he sought to administer the law, rather than make it—required the Rector-elect, Dean Kite of Hobart, to give an undertaking not to wear the chasuble.

37. After 1900 the Bishop of Sydney was no longer *ex officio* Primate. Judd and Cable, *Sydney Anglicans,* 141, 160, and 166; Robinson, "The Origins of the Anglican Church League," 21, 22, 157–64.

38. McIntosh, "Anglican Evangelicalism in Sydney," 358.

39. Cameron, "Aspects of Anglican Theological Education," 180.

The chasuble was a pre-Reformation vestment dear to Anglo-Catholics because it was a symbol of continuity with the Catholic Church. Evangelicals understood it to symbolise the priest as the mediator in the sacrifice of the Mass. The chasuble was illegal under Canon Law.[40] Wright and Evangelicals perceived it to be the thin end of the wedge of encroaching Anglo-Catholicism. Ritualistic practices had been developing since the 1880s at St James': there were a robed choir and servers, flowers, candles and a brass cross on the Holy Table, and since 1900, the chasuble. Kite was not prepared to give Wright an undertaking not to wear the chasuble (despite being a High Churchman he had never worn the eucharistic vestments). For a time Wright faced a great deal of hostility, both from a section of the St James' congregation and from the Press. He found it difficult to appoint a rector to the parish until he threatened parish leaders with the appointment of an Evangelical. At this they capitulated and a former Archdeacon of Wagga, WF Wentworth-Shields, became Rector.

The resignation of the Rev. FJ Albery, Rector of Christ Church, St Laurence, Sydney, in 1910, precipitated a similar crisis. The first historian of Christ Church wrote:

> 19th April is a day to be remembered by all friends of Christ Church, that historic and venerable stone building, whose steeple still points upward, like the Finger of God, amidst the toil and turmoil and rush of the modern world. We have seen how each succeeding priest has patiently taught the faith of the Holy Catholic Church through the changing years of an ever growing city, and how, by degrees, the symbolic and beautiful ritual of the Church has aided man to sense something in his outward devotion, reminding him of the glory of the Lord in this holy place ... But on this day, 19th April, 1911, these Vestments had to be laid aside, not to be used again till permission is given for their use ... At the Easter Vestry Meeting, the Churchwardens were authorized and directed to make public the statement which all may read in the church today, and here this important matter must be left "with the full intention that their use shall be reintroduced at the earliest possible opportunity ... under strong protest and without in any way admitting any right on the part of the Archbishop to exact such an undertaking from the priest duly chosen by the nominators."

The new Rector, the Rev. CM Statham,

---

40. Bray, *The Anglican Canons 1529–1947*, 12: "It shall suffice that the dress of the minister at all times of his ministration be a surplice of white linen of accustomed form, a scarf or stole of silk, and the hood belonging to his degree."

> ... had sought to sign the undertaking [not to wear the eucharistic vestments] under protest; this the Archbishop would not allow, but consented to write down upon the paper embodying the undertaking a note to the effect that it was to be signed without protest, thus making it quite clear that the signing was compulsory.[41]

Wright's stand effectively put a stop to the growth of Anglo-Catholicism in the Diocese of Sydney. All clergy licensed to parishes in the Diocese had to agree not to wear the eucharistic vestments and so the number of Anglo-Catholics willing to work in the Diocese dwindled.[42]

The other real threat for Evangelicals was Modernism—another name for liberal theology. Davies and Talbot were moderate Liberals and associated professionally and on a friendship basis with Dr Samuel Angus, a Presbyterian Professor at the United Theological Faculty of St Andrew's College. Angus had caused much disquiet amongst all conservative Protestants by his liberal theological position. They claimed he was a pagan philosopher who denied fundamental Christian doctrines.[43] Angus' book, *Essential Christianity*, indicates the sort of liberal theology he held. About the Atonement, he wrote,

> The truth of the Atonement lies not in the acceptance of one of the many competing verbal theories on the relation of the death of Christ to God and to man's sin. The truth of that doctrine lies in the religious apprehension of the fact that Jesus' death was the natural and inevitable end of a life wholly to do the will of the Heavenly Father ... The effective truth of the doctrine consisted in a recognition that the Atonement was not an isolated fact but the supreme illustration of the moral order, convincing us that the sacrificial life, which was the highest life for Jesus, is the highest life for his followers ...[44]

In another part of the same book he wrote:

> ... the essence of Christianity has too often been confounded with, or even based upon, alleged historic facts of debatable

---

41 Allen, *A History of Christ Church S. Laurence Sydney*, 104–5, 107–8. For many years the public statement could be read on a plaque in the church porch.

42. Judd and Cable, *Sydney Anglicans*, 160–64; Allen, *A History of Christ Church S. Laurence Sydney*, 85–89, 100–107.

43. Emilson, *A Whiff of Heresy*, 227–29; Judd and Cable, *Sydney Anglicans*, 227.

44. Angus, *Essential Christianity*, 110.

historicity (such as the Virgin Birth, the miracles, the physical Resurrection of Jesus, the bodily Ascension to heaven, . . .)[45]

Angus was a formidable scholar with significant influence and dangerously heterodox views. Evangelicals were pushed to their limits to counter him in theological debate.[46] A man like Angus showed how important it was to train evangelical clergy and laity to develop a robust biblical faith and to have the tools with which to counter others like him. There seems to be no evidence that Davies himself attempted to refute or counter Angus' views.[47]

During Davies' long tenure, Moore College students were fed a mix of theology. At least some visiting lecturers, like Digges La Touche, George Chambers and Corrie Glanville, were Evangelicals, but Davies himself did most of the teaching. ML Loane, later Archbishop of Sydney, recalls Davies' homilies in chapel on the Gospel of John, when on repeated occasions Davies never got beyond an examination of the first two words: *en arche* ("In the beginning").[48]

McIntosh, in his evaluation of three Moore College Principals, quoted Davies on Scripture:

> . . . [it] "is the documentary evidence" of both the "history and human experience" that attests "the fact of progressive revelation" (undefined) and "contains [sic] the substance of God's message to man."

McIntosh comments,

> Davies had not defined his term "progressive revelation" and he had said only that Scripture "contains" the substance of God's message to man . . . The big issue with Davies was the inspiration and authority of Scripture.[49]

In his Moorhouse Lectures Davies wrote in these terms about the Bible:

> But reverence [for the Scriptures] that is not intelligent runs great risk of becoming enslaved to a mechanical view of inspiration

---

45. Ibid., 12.
46 Emilson, *A Whiff of Heresy*, 175, 212–13, 225.
47. McIntosh, "Anglican Evangelicalism in Sydney," e.g. 442.
48 interview with MHC 5.2.1996.
49. McIntosh, "Anglican Evangelicalism in Sydney," 378 and 409. The term "progressive revelation" was used by liberals to refer to ongoing revelation by God, *beyond* the Scriptures. For Evangelicals, it refers to God's unfolding revelation *within* the Scriptures.

as a kind of dictation, degrading the living word of God into a collection of oracles and proof texts, leaving the reader open to the dangers of a hard literalism and a grotesque realism. People who drift into this attitude towards Holy Scripture really believe traditions about the Bible rather than the Bible itself. They do not see the Bible clearly, as it is, but in a kind of fog in which they go astray . . . It is among the literalists and the verbal inspirationists that subjectivism runs riot and strange heresies and schisms arise.

Another danger of unintelligent reverence is its tendency to obscurantism, which ignores the human element in Scripture, creates unnecessary difficulties and makes real difficulties greater by failing to grasp the principle of progressive revelation and by neglecting to relate the writings to their historical background.[50]

By contrast, TC Hammond, Davies's successor at Moore College, wrote, with beautiful clarity:

In the nature of the case, biblical inspiration is *verbal*, i.e. the God-breathed message of the writer is presented in *words*, words that were *approved* by the Holy Spirit as they were expressed by the writer. This is not to say that each word was *dictated* mechanically.[51]

Davies" teaching on the Atonement was distinctly liberal: in essence it was that "the death of Christ had an effect not upon God but only upon man."[52]

Wright's election to the See of Sydney was largely the result of the formation of a new evangelical party: the ACL (Anglican Church League). Canon Francis "Bertie" Boyce, an "astute political tactician" wanted to unite Evangelicals into a moderate group acceptable to all the Church parties, and able to influence the Australian Church. He wanted as broad a base as possible for future Anglicanism. Wright was accordingly their choice as Archbishop. The ACL is fundamental to an understanding of the Diocese of Sydney. It was not narrowly exclusive, but small, efficient and clergy-led. It promoted public lectures, revived *The Church Record* which became a

---

50. Davies, *The Church and the Plain Man*, 235–36.

51. Hammond, *In Understanding be Men*, 33.

52. McIntosh quotes J Gresham Machen (1881–1937), an American conservative evangelical scholar, almost Davies' exact contemporary. McIntosh, "Anglican Evangelicalism in Sydney," 427.

Sydney-based conservative evangelical paper, and most important of all, pre-selected candidates for elected positions in the Diocese. By 1921 it was careful to include High Churchmen in one quarter of the elected positions, though not the important ones. By 1933 the ACL issued its first formal "how to vote" ticket. ACL members won over 80% of the "strategic" positions in successive synod elections, and rarely was an ACL nominee defeated. Wright's aloof leadership and weakened health after the Great War gave this powerful body plenty of scope for its influence. It is arguable whether any Archbishop of Sydney has had substantial independent power since the rise of the ACL.[53]

The cataclysm of world war descended within the first decade of Wright's episcopate. For Archbishop Wright, the Great War (1914-18) was a holy war. Parish clergy who stayed at home while urging their young men to sacrifice their lives were made to feel apologetic about tending the flock at home and by contrast Dean Talbot won approval for his term of service overseas and glory for his bravery as a chaplain under fire at Gallipoli. Wright made a practice of farewelling troopships from Woolloomooloo in the early morning, consistent with his support for conscription as a moral issue, but these dawn visits left him with weakened health for the rest of his long episcopate. After the War pews emptied, partly because of the young men who did not return from war and partly because of unbelief. The end of the war brought home the realisation that Australia was becoming a pagan nation and that the Church's spiritual leadership had been rejected by many Australians.[54]

Wright died in 1933 after an episcopate of some 24 years. In reaction to his rather weak leadership, conservative Evangelicals wanted a strong man for their next Archbishop. AE Talbot, the Dean, and DJ Davies of Moore College were the President and Vice President of the ACL at the time of the election. They promoted Joseph Hunkin, Archdeacon of Coventry, who had the reputation of a Modernist (Liberal). He *was* a Liberal. According to J McIntosh: he had "made his mark as a liberal Biblical scholar," and was a member of the Group Brotherhood. It is possible that Davies and Talbot did not know how liberal Hunkin really was.[55] He failed even to make the short list in the election process. Given the state of Moore College at the time, it is no surprise that Davies' candidate would be rejected.

---

53. Judd and Cable, *Sydney Anglicans*, 165–70; Robinson, "The Origins of the Anglican Church League," 160–61.

54. Judd and Dickey, "John Charles Wright," 412; Judd and Cable, *Sydney Anglicans*, 178–82.

55. McIntosh, "Anglican Evangelicalism in Sydney," 342, 355, and 459.

The only other candidate was Howard Kilvinton Mowll, a missionary bishop in West China. Mowll was already well known in Sydney and much admired for his evangelical zeal. A big man, with great presence, he looked and acted like the leader Sydney conservative Evangelicals sought. Mowll (1934-1958) was Archbishop of Sydney for a quarter of a century. His episcopate, like Bishop Barker's, was enormously significant for the establishment of a strong evangelical Diocese. The election of Mowll made Davies very angry and he resigned from the ACL.[56]

Archbishop Howard West Kilvinton Mowll, right hand side

DJ Davies died in 1935 and Talbot died the following year, and with their passing the triumvirate of Wright, Davies and Talbot ended. Davies had been on all the major diocesan committees, and as a result was often absent from Moore College. In addition, his teaching had deteriorated over the years. Ill health, tiredness and constant opposition must have contributed to this. By the 1930s the College was in the doldrums. The College debt stood at £5,000; a new chapel, and more adequate financial provision for the staff were needed, and existing buildings would have to be rebuilt or extensively repaired.[57] When Mowll first saw the state of Moore College he wanted "to shake Moore College from head to toe," according to ML Loane,

---

56. Loane, "Howard West Kilvinton Mowll," 272–74; Loane, *Archbishop Mowll*, 1–12; Robinson, "The Origins of the Anglican Church League," 161.

57. ML Loane interview with MHC 5.2.1996; Loane, *A Centenary History of Moore College*, 140. *Sydney Year Book 1936*, 311.

whom Mowll sent to Moore College as a chaplain while Davies was still Principal.

Davies was distinguished by his personal kindness, his scholarly mind, his leadership of liberal Evangelicals who sought a *via media,* and his long term of office as Principal of Moore College. Obituaries spoke of a man who was "teacher, scholar and preacher ... also a sportsman and musician," who was "a keen student of the social problem," "a Christian, a scholar and a gentleman." [58]

Many clergy wept openly at his funeral and fifteen cars were needed to take away the wreaths, according to J West.[59] Perhaps, like Davies, they foresaw with dread the advent of a new kind of leadership in the Diocese. So ended the longest reign of a Moore College Principal. It is ironic that Davies' love of peace provoked division, and that years after his death there was still bitterness about the way in which he was treated by Mowll and his advisors.[60] Davies was possibly the last liberal Evangelical to exercise leadership in the Diocese. The ACL ensured that such men would no longer be influential. A possible 200 clergy were trained at Moore College under Davies. Davies' impact, through them, on Sydney parishes has probably never been evaluated, but there must have been a certain dilution of Evangelicalism in the Diocese of Sydney, as a result, up until the 1960s. The Memorialists (see below) were, for the most part, Sydney clergy who trained at Moore College under Davies.[61]

The first decade of Mowll's episcopate spanned the end of the Great Depression and the whole of the Second World War. He was a man of huge energy, and the Diocese was revitalised under his confident authority. Three areas where he made his mark indicate his particular focus as a Conservative Evangelical. First was his strong support for, and involvement with, Moore College. Academic standards were raised, the debt reduced, fundraising initiated and a dynamic new Principal appointed. The Irishman Thomas Chatterton Hammond (1877-1961) was not Mowll's choice for the College and Mowll did not want him as Principal.[62] Hammond (known as TC) was an outstanding scholar, gaining distinction at Trinity College Dublin, where

58. Shaw, "David John Davies," *Societas*, Michaelmas term 1935; Cakebread, *Societas*, Michaelmas term 1935.

59. West, "A Principal Embattled," 11.

60. MHC interview with Mrs. W Sharland October 1984. Mrs. Sharland taught at SCEGGS Darlinghurst as a contemporary of Mrs. Davies and expressed her sympathy for the newly-widowed Mrs. Davies whom she claimed had had to move out of the College house shortly after the archdeacon's death.

61. Judd and Cable, *Sydney Anglicans*, 238.

62. KJ Cable conversation with MHC, July 12 1998.

he trained for ordination, but unlike Davies, he was not a gentleman. He was an open-air preacher with the Irish Church Missions (ICM) and an active parish clergyman who "made things happen." In Dublin Roman Catholicism was his particular target. *Sydney Anglicans* aptly states that he was, "from a polarised religious environment in which controversy and polemics were the order of the day." He was almost 60 years old when he came to Sydney.[63]

Without doubt TC Hammond is one of the chief architects of Sydney Diocesan Anglicanism. A full biography of this most important Sydney leader is yet to be written, and there are some eight boxes of his notes, addresses and broadcasts in the Moore College Archives. His spiritual heirs are, with others, Broughton Knox (1916–1994) and Phillip Jensen (1945–). In common are a focus upon intellect, education and rational argument, a hard-hitting approach, and the absence of the Keswick kind of pietism.[64] *In Understanding Be Men*, the handbook of Christian doctrine published under TC Hammond's name, is still used and admired by Sydney Anglicans.[65]

As Principal of the College, and as writer, speaker and broadcaster, prominent leader in the Sydney Synod and as advisor to Mowll, he was very powerful. During his time at Moore College the number of students from other dioceses dwindled to insignificant proportions and non-Evangelicals, as a general rule, ceased to enroll.[66] Since by this time most Sydney clergy were now trained at Moore College, this meant a new narrowness of churchmanship for Sydney Diocesan clergy.

The second area of Mowll's influence also involved Hammond. The Memorialist Controversy of 1938 arose because it appeared to some that "diocesan policy was intent on making Sydney a closed shop for Conservative Evangelicals." The Memorialists were a group of 50 clergy who wanted to preserve diversity of thought and worship in the diocese. In a letter to the Archbishop, called the "The Memorial," they claimed that "uniformity of

---

63. Loane, *Moore College* 14–153; Treloar, "TC Hammond the Controversialist," 20–35; Nelson, "Thomas Chatterton Hammond," 150–53; Judd and Cable, *Sydney Anglicans* 233; Nelson, *TC Hammond*, 88–91. At Trinity College Dublin he won the Downes Prize in 1902 for Extempore Speaking, the Wray Prize in 1903 in Arts, and a Gold Medal in Philosophy. He had a prodigious and photographic memory, a very logical mind and the ability to express himself with great clarity.

64. See Packer, *Keep in Step with the Spirit*, 157–58.

65. According to DJ Goodhew in his entry for Douglas Johnson, in *Biographical Dictionary of Evangelicals*, 333, Johnson wrote the book but TC Hammond edited the drafts and put his name to the published work. This is open to question, according to PF Jensen.

66. Cameron, "Anglican Theological Education in Australia," 345–46.

churchmanship rather than unity in Christ was being cultivated." S Judd in *Sydney Anglicans* notes:

> They were very ordinary Sydney Clergymen who differed from their fellow clergy more in matters of personal temperament than in background and experience. They were as troubled by the excesses of biblical criticism and the advances of Anglo-Catholicism outside Sydney as their conservative brothers, but sought a charitable understanding between the different schools of thought and impartial treatment from those in authority and power in the diocese.[67]

Mowll, advised by Hammond, replied to the Memorialists with a brusque letter and questionnaire and refused to meet with them. It was, according to the authors of *Sydney Anglicans,* the most critical controversy of Mowll's episcopate. There was a stalemate, which was never resolved, and "the Memorial symbolised the final destruction of the consensus which had been forged nearly thirty years before." It was "the pinnacle of protest in the history of the Diocese," according to S Judd. Like the chasuble dispute with Wright, it left much bitterness, and is still recalled by some today as an example of high-handed Evangelicalism.[68]

A third significant area of Mowll's influence was the Church of England in South Africa.[69] There have been two Anglican churches in South Africa since 1870: The Church of the Province in South Africa (CPSA) and The [Evangelical] Church of England in South Africa (CESA). This anomaly springs from the strategy of Bishop Robert Gray, the first Bishop of Cape Town, to seek autonomy from the English church and to force Tractarian beliefs and practices upon his diocese. After Gray died, the Archbishop of Canterbury consecrated his successor as Bishop of both the CPSA and CESA parishes. Despite a court ruling in 1880 (*Merriman v Williams*) that CPSA was not part of the Anglican Church, the fact that CPSA was far bigger than CESA and owned large amounts of property, meant that in time CPSA (and not CESA) was recognized by successive Archbishops of Canterbury.[70]

Attempts in the 1930s to bring the two Anglican denominations together failed, not for want of general support by representatives of both CPSA and CESA, but because of opposition by CPSA bishops. While he was Archbishop of Sydney, Howard Mowll was indefatigable in his support for

---

67. Judd and Cable, *Sydney Anglicans*, 238–40.
68. J Cornish interview with MHC 14.9.2011.
69. See Cameron, *An Enigmatic Life*, 298–99.
70. This is still the case at the time of writing.

the Anglican Church in South Africa, and his influence ensured that CESA remained Evangelical.

Evangelicalism attracts extremists from time to time. One memorable example of this, with devastating consequences for individuals, was the movement, hatched at the University of Sydney, called "Sinless Perfectionism." It was a sect that sprang out of a combination of theological ideas from Brethrenism, the Inter Varsity Fellowship (IVF) and Keswick Evangelical theology. Its leader Lindsay Grant, a man of charismatic personality, believed that complete holiness, and an escape from the effects of sin, were attainable in this life. It shook the Inter Varsity Fellowship at the University of Sydney, during World War II in the early 1940s, and TC Hammond was one of the Sydney Evangelicals who strenuously opposed it. Grant subjected the group he gathered around him to a kind of bondage: he was a "tyrant with an overwhelming spiritual arrogance . . . it was a world that turned sour." Forty years later he and his former wife had little but "damaged people around them to show for their search for holiness."[71] In the wider context of the Diocese of Sydney, Sinless Perfectionism and the nasty taste it left, may well be the reason for the death of the holiness movement in the Diocese of Sydney.[72]

The Second World War (1939–1945) showed Archbishop Mowll at his best. He was quick to meet the nation's pressing new needs, regardless of resources. He saw what was needed and expected others to implement his directives. He established an Anglican National Emergency Fund (CENEF) to provide chaplains and church halls in army camps, as well as chaplains for the troops on active service. During the War there were 63 full-time and fifteen part-time Sydney Anglican Chaplains in the Armed Forces. Canteen units served meals to the troops in Sydney and Wollongong, and inexpensive accommodation was provided in the center of the city. Mowll did not neglect the parishes during the War. He continued to strengthen and extend them, especially by a major effort to secure church buildings that would serve outlying districts after the War ended.[73]

From Jane Barker to Hammond expressions of Evangelical piety may have altered, but the fundamentals remained the same. Running like a thread though those years, and stretching back to Johnson in 1788, is an expression of faith that transcends Anglicanism. Evangelicals tend to forge links with like-minded Christians, regardless of denomination, whether it is Jane Barker with the Dissenters, or Nathaniel Jones with other Protestants

---

71. Millikan, *Imperfect Company*, 9; DWB Robinson interview with MHC 2.10.2006.
72. Piggin, *Evangelical History in Australia*, Chapter 5.
73. Judd and Cable, *Sydney Anglicans*, 240–43; Loane, "HK Mowll," 274.

or, more recently, Rev. Dr Peter Jensen with one's local congregation. Jensen, while Principal of Moore College, stated: "in Sydney most people who take religion seriously will accord their first loyalty to the local congregation rather than the denomination and the worldwide church."[74]

This perspective, which may well have its roots in English Puritanism, angers fellow Anglicans. But it is no recent phenomenon. Evangelicals have always been unpopular with some sections of the Christian community, partly because of their discomforting energy to evangelise and also because of their use of Scripture as the yardstick of their faith. Both have contributed to a perception that Evangelical theology is inerudite, unsophisticated and naïve.

The Diocese of Sydney has not always been evangelical, nor monochrome in its churchmanship, nor have all its senior leaders been Evangelicals: as the episcopacies of Broughton and Barry reveal. The long tenure of Davies as Principal of Moore College and Talbot as Dean of Sydney are vivid reminders of that. Some strong and very powerful personalities, exercising leadership over a long period, consolidated the evangelical ethos of Sydney up to 1945: notably Frederic Barker, Nathaniel Jones, TC Hammond and HK Mowll. Two institutions are of paramount importance in nurturing Evangelicalism in the Diocese of Sydney: first is Moore College with its monopoly on clergy training, followed closely by the Anglican Church League which nominates people to key positions. The history of confrontations with Anglo-Catholics and Liberals indicates that Evangelicals took no prisoners. And *vice versa*. The issues were too important.

---

74. *Sydney Morning Herald* 20.10.1994.

Chapter 3

The Greatest Gift to Evangelical Anglicanism 1945–1950

THERE IS ONLY ONE biography of Howard Mowll and another will almost certainly never be written. ML Loane published his biography of Mowll in 1960, not long after the Archbishop's death.[1] He had access to Mowll's diaries and private papers but destroyed the private papers, at Mowll's instruction, after Mowll died. Loane stated in the Foreword to the biography, "Nothing that life affords is more uplifting or more enriching than to know intimately and to love devotedly a man who is both good and great: such a man was Howard West Kilvinton Mowll." Loane's beautiful sentences and loving treatment of his subject are heart-warming, but the biography lacks a critical edge. Mowll's huge influence over the Diocese of Sydney merits a more scholarly appraisal.

Howard Mowll was comparatively young when elected Archbishop of Sydney in 1933.[2] For the previous ten years he was a bishop in West China, and before that he had lectured for ten years at Wycliffe College, Toronto, an evangelical theological college in Canada. He came from a godly home and was one of six children. While reading theology and history at Cambridge University he became an active member of the Cambridge Inter-Collegiate Christian Union (CICCU). He was president of the CICCU (the conservative evangelical student group) in 1911 and 1912, when it split with the Student Christian Movement (SCM) over the inspiration of the Scriptures

---

1. Loane, *Archbishop Mowll*, 9–12. According to Loane, Mowll's diaries were bequeathed to his nephew, CK Mowll. The great mass of his private correspondence was all destroyed, unread, at his request.

2. He was born in 1890.

and their use in active witness.³ Mowll was greatly influenced by the very successful mission of RA Torrey to Cambridge in 1911. Torrey's mission revived the CICCU and reinvigorated spiritual life at the University. He also fired up Mowll's missionary vision and evangelistic enthusiasm. Mowll began speaking at open-air meetings and was a beach mission leader for CSSM (Children's Special Service Mission) in 1912. His spiritual style was that of Keswick and he promoted this for the whole of his life.⁴ One of his mentors was the scholarly Bishop EA Knox of Manchester, who was probably the leading Evangelical in the England of the 1920s and who had been a mentor also to Archbishop JC Wright, Mowll's predecessor in the Diocese of Sydney.⁵ Mowll met his wife Dorothy while serving in China. Her father was the Principal of the Diocesan Theological College in Foochow (Fuzhou), China. She sailed for China in 1915 and worked there for eighteen years. She and Mowll married in 1924.⁶ S Piggin describes her as

> A woman of great vision and determination, mixed attractively with merriment and vitality. She was in many ways the power behind the power, and the strategist behind the visionary, always carrying a notebook and pen with her everywhere so she could keep track of the flow of ideas.⁷

The Archbishop of Canterbury, Cosmo Gordon Lang, interviewed Mowll before Mowll came to Sydney as the new Archbishop. Lang warned him that he "had neither the gifts nor the training which the See of Sydney required." Apart from Lang's distaste for Mowll's particular brand of churchmanship, Lang's negativity had some justification: Mowll had never been rector of a parish, or even worked in one as a curate, and had not worked in England for twenty years.⁸ The latter might have meant that he was possibly out of touch with contemporary Anglicanism in England and therefore out of step with the leaders of the day. Lang was proved wrong: Donald Robinson, a future Archbishop of Sydney and who from boyhood knew Archbishop Mowll well, maintained that Mowll had "remarkable gifts of leadership, of vision, of getting things done."⁹ Stuart Piggin has described

---

3. Loane, *Archbishop Mowll*, 47.

4. B Dickey, "Howard West Kilvinton Mowll," 455–56; Loane, "Howard West Kilvinton Mowll," 272–74.

5. Robinson, "Some Personal Reminiscences of Archbishop Mowll" *The Anglican Historical Society Journal* 48: No 1, May 2003, 7.

6. Piggin, *Evangelical Christianity in Australia*, 128.

7. Ibid., 128–29.

8. Robinson, "Some Personal Reminiscences of Archbishop Mowll," 9.

9. Ibid., 7.

the Mowlls as "archetypal evangelical activists" who "are still revered as the greatest gift to evangelical Anglicanism in Australia's history."[10]

Shortly after his arrival as Archbishop of Sydney, following the death of Archbishop Wright who had been Primate, the Primacy was removed, for the first time, from Sydney, Archbishop Le Fanu of Perth receiving thirteen votes to Mowll's twelve. It was a measure of the Australian bishops' active dislike for Mowll's evangelical convictions, and for the evangelical Diocese of Sydney, according to Mowll's biographer.[11] Some fourteen years elapsed before Mowll's turn came to be Primate.

Mowll's commanding height and air of kindly authority made him a formidable leader. Few people could say "No" to him and win. One who tried to say "no" was Rev. F Shaw, whom Mowll wanted for his domestic chaplain. Shaw declined, and years later recalled what happened next:

> The matter didn't end there. Bishop Kirkby sent a message to Archbishop Mowll telling him of my decision. A few days after another message came from his Grace, brief and to the point. "What a blow. Tell Shaw to meet me at Church House the day I arrive." I kept the appointment and was asked if I could use the typewriter and if I could drive a car. I had to say yes to this. His Grace seemed pleased and added, "I'll find a flat or cottage at Darling Point in the vicinity of Bishopscourt for your mother and sister and you'll be able to see them on your days off. But you will reside at Bishopscourt. Shaw, I appoint you as domestic chaplain as from today" . . . His Grace was determined and I, speechless.[12]

Within a short time, not only had Mowll set Moore College back on its feet again and instituted the Archbishop's Winter Appeal to aid the poor and needy,[13] but he had revived the Home Mission Society (HMS) as one of the key bodies for forward growth in the Diocese, with Archdeacon RB Robinson as General Secretary. Under Robinson (Archbishop DWB Robinson's father), the HMS experienced growth, expansion and energetic activity, working in the Children's Court, with the unemployed, in hospital chaplaincies and parish visitation. Mowll appointed a chaplain for youth work, and a diocesan missioner, and within his first two years as Sydney's Archbishop, personally visited 138 parishes. He conducted 70 confirmation services within the space of a year. In September 1937 he and RB Robinson

---

10. Piggin, *Evangelical Christianity in Australia*, 128.
11. Loane, *Archbishop Mowll*, 136.
12. Robinson, "Some Personal Reminiscences of Archbishop Mowll," 9.
13. Loane, *Archbishop Mowll*, 134.

travelled to Cook in South Australia to open the Bishop Kirkby Memorial Hospital and visit the work of the BCA (Bush Church Aid). They were away for only ten days but they drove 3,500 miles. Robinson, who shared a room with him on this excursion, said that the Archbishop never seemed to go to bed at all: he was up when Robinson fell asleep at night, and he was still up when he awoke in the morning.[14]

In 1938 Mowll attended the Tarambaram Conference in South India. According to ML Loane this stimulated him to review the whole question of faith and witness in the world. That, coupled with his years in China, gave him a vision for mission to South East Asia. He was one of the first to perceive new opportunities in that region, and to lay the foundations for engaging with them. His chosen strategy was to support the Church Missionary Society (CMS), the evangelical missionary society of the Anglican Church in Australia. He revitalized it, giving it a new constitution and as its President, strong leadership.[15]

He was honored with the invitation to deliver the prestigious Moorehouse Lectures for 1947—the year in which he became Primate of Australia. He chose to survey the state of contemporary mission work in the world. The lectures are not those of a scholar but of a man passionate about taking the gospel of Christ into the world. They inspire and challenge. For example, he wrote,

> We have been seeing all the world as it appears on the stage of today. One fact upon which we are all agreed is that it is chaotic and insecure. Within the chaos stands the Church of Jesus Christ, with her feet on the Rock of Ages, and her eyes upward to behold the vision of the Face of the Lord. That the world might share that vision is the great task which confronts her in these darkening days.[16]

Mowll had a sharp mind, an amazingly retentive memory and a genius for organization. But his contribution to evangelical scholarship and his attitude to it are worth exploring, because changes in evangelical circles were afoot in the 1930s in England, which in time had profound effects in Sydney. There had been a great dearth of evangelical scholarship among Evangelicals in England up to this time, despite the threats from Tractarians on the one hand and from Modernism on the other requiring scholarly defence. Promising evangelical men were encouraged to go out to the mission field

14. Ibid., 136–41.
15. Piggin, *Evangelical Christianity in* Australia, 130; Cole, *A History of the Church Missionary Society of Australia,* 227.
16. Mowll, *Seeing All the World,* 87.

rather than to pursue their studies, teach in parishes and equip clergy in theological colleges. Mowll himself had refused the great CT Studd's invitation to leave his university studies and go to Africa.[17] But having completed his BA, after a stint at Ridley Hall prior to ordination, he pursued formal studies no further. He was made Professor of History at Wycliffe Hall, Toronto, in 1916, remaining there until 1922, with a brief stint in France as a chaplain in the First World War. He seemed to have spent all available spare time on mission and chaplaincy work.[18] His ten years as a bishop in China probably allowed him little time for scholarship. When he came to Sydney, he relied heavily on TC Hammond for scholarly advice.[19] He was foremost an activist.

The Diocese of Sydney was to benefit from a renaissance in biblical scholarship, mostly generated by a comparatively unknown man, Douglas Johnson, known as "DJ". Johnson as General Secretary of the IVF (Inter Varsity Fellowship) was a far-sighted strategist for the evangelical cause in England and beyond. Johnson was a medical practitioner, and also very well read and he stressed the need for Evangelicals to engage in intellectual debate if they were to be effective in evangelism. He was instrumental in establishing the Biblical Research Committee and Tyndale House, a center for conservative biblical scholarship in Cambridge; London Bible College and the publication arm of IVF—later Inter-Varsity Press.[20] His work did much to recall evangelicalism from anti-intellectualism.[21] Among those who joined the Biblical Research Committee were Stuart Barton Babbage and Broughton Knox. Broughton Knox was a contributor to the *New Bible Handbook* published in 1947, and joined the staff of Moore College in 1954.[22]

John Stott commented on "DJ" and his influence at a gathering at Tyndale House in 1992:

> "DJ" is one of the unsung heroes of the Christian Church in this country. He saw the priority need to recover evangelical biblical scholarship. It is probably to him more than anybody else that the original vision for Tyndale House was given.

---

17. Loane, *Archbishop Mowll*, 54.
18. Ibid., 62–83.
19. Piggin, *Evangelical Christianity in Australia*, 131.
20. Two conservative Sydney Evangelicals were Wardens of Tyndale House: Leon Morris 1960–1964, and Bruce Winter, who trained at Moore College, 1987–2006.
21. *Biographical Dictionary of Evangelicals*, 333; Piggin, *Evangelical Christianity in Australia*, 134.
22. Cameron, *An Enigmatic Life*, 71–72.

> When I was myself an undergraduate at Cambridge during World War II, the Divinity School was entirely liberal in its orientation. I believe there were no evangelical believers in any British university post related to Theology (even FF Bruce's influential career had scarcely begun) . . . If anybody was rash enough to read for the Theology Tripos, and managed to survive, it was regarded as a miracle or certainty (depending on one's theological position), a conspicuous example of divine providence.
>
> But now the situation has radically changed . . . There are, I believe, about 50 evangelical academics in university posts related to antiquities, Old Testament, New Testament, Theology, Ethics and Church History. And Tyndale House, its Fellowship, and its outstanding biblical library, constitute a unique resource for evangelical scholarship.[23]

In Sydney, Moore College was to be the primary beneficiary of the new evangelical scholarship and now that the War was over, the College grew ever larger. From 36 students in 1944, 44 in 1945, and 55 students by 1946, numbers had grown to the largest enrollment in its history.[24] The trend continued with 81 the following year and in the ensuing decades it continued to expand.[25] It trained more and more of the clergy of the Diocese. Of the 263 active clergy in the Diocese in 1945, 66% had been trained at Moore College. By 1950 this proportion had risen to 69%.[26] Moore College at this time had a very small staff, with TC Hammond as Principal and Marcus Loane, Vice-Principal, and a few tutors and visiting lecturers.[27] The students who enrolled were mostly not of a high calibre by educational standards. Many were returned soldiers—older and more experienced men than those who had enrolled formerly. At least one of them studied for his ThL concurrently with a BA at the adjoining campus of the University of Sydney.[28] The Diocesan clergy were far from a monochrome group: they were disparate in terms of their theological training, their background and their educational attainments.

Sydney had considerably more clergy than any other of the Australian dioceses. Numbers fluctuated year by year, but in 1950 Sydney had 259 active

---

23. Timothy Dudley-Smith, *John Stott*, 187.
24. *Sydney Year Book* 1945,105; *Sydney Year Book* 1947, 119.
25. *Sydney Year Book* 1947, 1949.
26. *Sydney Year Book* 1945, clergy listed.
27. Loane, *A Centenary History of Moore College*, 148–49.
28. My father, Richard Bosanquet, was such a man. He was ordained deacon and priest in 1949.

clergy, Melbourne was next with 193, then Brisbane and Adelaide with 157 and 124 respectively. There were 24 dioceses in Australia, and some, like North West Australia and Kalgoorlie had fewer than ten clergy to man their few but vast parishes. Not all the clergy of the other dioceses received theological education before ordination. Those from remote dioceses without the resources to fund a training college had either no formal training or they trained in England or at a college in another diocese. Each metropolitan diocese had its own college, as did some of the smaller dioceses, and in addition Bible Colleges were founded and subsequently thrived. The latter provided evangelical training but were not Anglican in identity.[29]

Where were the women in the Sydney Diocese in the first years after the war? The Lambeth Conference of 1920 had decided that women should be admitted to those councils to which laymen were admitted, but the very next year the London Diocesan Conference resolved that "It is generally inexpedient and contrary to the interests of the church that women should publicly minister in consecrated buildings."[30] In the Diocese of Sydney, Synod gave permission for women to join Parish Councils in 1921, but if what happened at St Swithun's Pymble is any guide, women were not members of Parish Councils for the next 50 years.[31] The first Anglican woman had been ordained in 1944 by the Bishop of Hong Kong. Her name was Florence Tim Oi Li. In the face of extreme opposition, including from Archbishop Fisher of Canterbury, Florence withdrew from priestly ministry.[32] The Sydney conservative evangelical newspaper *Australian Church Record* (*ACR*) was supportive of Bishop Hall, the Bishop of Hong Kong, noting that

> The necessities of wartime were precluding the holding of the service of Holy Communion in a large district in which the deaconess was exercising a pastoral ministry. The work under her charge had grown exceedingly so that the Church had to be enlarged and the Bishop has been faced with a seemingly impossible position: the Bishop has courageously followed what he believes to be the guidance of the Holy Spirit and has now ordained Lei Tim Oi to the priesthood . . . In other parts of the Anglican Church there has been of necessity a certain amount of hostile criticism of the good bishop's procedure, but the bishop's

29. Piggin, *Evangelical Christianity in Australia*, 91–92.

30. May 1921. Porter, *Women in the Church*, 20.

31. Sydney Church Ordinance Amendment Ordinance May 1921. Available online on Sydneyanglicans.net; Cameron, *Living Stones*, 153.

32. Kaye, *Introduction to World Anglicanism*, 157 and 158; Fisher to Bishop of Hong Kong 31.3.1945, 25.5.1945; Bishop of Hong Kong to Fisher 30.9.1945, Fisher Papers 11.

plea cannot be easily countered. When Lambeth meets again there should be an interesting discussion and some rigid notions affecting the Sacrament of Holy Communion may receive a strong criticism if not condemnation.[33]

This unsigned article was written by the conservative Evangelical DJ Knox or approved by him, as editor of *ACR*. While it is of interest as an indication of a level of opposition to Archbishop Fisher, it also reveals a readiness, by Sydney diocesan hardliners, to review women's ministry in order to support innovation for the promotion of effective Christian work. As the article noted, the search for new ways of Christian ministry had also, significantly, raised the issue of Lay Presidency (laymen and women presiding at the Holy Communion). Later, Sydney's promotion of Lay Presidency was to prove highly contentious in the Anglican Church of Australia.

Sydney has always had women in ministry. The avenue for a woman to formal ministry was via the Deaconess Institution. This had been founded by Rev Mervyn Archdall, a Sydney Evangelical. "Bethany," the deaconess training house, was set up in 1891 with a two-year course. Sydney was the first and most prolific source of deaconesses in Australia, according to Anne O'Brien, and there seems to have been nothing in any of the other dioceses which replicated Sydney deaconesses, in terms of their theological training and the scope of their work.[34]

While there were only 38 deaconesses working in Sydney parishes in 1944, there were a few new deaconesses by 1948.[35] They were expected to assist the rector of the parish and regulations for them and laywomen were set out each year in the diocesan Year Books.[36] They could lead services, but not say the Absolution or the Blessing or two of the Collects; they could read the lessons, with the approval of the minister; read Morning and Evening Prayer and the Litany only when no minister was present or if he were incapacitated; address the congregation (with the above provisos); speak to the congregation about missionaries or women's work and life only if the minister's permission were given or if this were reported afterwards to the Archbishop; not take part in the Holy Communion service except to

33. *ACR* April 5, 1945, 4. Rev DJ Knox was Canon Broughton Knox's father.

34. O'Brien, "Anglicans and Gender Issues," 279 in *Anglicanism in Australia. A History*, ed. Kaye. The deaconess movement had been founded at Kaiserswerth in Germany by Pastor Fliedner and his wife. Mrs. Thelma Schleicher, a deaconess trained in Dresden, married a CMS missionary and came to Sydney briefly. Their son Bernard became Principal of Moore College and their two daughters were the first two deaconesses in Australia —Breward, *A History of the Churches in Australasia*, 209–10.

35. *Sydney Year Book* 1949.

36. For example, *Sydney Year Book* 1944,169–70.

read the lessons. They were required to wear the cap and dress approved by the Archbishop. The uniform was a steely grey colour trimmed with navy blue —enough to extinguish any lurking beauty in the wearer. In addition to helping the rector, deaconesses were teachers, worked in the Children's Court and in the Home of Peace and ran hostels and a Girls' Home. They did a sterling job, with little public acknowledgement. But an article in *ACR* in 1947 warmly commended them. Noting "we have come a good way on our journey of the recognition of women's ministry" and that the ordination of a deaconess was "strikingly similar to the ordination of a deacon" the author wrote of

> . . . the great work these servants of God and the Church are doing for the comfort and edification of God's children and the bringing straying sheep and lambs to the Good Shepherd's fold. No one who has any knowledge at all of the devoted works of these handmaidens of the Church can have anything but praise and thanksgiving to God for the restoration of this Order of the Sacred Ministry.[37]

Lay women for the most part ran fêtes, made and served food, arranged flowers and cleaned the church, washed the ceremonial robes, belonged to women's church groups like the Guild and the Mothers' Union, "manned" the crèche, taught Sunday School and Scripture in the local public school and quietly served in the background. HM Carey has commented, "Women's involvement in religion was not considered because they were perceived to be consumers rather than producers of religious culture."[38]

Except when he was on one of his frequent trips away from Sydney, Archbishop Mowll wrote a monthly letter to his diocese in the *Sydney Diocesan Magazine*. That, and his Presidential Address to the Synod each year give some insight into his priorities. The cessation of the War brought a host of problems as well as new opportunities. In 1945, at the 26th Synod, his thoughts ranged from the cost of postage for sending food parcels to England to the new problem of immigration "a difficult and anxious problem." While he wanted "to stretch out our hand to all . . . who are willing and able to come here," he was concerned that the effect of altering "our White Australia Policy" would be no longer to exclude Japan with her vast population. He perceived that the main problem would arise with immigrants from a different cultural and economic background and thought that we needed to carry out a policy "as little offensive to our Asiatic neighbours as possible."

---

37. *ACR* September 11, 1947, 8; I found nothing in the Archbishop's public statements that encouraged or commended the deaconesses.

38. Carey, *Believing in Australia*, 118.

Without actually saying so to the synod, he preferred British immigrants: "Naturally, we look to those who have been long nurtured in our faith and our own literature as offering the best material with which to realize our hopes." Sunday observance had dropped, the divorce rate was climbing, and lawlessness, alcoholism and gambling were significant social problems. He wanted to increase the number of church schools and he encouraged lay people to assist the clergy in teaching Scripture in schools, and in parish visiting.[39] The tasks of providing for new housing districts, planning for new church buildings, relocating wartime chaplains into parish work, and securing a better future for Aboriginal people lay ahead. He wrote,

In view of the fact that an increasing number of the Australian electors is becoming conscious of the debt owing to the Aboriginal population of this continent, and feeling increasingly ashamed of the treatment that has so often been meted out to them in the past, and that they are aware of the unsatisfactory nature of the policies pursued towards them in different parts of Australia, and feel it increasingly a matter of conscience that every possible step be taken to secure the future of these people on a equitable basis, are you prepared to ask your member of Parliament the following questions:

1. Are you prepared to pledge your support for any policy which aims to do full justice to the Aborigines as fellow human beings and fellow subjects of the King, irrespective of vested interests against them?
2. Are you prepared to vote for the bringing of all Aborigines in Australia under Federal control, or, as an alternative, under a policy framed by Federal authorities, but administered by the States?
3. Are you prepared to vote for a unified policy which aims at the social betterment of the Aborigines, their education along lines which will fulfill their real needs, and the granting finally of full citizenship to those who are fitted to receive it?[40]

Because he was an Englishman, Mowll noted recent events at Home: Churchill's loss at the polls, the arrival of the Duke and Duchess of Gloucester in Australia, and the elevation of Dr Geoffrey Francis Fisher to the See of Canterbury in 1945. His comment on the appointment was, "there has seldom been an appointment to Canterbury of a man so little known to the Church overseas."[41] He warmly commended the formation of the World

39. *Sydney Year Book* 1946, 35.

40. *SDM* September 1946, 3; in 1949 Aboriginals in NSW, South Australia, Tasmania and Victoria gained the right to vote in state and federal elections; in all states for federal elections in 1962; and in state elections in Queensland in 1965.

41. *SDM* February 1945, 3.

Council of Churches, becoming the first President of the Australian branch in 1946. He attended the inaugural Amsterdam meeting of the WCC in 1948.[42]

Mowll was a great traveller: the ten-day trip to South Australia in 1937 was only the beginning. He was an indefatigable visitor to the parishes in his care, and after becoming Primate, to every one of the other dioceses in Australia.[43] There was the visit to South India in 1938, to the USA in 1947 for the first international IFES conference, and to Amsterdam the following year for the WCC. His visit to Western China was by aeroplane and occasioned long letters in the *Sydney Diocesan Magazine* detailing the events of this trip to his faithful readers back in Sydney. The trips were purposeful: to understand the situation of the people he visited and to build bridges of friendship with them. The purchase of "Gilbulla" in 1949 aligned with this strategy. Set in dairy farming country on the rural outskirts of Sydney, this former Macarthur property was purchased for various reasons, chief among which was "to enable the Archbishop to meet clergy, church officers and members of the Church in conference or retreat."[44] For the next 50 years people of all kinds of age and churchmanship met at "Gilbulla" and this property, in an incalculably significant way, enabled people of different points of view to talk with each other and to grow to know the other as a fellow human being—a Christian one at that. [45]

The CENEF Memorial Center in Castlereagh Street had been opened by the Governor-General with the Duchess of Gloucester present, in October 1946. This again stood as a symbol of Mowll's big heart. Its purpose was to continue the good work carried out during the War of providing meals, friendship and counsel to ex-servicemen. In addition, looking to the future, the upper floor would provide a meeting place for the young people of the city. In this post war era CENEF began to redirect its resources into youth work and purchased a conference site at Pork Hacking in 1947. Since 1942, with the appointment of the Rev. Graham Delbridge as Chaplain for Youth, there had been very lively work with young people, through

---

42. *Sydney Year Book* 1946, 41; Piggin, *Evangelical Christianity in Australia*, 133

43. Ibid., 132.

44. ACR July 27, 4.

John MacArthur (1767–1834) was soldier, entrepreneur, and pastoralist. His agricultural establishment Camden Park (on which "Gilbulla" stood) comprised over 60,000 acres. He is remembered chiefly for the establishment of the wool industry in Australia, although "ultimately it was to the persistence and loyalty of his wife and sons that Macarthur owed the greater part of his reputation." Margaret Steven, "John Macarthur," 159.

45. West, *Gilbulla 1899–1999*.

missions, through an increase in the number of branches of CEBS (Church of England Boys' Society), and through the HMS Service Bureau which helped coach for the matriculation, gave vocational advice and found jobs for young people. In addition, the HMS coordinated its work with that of the diocesan Board of Education and parish youth groups.[46]

Independent of Mowll but it would seem, fully supported by him, was the *Australian Church Record*, edited at this time by DJ Knox. Its bi-monthly issues were packed with news about the other dioceses of Australia, book reviews, news and running commentaries on church affairs, as well as letters to the editor. There were teaching articles in every edition: about Evangelicals' Reformation heritage, about Roman Catholics, and especially about aspects of theology. The young Turks who joined the Moore College staff, notably DB Knox and DWB Robinson were active contributors and gave the newspaper an intellectual approach, which was both stimulating and challenging. While it is difficult to know how many Sydney Diocesan people read the *ACR*, it was without doubt a formidable organ promoting the conservative evangelical position.

Mowll's first encounters with Archbishop Fisher of Canterbury (1945–1961) were unfortunate. They clashed over the Church of England in South Africa and—at arms' length—over what became known as "The Red Book Case." In 1948, Mowll travelled to Cape Town to confirm 37 CESA young people, since the CESA had no bishop. A former editor of the *Church Times* wrote that

> Unless Mowll was acting with the tacit consent of the Archbishop of Cape Town . . . the incident looks like a peculiarly dirty and distressing instance of Anglican disloyalty. Why ever can't we hang together instead of trying to emulate Kipling's adjutant who mounted his horse and rode off in both directions at once?[47]

The Archbishop of Cape Town wrote to Fisher that Mowll had conducted the confirmations with his written permission. In fact he had asked Mowll to preach but Mowll declined because he was too tired. Archbishop and Mrs. Mowll had tea with him—which sounds amicable enough.[48] Fisher acknowledged that all was in order, after all, but in a letter to Bishop Leonard Fisher of Natal (the Archbishop of Canterbury's brother), he wrote that

---

46. Judd and Cable, *Sydney Anglicans*, 246.

47. The Rev. Dr GL Prestige to Fisher 12.1.1948, Fisher Papers 39: Lambeth Palace Archives. Frappell, *Anglicans in the Antipodes*, 269–342.

48. Archbishop of Cape Town to Fisher 30.1.48, Fisher Papers 39.

what Mowll had done was an invasion of another bishop's diocese.[49] This kind of territorial dispute was to become a cause for resentment towards Sydney Evangelicals in later decades.

The first Bishop of the CESA, Bishop Fred Morris, clashed with Fisher the following year. Formerly the Bishop of North Africa, and not yet Bishop of the CESA, Morris was urged by Fisher in 1949 "with all the power I can command not to visit that church [CESA] or to take confirmations for it."[50]

Morris' reply to Fisher explains clearly the position of the CESA people in South Africa:

> I think you are judging unfairly against this body [the CESA]. It seems to me that this church is loyal to the Church of England as judged by the Word of God, the Articles and the Book of Common Prayer. The Church of the Province has been disloyal to the Church of England and has professed her aim which is to prepare her people for re-union with the Roman Church, practising auricular confession, transubstantiation, adoration of the Virgin Mary etc. How can the Church of England in South Africa accept the ministration of those who hold such beliefs?
>
> It is not a pleasant situation for the leaders of the Church of England in South Africa; they have been robbed of what was due to them and are being treated as schismatics by those to whom they are most loyal.[51]

Mowll wrote to the Archbishop of Cape Town the following year. He prefaced his words with the assurance that he was not writing "in a spirit of hostility." He went on to say:

> The Church of the Province of South Africa has not honoured its promise to allow each congregation which joined the Church of the Province of South Africa to continue to worship in its own way. For example at St Peter's Mowbray—certain changes, in themselves are of minor importance, but a general trend of the services was towards a less evangelical churchmanship.
>
> The Church of the Province of South Africa was not recognized as Church of England by Chief Justice Sir George Villiers and this was substantially upheld by the Judicial Committee of the Privy Council . . . Also the Bishop of Natal's two cases in 1865 and 1866 and Merriam v Williams in 1882. Lambeth created a new situation by the formation of the wider Anglican

---

49. 30.1.1948 and 3.3.1948, Fisher Papers 39.
50. Fisher to Mowll 8.1.1949, Fisher Papers 51.
51. Morris to Fisher 26.1.1949, Fisher Papers 51.

Communion and the Church of the Province of South Africa was drawn into that . . . the most hopeful course is to wait until the lapse of time removes one or two fanatical old stagers, and then perhaps the schism may be healed.[52]

Despite Mowll's hopes and olive branches, the schism has not healed and, as in former decades, the CESA was not invited to the Lambeth Conference of 2008. Archbishop of Canterbury George Carey (1991–2003), an Evangelical, makes it clear in his autobiography that the CPSA is the recognized Anglican Church of South Africa within the Anglican Communion. He does not even mention the CESA.[53]

The other matter in which Mowll and Fisher clashed, though at arms' length, was the Red Book Case. This dominated the greater part of the 1940s for Australian Anglicans and gave Evangelicals a name for litigiousness, not for the first time.[54] It was, until the climax of the women's ordination debate in 1993, the most significant litigation involving the Anglican Church in Australia.

The matter began in 1944 with a complaint, filed in the Equity Court of NSW, by 23 laymen from the Diocese of Bathurst, against the Bishop of Bathurst, Thomas Lomas Wylde. He had published and circularized an unauthorized prayer book, bound in red—hence its name the Red Book. The initial complaint was that the book contained heresy in the service of the Lord's Supper where a number of prayers and rubrics pointed to a Roman Catholic doctrine of Transubstantiation.[55]

The laymen had initially written to Archbishop Mowll but he referred the case to TC Hammond. It has been argued that if Mowll had been more experienced and had the confidence he later acquired as Primate, he might well have resolved the case without recourse to litigation.[56] Hammond, as we have seen, was not necessarily a good diplomat. Wylde rejected the lay-

---

52. Mowll to Archbishop of Cape Town 8.5.1950 and 28.6.1950, Fisher Papers 69.

53. Carey, *Know the Truth*, 277.

54. Evangelicals sought to uphold Reformation doctrine, enshrined in the 1662 *Book of Common Prayer*, by resorting to legal prosecution of Tractarians who departed from this. In a number of notable cases Tractarians were actually imprisoned for ritualistic practice. The matter of Gorham vs. the Bishop of Exeter (1847–1850), the first great decision on a matter of doctrine since the Reformation, was the first of such court cases whereby Evangelicals sought to defend doctrine. Gorham, an Evangelical, was an opponent of the doctrine of baptismal regeneration. See Chadwick *The Victorian Church Part I*, 250–59; Cornish, *A History of the English Church in the Nineteenth Century*, 130–54.

55. Transubstantiation is the doctrine that the body and blood of Christ become localized in the bread and wine after the prayer of consecration.

56. Teale, "The 'Red Book' Case," *Journal of Religious History* XII (1 June 1982), 87.

men's complaints and refused to withdraw his prayer book from circulation. Hammond and the Relators (the 23 laymen) engaged H Minton Taylor of the law firm Allen, Allen and Hemsley. After three years the initial charges were dropped and the hearing of a new claim commenced in September 1947. This new claim was that the use of the Red Book was a breach of the trusts applicable to church property in the Diocese of Bathurst held upon trust for Church of England purposes.

The hearing occupied seven sitting days of the court. Mr. Justice Roper in his judgement of February 1948 upheld the laymen's claims against Wylde. Wylde then took the case on appeal to the High Court, where he lost, but with the four judges divided evenly on the matter. The High Court ruled that an injunction against the use of the Red Book applied only to 20 churches in the Bathurst Diocese, whose trusts had been approved by the Equity Court. This effectively made the victory of the Relators a Pyrrhic one, especially as the Red Book was subsequently reprinted and published in Victoria and some 10,000 copies sold.[57] RW Kitto, Wylde's barrister, observed that the Red Book Case left the Church exactly where it was before litigation began. The case exposed the need for Prayer Book revision and exacerbated the unhappy divisions between various sections of the Anglican Church. Since Sydney was the epicenter of the trial, the Sydney Diocese, already regarded as something of an oddity, was further marginalized.

The Red Book Case is fascinating because of the anomalies it illuminated, for the problems it raised and for the divisions it etched more deeply in the Church of England in Australia. Wylde's Red Book was only one of a number of such prayer books at the time but he had the misfortune to come up against a significant number of laymen who made effective protest to someone in power: Mowll himself. Hammond's papers are lost, but it would appear that he took the matter up at Mowll's behest because he perceived an important issue was at stake. He and Mowll may well have done nothing about illegal prayer books had not the 23 Relators precipitated action. The issue was theological: the Red Book represented a departure from Reformed practice.

The fact was that nobody adhered strictly to the 1662 *Book of Common Prayer*—including Hammond as Rector of St Philip's Church Hill—so a resort to litigation over the use of the Prayer Book was a double-edged sword.[58] For Wylde, the heart of the matter was the *ius liturgicum*—the right he claimed as a bishop to prescribe liturgical forms and ceremonial other than that laid down in the *Book of Common Prayer* or by Act of Parlia-

---

57. Davis, *Australian Anglicans and their Constitution*, 113.
58. Galbraith, "Just Enough Religion to Make us Hate," 181.

ment. He and Francis Batty, Bishop of Newcastle, also strongly criticized the Evangelicals' resort to secular litigation. Despite this, when Wylde lost the initial case, he too resorted to litigation when he took the case on appeal to the High Court.

Litigation in the Red Book Case was an attempt to stem the tide of Anglo-Catholicism and there seemed no alternative option. As with the Diocese of Sydney's application to the state courts in 1993, over the legality of ordination of women to the priesthood, the case was determined, not by reference to Anglican Canon Law, but to law relating to the use of property held on trust for the Anglican Church. Like the Roman governor Gallio of Acts 18, the State on both occasions was determined to keep clear of theological disputation.[59] At the heart of the issue was a question about the right of Anglicans to deviate from the *Prayer Book*. This was a continuing theme for the remainder of the century. It is important to remember that the Diocese of Sydney was not formally involved in the Red Book Case: the Archbishop did not involve himself in the matter (and was criticized for this by Mr. Justice Rich when the High Court heard the appeal), nor was the Sydney Diocesan Synod involved.[60] There were articles about it in *ACR* but this was not an official organ of the Diocese.[61] The Relators were from the Diocese of Bathurst and the hearing was held in Sydney simply because that is where the court which heard the case sat to hear the matter.

The Red Book Case demonstrated that the Church of England was the church of the laity as well as the clergy. Laymen had "taken on" a bishop and won. They found out that they had some effective power in shaping Anglican polity. The matter also showcased Broughton Knox, who was called as an expert witness. He acquitted himself very well, and made his mark as an astute, doctrinally sound, emerging leader. In the eyes of non-Evangelicals and Anglo-Catholics he appeared as dangerously litigious and his contribution, early in his career, in the Red Book Case defined him to such people henceforth as a man to treat with caution.[62]

Archbishop Fisher also became involved. He was sympathetic to Wylde. He wrote of "our English commonsense" in a situation where the use of various lectionaries and service forms was "experimental" but could be challenged in the courts. "I am sorry," he said, "that you should have to face

---

59. Acts 18:14–15.

60. Wylde, *The Bathurst Ritual Case*, 237.

61. *ACR* 9.10.1947, 26.2.1948, 20.4.1948, 26.8.1948, 16.12.1948, 23.1.1949, 24.2.1949, 7.4.1949, 19.5.1949 and 16.6.1949.

62. Cameron, *An Enigmatic Life*, 97–104.

a test case."[63] After Wilde lost the appeal, Bishop Batty of Newcastle wrote to Archbishop Fisher, "Most important of all, it seems to me that the issue of the case has made it wildly improbable that any such action will ever be taken again."[64]

He was right. He was referring to the possibility of Sydney's resort to law in opposition to the Church of England in Australia becoming autonomous. Underneath the Red Book Case lay a much bigger issue: that of the long struggle to untie the apron strings with the Mother Church—the "Nexus" of Australian Anglicans with the Church of England in England.

---

63. Fisher to Wylde 18.10.1947, Fisher Papers 39.
64. Batty to Fisher 4.4.1949, Fisher Papers 51.

Chapter 4

Loyal Sons of the Reformation
1950–1958

Nowhere is the distinctiveness of the Diocese of Sydney seen more clearly than in the long-drawn-out business of establishing an autonomous Anglican Church in Australia. John Davis in his definitive work *Australian Anglicans and their Constitution* emphasizes this in his introduction. He writes:

> The question of what is to be done with issues that divide has been with this church almost from the beginning. Interestingly, almost all of them have been to do with accommodating the diocese of Sydney . . .
>
> No organization based on an association freely entered into—like a church—can survive intact if a major change to existing practice or belief is pushed through over the sustained objection of a substantial minority . . . The explicit recognition of the pre-eminent place and power of the diocese of Sydney in the overall structure of the Australian Church stands sharp and clear.[1]

Until 1962 Australian Anglicans were tied to the Church of England, in England. The degree to which they were legally bound to England was sometimes a matter for conjecture, and at times grave concern. For some Australian Anglicans, the Nexus was a guarantee of adherence to conservative Reformed theology, although as the years passed and liberal theology gained increasing traction, especially after World War I, the Nexus began to appear more like a ball and chain to conservative theologians.

---

1. Davis, *Australian Anglicans and their Constitution*, 3.

The beginning of the quest for autonomy can be dated to Bishop Broughton's calling of a conference of all Australian and New Zealand bishops in 1850. The place was Sydney. It was the first such meeting to be called in modern times and the development of synodical government dates from this meeting (and a similar one held in Toronto shortly after).[2] Broughton's aim was to create an autonomous local church with a constitution originating in the will of the local people, not by the fad of the parliament of the day.[3] The constitution committee foundered over a theological issue—baptismal regeneration. Broughton died shortly afterwards.

Ten years later, Broughton's successor, Frederic Barker, held a conference which formed a committee to draw up a constitution for the Diocese of Sydney. In this, he reflected the diocesanism that has ever since characterised the Anglican church in Australia: a country of huge distances and increasingly self-contained and inward-looking dioceses, each, with the exception of Melbourne, growing monochrome in their theology and practice, partly because of their isolation from each other.[4] JTR Border, in his book *Church and State in Australia 1788–1872: A Constitutional History of the Church of England in Australia*, refers to Barker as a man of "extremist churchmanship," whose policy led to the estrangement between dioceses. He was, wrote Border,

> . . . a weak, cautious and unimaginative administrator and he must be regarded by all constitutional historians as the "tragic bishop" of the Australian Church. On him lies the responsibility for the century-old constitutional divisions in the Australian Church which have been both its bondage and its shame.[5]

Border came from the High Church Armidale Diocese. His criticism of Barker rings strangely to a Sydney Anglican's ears. The divisions to which he refers existed long before Barker arrived.

These date back to the Anglican Church created by the Elizabethan Settlement of 1559—a compromise—and as such, it contained the potential for dissatisfaction in later years. Some 30 years later, towards the end of Elizabeth's reign, Richard Hooker wrote *The Laws of Ecclesiastical Polity*. Published in 1593, and though little-read at the time, it was, according to Diamaid MacCulloch, "one of the chief starting points for England's move away from mainstream Protestantism." The Archbishop of Canterbury of

---

2. Ibid., 13.

3. Shaw, *William Grant Broughton*, 241.

4. Even Sydney and Newcastle, 160 kilometers apart, were a considerable distance from each other in the days before fast transport.

5. Davis, *Australian Anglicans and their Constitution*, 15–16.

the time, John Whitgift, "scourge of Puritans" had asked Hooker to write a book which would assist him in his campaign against the Puritans. *The Laws* was the result. In *The Laws* Hooker managed both to defend and to undermine the Elizabethan Settlement. He defended it to the point that, as MacCulloch says, "After reading it, one feels that if the parliamentary legislation of 1559 had laid down that English clergy were to speak standing on their heads, then Hooker would have found a theological reason for justifying it."[6] But Hooker also undermined the Reformed position. While careful not to challenge Reformed propositions too directly, Hooker re-emphasised the role of the sacraments and liturgical prayer at the expense of preaching. The whole purpose of his book was to widen the *adiaphora:* the number of matters about which Christians might hold different views. His work was "a protean source for future commentators," according to MacCulloch, and he is esteemed by many Anglicans today as supreme among the great formative theologians of Anglicanism.[7]

Hooker died early, but one of his friends, Lancelot Andrewes, became very influential as a preacher and writer. Under his influence, Charles I became a devout High Churchman (or Arminian, as was the contemporary term).[8] His theology was not part of the mainstream theology of the Reformation.

Puritans were those who supported the Reformed position, although not all those who were Reformed were Puritans. After the Puritan victory over King Charles I in the Civil War and their subsequent rule when Oliver Cromwell was Lord Protector (1649-1658), clergy of the re-established Church of England in 1662 mostly turned their backs on Calvinist or Reformed Protestant theology which had been the "overwhelmingly" dominant theology in England until the 1620s. But the 1662 *Prayer Book*, which was the Prayer Book which they used as members of the Anglican Church, was substantially Reformed, being Cranmer's creation of over a century before.

When Charles II became King (1660-1685), he required all those who held public office to take Holy Communion in the Anglican form. Those who refused were called Dissenters and on the 90th anniversary of the Massacre of St Bartholomew's Day, in August 1662, some 3,000 clergy, together with lay people who were of the same mind, departed from the established church. MacCulloch comments: "This was a persecution of Protestants by

6. MacCulloch, *Reformation*, 503-7.

7. See Kaye: *An Introduction to World Anglicanism*, 213; Kaye, *A Church Without Walls* 20-1, 27; Ward: *A History of Global Anglicanism*, 21; Avis, *The Identity of Anglicanism*, 6; Carnley *Reflections in Glass*, 141-2; "The Way, The Truth and the Life." 4.

8. MacCulloch, *Reformation*, 510 and 515.

Protestants unique in Europe in its intensity and bitterness: another major question-mark against the complacent English boast of a national history of tolerance."[9]

With reference to Australian Anglicans attempting to function within one ecclesial organization, Davis notes:

> The briefest of observations of Anglican history since the Reformation, wherever it has found expression, provides examples of considerable "institutional strain" with occasional secessions or outright schism. The most obvious examples of these limits of comprehensiveness would be the expulsion of the Puritan party after the Restoration, the departure of the non-jurors a generation later, the failure to cope with the Methodist movement within the Church of England and the inability of some Anglo-Catholics after 1833 to remain in communion with Canterbury.[10]

And so to Australian Anglicans working with great difficulty on a constitution, and the position of Sydney in this long, drawn out labor.

Two issues were often confused in the debate about a constitution: the first was about autonomy from the English church, and the second concerned unity and a centrally governed Australian church. Sometimes one was forgotten as the other was pursued. Some bishops at the early conferences (the Tractarian Bishop Short of Adelaide, for example) wanted a consensual compact while others wanted autonomy enacted by law (the evangelical Archbishop Perry of Melbourne, for example). There was also the question of exactly who was an Anglican. Anglicans were defined as those in communion with the See of Canterbury.[11] The so-called Lambeth Quadrilateral, setting out the basis of common belief, was approved at the Lambeth Conference in 1888. The four articles of the Quadrilateral were:

1. The Holy Scriptures of the New and Old Testaments, as "containing all things necessary to salvation" and as being the rule and ultimate standard of faith.

---

9. Ibid., 531.

10. Davis, *Australian Anglicans and their Constitution*, 57. "Non-jurors" were a group of Anglican clergy who, after the "Glorious Revolution" of 1688 in which Parliament deposed King James II and installed William and Mary, refused to take an oath of allegiance to the new monarchs, believing that they would violate their oath to the previous king.

11. According to Davis, *Australian Anglicans and their Constitution*, 26. This definition put the CESA in an anomalous position.

2. The Apostle's Creed, as the Baptismal Symbol, and the Nicene Creed, as the sufficient statement of the Christian Faith.

3. The two Sacraments ordained by Christ himself —Baptism and the Supper of the Lord —ministered with unfailing use of Christ's Words of Institution, and of the elements ordained by Him.

4. The Historic Episcopate, locally adapted in the methods of its administration to the varying needs of the nations and people called of God into the Unity of His Church.

Strangely, this document does not mention the formularies: the *Prayer Book*, the *Ordinal* or the *Thirty-Nine Articles*, which are peculiar to the Church of England.

Attempts were made to draft a constitution following the legal opinions of 1911 and 1912, which had been sought as to the legal position of the Nexus. Learned opinion was that the legal state of the churches in Australia was *not* autonomous. Under successive chairmen: Bishop GM Long of Bathurst, Bishop JS Hart of Wangaratta, and Bishop F de W Batty of Newcastle, successive constitutions were drafted, in 1926, 1932, 1936, 1939, 1946, 1951 and 1955.

All dioceses except Sydney accepted the first draft (1926). Archbishop Wright's objections were: "as an evangelical clergyman I could not have possibly assented to the constitution unless I thought that it protected the Protestant and Reformed character of the Church."[12] There was talk by observers, even before the voting, of Sydney forming a separate Sydney church.[13] But Sydney was not alone in its objections and concerns. Conservative Anglo-Catholics, mainly in Queensland, were grateful for Sydney's stand. Their objections were different from Sydney's, however. Their concern was that the draft constitution gave secular entities, not churchmen, the final power in two areas: the proposed Appellate Tribunal, of which the majority was lay lawyers (not bishops) and an Act of Parliament to protect the church from itself.[14]

Bishop Hart called the Diocese of Sydney "the lion in the path of unanimity." Bishop Long wrote of the difficulties of the 1920s:

> Future generations will probably ask wonderingly: "Why were Anglicans so conservative in the nineteen twenties?" "Why could they not have shown a little more trust in us who succeed them?"

12. *ACR* 31.1.1957, 6.
13. Davis, *Australian Anglicans and their Constitution*, 66.
14. Ibid., 67.

> Let us hope that some just and learned historian will arise to tell them that the majority of Anglicans were not distrustful and crustily conservative, but that we loved unity and hated schism, and laid upon that altar some things very precious to us, believing that a later generation would retrieve our sacrifices from the altar where we laid them out."[15]

For Long and many others, unity was paramount. That is why the constitutional committee continued to try to work with the Diocese of Sydney and others who did not vote in favour of the draft constitutions. Sydney was not necessarily shy of schism, and for this Diocese unity on faulty theological foundations was worse than schism.

Sydney agreed to the 1932 draft. It was the Catholic wing of the church which opposed it. But the advent of a new archbishop to Brisbane, JWC Wand, who introduced changes relating to the authority of the *Thirty-Nine Articles*, meant that Sydney also withdrew its support. The advent of TC Hammond to Sydney, who, according to Davis, was more than a match for Wand, increased the heat of the debate in the 1930s.[16]

Minton Taylor, one of the many able Sydney lawyers to involve himself with analysis of constitutional drafts, commented that there were two opposing schools of thought: either "that the faith was committed to the bishops and not the Church, or that the faith was committed to the Church." Bishop Batty observed that Sydney wanted "to tie the Church in Australia irrevocably to the standards of faith and practice formed in the sixteenth and seventeenth centuries in England."[17] This was a fair comment at the time, but one which was to be less true as Sydney departed from liturgical use of the *Book of Common Prayer* in later years.

By the time of the 1946 draft, nothing seemed to have changed. TC Hammond was conjecturing about forming a new Church of England; the *ACR* wrote: "a knife is to be put at the throat of loyal sons of the Reformation . . . We cannot . . . surrender our birthright."[18] Bishop Johnson of Ballarat wrote:

> What Sydney is asking for is that we should rivet upon ourselves for all time the very fetters from which we set out to escape over 30 years ago . . . Is the Church of England a sect or denomination

---

15. Ibid., 6, quoting the Bishop of Bathurst, in *Adelaide Church Guardian* 8.6.1928, 6.
16. Ibid., 77, 80–90.
17. Ibid., 92–93.
18. *ACR* 6.9.1945, 9.

which 300 years ago adopted a set of unalterable standards which must be preserved for all time by the process of law...?[19]

But the *Book of Common Prayer* and the *Thirty-nine Article of Religion*, dating from 1662, are where Sydney finds its identity.

Despite what seemed to be unchangeably entrenched positions, there was marked progress during the next few years. A number of things had changed. First, the English were planning to revise their canons, and this might well mean that unacceptable clerical garb, for example, would now be lawful. Links with England were now to be seen as less of a protection for Reformation principles than formerly. Second, the outcome of the Red Book Case strengthened Sydney's hand. Third, TC Hammond decided to support autonomy, and persuaded Archbishop Mowll to do so. Fourth, the residential conferences to discuss the new draft constitution were a place for people to understand each other, grow to appreciate one another, and even trust one another a little more. Bishop Batty and TC Hammond became friends, as did Archbishop Moline (Perth) and Archbishop Mowll. These were indeed friendships across a divide.[20]

The final impetus, and perhaps the greatest, was the visit of the Archbishop of Canterbury, Geoffrey Fisher, to Australia, in 1950. Mowll was now Primate, and chaired the General Synod when Fisher was present. Fisher made it clear that Australia must have its own constitution. As well as strongly urging Australian Anglicans to break the impasse, he drafted suggestions for a constitution while on his sea voyage home to England. Fisher's analysis of the Australian Anglican church to the Australian House of Bishops was that of an informed and authoritative outsider's perceptions of the situation. He was strongly in favour of a strong central body to "stand behind the provinces and archbishops and indeed control them."[21] He recommended that there be an Archbishop of Australia: this, in Fisher's view, would relieve the Sydney-Melbourne tension, and the High Church-Low Church tension. He said that the first necessity was for a constitution. It would be fatal if the Church in Australia did not have one—it must make another attempt. He advised that Sydney should be given every safeguard.

His notes state that he said:

> Fear must be replaced by trust. If Sydney is afraid, it is not altogether surprising. As I have gone through Australia I have seen

19. Davis, *Australian Anglicans and their Constitution* 106, quoting Bishop WH Johnson of Ballarat, in *The Church Standard*, August 24 1945, 6.

20. Davis, *Australian Anglicans and their Constitution,* 141–43.

21. Memo regarding Fisher's speech to the Australian House of Bishops, Fisher Papers, Papers 74.

> monochrome dioceses and even monochrome provinces of an advanced Anglo-Catholic type: if that is reaction from Sydney's Irish Protestantism, Sydney is a reaction from them. In fact, they go on reacting to one another. Where is the central tradition firmly established? Look at the theological colleges: Moore College is firmly rooted at the Low Church end. St Michael's Adelaide with the whole weight of Kelham behind it. The danger of monochromity is acute. In Queensland and Adelaide I got a strong impression that before very long hardly a clergyman would survive who was not an Anglo-Catholic, and it must be added that on the whole the later generations of Anglo-Catholics are a good deal inferior to their predecessors.

He noted: "They took it extremely well and were really rather exhilarated by having a number of blows straight from the shoulder, and I am inclined to think it was the best thing I did in the Antipodes."[22] From this memo it is clear, by the way, that Sydney was unique because it was *evangelical*.

Fisher sent his redraft of the constitution off to Batty with the disclaimer that it was done in a lighthearted spirit and without re-reading what he had written. The key suggestion he made, which seems to have been the tie breaker was: "all liberty should be given to a diocese to contract out of any canon so far as its own internal life of faith, ceremonial, discipline etc. is concerned."[23]

Batty as Chairman of the constitution committee thanked Fisher for his "amazingly kind" enclosure. It had come at a "most opportune time." He added, "If the existing draft were remoulded nearer to Sydney's heart it would be rejected by all the dioceses of Queensland and West Australia"![24] Batty's "Hymn for the Constitution Committee" written in 1950, and safely stored in the Fisher Papers at Lambeth Palace Archives, is a gem. Sydney was not the only butt of Batty's humour.

> A few more synods held
> A few conventions more
> And we shall be most probably
> Just where we were before.
> When Newcastle has done
> The utmost that he can
> The proper study of mankind

22. Ibid.
23. Fisher to Batty 15.2.51, Fisher Papers 74.
24. Batty to Fisher 1.3.51, Fisher Papers 74.

Will surely still be Mann.²⁵

A few more efforts made
To please the Sydney group
And we shall very likely be
Completely in the soup.
And on the other hand
If Queensland sets the pace
The Reformation might as well
Have never taken place.

A few more herrings drawn
Across the main debate
And we shall be back where we were
In 1928.
We'll still await the day
When all the clergy come
To trust the Bishops and concede their *jus litugicum*.

A few amendments moved
To section 54
And we shall reach undoubtedly
The controversy's core.
When all is said and done
This is the matter's pith
Shall we be ruled by reason
Or by Canon Langford Smith.²⁶

Not all Sydney leaders were convinced that the 1955 draft constitution should be accepted: a number of bright young men, including David Broughton Knox (to be Principal of Moore College from 1958 to 1985) and Donald Robinson (Archbishop of Sydney 1982–1993) expressed their opposition cogently. Over the years the *ACR* was assiduous in tracking matters small and great in the tortuous process of reviewing drafts of the constitution. For example, the editorial of 3 March 1955 stated that the new

---

25. WJG Mann was a leading layman, barrister, and Chancellor of the Diocese who opposed the Constitution in the 1920s because it could be altered. Judd and Cable, *Sydney Anglicans*, 211; Cameron, *SCEGGS*, 125.

26. Fisher Papers 79. Neville Langford-Smith, a Sydney clergyman, became Bishop of Central Tanganyika in 1960.

constitution contained contradictory principles: first that the ecclesiastical unit is as wide as the nation, and second that the diocese is the true unit of the church. It began with one principle (that of a supreme central legislature) and assimilated another, contrary principle without abandoning the first. If the diocese is the unit, why have a completely new constitution at all? It would have been much better and simpler to amend the old, when needed, than to adopt a completely new, inconsistent constitution.[27] Robinson's verdict on the constitution is memorable:

> We only remain united by maintaining two denominations in one organization and allowing members of both to call themselves Anglican. But the real problem we have to face is that there is no unity between these two divergent views at the level of local worship, which is the only valid test of unity. While this remains the case, the alleged comprehensiveness of the Church of England is a chimera.[28]

Before the Sydney synod approved the draft Constitution, the *ACR* carried a prescient and clear article explaining the position of the Sydney Diocese. Sydney's *identity* was at stake. The article noted the size of the diocese and the imbalance of representation at General Synod; the cost of concessions it had made to the draft constitution, and the strong likelihood of isolation under the proposed new laws. It stated:

> The Diocese of Sydney has always occupied a unique position among the dioceses of Australia in regard to proposals for a new constitution. It is the mother diocese of Australia, and although now the smallest but one in extent it is still much the largest in numbers. Its size and importance places a proportionately large responsibility on its synod to decide wisely and cautiously what it deems best for the Church in Australia. Its caution is increased by the fact that the voting strength of its delegates in General Synod is only a fraction of what its numerical strength warrants. This means that a very large number of Anglicans are most inadequately represented.
>
> The tendency toward ritualism and the loosening of Reformation standards which has largely characterized the Anglican Communion over the past century means, in general, that Protestant churchmen have least to gain and most to lose by a new constitution in Australia. It is not therefore surprising that the initiative in constitutional reform has not come from Sydney.

---

27. *ACR* 3.3.1955, 2. This may well be Robinson's work.
28. Davis, *Australian Anglicans and their Constitution*, 149.

Sydney's role has usually been that of being asked to agree to a change which it did not desire or request, and which may be fraught with uncertainty in effect. Similarly, while debates on the successive drafts have included any references to "concessions" to this or that party, such concessions have in reality been all on one side. It is difficult to see that any concessions are made by the present draft constitution to the predominantly Protestant and evangelical diocese of Sydney ... They are not concessions compared with what the diocese at present legally enjoys under the existing constitution.

Of the 3½ million members of the Church of England in Australia, 1½ million or 43% live in NSW. In fact, just under a third of the Anglicans of Australia live in the diocese of Sydney.

The significance of these figures is seen when the adoption of the proposed new constitution for the Church in Australia is contemplated. For in the eyes of the law the new constitution would wind up the Church of England in NSW and inaugurate a new church. Of course, churchmen are at liberty to act in this manner, but they cannot then continue to use the property given to the Church of England without an Act of Parliament, taking it away from the Church of England and giving it to the new church. It is hard to imagine Parliament passing such an act if there is an appreciable body of persons who object to their property being taken from them.

Certainly, if the Diocese of Sydney does not approve the constitution, it is not practical politics to expect Parliament to pass such an act. This means that if Sydney does not accept, NSW does not go into the constitution, and if NSW, with almost half the Anglican population in Australia within it, does not implement the proposed constitution, it is not likely that the rest of Australia will want to do so.

It is sometimes said that if Sydney does not accept the constitution, it will be isolated as a diocese. But the above considerations show that this fear is without substance. On the other hand, the danger that Sydney will be isolated is real under the provisions of the proposed constitution, which allow the church a wide latitude of change in an Anglo-Catholic direction (at present illegal), while permitting each diocese to reject such change. The consequence is likely to be a widening gulf between the outlook of the Diocese of Sydney and that of the rest of the church in Australia. Sydney will become isolated within the constitution and tremendous pressures will be generated to make it abandon its evangelical position and conform to the theological outlook prevalent in the rest of Australia.[29]

The Sydney Synod approved the draft constitution in 1957. The approval of each diocese was necessary for the constitution to be adopted, and Adelaide held out until September 1961—the last diocese to approve it. The Constitution was adopted in 1962, when the Church of England in Australia came into being.[30] By then Archbishop Mowll was dead.

The decades-long debate over a Constitution was essentially about *identity*. For Sydney, it raised the issue of who we really are and why we care about certain principles. Who and what threatened our identity? Liberal theology and Anglo-Catholicism were identified as the key enemies to remaining an evangelical diocese and in consequence were opposed consistently and tenaciously. Unless this is recognized, many of the old controversies appear to contemporary minds to be strange and even bizarre. The threat to who we are makes Sydney defensive and also forces us to experiment.

The 1950s were a time for the Sydney diocese of enormous challenge and growth, as the post-war population expanded rapidly. This was the era in Australia when the Liberal Federal government under Robert Menzies held office for sixteen continuous years (1949–1966). It was a period of very stable government since senior ministers remained in office for long periods and there was continuity of policy. The Labor Party was smashed by the Petrov Affair and divided in two after 1955 by the creation of the Roman Catholic, anti-communist DLP.[31] On an international scale, the Korean War began in 1950 and continued until 1953. 17,000 men served in the war and 339 lost their lives. Another 1,200 were wounded. The year after the Korean War ended, the hydrogen bomb, the most destructive weapon man had ever invented up to that time, was exploded. The long reign of Queen Elizabeth II began in 1952. Menzies, "an accomplished and avuncular courtier" welcomed the new Queen and the Duke of Edinburgh in a prolonged tour of Australia in 1954.[32] Australia was still very British in affection.

Many "migrants" came to settle in Australia from a great variety of European nations, as well as British people. The post war Baby Boomer generation was born. Census figures for 1954 show that there were now 7,651,802 Australians. This figure excluded Aborigines. New South Wales

---

29. *ACR* 14.3.1957, 4.

30. The Church of England in Australia changed its name to The Anglican Church of Australia in 1981.

31. Bolton, *The Oxford History of Australia 5*, 139–145.

32. Ibid., 140.

was the most populous state, with 3,423,529 inhabitants. Of that number, 1,466,571 claimed to be Anglicans—about one fifth of the total population.

The 1950s in retrospect were the age of a return to piety. The late 1940s and 1950s witnessed the greatest church growth that Britain had experienced since the mid 19th century.[33] In *The Death of Christian Britain*, Callum Brown notes,

> Traditional values of family, home and piety were suddenly back on the agenda between the end of the war and 1960. The churches benefited immediately. During the late 1940s and the first half of the 1950s, organized Christianity experienced the greatest per annum growth in church membership, Sunday school enrollment, Anglican confirmations and presbyterian recruitment of its baptized constituency since the 18th century ... Marking the mood, religious revivals spread across Britain, aided by new technology and new forms. The Billy Graham crusades of 1954–6 were especially noteworthy, producing mass audiences ...
>
> Accompanying all of this was a revival of tract distribution and district visiting on a scale not witnessed since the late Victorian and Edwardian periods ... Attendances at the Greater London crusade in 1954 represented 21.2 of the resident population, whilst attendances in Glasgow represented 73.7 per cent of the city's population.

The phenomenon was repeated in Australia, and in Sydney. During the 1950s the population within parishes grew, as did their number. In Sydney in 1950 there were 173 parishes: by 1958 there were 220. In addition there were 219 branch churches in 1950 and 232 branch churches by 1958. Within the parishes children flocked to Sunday School and bishops presided at huge confirmation services. For instance, at St Thomas', Kingsgrove, there were 140 confirmees in August 1959, and 900 children enrolled in the Sunday School.[34] New areas stretched the diocesan resources. The *ACR* reported in March 1958:

> There is probably no greater domestic challenge before the Australian Church today than that of the huge new housing areas which have developed in all the major cities in recent years. Nowhere is that development more clearly seen than in the new housing areas of Sydney, where many thousands of homes have been built, and many more on schedule.

---

33. Brown, *The Death of Christian Britain*, 170.
34. *ACR* 20.8.1959, 6.

> In Sydney the development of new housing is particularly noticeable in church districts like Villawood with Old Guilford and East Fairfield; Sefton with Birrong; Regent's Park and Chester Hill; or in parishes like Carlingford, which includes the Dundas Valley estate, visited last week by her Majesty Queen Elizabeth the Queen Mother.
>
> Almost fantastic development has taken place on the NSW south coast, where Wollongong has expanded into a huge industrial city with suburbs stretching for many miles. A recent estimate of the population of the City of Greater Wollongong was 100,000. Town planning authorities believe that within five years this figure will have doubled . . .
>
> In the Diocese of Sydney, the Home Mission Society has done much to help the work in new districts . . . a spokesman for the society said: "In new areas, the financing of the work is not easy because of the disinterest of the majority of people. The new housing areas are mission fields indeed, and the Church as a whole must be responsible. We must do more and more in sending missionaries to these fields at our own front door."[35]

For Evangelicals in the diocese of Sydney, "mission" meant preaching and teaching the good news of salvation through Christ's death and resurrection. It was not primarily about getting people to go to church, but about repentance, faith in Jesus Christ, and living a new life in obedience to Christ. The churches were where people's faith was nurtured, as well as places where the gospel was taught. Archbishop Mowll threw his vast weight behind mission in his diocese. His appointment of the Rev. Graham Delbridge in 1942 as Chaplain for Youth had borne lots of fruit. By the time Delbridge resigned in 1952, the diocese had purchased two properties at Port Hacking, "Chaldercot" and "Rathane." Mowll called them "the hub of diocesan youth work" and an estimated 5,000 young people annually spent a weekend or longer there. A Youth Leaders' Training Course had been operating for seventeen years, by 1952, with about 100 young people attending these courses annually.[36]

Mowll initiated a Diocesan Mission in 1951, after conferring with his clergy. The mission aimed at reaching the 70% of the community not actively attached to any church, and concentrating on the "New Districts." A Children's Week, Youth Weekends, and Family Services were planned.[37] Individual parishes held missions from time to time, and notable English

---

35. *ACR* 6.3.1958, 1.
36. Archbishop's Letter *SDM* April 20, 19–20.
37. Ibid., September 20, 123.

evangelists were invited to Sydney: Canon Bryan Green in 1951 and the Rev. John Stott in 1958, for example. Green's visit attracted 75,000 people, crowded into the Cathedral and the Town Hall, with more listening to him on the radio. 3,000 signed "witness cards" professing to have put their trust in Jesus Christ.[38] John Stott led a mission at the University of Sydney in August 1958, then in Melbourne, organised by the evangelical students from Melbourne University.[39] Howard Guinness at St Barnabas' Broadway, a step away from the gates of the University of Sydney, led student Bible studies and conducted university missions.[40] The Rev. Bernard Gook, Diocesan Missioner and a fellow Briton, led conferences on evangelism.[41] These men and their work were commended in the annual Presidential Address Mowll delivered at the Sydney synod.

Although not Anglican institutions as such, the Children's Special Service Mission (CSSM) and Scripture Union (SU) were strongly supported by Evangelicals in the Sydney diocese. Mowll was World President of CSSM.[42]

Beach missions were a CSSM initiative and were planted in camping areas up and down the NSW coast for the ten days after Christmas. They aimed to reach holidaymakers, especially children and teenagers, with the gospel. Throughout Australia in 1959 there were over 50 beach missions and in NSW over 600 young people served on 23 CSSM teams along over 1,100 kilometers of coastline stretching between Evans Head and Lake Tabaine. The bad weather that year meant that meetings were held inside the tents, instead of outdoors, and the *ACR* reported that the closer contact produced "was one external reason for the particular fruitfulness of this summer's missions." The work of Scripture Union took over where the beach mission teams left off, providing inquirers with notes for daily Bible Reading. Toowoon Bay Beach Mission reported a record 128 subscriptions for 1959.[43] Camp Howard, another initiative of the Diocesan Youth Department, was established in 1956. Bible teaching and direction in Christian living were at the center of the program. The holiday camps proved very popular from the

---

38. *ACR* 7.8.1958, 1.

39. Ibid., 12.6.1958, 1.

40. Presidential Address, *Sydney Year Book* 1954, 49.

41. Ibid., 1957, 46.

42. Mowll's engagement diary in the *Sydney Morning Herald*, 20.8.1938 re the CSSM Annual Meeting 1938; also *Morning Bulletin*, Rockhampton, 5.5.1945. His predecessor in this position was Bishop Taylor Smith, who died in 1938. Loane, *Archbishop Mowll*, 68.

43. *ACR* 19.2.1959, 3.

start—in the January of 1957 an estimated 1,000 schoolchildren attended Camp Howard holidays at Port Hacking.[44]

The outcome of all this activity is difficult to quantify. Statistics from the diocesan Year Books of the 1950s indicate considerable growth in the number of active clergy, parishes and the proportion of Sydney clergy who had trained at Moore College.[45] It was a struggle for parishes to accommodate congregational growth and there was a surge of church hall building. For example, in 1957 seventeen new church halls were opened as well as five new churches. There was even a diocesan "mobile church"—a van from which a service could be conducted, in areas where no church as yet stood.[46]

In his Synod Charge of 1952 Mowll urged Sydney people to take up the challenge of evangelism with the rapidly growing population. Having given precise details, he ended his speech with a plea:

> The growth of the population, the new housing areas, the influx of migrants all provide a tremendous opportunity for evangelism. If the impact of the Gospel is not brought to bear upon the homes in these new suburbs in their early days, the opportunity may pass. If, however, energetic efforts are made now, they will bear lasting fruit. Church people, in the name of the Church, must give time to visit newcomers, and, when possible, might open their homes for Sunday School or a Church Service."[47]

The laity were being mobilized in the face of this great need. Perhaps this was a phenomenon in itself.

Several years later the indefatigable Mowll urged parishes to look beyond their boundaries. At a Diocesan Festival he said:

> I beg of those responsible to be truly Christian in the breadth of their outlook and understanding of the needs of others. We

---

44. Presidential Address, *Sydney Year Book* 1956 p47; *ACR* 6.12.1957 p9; *SDM* October-November1956, 36.

45. Statistics for 1950s from *Sydney Year Books* 1950 and 1960:

	1949	1959
Active clergy	259	290
Parishes	173	188
Moore College trained	179 (60%)	250 (86%)

46. *Sydney Year Book* 1954, 48; Archbishop's Letter, *SDM* July-August 1956,13.

47. *SDM* 20.7.1952, 74.

must resist the temptation to supply our many parochial needs first and only give what is over to the pressing needs of the housing areas.

What is the good of our improving buildings in our parishes and providing other amenities if these new areas are growing up without help? This tremendous need has not properly been realized. If the gospel is to be spread it is urgent that we should purchase sites in the new communities that are being developed and that we should build the necessary facilities.

The *ACR* added:

In the District of Corrimal, for example, while the number of schoolteachers has increased from 60 to 230, and doctors from 7 to 31, the number of clergy in the same period has only increased from 4 to 5.

The District of Villawood, where a Curate-in-charge ministers with the help of a deaconess, has 5,000 new homes, with 20 new families moving in each week. There are eight primary schools with 2,600 Anglican children to be instructed. Over 40 school classes are taken each week.[48]

Two ways in which Mowll sought to address the challenges of growth were by the Every Member Canvass, which was a fundraising venture, and by supporting growth at Moore College. Individual parishes were able to choose whether to participate in the Every Member Canvass, run by the Department of Promotion under the HMS umbrella. The Rev. RS Walker ran the program, starting in 1956, and while it was somewhat controversial, its aims, according to Mowll, were the deepening of Christian fellowship, and the full commitment of each member of the church to Jesus Christ and his kingdom. Participants were asked to pledge a certain amount of money during the year. "Stewardship" was to be emphasized in teaching from the pulpit.[49] More than half the parishes participated, and some large sums of money were raised over the next few years. To some extent, the energy put into fundraising was diverted from energy for evangelism, and even undermined it, when "nominal" Christians were approached to make a financial contribution to the work of the church.[50]

Mowll's strong support for Moore College had not waned. It was the key to evangelism in his diocese. So in 1952, having reviewed the phenomena of growth in Sydney, and also the terrifying fall in the number of clergy

---

48. *ACR* 24.5.1956, 1.
49. Archbishop's Letter, *SDM* July-August 1956, 6.
50. Judd and Cable, *Sydney Anglicans*, 261–62.

in England—some 6,000 fewer than in 1914 and 3,000 fewer than in 1940—he wrote:

> The importance of Moore College as the centre of theological training for the Ministry in the Diocese is very great. Eighty per cent of the clergy at work in the Diocese received their training at Moore College. Since the War, there have never been fewer than 60 students in the College, and two new wings have been built to provide adequate accommodation for resident students ... A third wing is now in course of construction ... The present rate of supply, which might have been adequate to maintain the ministry of the Church in pre-war days, is quite inadequate to meet the new demands of the post-war increase of population ... It is as urgent as it has ever been that properly qualified young men should be encouraged to think in terms of a vocation to the Ministry.[51]

Moore College celebrated its centenary in 1956. The College enrolled its 985th student that year and the following year had 101 students on campus—the largest number in its history.[52] Marcus Loane had been appointed Principal in November 1953, on the retirement of TC Hammond. After Loane was made an Assistant Bishop in 1958, Broughton Knox became Principal. Knox, who remained in that post for the next 25 years, was to turn Moore College into an evangelical powerhouse in terms of the numbers of clergy it trained, and the scholarly evangelical work its faculty and alumni produced.

In the 1950s Mowll presided over huge social change: a growing prosperity, the advent of the motorcar, of television, of aeroplane travel. His monthly letters to his diocesan family were full of concern about social issues, whether gambling or the ill effects of the misuse of alcohol, or the influence of television. His focus was broader than evangelism *per se*. His strenuous travel commitments also point to a man eager to see and learn and understand, especially after his election as Primate (1947). He became President of the Australian Council of Churches in 1946 and as a delegate to the World Council of Churches inaugural assembly in Amsterdam in 1948 he had, and continued to have, a strong involvement in the ecumenical movement. His missionary zeal also pulled him beyond his Anglican boundaries. Travel, whether within Australia or internationally, gave him bonds with a diverse group of people. No one could have described this evangelical leader as parochial.

51. *SDM* 1952 July 20, 76.
52. Hodgson Register. *ACR* 28.2.1957.

His second visit to China in 1956 was a wonderful climax to all his travel, and took him back to his workplace of over a quarter century before. It was at the invitation of the Chairman of the House of Bishops and Mowll's purpose was to renew contact with the Chung Hua Sheng Kung Hui—a member church of the Anglican Communion. The Mowlls visited Howard Mowll's old diocese of Szechwan. People there, he thought, had not seen a Westerner since the last missionary left. He renewed contacts with old friends, was encouraged to hear that the church was "not only holding her own, but in some places, the Church attendance was increasing and new churches had been opened." Mowll did not go out of his way to sniff out difficulties of the Communist regime and in this he was politically naïve. He wrote that he saw no evidence of anti-Western indoctrination and little "indication of widespread liquidation"![53] This was the very year in which Mao Tse Tung initiated his twelve-year plan for agriculture, the target being to triple the grain output of 1936, the highest-ever. As peasants were already living on a knife-edge, millions, at a minimum, would be tipped into starvation and death.[54] Mowll strongly encouraged Sydney Anglicans to pray for the Christian Church in China, that he and the other delegates would stir up "a great outpouring of prayer for the Chinese Church, which had been preserved during those difficult days." Mowll's ongoing links with the church in China gave him the vision for missionary work closer to home: CMS work in South-East Asia.

One rather striking feature of the Mowll era was the annual Reformation Rally. Inaugurated in 1929, the rallies were a pungent way of reminding Sydney Anglicans of their hard-won Protestant heritage. Over 300 people attended the rally of October 1956, held close to Reformation Sunday (the 22nd Sunday after Pentecost), which was held in the Chapter House. That year the chairman of the rally, Mr. Norman Jenkyn QC, spoke of the benefits the Protestant Reformation had conferred, especially mentioning the emphasis on the right of direct access to God by the soul. Bible reading and prayers followed, then there were two addresses: the first by the Dean, the Very Rev. EA Pitt, on "Thomas Cranmer the man" followed by the Rev. DWB Robinson, on "Thomas Cranmer: his message." It was the 400th anniversary of Cranmer's death. The *ACR* always noted the annual rallies and from time to time ran articles about the Reformers.[55] Sydney Evangelicals were not the only ones commemorating the Reformation annually. We

---

53. *SDM* Feb-March 1957, 62–63.

54. Chang, and Halliday, *Mao. The Unknown Story*, 415. This biography of Mao contains no references to the treatment of Christians.

55. *ACR* 25.10.1956, 16.

know from newspapers of the day that Brisbane, Townsville, Melbourne, Hobart, and possibly Adelaide also held Reformation Rallies, and that they continued into the 1950s.[56]

The issue of the place of women in the church was beginning to warm up. The ordination of Florence Tim Oi Li in 1944 by the Bishop of Hong Kong had ended in Florence's withdrawal from priestly ministry but she was a lonely signpost to future change. After the War was over, various groups turned their minds to the question of appropriate women's ministry. The first ordinations took place: in 1948 three Danish women were ordained as pastors of the Danish Church. The *Sydney Diocesan Magazine* noted "the ordaining Bishop vigorously defending against much criticism this unique act, claimed that women exercised a real ministry in the life of the early church."[57] A decade later the Church of Sweden voted by a majority of 69 to 29 to accept women as ordained ministers, despite fears of schism.[58]

In England, in 1947, a committee appointed by the Archbishops of Canterbury and York to inquire into theological training of women "for service in the church" recommended a determined effort to recruit educated women and that a new theological college offering a two-year course be established for them.[59] It is possible that nothing came of this plan. At much the same time the World Council of Churches established a Commission on the Life and Work of Women in the Church.[60] In 1954 the Archbishops of Canterbury and York re-affirmed the Order of Deaconesses as the one order in the Church of England to which women were admitted by prayer and the laying on of hands of the bishop. This was a kind of ordination, and gave such a woman "distinctive and permanent status in the Church," and thenceforth she was dedicated to "lifelong service and ministry."[61]

In the *ACR*, in 1951 "Kanonikos"—whoever that was—wrote an article entitled "Should women be priests?" He noted that "women had a real part to play in the ministry of the early church. The question is, were there some functions of the ministry which women were not permitted to exercise?" He concluded that Paul's injunctions to women (I Corinthians 14:33ff and

---

56. *Nambour Chronicle and North Coast Advertiser* e.g. 4.11.1938, 4; *The Courier-Mail*, Brisbane e.g. 2.11.1953, 5; *The Argus*, Melbourne e.g. 4.11.1936, 5; *The Mercury*, Hobart, e.g. 5.11.1936, 5; *Townsville Daily Bulletin* e.g.30.10.1943, 4. Sydney's rallies continued into the early1960s—*Southern Cross* advertised one for 1964: September issue 1964.

57. *SDM* 20.8.1948, 166.

58. *ACR* 16.10.1958, 3.

59. *SDM* 20.8.1947, 15.

60. Ibid., 20.10.1949, 161.

61. Ibid., October 1955, January 1966, 75.

I Timothy 2:12) are based on the principle that women should not exercise authority over men. He stated,

> In view of the fact that the Apostle does not prohibit praying or prophesying, we may reasonably infer that "not to speak" means that women should not be teachers or preachers in the congregation. It also follows from the principle that women should not have the oversight of a congregation.[62]

This was a different perspective from an article some six years earlier in the same newspaper. On that occasion the anonymous writer described the Bishop of Hong Kong's action in ordaining a woman as "noble audacity" because he refused to place "what is after all only an ecclesiastical convention" before the spiritual necessities of the children of God.[63]

Some of the views about women's ministry seem sad and comic to 21st century eyes. A clergyman from Victoria, in a letter published by the *ACR*, having noted how much he owed to his mother, went on to say that the rights of women "inevitably lead on to the rights of children to equality also. This is seen in the undisciplined child of today," and that the fight for women's rights "is a sure sign of national decadence." He noted that "a few Deborahs and Huldahs emerge occasionally like Dorothy Sayers and Maude Royden but they only emphasis the failure of their contemporary males."[64]

Nora Tress, of Chatswood, Sydney, wrote a letter in response:

> An alternative heading to this letter might have been "O Vain Man." I . . . would like to know what Mr. Lousada would really like to do with us. Would he veil us again and restore us to the sanctity and seclusion of the Easterns? Does he really wish to deprive us of the right to vote, the right to hold any sort of executive position, or the right to voice an opinion in the public affairs of this world, spiritual or material?
>
> It is a serious charge to make us responsible for national decadence, and I meekly protest against being classed with the unruly children of our modern age! It all sounds like the old, old, story of Adam blaming Eve for all that has gone wrong with the man-governed world.
>
> . . . If Mr. Lousada's feelings are interpreted correctly, I gather he may not care very much for deaconesses. Perhaps he would disallow them altogether (seeing they are permitted to do next to nothing anyway) and I suppose that all lady missionaries

---

62. *ACR* 8.3.1951, 12.
63. Ibid., 11.9.1947, 8.
64. Ibid., 8.9.1951, 9.

should be withdrawn from the field, and female Sunday School teachers used only with discretion.

I wonder when the gentlemen who are followers of Mr. Lousada's creed will recognize that God has bestowed upon women gifts and talents which may only be fully used in his service if given positions of responsibility. The placing of women under the authority of man came about as one of the results of the Fall. When the Saviour was born of a woman her emancipation began and has gone on down through the Christian era. I feel sure that with the Second Coming of our Lord it will be completed, and she shall be restored to the position God intended her to have before her first great transgression.[65]

The issue of women's ministry raised unsettling questions about Scriptural interpretation and would become deeply divisive among Christians in the following decades, partly because it was emotive and partly because many conservative Evangelicals saw it is much more than a problem of church order: for them nothing less than the authority of the Bible was at stake. Those conservatives who opposed the ordination of women held their convictions from a sincerely held view of the Bible. Archbishop Peter Jensen has stated: "Holding a conservative position is very difficult. It requires courage and faithfulness."[66]

One woman with a high profile and a busy ministry as a diocesan leader was Dorothy Mowll. A keen sportswoman in her youth, a passionate supporter of mission work and a talented linguist, she was a woman of remarkable gifts. As wife of the Archbishop of Sydney she was his great support, but also used her position to "make things happen." She was tireless in helping to organize the biggest gathering of Anglicans ever seen outside England for the Broughton Centenary of 1936. During the Second World War she directed and worked alongside some 2,000 women in helping servicemen with canteens, meals and hostel accommodation while they were on leave. She was awarded the OBE in 1956. She planned the CENEF Center and was a warm supporter of Camp Howard. After her death just before Christmas in 1957, the *Sydney Diocesan Magazine* wrote a long tribute to her. It is an amazing measure of the degree to which Dorothy Mowll was loved and appreciated. The article stated:

> She was an astoundingly successful organizer and leader, a visionary yet with her feet planted firmly on the ground, a woman utterly determined to complete every job given her to do. But

---

65. Ibid., 22.3.1951, 10.
66. Archbishop Peter Jensen interview with MHC 4.3.2015.

for all that she was greatly beloved by those who worked with her. In one sense they could never quite keep up with her. She had a vision and a determination far beyond the average, and so was able to take the seemingly impossible tasks in her stride . . . She was a gifted conversationalist . . . She was at home in any company and made the same vital impression wherever she went.[67]

Howard Mowll himself was nearing his final years and died within a year of his wife's death. He noted in his Archbishop's letter of October 1955 that at the recent General Synod, which he as Primate chaired, a motion moved by the Bishop of Ballarat and seconded by the Bishop of New Guinea, read

> That this Synod extends its gratitude to His Grace the Primate for his leadership in the life of the Church in Australia and records with thankfulness the fact that since the last Session of General Synod the Primate has visited every Diocese in the Commonwealth, including New Guinea and assures His Grace that his visits have been greatly appreciated by the Dioceses and have materially helped to bring together the Churches in unity and concord. It renders thanks to God that, under the leadership of His Grace, the Church is developing a wider vision of its mission task.

It was a timely motion, since although the movers were not to know, this was his last General Synod.[68]

Mowll's indefatigable travelling was beneficial for the unity of the Australian Anglican Church. He created personal bonds wherever he went. In consequence, the sometimes fierce and bitter wrangles over the Constitution were less damaging than they might have been. Mowll seems to have had a gift for cultivating good, warm relationships. One example is the manner in which he maintained cordial relations with Archbishop Fisher (whose correspondence reveals a healthy respect for Mowll), despite the differences between them.[69] The relationship was at it most strained in 1955 when GFB Morris finally became Bishop of the CESA. After Morris's election, Fisher claimed Morris was a "schismatic" and issued a statement that "Unless Bishop Morris withdraws from this position I must regard him as having put himself out of communion with the See of Canterbury and

---

67. *SDM* February 1958, 192–206.

68. Ibid., October 1955, January 1956, 72.

69. For example, Fisher memo 9.8.1948, Mowll to Fisher 14.8.1948 and Fisher to Morris 8.1.1949. Fisher Papers, 39.

outside the fellowship of the Anglican Communion."[70] Morris was quoted in the *Manchester Guardian*:

> No good purpose can be served by seeking to discredit the Church of England in South Africa or by threatening to expel me from communion with the See of Canterbury. It is a form of persecution which will bring discredit on those who practise it. There can be no agreement or concordat with the "Church of the Province" which has deliberately eliminated the Thirty-Nine Articles, promotes a manual such as "The Mass our Sacrifice," advises the invocation of the saints, prayers for the dead, and other pre-Roman practices.[71]

Throughout his long episcopate Howard Mowll was tireless in his support for the CESA and one of his gifts to the wider Evangelical Anglican world is the survival and growth of the Church of England in South Africa.[72]

Howard Mowll died suddenly on 24 October 1958. This writer's mother cried when she heard the sad news. He was a father to the people of the Sydney Diocese: loved, respected, utterly dependable, revered. Many could not remember a time before him. Canon DJ Knox, the most senior clergyman of the diocese, and a tough man, wrote:

> My first involuntary reaction was to cry out when losing so suddenly our friend and leader. Perhaps his outstanding characteristic was unfeigned and unchanging friendship. A loving heart prompted continual acts of thoughtfulness. No one will ever know the extent of his private benefactions. But the Archbishop was at the same time a resolute and determined leader of men; a man greatly to be admired for fortitude and courage; and he led in the right direction, for his heavenly Master was ever in his eye and his Master's book of instructions was ever in his hand.[73]

He was described in an obituary as an outstanding missionary statesman . . . "honored and loved by churchman of all shades of conviction and outlook." He was the sixth in the line of bishops in the Diocese of Sydney and at his death he was the most senior diocesan bishop of the Worldwide Anglican Communion. The editor of the *ACR* stated "there is no doubt that

---

70. 4.10.1955, Fisher Papers, 154.
71. *Manchester Guardian*, 4.10.1955, Fisher Papers, 154.
72. MHC interview with Bishop Frank Retief 9.7.2004.
73. *ACR* 30.10.1958, 1.

the verdict of history will declare that his name must be linked with that of Bishop Barker as the greatest bishop who has yet presided over the diocese."

Chapter 5

The Last of the Englishmen: the Gough Years 1959–1966

Hugh Rowlands Gough, elected to succeed Mowll, was no stranger to Sydney. His credentials were impressive and he was a well-built, handsome man with a confident, resonant, educated English voice. He possessed great presence and looked every inch an archbishop.

At the Election Synod of November 1958, the select list of nominations for the position of Archbishop of Sydney had contained eight names: most of them of men of outstanding ability. As well as HR Gough, there were: the Very Rev. Dr SB Babbage (Principal of Ridley College, and Dean of Melbourne), Bishop Donald Coggan (Bishop of Bradford and afterwards Archbishop of Canterbury 1971–1980), the Rev. John Stott (Rector of All Souls' Langham Place, London), the Rev. MAP Wood (Vicar of St Mary's, Islington) and Mowll's co-adjutor bishops WG Hilliard, RC Kerle and ML Loane.[1] Possibly because some declined the honor, the final list comprised the three co-adjutor bishops and Gough. Stott declined to commit himself to consent to an invitation to be Archbishop of Sydney, if elected. Most illuminating is his strong support for Marcus Loane, whom he considered the most likely successor to Mowll. He wrote, "he is head and shoulders above me as a candidate."[2] The Sydney conservatives were unable to agree on a single nominee, so the conservative vote was divided among the three co-adjutor bishops, while the non-conservatives supported Gough. Perhaps the synod was not yet ready for one of their own, rather than an Englishman, to be their new Archbishop.

1. *ACR* 11.12.58, 5.
2. Dudley-Smith, *John Stott.* 323–24.

Bishop Gough received the required majority of votes in both houses of the synod, and was unanimously invited to become Sydney's seventh Bishop. He was the son of a former rector of St Ebbe's Oxford and married to Madeleine, the eldest daughter of the Twelfth Baron Kinnaird.[3] His evangelical credentials were strong. Like Mowll, he had been president of the evangelical student union CICCU at Cambridge, and for five terms (1926–1927). He had a distinguished career in the Second World War, having been mentioned in dispatches as a chaplain during the War, and awarded the OBE in 1945. While Archdeacon of West Ham, London, and then Bishop of Barking in the diocese of Chelmsford, he developed good administrative skills in re-building after the ravages of the War. He was chairman of the Evangelical Alliance of Great Britain, and most significantly he chaired the 1954 Billy Graham Crusade in London—the only English bishop to support the Crusade wholeheartedly.[4] He had been Bishop of Barking for ten years and was 54 years old when the call came to the Diocese of Sydney.

Archbishop Hugh Rowlands Gough

3. *ACR* 2.6.1966, 1; Harrison, "A consideration of some of the changes occurring during the episcopate of the Most Rev. Hugh Rowland Gough."

4. Loane, Obituary: The Right Rev. Hugh Gough, *The Independent*, Saturday, 29 November 1997; Judd and Cable, *Sydney Anglicans*, 264.

Sydney people knew him from a recent visit. At Mowll's invitation he had come to Sydney in 1957 to take part in the Sydney Clergy School, *en route* to lead a mission in Canada. Mowll must have thought highly of him as, back in 1936, he had invited Gough, after Dean Talbot's death, to be Dean of Sydney.[5] Mowll may well have been thinking of Gough as a suitable successor to be Archbishop of Sydney, when the time came. Certainly, as early as 1951, Broughton Knox, in England at the time, wrote to his parents that Hugh Gough was a possible successor to Mowll. Not a brilliant orator, but he "speaks direct and with weight," was his opinion.[6] Archbishop Fisher also was impressed by Gough, and Gough was his preferred man for appointment as the Bishop of Barking.[7] But Fisher thought that Gough was the wrong man for Sydney.[8]

Marcus Loane wrote mini biographies of many Sydney clergy. For example *Mark These Men* records the lives of 25 men who served the Diocese from the 1930s to the 1970s. Significantly, Hugh Gough's name is not among them, except in a passing reference or two.

There are a couple of telling anecdotes about Hugh Gough. He summoned Athol Richardson, a Judge of the Supreme Court and President of the Anglican Church League, to a meeting. Richardson instructed his secretary to reply that if the Archbishop wished to see him, his secretary would arrange a meeting at Justice Richardson's chambers at a time suitable to both parties. Gough responded and Richardson replied with much the same message. This went on for some months. Eventually Richardson, a small man, went to see Gough. Gough seated Richardson in a chair opposite his desk. In that position Richardson's eyes were roughly on a level with Gough's desktop. Gough sat on the other side of his desk. His opening words were that the ACL must be abolished. Richardson stood up and replied: "Sir, you neither understand who I am nor the ACL," and departed, slamming the door of Gough's office behind him.[9]

A senior clergyman recalls the time he spoke to a handyman employed at Moore College. This man was very competent and had come to Australia from the north of England. He said that he had been asked to do some repairs for the Goughs at Bishopscourt. The next time they met, the clergyman asked him how he had fared at Bishopscourt. The reply was that when

---

5. *SDM*, June 1957 115, and July 147.

6. DB Knox to his parents 7.6.51 and 4.11.51. Quoted in Cameron, *An Enigmatic Life* 119.

7. Fisher to SH Denman 13.11.58, Fisher Papers 194.

8. Reid, *Marcus L Loane*, 49.

9. N Cameron to MHC 7.11.12. Richardson's account to NM Cameron.

he arrived, a housemaid had told him that if he wished to visit the lavatory, he must ring a little hand bell. "Why?" he asked. "Because we don't want tradesmen wandering about the corridors here," she said. He responded that he was not going to ring any little bells when he wanted to visit the bathroom. The class system was the very reason he had left England.[10]

Soon after his arrival in Sydney, Gough alienated himself from the Sydney leadership. In a number of ways Gough was the proverbial square peg in Sydney. His autocratic manner, befitting a bishop in England, made him appear aloof. Able but not reflective, he was a church leader whose lack of theological scholarship set him apart from the bright young men with whom he clashed—especially DB Knox and DWB Robinson. His theology has been described as "not far from what you might call 'camp-fire religion."[11] Archbishop Fisher agreed. Prior to Gough's election, he had written to the Most Rev. Frank Woods, Archbishop of Melbourne : "Gough is a very nice man . . . but . . . without Loane's asset of considerable learning, and I should not feel able to press him upon the Sydney people."[12]

Hugh Gough clashed with young Turks DB Knox and DWB Robinson over the Constitution, and this had long-term consequences for the identity of the Diocese. Archbishop Fisher had, as we have seen, kick-started the Constitution into life back in 1950. By the time Hugh Gough was Archbishop of Sydney, the Constitution was all but finally ratified and in 1960 the State Parliament was to ratify it as the Constitution Act. It was at this point that four Sydney Evangelicals wrote to the Attorney General to request that the bill be held up and at least modified. The four men were DB Knox, DWB Robinson, KN Shelley and the Rev. JRL Johnstone—the latter being the initiator of the letter. The Attorney General declined to act and the bill was duly passed. The letter stirred up a great deal of anger and Gough took the matter very seriously indeed.

Dean Pitt, an Englishman who had nominated Gough for Sydney, was in touch with Fisher, as was Gough.[13] The correspondence makes fascinating reading, revealing the level of hostility Pitt and Fisher held towards Sydney Evangelicals. Pitt wrote to the Attorney General, RR Dowling, sending a copy to Fisher.[14] In it he criticized the Evangelicals' letter as "an act, of course, of the grossest discourtesy and disloyalty" because they had not informed

---

10. Interview with MHC 8.11.12.

11. Barnett interview with MHC 22.4.2002. What Barnett heard said of Gough, rather than his own words about Gough.

12. Quoted in Reid, *Marcus L Loane*, 49.

13. Pitt to Fisher 14.11.1960, Fisher Papers, 235.

14. Ibid.

the Archbishop of their intentions. He mentioned that "a certain faction have attempted to dominate our Diocesan Synod, and have insisted that the Synod have the last say in everything." He also wrote that the approach of these men to the Attorney General had "deeply upset the Archbishop."

Fisher described the men to Pitt as "obdurate clergy who have lost all feeling for Our Lord's spirit of evangelism, and have become mere politicians handling the word of God deceitfully."[15] Pitt replied:

> . . . I am sure these people will not get away with it but great harm is being done to the name of the church. They hanker for martyrdom and I say let them have it! Or send them to South Africa for Fred Morris.
>
> We may well have an unpleasant battle with some of our people because the political machine of the Protestant underworld is in good working order. However I am having to lower myself into organizing shock troops . . .
> I am sure we must get rid of Dr Knox and Robinson from Moore College, which is the key to our problem.[16]

TC Hammond he described as "a great trial to any Liberal thought" in the same letter.

For all the grandiose claims as to the value of the Constitution, a senior Brisbane layman who had been a member of the Constitution Committee from the early 1950s, described the Constitution as

> One of the most rigid, frustrating and ineffectual constitutions ever devised, which makes that of the United Nations look like a dictatorship by comparison. One distinguished lawyer said "it is not a constitution, but a colander, full of holes." No doubt the holes were the many ways of escaping, deferring, or avoiding the effects of the constitution.[17]

Fisher and Gough both dealt with DB Knox in their own separate ways. In his letter to Knox, Fisher brought out the big guns. He spoke of "a point beyond which obstruction cannot be the will of the Holy Spirit" and of the "immense importance for the whole Church in Australia that it should become self-governing under its own Constitution." This was, Fisher wrote, because "it comes straight from the principles of the New Testament and the

---

15. Fisher to Pitt 22.11.1960, Fisher Papers, 235.

16. Pitt to Fisher 2.12.1960, Fisher Papers, 235.

17. Ronald St John in *Church Scene*, 12.3.1982, 4. Quoted in Davis, *Australian Anglicans and their Constitution*, 172.

Apostolic Age and the Sub-Apostolic age." He wrote about the Imperialism of Rome which he was "perfectly sure is false to the Apostolic pattern . . . and must be broken."[18]

Knox's courteous and well-reasoned reply pointed out that the new Constitution was "the only constitution that I know of in the Anglican Communion which does not make the principles of the Reformation Settlement of the Church of England an unalterable part of the constitution." He also stated that the letter to the Attorney General was a private one, and that it was only after the four men learned that the Attorney General had been given to understand that the support for the constitution was unanimous, that they felt it their duty to inform him of the facts.[19]

Far more serious than Fisher's displeasure, was that of Archbishop Gough. He wrote to them saying he had been "grievously hurt" by behaviour which was "most discourteous and most disloyal." The four men had lost his confidence, and Knox, as Principal of Moore College, was singled out for the most severe reprimand.[20] These four men, however, were good men to whom Sydney owes her evangelical life.[21] Marcus Loane noted in his book *Men to Remember* that Gough gave the men no chance to defend themselves or offer any explanation. Loane's opinion was that Knox received particular opprobrium because he held the most power: as Principal of Moore College, as a very active member of the Anglican Church League and as an opponent of the Constitution. Loane concluded, "Broughton Knox . . . went back to entrench himself in Moore College and to erect his barricades against all possible interference."[22]

What seems to have happened during Gough's short episcopate is a strengthening of Evangelical identity. Faced with an Archbishop who did not see eye to eye with them, who was seen to be linked to Fisher and Pitt, evangelical leaders deliberately strengthened their arm. Three institutions grew in influence and further defined their evangelical identity under Gough's episcopate: the *Australian Church Record*, the Anglican Church League and Moore College. Each was empowered by DB Knox's very considerable involvement.

Broughton Knox had been writing articles for the *Australian Church Record* since the Red Book Case of the 1940s. At Moore College, a box

18. Fisher to DB Knox 13.12.1960, Fisher Papers, 235.

19. DB Knox to Fisher 21.12.1960, Fisher Papers, 235. The vote had been 88 to 49, according to Knox

20. H Gough to DB Knox 8.11.1960 1993/10/2 Archbishop's Office-Correspondence Diocesan-Constitution 1955–1960, *Sydney Diocesan Archives*.

21. Peter Jensen interview with MHC 4.3.2015.

22. Loane, *Men to Remember*, 42–3.

contains bound copies of *ACR* running from 1948 to 1957. While the *ACR* regularly published unsigned articles, Broughton's handwritten notes on the bound copies indicate authorship. In those days he was a major contributor to *ACR* and there is no reason to think that this did not continue into the following decades. He wrote at least eighteen articles in 1956–7 opposing the draft Constitution. With regular articles by Donald Robinson, Marcus Loane, and TC Hammond until the time of his death, the newspaper was a powerful organ for conservative evangelical views. Articles on the Reformation were a regular feature, and the tone was didactic. Such an article, by "A Special Correspondent," was "What are the Causes that Split Anglicans?" Its conclusion was that:

If Anglicans could agree on the final authority, Bible or Church, there would be every possibility of different schools of thought getting together to discover what doctrines that authority ultimately endorsed. But so long as these are two authorities to which Anglicans give their allegiance, explicitly or implicitly, there is no possibility of compromise or of reconciliation. The general maxim of Jesus applies here: "Ye cannot serve two masters." A policy of comprehension in this ultimate matter of authority is an attempt at an impossibility.[23]

Closer to the bone, there were articles critical of Michael Ramsey, Archbishop of York (and later of Canterbury, following Archbishop Fisher). Such an article, written in 1961, was headed "Evading the Reformation." It stated:

> The Archbishop of York, Dr Ramsey (a recognized Anglo-Catholic leader) has probably inaugurated a new Anglo-Catholic approach to the Reformation in his sermon at Edinburgh at the beginning of the quarter-centenary celebrations for the Scottish Reformation. He suggested that the Reformation continued in the Church of England until 1662, when the Prayer Book received its final revision.
>
> This suggestion has the advantage from the Archbishop's point of view of including the Caroline divines of the school of Archbishop Laud, who reacted against the doctrines and attitudes of Tudor times in a High Church direction. We can therefore expect to find much made of this idea in future Anglo-Catholic discussion of the Reformation.
>
> But it will not do. The Reformation of the Church of England in doctrine, worship and order was completed early in the reign of Elizabeth I and not subsequently modified to any significant

---

23. *ACR* 9.1.1958, 7.

extent. In 1661 and 1662 the Thirty-Nine Articles were left untouched, and though the Prayer Book was amended extensively, every amendment was one of detail; in principal the Prayer Book of 1552 remained in force.

This is not to say that Carolines would not have liked to make alterations of substance; they would. But in fact they did not.

They themselves were fully aware that the Reformation was a past event, and that their work was on a smaller scale, even when they were revising the Prayer Book, as can be seen from the Preface to the 1662 Book (particularly the passage which says: "Accordingly we find that in the Reign of Several princes of blessed memory since the Reformation . . . "—which clearly implies that the Reformation was long since past).

The formative and normative period for Anglicanism is from 1547 to about 1560.[24]

Bruce Kaye, in *An Introduction to World Anglicanism* notes that Anglican Churches look to the documents of the English Reformation as authoritative sources for Anglican doctrine. Paul Avis in *The Identity of Anglicanism* states that no single period of Anglicanism is definitive. In his view Anglicanism is a continuous story: we cannot freeze-frame it and say, "This is definitive Anglicanism."[25] This is the crux of much of the controversy about the nature of Anglicanism.

The *Australian Church Record* moved closer to home in February 1962. Under the banner headline "Australian Evangelicals address Islington Conference," still in big print were the words: "Addressing the 128th Islington Clerical Conference, the Archbishop of Sydney, Dr Gough, expressed his concern lest Evangelicals should feel "bound hand and foot" by the Reformers."[26]

The most outspoken *ACR* article was probably the one in 1963, under the provocative heading "Another English Archbishop." The article was written after the announcement of the new Archbishop of Perth, who is not even named in the article. Having acknowledged that Australians are in the debt of the Englishmen who came out here, particularly in the early days, the writer continued:

> It must be disappointing to all who long to see it autonomous not only on the constitutional level but also in its life and work

24. ACR 19.1.1961, 4.
25. Kaye, *An Introduction to World Anglicanism*, 233; Avis, *The Identity of Anglicanism*, 160.
26. ACR 15.2.1962, 1.

that the unbroken tradition of importing Englishmen as Archbishops has been continued by the Diocese of Perth. The new Archbishop, like every other Australian Archbishop, is to be an Englishman.

No reasonable person would object to the appointment of a man, who like the former Archbishop Booth of Melbourne, had served the whole or even a substantial part of his ministry here before becoming Archbishop.[27] But whatever the special gifts of those who come here for the first time as Archbishops, it is hard to see how they can give an effective lead in the peculiar conditions which obtain in this country until they have been here for a considerable period . . . The tradition of appointing Englishmen seems to be wearing thin in vice-regal circles. Is it not time that we dropped it?[28]

This seems like a thinly veiled criticism of Archbishop Gough, the last English Archbishop of Sydney.

Broughton Knox's second sphere of influence was the Anglican Church League.[29] He used the ACL to oppose the draft Constitution with great efficiency. He warned Sydney members of the General Synod that the Constitution would mean "in due course, the end of evangelicalism in our church, for in 50 years the General Synod will have a stranglehold."[30] His letter to the Attorney General was the culmination of a long campaign to oppose the Constitution because of his belief that Evangelicalism was at stake. Broughton Knox created an alternative power base in the ACL. Knox's alienation from the archbishop of the day and his strong dislike of centralism (whether in the Anglican Church of Australia or in the Sydney Diocese), plus his growing influence as Principal of Moore College, made the ACL a formidable force to be reckoned with.

Under Broughton Knox, Moore College became the powerhouse of the Diocese of Sydney. Following TC Hammond, Marcus Loane had been College Principal from 1953 until his appointment as Bishop Coadjutor in 1958. Broughton Knox was his successor, and became Principal in 1959, his appointment being one of the last decisions Archbishop Mowll made before his death.

---

27. JJ Booth, an Evangelical, was Archbishop of Melbourne 1942–1956. He came to Australia from England at the age of eighteen, and trained at Ridley College, Melbourne. Cameron, "Aspects of Anglican Theological Education," 192.

28. *ACR* 28.3.1963, 4.

29. See Chapter 2.

30. DB Knox to HK Mowll 14.10.1955, quoted in J Davis, *Australian Anglicans and their Constitution*, 151.

When Knox took the reigns at Moore College, the College was poised for expansion and change. The Sydney Billy Graham Crusade of 1959 brought a rise in student numbers and in 1960 44 new men were enrolled. Women also studied at Moore College, attending in increasing numbers.[31] Knox initiated a College Appeal, built new buildings and expanded the College site. His policy of purchasing local real estate, mostly terrace houses, resulted in the acquisition of 63 new properties by 1971. He expanded the College Faculty, relying on appointing local men rather than imports. In encouraging his staff to read for doctorates at universities in England and the USA, and in introducing a fourth year of study he raised academic standards. Many believe he brought a new academic rigour to the lecture room, though some dispute this.[32] An intentional focus on scholarship and learning replaced the earlier pietism of Mowll and Loane. The focus of teaching was Biblical Theology.[33] The College library grew to become a magnificent resource for the College and for scholarly research. Knox started a school of preaching to promote the art of biblical exposition. Sydney preachers are sometimes criticized for being generally a "dull lot." Whether or not that is true, Moore College and the training it gives its preachers is the most likely reason.[34] Knox introduced annual College missions, which still continue and which gave students experience in evangelism in the parishes of the diocese. Broughton Knox's anti-episcopal stance was general knowledge, as was his lack of interest in liturgy. The latter was to have serious consequences for Prayer Book use in the Diocese.

In the remaining years of Gough's episcopate, Gough and Knox seemed to have a reasonable working relationship, one that enhanced Knox's influence and the steady growth of Moore College. Knox regularly out-manoevered Gough and made the most of Gough's lack of interest in diocesan nuts and bolts. In the early 1960s Knox would contact Gough to ask permission to enter into a contract for purchase of a property. "For goodness" sake, don't worry me with the details, just go ahead and buy the stuff" was the Archbishop's usual response.[35]

Knox's influence on the contemporary shape of the Sydney Diocese is immense, partly because he was at Moore College for a quarter of a century.

31. Cameron, *An Enigmatic Life*, 206.

32. Ibid., 185–206.

33. Biblical Theology is the name given to a form of theology introduced by (though not invented by) Donald Robinson at Moore College. It studies the development of the Bible through salvation history, accompanied by an exhaustive study of the biblical texts in their original languages.

34. Rev. Dick Lucas to MHC 31.7.2007; J Cornish interview with MHC 14.9.2011.

35. Cameron, *An Enigmatic Life*, 194.

While there were students at the College who disliked him, there were many, who later became diocesan leaders, who revered him. This was a puzzle to Knox's contemporaries. The brothers Peter and Phillip Jensen are among the many Sydney leaders who revered him. Under Knox Moore College became almost exclusively the training college for Sydney clergy: few Sydney clergy trained elsewhere and few from other dioceses trained at Moore. This had a number of consequences, one of them being that Knox and his staff influenced the parishes and the laity in a new and very thorough way, increasing the distance between Sydney people and those from other dioceses.

The two most significant events during Gough's episcopate were the Billy Graham Crusade of April 1959 and the Archbishop's Commission, set up in 1959. There is a certain irony in this. The Billy Graham Crusade took place a month before Gough arrived in Sydney. The effects of the Crusade were, however, very important for the Diocese in Gough's time. The recommendations of the Archbishop's Commission, though the Commission was Gough's brainchild, were not implemented during Gough's time in Sydney.

Sydney was not alone in welcoming Billy Graham, the American evangelist, in 1959. His Australian visit included Perth, Adelaide, Melbourne, and Brisbane as well as Sydney. In each city thousands of people gathered to hear him. A total of 106,800 attended in Perth; 253,000 in Adelaide; 719,000 in Melbourne; 291,000 in Brisbane and 980,000 in Sydney. Stuart Piggin has written,

> To that point it was the largest, most successful evangelistic campaign in human history —and it happened in the land of the amiable pagans. "Never again will I doubt that the Gospel is the power of God," wrote Bishop Kerle, overawed, "nor that men's lives can be changed through the foolishness of preaching."[36]

The Crusade of 1959 began in Melbourne, where the greatest crowds for the first week of any Billy Graham Crusade attended. The size of the crowd forced the organisers to change the venue from the West Melbourne Stadium to the newly completed Myer Music Bowl. As was his practice at all his crusades, at the close of his address Dr Graham invited his audience to come to the front to "dedicate their lives to Christ, and say "I will" to the Lord Jesus." Of those who did so, 60% were those who committed themselves to Christ for the first time, while the remaining 40% were rededications.[37]

Sydney's preparation for the Billy Graham visit included a great deal of prayer. The *ACR* reported,

---

36. Piggin, *Evangelical Christianity in Australia*, 168.
37. *ACR* 5.3.1959, 1.

The most important part of the work of preparation has been the prayers of God's people. In addition to the normal meetings for prayer in the churches, the Crusade has been constantly remembered in special groups that have made time to come together with this purpose. Perhaps the most outstanding development in this regard has been the Women's Prayer groups. At the time of going to press there are over 4,500 groups meeting in over 3,000 homes in the metropolitan area. The average attendance is between six and eight.

And for places further afield such as Wollongong, some 90 kilometers south of Sydney, special arrangements have been made to transport large numbers to the Showground each night and also to have a direct landline to the Town Hall annex.[38]

In Sydney, the Protestant churches had joined together to organize the Crusade. Bishop Clive Kerle seems to have played a major part in the leadership, and a former Governor of NSW, Lieut. Sir John Northcott officially welcomed Dr Graham to NSW. The stated objects of Billy Graham's evangelistic campaign were to:

1. Get Sydney and NSW talking about religion.
2. Revitalise the churches and "Christianise the Christians."
3. Awake a new sense of social consciousness and responsibility of Christians to love their neighbours as themselves.
4. Bring men to a vital knowledge of Jesus Christ as the answer to their every problem.
5. To bring hope in an age of despair and to show that there is meaning to life and history.[39]

The short-term results of the Crusade are seen clearly in the microcosm of a Sydney parish. The Curate in Charge of a new housing area, the Rev. Silas Horton, of Regent's Park and Birrong, commented:

> It is just a week since the Billy Graham Crusade began and already there have been great blessings. We are not a big church, averaging about 30–35 each service . . . and we live on the outer fringe of the metropolitan area.
>
> The first response was the handful who offered for counsellor training. These in themselves have become the key workers in pre-Crusade activity in the parish. Secondly, neighbourhood

---

38. *ACR* 2.4.1959, 3; *ACR* 16.4.1959, 1.
39. *ACR* 16.4.1959, 1.

prayer meetings have proved a means of spiritual strength to the comparatively small number who have attended . . . Thirdly, census visitation introduced many to the thrill of getting out to meet and invite people to heed the things of God . . . Next, referrals from the Crusade have now exceeded 20 and amongst the first decisions have been church officers and key members. Individuals, married couples, teenagers, have all begun new lives through this personal encounter with Jesus Christ. The whole parish is now swinging into additional Bible study and prayer groups to cater for the needs of these new Christians and old Christians who have rededicated their lives to Christ. Lastly, there is a new vision and spiritual interest, new friendliness and co-operation in our church life.[40]

Clearly, sound preparation beforehand, especially that of training counselors and praying energetically, had ensured that hearts were ready for the Spirit of God to work through Billy Graham and his team. Equally clearly, those whose spiritual lives were touched by the Sydney Crusade needed the support of their local church. Those churches which cared for the Graham converts would see long-term growth, individually and corporately. The influence of the Graham Crusade was, in consequence, no flash in the pan, but for a significant number of Sydney Christians, the occasion when they found life-changing faith in Christ. Archbishop Peter Jensen is one such person.[41]

Stuart Piggin has noted how the Crusade affected the community. For example, for a number of years concurrent with, and following the 1959 Billy Graham Crusade, the number of convictions for crime slowed; in the year following the Crusade the number of illegitimate births declined; and from 1960–1 there was a 10% reduction in the consumption of beer. There is anecdotal evidence of many a dormant conscience awakened.[42]

Graham had his critics. Most notably for Anglicans, Archbishop Fisher was very reluctant to associate himself with the 1954 London Billy Graham Crusade. Correspondence back and forth from Fisher to Graham and his staff is illuminating.

Kenneth de Courcey wrote to Fisher re the amazing results of the Crusade at Harringay:

> The results for our church and for the Nation might be profound and far-reaching if you felt you were able to put yourself

---

40. *ACR* 3.4.1959, 1.
41. PF Jensen, Address to the ACL Synod Dinner 2000, www. acl.asn.au.
42. Piggin, *Evangelical Christianity in Australia*, 169–70.

unhesitatingly at the head of, what is, I believe, the beginning of a national surge back to the Churches . . . My great anxiety now is to see you at the head of the great awakening.[43]

Billy Graham also wrote to Fisher, inviting him to take the prayer at the closing meeting of 22 May, at Wembley, saying, "This closing day will be one of the largest Protestant gatherings in the history of Britain."[44] Fisher accepted the invitation to attend but stated that he would prefer to say a prayer and give the Blessing at the conclusion of the meeting, rather than extempore prayer before Graham's address.[45] He was cautiously supportive of Billy Graham in response to a critical opinion of the evangelist, writing, "What he does can do nothing but good . . . and . . . he hands on all who come to seek his advice at once to their Churches.[46] On the other hand, when asked to support a motion in the Church Assembly re "follow up" of converts and inquirers at the Billy Graham Crusade, he argued against it.[47]

The reluctance of the Archbishop of Canterbury to take the leadership in supporting the Billy Graham Crusade is reminiscent of the Establishment's rejection of John Wesley in eighteenth century England. There were, and are, strong critics of Billy Graham among Australian Anglicans. Bishop EH Burgmann of Canberra and Goulburn called Graham's view of the Bible "idolatrous," and another bishop, TB McCall of Rockhampton, wrote in his diocesan magazine that aspects of the Graham crusades were "objectionable, dishonest, distressing, and disgusting."[48] Graham is still blamed for the Diocese of Sydney's current identity.[49] The underlying criticism is the same as that levelled at Evangelicals, because Graham is an Evangelical. Graham's commendation of Bishop Loane and Bishop Kerle and their strenuous support for the Crusade and the "follow up" are a striking contrast to Fisher and some Australian bishops from other dioceses.[50]

The NSW Council of Churches passed a resolution about the recent Crusade, which read:

> The Council of Churches in NSW wishes to express to Dr Graham and the members of the team its most sincere gratitude for their unsparing labours in the gospel during the Sydney

43. K de Courcey to Fisher, undated 141, Fisher Papers.
44. B Graham to Fisher 5.5.54 141, Fisher Papers.
45. Fisher to B Graham 6.5.54 141, Fisher Papers.
46. Fisher to Williamson 21.5.54, Fisher Papers.
47. Chaplain (probably Fisher's chaplain) to RD Say 5.5.1954 141, Fisher Papers.
48. Piggin, *Evangelical Christianity in Australia*, 162–3.
49. MHC conversation with a middle church Anglican October 2012.
50. *CR* 14.5.1959, 1. Gough was yet to arrive in Sydney to take up his position.

Crusade. Not only has the Church been reminded of the primacy of Evangelism, but we have experienced a glorious unity and fraternal spirit on the basis of this great effort to confront the people with the claims of Christ.

The Crusade has proved to be a mighty working of the Spirit of God in the lives of hundreds of thousands who have heard the preaching; in the unprecedented witness to the great truths of the Gospel and in the revelation of the deep hunger for spiritual reality which the Crusade has revealed . . . The Council hopes that this great quickening of spiritual awareness and unity will continue to express itself in terms of Christian Social Witness, which is itself inseparable from effective Evangelism.[51]

During Gough's episcopate other evangelists visited Sydney: Leighton Ford (of the Billy Graham Crusade) in 1961; and David Sheppard, the English cricketer in 1963. The visitor who has had the most particular and sustained effect on the Diocese of Sydney from the 1960s onwards is the Rev. John Stott, Rector of All Soul's, Langham Place. John Stott was a huge influence on Sydney Evangelicals through his many visits, his powerful addresses at the annual Katoomba CMS Summer School, his university missions, and his many books. He was a brilliant strategist for Evangelicals worldwide.[52] He has been called "the father of modern expository preaching."[53] In 2005 *Time* magazine named him as one of the "100 most influential people in the world" and the architect of the evangelical movement in the 20th Century.[54] Ruth and Billy Graham wrote of him, "John Stott is the most respected Evangelical in the world today, and has been a standard, or role model, for thousands of clergy. We consider him one of our warmest personal friends."[55] John Stott stayed in Sydney, on his first visit in June 1958, with the Loane family, then living at Moore College. This was the beginning of a long friendship with Marcus and his family. While on that first visit, Stott called on Archbishop Mowll, describing him as "a very dear old boy, a staunch Evangelical, perhaps a bit of an autocrat, but very sweet and gracious."[56]

Stott's first mission at Sydney University was very well attended, with the Wallace Theatre (seating about 600) packed to overflowing for Stott's

51. ACR 28.5.1959, 1.
52. He wrote over 50 books translated into 65 languages.
53. Barnett interview with MHC 17.11.2010.
54. Chapman, *Godly Ambition*, 158; LifeCoach4God at verticallivingministries.com/John Stott.
55. Dudley-Smith, *John Stott*, dust cover.
56. Quoted in Dudley-Smith, *John Stott*, 400.

daily lunchtime lectures, and with a 1000 people crammed into the Great Hall on the final Sunday evening. These were impressive numbers for what was a small university of about 12,000 students in those days. Stott was there primarily as a missioner, his theme, "What think ye of Christ?" Not only were many lives changed by his powerful message, but the team of assistant missioners learned a great deal from Stott, as well as being warmly encouraged in their own task of evangelism.[57] Stott visited other Australian cities in 1958: Melbourne, Brisbane and Perth. By the early 1980s he had visited Sydney at least seven times. Evangelistic work among university students was a highly strategic activity, since the students were the professionals and leaders of the future. They were also at an age where they were making life-changing decisions and were open to hearing the challenge of the gospel. Mowll had seized this opportunity at Cambridge, as a student there, as had many others after him. Stott was one of a long line of missioners to the universities.

His book *Basic Christianity*, published in 1958, became the definitive evangelistic paperback for at least a generation. By 2012 it had been translated into 54 languages and had sold millions of copies worldwide. This is one of the many letters Stott's biographer notes in response to *Basic Christianity*

> Dear John,
>
> Thank-you for writing *Basic Christianity*. It led me to make a new commitment of my life to Christ. I am old now—nearly 78—but not too old to make a new beginning.
> I rejoice in all the grand work you are doing.
>
> Yours sincerely, Leslie Weatherhead[58]

The *ACR* promoted Stott, publicizing his visit in 1958 and printing his views on significant issues.[59]

The year after Stott's visit, and the month after the Sydney Billy Graham Crusade, Archbishop and Mrs. Gough arrived in Sydney, in May 1959. In the September of the same year, Gough was elected Primate of Australia. At his first Synod he announced his intention to appoint an Archbishop's

---

57. Ibid., 399–400, 403–5.

58. Chapman, *Godly Ambition*, 5; Dudley-Smith, *John Stott*, 456–57. Leslie Dixon Weatherhead (1893–1976) was an English Christian theologian in the liberal Protestant tradition. He served as minister of the City Temple, London, for nearly twenty-five years. He was author of numerous books, including *Life Begins at Death*, *The Will of God*, and *Prescription for Anxiety*, all published by Abingdon.

59. *ACR* 8.12.1959, 4. One such was "Prayer Book Revision," *ACR* 8.12.1959, 4. Another was on Evangelicals, *ACR* 8.6.1961, 7.

Commission which was to be along the lines of recent English ones. It was to be a survey of administrative organization, property and finance.[60] At the time Sydney had 290 active clergy (Melbourne had 250), 86% of whom had trained at Moore College. There were 188 parishes and 234 branch churches. Sydney was the wealthiest of the Australian dioceses. Her assets were vast but she was short of money.[61] The assets were in the form of large estates, but the Diocese had not been a good housekeeper and had failed to husband its resources in a business-like manner to obtain the greatest financial benefit from them.[62]

Originally land grants from the government of the day, some 150 acres comprised the church's glebes. They included the Bishopsthorpe Estate, St Mark's glebe, St Philip's glebe, St James's glebe and the Cathedral site in the center of the city. The total value of this land amounted to £7,401,766 in 1964 and the earning rate on this capital was a tiny 1.34%.[63] The reason for this situation was, in part, that the glebe lands had been leased for 99 years at ground rents, which, by the time of the Commission, and with the "tremendous" inflation of the previous 25 years, were "ludicrously small." The cottages on the site of the Endowment of the See (The Bishopsthorpe Estate) were dilapidated and would cost money to repair. There had been no central body governing the finances: the bodies managing the glebe estates were inefficient and the whole administration of diocesan finance needed to be overhauled.[64]

The Archbishop invited a group of fifteen clergy and lay men to form the Commission and to carry out their survey. He stated:

> I had no idea as to the heaviness of the burden I was asking them to carry. The more the Commission studied the situation, the more difficult and obtuse it appeared . . . Implicit in some of the statements and recommendations are criticisms of the past and present story of the Diocese and it could not be otherwise. . . We are all proud and thankful for the heritage that has been handed down to us by those who have gone before us, but we would not be treating them with the honour they deserve if we shut our eyes to facts and imagine that all has been or is perfect.

---

60. *Sydney Year Book* 1960, 226.
61. *Report of Archbishop's Commission*, 60.
62. Ibid., 60.
63. Ibid., 78–79.
64. Ibid., 81–82.

The Last of the Englishmen: The Gough Years 1959–1966   95

Complacency is one of the most unpleasant forms of pride, and pride is a deadly sin.[65]

Jones, Lang, Wooton & Sons, had been commissioned to investigate the properties held by the Diocese and in October 1959 the firm sent its report to the Archbishop. It was damning. The Diocese held a huge portfolio: 923 properties in all. Most of these ought to have had schedules of tenants' disrepair, which meant that the Diocese would have been spared a repair bill of some £461,500.[66] Rents should have risen with the appreciation in property values, but had not. In addition, a law passed in 1930 had allowed rents to be reduced by 22½%, and the Diocese was the only landholder known to JLW who had not applied for reinstatement of the full rent. None of the tenants was obliged to insure the properties they leased, so in the event of fire, the Diocese would be the loser. There was no attempt to ensure that the glebe lands were correctly zoned, neither were restrictive covenants on land adjoining the Church lands observed, with the result that inappropriate buildings had been erected on these sites. The Glebe Trustees had recently sold a piece of land for £100, which the Valuer General had assessed at £25,000! The main reasons for this chaotic situation of mismanagement were that the records were in disarray— 431 records could not be accounted for; and administration was inadequate: the overworked staff were not to blame but there was a lack of concentrated study of the problems at executive level.[67]

The Report of the Archbishop's Commission, containing analysis and recommendations, ran for 275 pages, while the summary of recommendations ran from pp 111-121. The second half of the Report looked at the Diocesan schools: eighteen in all. The survey covered finance, staffing, subjects offered and examination results, the question of founding new schools, and the question of whether the schools were fulfilling their real functions. Of interest here was the question "How can boys' schools produce more dedicated Christians?" and "Candidates for the ministry—do the schools produce enough?"[68] The Principal of Moore College provided an analysis of the origin, by type of schools, of the students who entered the College in the period from 1937 to 1964. Except for the period 1945-1949, state schools were overwhelmingly better represented. For example, in the period 1955-1959, 110 students came from state schools, but only fifteen from Anglican schools.[69] This raised the question of the value of Anglican schools,

65. Ibid., 4.
66. Graphic photos were included in the Report, with comments underlining the properties' dilapidated state.
67. Jones, Lang, Wooton, "Report."
68. *Report of Archbishop's Commission,* 270 and 220.
69. Ibid., 221–22.

costly as they were, and becoming more so. Also the extent to which the schools were demonstrably Christian: places where there was a conscious focus on evangelism and teaching about the Christian way of life.

The Report also assessed the requirements of the diocese: not only should the administration of its wealth be addressed, there were also huge needs requiring substantial sums of money to be spent. In the new, expanding areas of the Diocese, 60 new churches were needed; 35 needed replacing; 32 required extensions; and 72 required major repairs. The bill for this was an estimated £2,269,000.[70]

The Report was tabled at the Synod in 1964. In 1965 a special session of Synod met to debate the Report and act on it. Three resolutions were passed:

1. That the Church Property Trust be reconstituted and reorganized[71]
2. That a Sydney Church of England Investment Trust be established
3. That a Church Information Center be established

Gough departed fifteen months later, and full-scale implementation of the Report lay some years ahead. The authors of Sydney's Diocesan history have commented:

> Such a Commission promised to open a Pandora's box: criticism of past and present decisions of church leaders was inevitable and it was likely to reveal problems of which the average churchgoer and synod member were unaware ... There was little in the Commission's findings that a secular corporation would have queried; indeed they represented the application of modern financial and managerial methods to the church's business. The only typically ecclesiastical touch was the slowness with which they were applied.[72]

Gough's time as Archbishop was marked by a groundswell of change: social, ecclesiastical, theological, educational, moral, and even musical. The secularism of the late twentieth century and twenty-first century quickened its inexorable growth in the mid 1960s. Alongside other churches, Anglican numbers had begun to fall.[73] There was even the prospect that the Anglican

---

70. Ibid., 51.

71. The Sydney Property Trust is the Sydney Diocesan body which owns parish properties including church buildings, halls and rectories.

72. Judd and Cable, *Sydney Anglicans*, 268.

73. The 1933 Census figures showed 38.69% of Australians were Anglican but by 1961 the figure had fallen to 34.91%. Those with no religion rose from .02% in 1933 to .65% in 1961.

Church might amalgamate with other Protestant churches.[74] In an environment of increasingly accelerating change Gough had the added burden of being an uneasy fit as Archbishop of Sydney. Towards the end of 1965 a feature article in the *ACR* highlighted aspects of the Archbishop's unease. The article drew attention to his monthly letter in *Southern Cross*. Headed "ARCHBISHOP WARNS SYDNEY: 'DON'T BE SPLINTER GROUP,'" the article reported (mostly accurately) what the Archbishop had written.[75]

> The Archbishop of Sydney in his monthly letter warns of the danger of Sydney Diocese becoming a "small and increasingly ineffective splinter group of the Church." The future of such a group would be "very doubtful" is the Archbishop's view. The Archbishop made these comments in connection with next year's meeting of General Synod, which, he said, would have to take action on many matters, some of which may be "of a controversial character." The Archbishop went on: "I am rather concerned as to what the attitude of our own diocese will be in such matters. I think it true to say that this diocese will find itself at a crossroads.
>
> "We decided to support the New Constitution but are we willing to follow the implications of that decision? The decision really is whether this diocese will enter fully into the life of the whole Church of England in Australia (and indeed of the whole Anglican Communion) or will it insist on its rights of independent judgement and shut itself away in exclusiveness as a kind of semi-independent branch of that Communion."
>
> Posing the question as to whether we are Evangelical Anglicans or Anglican Evangelicals the Archbishop said that when he first came to Australia he made it clear that "I am an Anglican first but one who believes that the Evangelical interpretation of Anglicanism is the right one and that true Evangelicalism is Anglicanism in its purest form."
>
> "Unfortunately," the Archbishop concluded, "there is a type of Evangelical Anglicanism prevalent in England and elsewhere today which is more Calvinistic than Anglican."

The latter statement is clear indication that Sydney Diocese is not unique, just differently connected. The article continued:

> Turning his attention to the question of Church Union Dr Gough asked: "What really is our attitude to the question of

74. *ACR* 18.11.1965, 1; *Southern Cross* November 1965, 2–3.

75. The inaccuracies have been replaced in italics by the original text from the *Southern Cross*.

Church Union? We talk a great deal about this being our goal and some speak as if it were just around the corner. But most of us act quite differently. We spend laborious efforts on Prayer Book Revision which could be entirely obsolete if we join a *United Church of Australia*. We spend long hours in debating in committees about many matters which are purely Anglican, e.g. method of electing the next Primate, the formulation of new dioceses and regulations concerning divorce. All these and many others could become redundant if we are serious about joining a United Church during the next few years.

"I do not profess to know the answers to these questions but I draw attention to the problems because certainly we are behaving in an astonishingly inconsistent manner which puzzles the world and gives concern to our brethren in other Churches."[76]

These are the words of a very frustrated leader. General Synod, of which he as Primate was Chairman, was doubly hard if he were at odds with his own diocese. Moreover, he did not seem to understand that the New Constitution had created new problems and exacerbated division rather than bringing unity. The growing Calvinism (under DB Knox at Moore College) was like a sharp pencil giving new clarity to Sydney's theological position, setting it apart from the rather fuzzy theology that being Anglican first and Evangelical second is likely to encourage. Calvin and Cranmer may have been closer than he liked to think.[77] In addition, there was naturally a high level of frustration that all the planning and all the committee work to which he had devoted his time might be fruitless if swept away by an amalgamation with other Protestant churches. How could he lead such an unruly mob, especially as leaders like Knox, Robinson and Loane were generally a step or two ahead of him?

Change was in the air. It seemed to pervade every corner of life. In the Anglican Church, the strong groundswell of support for ecumenism led to discussion of amalgamating Protestant denominations. Evangelicals were generally not in favour, seeing compromise as the price for union, and, if the Roman Catholic church were included, the "surrender of Evangelical truth and all the Protestant Reformation gained," according to a report in the *ACR* in 1965.[78]

---

76. *ACR* 18.11.1965, 1.

77. MacCulloch, *Thomas Cranmer*, 618–19. Thomas Norton, Cranmer's thoroughgoing Evangelical son-in-law, translated Calvin's *Institutes* into English, publishing them in 1561. *Ibid.* 610, 619–20.

78. *ACR* 22.4.1965, 7.

The idea of revising the 1662 *Book of Common Prayer* was not new. Though beautiful, the language of Cranmer's Prayer Book was centuries out of date. Anglicans differed over its theology. The controversial 1928 Revised Prayer Book, influenced by Anglo-Catholic theology, allowed prayers for the dead, reservation of the sacrament and "vestments." The British House of Commons rejected it twice, in 1927 and 1928.[79] In Sydney, fears that the Church of England in England was slipping from its Reformation moorings had prompted TC Hammond and Mowll to support the move for a Constitution for the Australian church. Even before the Constitution had come into effect, as early as 1948, the Sydney Diocese had started to look at *Prayer Book* revision, forming a Select Committee for the purpose.[80] A decade later, Donald Robinson moved a synod resolution recommending *Prayer Book* revision and in 1962 a *Prayer Book* Commission was set up by the General Synod.[81] Meanwhile in Presidential addresses Archbishop Gough cautioned against deviations from the *Prayer Book* and experimental forms of worship. He stated that the General Synod was the body to authorize any experimentation and liturgical revision required liturgical experts, not parish clergymen.[82] Clergy were forbidden to prepare their own forms of service. This caution proved to be Canute-like in its effectiveness.

A related issue was church music. It is a mystery why music in churches has changed so radically in the past 60 years. From organs to bands, from hymns to songs, from choirs to their virtual elimination. We can point to television, the rise of rock music and the popularity of electric guitars and drums, to radio and pop music, all dating from the Sixties. But the radical shift in musical preference by the majority of churchgoers under the age of 50 is something of a phenomenon in itself.

Some pointers towards the future come from an opinion survey run by Warwick Olson, the editor of *Southern Cross*, in 1965. He invited musicians, clergy and lay leaders to offer their opinions on church music. Nigel Butterley, the composer, wrote that there would be no real renewal in church music until there was renewal in the liturgy itself. He complained about the anachronism of using the Tudor English of the Prayer Book—it made Anglican psalm singing "so often seem pointless." He, like others in the opinion survey, questioned singing alternating versicles and responses and questioned the role of the choir. He wrote:

---

79. Judd and Cable, *Sydney Anglicans,* 210.
80. *Sydney Year Book* 1949, 120.
81. *Southern Cross* February 1963, 17.
82. *Sydney Year Book* 1966, 264.

> A fundamental question is that of the relative function of choir and congregation. It must be asked to what extent a parish choir should exist as a separate entity, and whether its most important task, that of leading the congregation's worship, should not cause us to question the suitability of the chancel as the place for the choir to sing from.[83]

Owen Dykes, a dynamic Sydney clergyman, wrote: "To hear the versicles, responses, canticles and psalms "sung" in many of our churches is a test of one's endurance and sense of humour." Helen Channon, organist at St Faith's Narrabeen, wrote prophetically: "the whole question of church music is a vexed one, and one of the most difficult problems facing the Church in a challenging world." Disc jockey Ross Brown put his finger on the evangelical approach to music in churches. It could and should be a means of evangelism. He wrote:

> I consider that the music of the Church is uninspiring, droll and achieves nothing—especially as a means of evangelism. Most people who oppose the changing of the Church's music would be those people who are using the Church as a refuge against a modern and progressive world, finding security in the old fashion. Music is an international language that breaks down barriers and, given the opportunity, could be put to work for the Church instead of lying dormant.

He recommended the Aboriginal singer Jimmy Little (whose songs were on the Top 40 chart) and The Joy Strings—an English Salvation Army group— "each year successfully reaching thousands of people." A fellowship leader wrote:

> "O come let us sing to the Lord" (with a new tune). Can you imagine a world without music? Most of life is centered about some form of rhythm. Think about it next time you're walking, or washing clothes in the washing machine. The rhythm changes according to environment and circumstances. Then we walk through the doors of the church and slow down like an unwound clock. Why?

He wrote of things that "inspired or aroused interest" being "taboo." There are parallels here with Luther and the Wesley brothers and the reason for their musical innovations.

Pentecostalism became a new force in the Sixties. Young people in particular were drawn from Anglican Churches, attracted by its exuberant

---

83. *Southern Cross* October 1965, 10–14.

meetings, bright singing and happy atmosphere.[84] The question Evangelicals asked was, "Is it Scriptural?" The *ACR* took the Pentecostal movement very seriously, reprinting articles on the subject from the *English Churchman*.[85] The author, the Rev. R Bell, reasoned that the power of working miracles did not extend beyond the apostolic age, that there was no Scriptural warrant for the "Second Blessing" and he wondered if Pentecostalism was a form of heresy.[86] The *ACL* was strongly opposed to the movement, as evidenced by its response to a missionary convention at Picton Anglican Church being "used as a cover for . . . a Pentecostalist Teaching Mission." The editor commented, "Wherever the Pentecostalist movement has spread it has proved a divisive force."[87]

Many young people were unsure of a right response to the Pentecostal/Charismatic movement. They did not want to label its members liars and they did not want to disobey the Scriptures as interpreted by leading Evangelicals. The movement prompted Paul Barnett and Peter Jensen to coauthor a book titled *The Quest for Power*. The title says it all.

A controversial book, *Honest to God*, by JAT Robinson, the Bishop of Woolwich, made headlines in 1963. It eroded many of the fundamentals of Christian doctrine, including Christ's Incarnation, Resurrection and Atonement on the cross. The London *Daily Mail* commented that if Dr Robinson were right, "the Athenasian Creed would become meaningless, the Virgin Birth and the Resurrection unacceptable.' If the Bishop wished to explore his "extremely remote theory," the national daily continued, then "one wonders . . . whether he should continue a bishop." The *ACR* stated, "*Honest to God* will cause offence to many Christians who read it. But a reading of it should be accompanied by a recollection of the conspicuous failure of the Church of England as a whole to make Christianity meaningful to this generation."[88]

Marcus Loane commented in his inimitable way on both Pentecostalism and *Honest to God*. He called them "vogue theology." He said,

> *Honest to God* suffers from the basic difficulty which is common to all humanism: it discards the authority of the Bible as a divine revelation of truth, and that leaves it without the one criterion that matters in theology as distinct from philosophy

And of speaking in tongues:

84. *ACR* 16.7.64, 2–3.
85. The author of the articles, the Rev. R Bell ALCD, relied almost exclusively upon BB Warfield.
86. *ACR* 18.6.64, 2.
87. *ACR* 24.3.66, 2.
88. *ACR* 11.4.1963, 1.

> Cold winds from the arid wastes of speculative philosophy are not alone; there are also wild winds from the restless surge of charismatic experience.

He believed that they might be rooted in the psychology of an abnormal condition. They were certainly not for public display. That was deplorable.[89]

Change came also in positive ways. One notable example is the growth of the CMS Summer School. When appointed General Secretary of the NSW state branch of CMS, in 1955, Rev Geoff Fletcher promoted the CMS Summer School, held every January for a week, at Katoomba.[90] During his nine years as General Secretary, the numbers grew from 211 to 1,200.[91] The Summer School was a way to learn first-hand about CMS mission work in the world, to meet fellow Christians, and to hear biblical teaching. John Stott became a frequent visiting speaker at the CMS Summer Schools.[92] The Summer Schools had a unifying effect on the diocese as people gathered together from hundreds of parishes and they remain a potent influence on Sydney Diocesan life.[93]

Another area of change, mostly still very slow, was the place of women in the Anglican Church. Overseas, women were continuing to take up church leadership for the first time: in Hong Kong, in 1963, Deaconess Jane Hwang was appointed Vicar of the new parish of St Thomas' Shekkipmei, Kowloon. She was also headmistress of a primary school for 1,000 children, and although she could not be ordained to the priesthood, the Bishop of Hong Kong described her as "a Christian woman with all the priestly gifts poured out upon her by the Spirit of God."[94] Later that year, the Archbishops of Canterbury and York appointed a committee to examine the "whole question of women and holy orders."[95] In September 1965 the Montreal synod voted in favour of women having full delegate status to the Montreal Synod. The voting was close: 129–136.[96]

Back in Sydney, in 1962 the impressive number of 60 women studied theology at Deaconess House, some of whom performed very well in their

---

89. Presidential Address, October 1966, *Sydney Year Book*, 1967, 274–5.

90. It moved to the Katoomba Convention site in 1960—Braga, *A Century Preaching Christ*, 116.

91. S Braga, *A Century Preaching Christ*, 116, 128; Cole, *A History of the Church Missionary Society*, 227–229.

92. Ibid.,, 233 and 276; Dudley-Smith, *John Stott. A Global Ministry*, 177–8.

93. PF Jensen interview with MHC 23.11.2010.

94. *Southern Cross* July 1963, 16.

95. Ibid., November 1963, 17.

96. Ibid., September 1965, 16–17.

final examinations. One of these was Margaret Rodgers, who was awarded a First Class pass.[97] Many of these women became missionaries, others worked in schools, and others worked in parishes.[98] Sydney trained a significant number of women and they were active in ministry across Sydney parishes and beyond.

Joy Parker had a column in *Southern Cross*. An intelligent and strong woman, she later became Head of Tara, an Anglican school for girls in Sydney. In November 1963 she raised some provocative issues in an article headed "The Place of Women in the Diocese." She noted that in church services, although there was always a majority of women, even deaconesses rarely played any significant part. This was despite the fact that "in their own organisations women competently conduct services of worship." She asked was it scripturally correct for women to seek ordination. Such a question "requires our prayerful consideration." She further noted that male committees controlled the affairs of a congregation "largely composed of the so-called 'unfathomable' sex." She asked: "is it unscriptural to have female representation on committees?"[99]

Deaconess Mary Andrews, the Principal of Deaconess House, and a woman who had run churches in China, pulled no punches in a brilliant article for *Southern Cross* in October 1964. She began:

> If Synod is the parliament of the Church—and wholeness of the Church can only be achieved when every part of its membership can participate fully—then women have a place on Synod.

She argued that the Church was not at present making the fullest use of woman power in mission, that women who needed help are not getting help because there are no women to represent them on Synod, that there has been "a revolutionary change" in the status of women. She continued,

> Women have come to think differently about themselves, encouraged by secular writers and thinkers. There has been a great lack of understanding and very limited imaginative writing on the place of Christian women in the modern world and in the Church in spite of the part women played in the ministry of the Lord and the early Church.
>
> On the whole, Christian women accept the judgement of men on most subjects dealing with the Church . . . However, there are women in the Churches who feel their work for Christ

---

97. *ACR* 13.2.1963, 1.
98. Ibid., 6.5.1965, 2.
99. *Southern Cross* November 1963, 10.

lies in Society for their situation is not understood in the Churches. In the Church women are seldom stimulated to use their varied "gifts" and it is doubtful whether the variety of their gifts is even recognized.

She cited the example of Florence Nightingale who said of the Church: "She neither gave me work to do for her, nor the education for it." She noted that the franchise for women improved their situation, and that of their children, greatly. She reminded her readers that the 1919 Enabling Act in England gave the women the right to be elected members of parish councils. Her most telling point came next:

> Over the centuries women have wielded a private influence with very great skill and many still prefer it to any form of public responsibility. But the choice between influence and responsibility is one that women have to make and the Church has to make in relation to women.

A Mrs. Clark of Blaxland wrote a letter to *Southern Cross* the following month:

> I hope that Deaconess Andrews will be our first Synodswoman for the Diocese of Sydney and I am sure her example would point the way to further representation in what deeply concerns us, the spiritual progress of our children and the well-being of women participating in Church life.[100]

In 1965 the Sydney Synod voted on whether there should be women in the Synod. The vote was "yes" 161:129—a healthy majority. Women were promised a place there by 1972.[101]

An *ACR* interview with a parish rector in 1963 sums up the prevailing view of the place of women in the church at the time. Question: "We have been talking about the place of men in the parish; have you ever thought of having women on the Parish Council?" Answer: "This has been talked about. We're able to say we have sufficient men. I doubt very much whether we would find women anxious to join the Parish Council or Church Committee."[102] With encouragement like that, most women would have preferred to use their gifts elsewhere.

Hugh Gough resigned as Archbishop of Sydney in June 1966, after the relatively short term of seven years in office. The reason given was ill

---

100. Ibid., November 1964, 17.

101. Ibid., November 1965, 7–9.

102. Ibid., March 1935, 5. The Rev. Reg Langshaw, Rector of St Anne's Ryde since 1935, was the clergyman interviewed.

health and doctor's orders to take six months' rest. The *ACL* paid tribute to his support for the first Graham Crusade in England, which "was widely believed to have cost him preferment" and for his outspoken views on social issues, including support for the Australian government's policy on Vietnam, and for his extensive travel throughout Australia and overseas.[103] The *ACL* promised that their next issue would devote itself to Gough's time as Archbishop, but no such article ever appeared. Bishop Loane, now the Administrator of the Diocese, wrote a warm appreciation of Archbishop Gough in the June issue of *Southern Cross*, noting his personal charm, his appointment of the Archbishop's Commission, his courage and his "vigorous encouragement to every new avenue of ministry."[104] Gough wrote a warm farewell letter to the diocese in July 1966, in *Southern Cross*. He wrote, "We have come to love Australia and it is hard to leave you all."

It was asserted at the time, and since, that there was another cause of Gough's departure. This has been in the public domain for some time.[105] The protagonists are now dead, so the picture is unclear to some extent. The alleged cause was the subject of a complaint by a leading Sydney Anglican layman and businessman, who resided in Double Bay, a wealthy Sydney suburb near the location of Bishopscourt, where Gough and his wife lived. The complaint, made in late 1965 or early 1966, was to the effect that an improper relationship had developed between Gough and a married woman whom Gough had met at a local tennis club. The complaint was made to the Archbishop's chaplain who referred it to Bishop Loane, the Archbishop's most senior Assistant Bishop.[106]

The Rector of Darling Point was instructed to seek Gough's immediate resignation. What exactly happened then is unclear. However, Gough left Sydney on 20 February 1966, by ship, for London. He intended to consult his doctor and then proceed to Jerusalem in order to attend a conference. The doctor recommended six months' rest and a copy of the doctor's letter was attached to a letter of resignation sent by Gough to Loane in March 1966. Loane intended to table it at the meeting of the Standing Committee of the Sydney Diocese in March.[107] But Gough contacted Loane on the morning

103. ACR 2.6.1966, 1 and 7.

104. *Southern Cross* Supplement June 1966, p iii.

105. The *Sydney Morning Herald* 8.1.2013, 10. In the obituary for Stuart Babbage, Tony Stephens quotes EG Whitlam, who stated in 2004 at the launch of Babbage's *Memoirs of a Loose Canon*, that Hugh Gough "had been exposed as an adulterer."

106. Notes from the diary of Archbishop Philip Strong Friday 10 June 1966: "It seems that our worst fears are confirmed and it was infatuation with a married woman."

107. The Standing Committee is elected by the Synod and meets monthly during the year when Synod is not meeting. Synod as a rule meets for about 5 days once a year.

of the meeting asking him to withhold the letter. Loane did so. Gough then made a public statement that he planned to return to Sydney in June 1966 and resume his office.[108] Exactly what happened after that is unknown, but at the May meeting of the Standing Committee a resignation was tabled and the See declared vacant. Although those directly involved are dead, there is secondary evidence that the complaint of the layman was justified.[109]

Like the Anglican Church in general, the Diocese of Sydney, then and now, regards adultery, whether in the legal sense or in the biblical sense (Matthew 6:28) as sinful. That Sydney Evangelicals were prepared to ask their Archbishop to resign because of an alleged sexual liaison is very significant. In the years to come, questions of sexuality and sexual propriety would be at the center of Anglican storms. The evangelical attitude to extra-marital sex stands in contrast to the views of Muriel Porter of Melbourne, a long-time member of the General Synod and trenchant critic of the Sydney Diocese. In her book *The New Puritans* (2006), she writes: "I acknowledge the value of other sexual relationships than formal marriage, such as committed *de facto* and homosexual partnerships . . . I believe an open attitude to faithful, committed same-sex partnerships is also compatible with Scripture."[110] She is critical of the Sydney Evangelicals "exaltation of family [where] there seems to be a concern for male purity."[111] Later she states of the Sydney evangelical position: "Any form of sexual activity outside marriage, and same-sex activity in particular, is overtly regarded as impure, especially in the clergy."[112] "The rigour of Sydney Diocese's expectations . . . comes close to requiring moral perfection."[113]

Gough's episcopate ended suddenly and somewhat mysteriously. In one sense, and from his point of view, it was a failure. He had alienated Sydney's leaders, was out of step with Sydney's ethos, and left before the recommendations of his Commission had been implemented. On another view, however, it was a most significant time of growth for Evangelicals in Sydney, and to a large extent Gough had contributed to this. His Commission would prove to be a very important instrument to overhaul diocesan administration, enabling it to function far more effectively. The Billy Graham Crusade

108. Loane, *Men to Remember*, 87–88; *ACR* 2.6.1966, 1; *Southern Cross* June 1966, 10.

109. Alicia Watson interview with MHC 2.5.11. Watson's aunt later married the husband of the woman with whom Gough had the relationship. M Rodgers interview with MHC 9.5.11.

110. Porter, *The New Puritans*, 116.

111. Ibid., 113.

112. Ibid., 147.

113. Ibid., 148.

of 1959, though not his initiative in Sydney, and in fact occurring just before he took up his Sydney post, was like a giant wave through Sydney, its power unleashing what some have called a revival.[114] Some of Sydney's most influential leaders were converted in the 1959 Crusade, many churches had an influx of new Christians, and current members were re-invigorated. During this decade CMS Summer Schools and visiting Evangelicals from the other side of the world continued the encouragement of evangelical Christians, new and old, through evangelism and Bible teaching. Somewhat ironically, the direct result of clashes with Gough meant the flourishing of evangelical institutions in the Diocese. The ACL, The *Anglican Church Record* and Moore College each developed into high-powered stewards of the evangelical cause during the Gough era. Opposition energized them. During this time, parishes continued to grow in size and number and offertories increased significantly.[115]

---

114. Piggin's study of revival in *Spirit of a Nation*, Chapter 7, concludes that the Billy Graham Crusade in Australia in 1959, "was a revival, all right, and a great one," 171.

115. *Sydney Year Book* 1960, total parishes: 188.
Total receipts of the Standing Committee:
1959: £34,154.9.10—*Sydney Year Book* 1960, 272–3.
1966: $159,085—*Sydney Year Book* 1967, 324–5.

Chapter 6

One of our Own at Last: Marcus L. Loane 1966–1982

SYDNEY EVANGELICALS DO NOT emerge untarnished by the Gough years. The desire to win every battle, as exemplified by their last-ditch stand over the Constitution, is an example. Sometimes to lose is to win and to win is to lose.[1] Hackles were raised: mistrust and dislike characterized the relationship between Archbishop Gough and leading clergy from the moment he arrived. Some of this was avoidable, and so is regrettable. The combative spirit of DB Knox and members of the ACL is not attractive to those who ask how this approach was consistent with Christian love.

Marcus Loane (later Archbishop Sir Marcus Loane) was a thoroughgoing Evangelical and a member of Sydney clergy's elite inner circle. Greatly respected, absolutely steadfast in holding to Reformed theology, he nevertheless was a man of peace. He is one of Sydney's great metropolitan bishops, standing alongside Bishop Barker and Archbishop Mowll. He was Archbishop for fifteen years, in an era of turbulence in both the secular and Anglican worlds. During this time he united and strengthened his own diocese. Its connections with the other dioceses of Australia were the healthier for his influence.

---

1 ED Cameron conversations with MHC March 2013.

Archbishop Marcus Lawrence Loane

In a plea for church unity he concluded one Presidential Address to his synod:

> Personal piety, practical enterprise, excellence in scholarship, qualities of leadership, are too seldom found in equal measure, and the result is that disproportion easily develops in relations or attitudes. We ought never to build up things that are trifles into issues about which we then hold passionate convictions; at the same time, we will never find real family fellowship in a movement that is based on concession or compromise in vital matters of truth. We must seek the welfare of the whole Church

in a movement of God's gracious Spirit, which will harness freedom in things that are indifferent to a responsible concern for the glory of God and the doctrines of grace.[2]

The qualities, in equal measure, of personal piety, practical enterprise, careful scholarship and leadership aptly depict aspects of Loane himself, according to those who knew him and worked with him.[3]

Born in 1911, Marcus Lawrence Loane was 54 when he was elected Archbishop of Sydney. He was educated at The King's School, then at the University of Sydney.[4] While still at the university he enrolled at Moore College and after he had completed the College's two-year course, he was asked by Archbishop Mowll to be a chaplain to the Moore College students. The appointment was significant. The Moore College Principal, DJ Davies, was a tired man and ill, but more importantly, held unacceptably liberal theology. Mowll saw in Loane a young man who would help him in his plan "to shake Moore College from head to toe," as Loane put it.[5] Mowll's influence upon Loane continued to be very strong throughout Mowll's episcopate. It seems that Mowll saw in Loane, not only a "sound man" in terms of his theology, but also a good pastor, a man who would be able both to empathize with the students and provide helpful spiritual counsel.

After ordination to the priesthood in 1936, Loane spent time in parish ministry in England, then on the outbreak of war in 1939 he and his wife Patricia returned to Sydney, where Loane was appointed Vice-Principal of Moore College. He then left the College to serve as a chaplain in the army in New Guinea from 1942–1944. While there his experience of the Church broadened, especially through his contact with Philip Strong, Bishop of New Guinea. Strong, an Anglo-Catholic, who later became Archbishop of Brisbane and Primate of the Anglican Church of Australia, liked Loane, describing him as "a very nice fellow indeed and a very earnest Evangelical of the best type . . . very charming person."[6] Loane's first biographer commented:

> Loane's experience as a chaplain had enabled him to see Bishop Strong and other churchmen in their own setting and to value their worth. Their sacramental emphasis was not his, but he

---

2. *Sydney Year Book 1980*, 234.

3. ED Cameron conversation with MHC 28.5.2013.

4. He was awarded BA (University of Sydney) in 1932, the ThL (Moore College) in 1933, MA in 1937, the DD (Wycliffe College Toronto) in 1958 and the KBE in 1976.

5. ML Loane interview with MHC 5.2.1996.

6. Reid, *Marcus L Loane*, 24. A new biography of ML Loane was published in October 2015: Alan Blanch, *From Strength to Strength—A Life of Marcus Loane*.

could not deny the reality of faith and commitment, which in some cases had been sealed with a martyr's death.[7]

Loane was briefly attracted to missionary work, but he realized that all he really wanted to do was to work at Moore College. Mowll secured his discharge from the army and he returned to the College, resuming his position as Vice-Principal. When TC Hammond retired in 1953, Loane succeeded him as Principal of Moore College. Some six years later, Mowll appointed Loane a Coadjutor Bishop of Sydney and it was at this time that Broughton Knox became Principal of Moore College.

Loane was elected Archbishop of Sydney in August 1966 by an overwhelmingly strong vote of both clergy and laity.[8] He was the first Australian to be elected Archbishop of Sydney. The *ACR* captures his strong sense of history in the making, as Loane entered the Synod meeting place:

> On his entry into the Chapter House, a long, standing ovation was given to him. Although, as always, master of the situation, Bishop Loane was visibly moved by the sense of the historic importance of that moment in his life.[9]

The *ACR* was conscious of the wider Anglican Church when it stated, in bold type,

> While news of the election of the Rt. Rev. Marcus Lawrence Loane as eighth Archbishop of Sydney has been received warmly by Evangelical Christians of all denominations it has also been welcomed by many Anglicans of schools of thought different from that of Bishop Loane himself.

The two reasons for this, according to the *ACR*, were that Loane was an Australian, and the second was that, following the vote, although a considerable segment of Synod voted against him, the call issued to him to become Archbishop was unanimous. In fact, the clergyman who seconded the motion calling Loane to the Archbishopric had previously moved the nomination of another man, and was of a different kind of churchmanship from Loane. The comment from the *ARC* about the warm reception of Loane's election "by Evangelical Christians of all denominations" is very important. The Diocese of Sydney and the Archbishop of Sydney have their own constituency. This constituency is nothing less than the worldwide network of Evangelical Christians. Sydney Diocesan work has been

---

7. Reid, *Marcus L Loane*, 24.
8. *ACR* 28.7.66 1; Clergy: 162 (total other: 72); Lay: 232 (total other: 134).
9 *ACR* 28.7.66, 1.

interdenominational, probably since Barker's time, and according to Archbishop Jensen, the Archbishop of Sydney is a *de facto* leader of Evangelicals in Australia and in the world.[10]

Towards the end of his term of office, Loane wrote a series of mini biographies of the people who shaped his life.[11] They were all men; all but one of the six were ordained and he met them while still a young man. Three were Sydney Diocesan men: Mowll, David James Knox (father of Broughton Knox) and Richard Bradley Robinson (father of Donald Robinson). Mowll's influence on Loane was considerable. Archbishop Mowll was a benevolent autocrat and Loane, somewhat in the Mowll tradition, is said to have treated his bishops as a headmaster with his prefects.[12] Like Mowll, he was a great traveller, and when he became Primate, he visited every diocese in Australia (at the Diocese of Sydney's expense). Of Mowll, Loane wrote: "He opened my eyes to a far wider world of thought and vision than I had known. For me, he was the Archbishop *par excellence*."[13]

DJ Knox had been Loane's boss when Loane worked for him as his curate. Loane described him as "like a father" and indeed Knox became Loane's father-in-law when Loane married his daughter, Patricia Knox. While Loane described Knox as "a man of exceptional integrity, profound sincerity, and a transparent devotion to Christ," Knox was also a tough, choleric and sometimes pugnacious man.[14]

Archdeacon Richard Bradley Robinson impressed Loane with his warmth. Loane wrote of him, "The warmth of his welcome at our first meeting never grew less and I can say how much it meant to me to be taken so fully into his confidence and trusted so much by him when I was young."[15] All who remember Archdeacon Robinson (known affectionately as "Robbie") would agree on his kindness. A right hand man in the Mowll regime, he managed to be both gracious and unswervingly faithful in his evangelical stance.

The other three influences on Loane were a Melbourne Evangelical, Horace John Hannah; a Scot, the Rev. George Mackay; and Canon Talbot Greaves, an Englishman. Hannah impressed him with his passion

---

10. PF Jensen interview with MHC 4.3.2015.

11. *Southern Cross* September, October and November 1981.

12. ED Cameron conversation 22.3.2013.

13. *Southern Cross* September 1981, 25; Presidential Address to General Synod 1981 by the Most Reverend ML Loane KBE, MA, DD, Primate of Australia, 5.

14. J Reid, *Marcus L Loane*, 5–6; conversation with Joyce Hays (neé Bosanquet), 2005. As a child Joyce attended St Paul's Chatswood with her brothers until DJ Knox angrily and unfairly blamed her brother Geoff for a misdemeanor. They never returned.

15. *Southern Cross* September 1981, 25.

for reading and books and his support for missionary work. Like Loane, who walked the Kokoda Track, he was "a great walker." Most important of all, he wrote to Loane every week for nearly 20 years.[16] The Rev. George MacKay was a very powerful preacher, and on a visit to Sydney in 1929, took a personal interest in Loane, encouraging him in his studies. He made no secret of his hope that Loane would eventually be ordained.[17] Canon Greaves, "a man of rare sagacity . . . linked with a humble, loving, Christ like spirit" made Loane so welcome that his home in Sevenoaks became home away from home for Loane when he visited England.[18] With the exception of DJ Knox, all Loane's mentors were, it seems, gentle men. It is noteworthy that he did not name TC Hammond among the men who shaped his life, although he worked closely with TC at Moore College when he became a member of the Moore College staff.[19] In his history of Moore College, Loane described TC as "fescennine."[20] This little-known word buried like an explosive in his tribute to TC Hammond is probably one of the rare occasions when Loane was strongly negative about a fellow clergyman, if he and the Oxford Dictionary agree as to the meaning of the word.

The Loane era, while a stable and more peaceful one than those which preceded and succeeded it, within the Diocese and the Anglican Church of Australia, was a turbulent time for Australians. Australia's involvement for ten years in the Vietnam War (1962–1972) required sending out more than 50,000 personnel and 521 Australians were killed.[21] Australia's commitment to the war, the conscription of young men as soldiers, and the queries as to whether this was a war in which this nation should be involved sparked anti-war protests. Leading churchmen were divided as to whether to support the war.[22] Loane's approach was to pray: for the establishment of good government for the Vietnamese people, and for Australian servicemen

16. Ibid., November 1981, 26–37.

17. Ibid., October 1981, 18–19.

18. Ibid., September 1981, 25.

19. Letters to DB Knox indicate that neither man liked TC Hammond much. See also footnote 11 in Cameron, *An Enigmatic Life*, 97.

20. Loane, *Moore Theological College*, 153. The *Shorter Oxford Dictionary* entry for fescennine: "pertaining to scurrilous dialogues in verse; licentious, obscene, scurrilous." According to Archbishop Jensen, others would disagree with Loane's assessment: PF Jensen to MHC 14.4.15.

21. Australia's Involvement in the Vietnam War—Fact sheet 117, National Archives of Australia.

22. Archbishop Ramsey, some Australian Anglican and Roman Catholic bishops, as well as the Methodist leader Rev Alan Walker, opposed the war. *The Anglican*, 6.4.1967 and 27.4.1967.

"sent to bear the brunt of constant and heavy fighting."[23] The aftermath of the war brought some 100,000 refugees to Australia, a small proportion of whom came as "boat people."[24] They and subsequent refugees were unlike the great majority of immigrants to Australia before the Second World War. They were not British and they were not Anglican. During Loane's "reign" the percentage of Anglicans in Australia fell from 34.9% to 26.1%.[25] This figure refers to nominal Anglicans. The actual number of Anglicans in Sydney attending church probably rose, as the number of parishes increased substantially.

Other memorable events of the era were the mysterious death of Prime Minister Harold Holt (19 December 1967), the Six Day War between Israel and Arabs, the assassination of Martin Luther King in 1967, the assassination of Robert Kennedy in 1968, the moon landing in 1969, Watergate in 1973 and the wedding of Prince Charles, heir to the British throne, to Lady Diana Spencer in 1981—the first time, according to Loane, that the marriage of a Prince of Wales had been celebrated since 1863.[26] There were no fewer than four different Archbishops of Canterbury during Loane's term as Archbishop. Michael Ramsey succeeded Archbishop Fisher in 1961 and retired in 1974. His successor was the scholarly Evangelical Donald Coggan who in turn was succeeded by Robert Runcie in 1980. Both the Queen and Archbishop Coggan visited Sydney in 1977. Coggan had already visited Sydney twice before, while Archbishop of York, and at Loane's invitation.[27]

Perhaps the most significant arrival was non-human: the computer. Although room-sized computers were introduced to Australia as early as 1949, census data were first processed electronically in 1966 and the Apple II personal computer, the size of a typewriter, was released in 1977, the first of the "consumer computers."[28] In the Diocesan magazine *Southern Cross* systems analyst David Totterdell presciently wrote that the utilization of computer technology presented an acute challenge to the Christian community, the issues being "unemployment, privacy and economics." [29]

During its short but dramatic years in power the Whitlam Labor government (1972–75) enacted radical legislation, which facilitated enormous social change over subsequent decades. Lindsay Tanner, a Labor politician,

---

23. *Southern Cross* July 1967, 4.
24. About 2,000.
25. http://www.abs.gov.au/ Special Feature: Trends in religious affiliation.
26. *Southern Cross* July 1981, 12.
27. *The Anglican* 10.6.1969, 1.
28. http://www.australianhistory.org/technology-timeline; inventors.about.com
29. *Southern Cross* November 1978, 18.

has written that the Whitlam Government shaped modern Australia because the landmark social justice campaigns of the 1960s came to fruition under Whitlam.[30]

The most critical legislation, from the viewpoint of conservative Christians, was enacted in 1975: the Family Law Act, which included no fault divorce; and the Racial Discrimination Act. While the 1975 Racial Discrimination Act was a Federal Act legislating specifically against racism, state legislation concerned with other types of discrimination soon followed. The New South Wales Anti-Discrimination Act 1977 (NSW) included sexual discrimination, and here homosexuality and transgender were specified. South Australia had been the first state to decriminalise homosexuality, in 1972. The anti-discrimination legislation regarding homosexuality was a big leap. Homosexual practice moved, almost in one bound, from being a centuries-old criminal offence, to being accepted to the point where any kind of discrimination (there were some exceptions such as in schools) was legally culpable.[31] In NSW the cart seems to have come before the horse: homosexuality was decriminalised in 1984, but the 1977 anti-discrimination legislation on the grounds of sex preceded it.

Legislation relating to homosexual practice and its consequences for social institutions, including school and churches, continues to be dynamite. It has proved to be the single most divisive issue in the Anglican Church of Australia in the twenty-first century, and in the worldwide Anglican Communion.

The new approach to homosexuality was a frequently discussed issue in the *ACR* during these years. Over the following 40 years it has not ceased to surprise conservative Christian people that behaviour so clearly condemned in both Old and New Testaments should be now deemed by some to be acceptable behaviour, within and outside the Christian church.[32] As early as 1971 the Synod of the Diocese of Melbourne voted in favour of a request to the Government to legalise homosexual acts committed by consenting adults in private. The Victorian Attorney-General, Mr. Reid, condemned the synod's recommendation and said he would not recommend

---

30. http://www.themonthly.com.au/gough-whitlam-95-years-comment-lindsay-tanner-3477.

31. http://aic.gov.au/documents/F/2/E/%7BF2ED9BD3-0314-4EAA-AD03-410635E620DE%7Dti29.pdf No.29 Homosexual Law Reform in Australia, 1991, Melissa Bull, Susan Pinto and Paul Wilson.

32. Key references, either directly or by implication, are: Leviticus 18:22, 20:13; Deuteronomy 5:18, Romans 1:18–32, I Corinthians 6:9, 13 and 18; Galatians 5:19, Colossians 3:5, Revelation 21:8, 22:15; Porter, *The New Puritans*,134–5.

changes in the provisions of the Crimes Act concerning homosexuality.[33] Reid went on to say that any lessening of penalties, or changes to the law would be an encouragement to acts of homosexuality. "In my view," he said, "this is a sign of degeneracy in any community."[34]

The *ACR* quoted an article in English newspaper the *Church Times*, about the Preface in *Crockford's Clerical Directory 1975–6*. Anonymous, but described by the publishers as "a person of distinction," the writer of the Preface devoted nearly a page to the subject of homosexuality. He wrote,

> At a time of moral confusion and of growth in moral sensitivity, it is not surprising that those who are by nature homosexual should claim the right to live according to their nature; and at a time when many in the church recognise the need to be realistic and compassionate about the world as it actually is, it is not surprising that "gay lib" has been given a hearing. All this constitutes a growing pastoral problem.
>
> A special standard was to be expected of the clergy, who are so often entrusted with the care of the young and with counselling about marriage.
>
> In practice this must mean that no priest with homosexual leanings should ever feel free to give any physical expression to them; the self-control must be iron. Priests who uphold this traditional standard of self-discipline and self-sacrifice are wise not to describe themselves as "homosexuals." The word has many meanings, and most of them are still (to the public) corrupt.[35]

Marcus Loane in an early Presidential Address to the Sydney Synod went to the heart of the issues Christians were grappling with, in such a time of moral change

> The question must arise as to how far it is proper for the Church to expect the State through its laws to uphold the standards of morality, which have their roots in the soil of God's Law. It is clear that men must agree on what is right and what is wrong, or there can be no law at all. This means that a common morality is part of the price which society must pay for the sake of common welfare. But is such a morality to be governed by the permissive attitudes and changing fashions of each generation? Or is it to reflect the great unchanging majesty of what we call the law of

---

33. http://aic.gov.au/documents/F/2/E/%7BF2ED9BD3-0314-4EAA-AD03-410635E620DE%7Dti29.pdf Aspects of homosexuality were decriminalised in Victoria in 1980.

34 *ACR* 4.11.1971, 9.

35. *ACR* 25.11.1976, 5.

God? Perhaps I may express the alternatives a little differently. Should men be free to do what they like so long as what they do does not develop as a corrosive in the life of society? Or should the law define the real standard of right and wrong, and then impose it on the whole community? There is no doubt in my mind that the latter is the ideal; but to achieve it requires the constant education of society in sound moral principles. And such education is the particular contribution, which the Church ought always to be making.[36]

One Sydney Anglican who was trying vigorously to educate and influence both Christians and the general public was Broughton Knox. His weekly broadcasts on radio 2CH, later available as pamphlets, his articles, and his letters to his local MP were admirable endeavours to engage with secular morality. On the matter of homosexuality he asserted that the homosexual could find no moral principle to guide his actions. To condone the practice was to destroy the basis of sexual morality *in toto*. The question, "Am I my brother's keeper?" must be answered with a "Yes!"[37]

The homosexual issue was linked, to some extent, with the question of women's place in the Anglican Church. Some of those who espoused women's ordination to the priesthood were seen sooner or later to support the position that "it's OK to be gay." While to many thinking Christians the Bible was not unequivocally clear on the women's ordination matter, it was quite, quite clear on homosexual practice. Without doubt the awareness that the two controversial issues were linked made conservative Evangelicals in the Sydney Diocese very fearful that if women were ordained as priests, then the next inevitable step would be the condoning of homosexual practice and so-called "gay" marriage. The only real links seem to this author to be that both are about gender, and about inclusion or exclusion in the Anglican Church.[38]

The women's ordination movement was part of a wider movement in Australia and the West. The second wave of feminism occurred in the 1970s (the first had been in the 1890s) marked by and stimulated by publication of such influential books as Germaine Greer's *The Female Eunuch* (1970) and Anne Summer's *Dammed Whores and God's Police* (1975). There were significant changes to women's status and role in society at this time: for example, the steady rise of the number of women in the workforce,

---

36. *Sydney Year Book*, 242-3.

37. "The Christian doctrine of sex" 9.7.1972 and "The Last Tango," 4.3.1973, The Protestant Faith, Box 80a.

38. Sydney Anglican leader conversation with MHC in the 1980s.

Commonwealth legislation awarding women equal pay (1972), the establishment of the Women's Electoral Lobby (1972) and the introduction of courses in the universities focusing on women's issues.[39]

Neither the proponents of women's ordination nor those who oppose it possess the luxury of a watertight case for their position. Sydney Evangelicals want to obey biblical teaching on the subject, but there is no unanimity of interpretation among them. Different people come away from the biblical text with different conclusions. This may result partly from a desire for the text to reinforce their particular position. In addition, much or even most of the analysis on the subject seems primarily designed to *persuade*. Rarely are the texts laid out and examined with scholarly detachment. In fact, the opposite is true: many books and articles verge on the polemical in tone. The issue is noteworthy for the emotion it arouses. The debate has been long, arduous, and above all, hurt and angry in tone.

There really is no watertight case for either side. Those who try to obey Paul's commands relating to women in church leadership find it impossible to do so with absolute integrity. For example, some of those women who maintain that a woman should not preach have written books and spoken in the synod. The fact that our culture is different from that of first century Palestine makes it very hard to know where exactly the eternal principles lie. People have resorted to drawing lines in the sand. Equally difficult is the position of those who espouse women's ordination as a right. There are a number of Pauline injunctions, which have to be explained first in order to hold this position with integrity.

One step in the right direction is to be aware of the methodology being used. There are, for example, two kinds of perspective which people tend to employ: viewing the women's ordination issues either from a worm's eye view (microscopically close) or a bird's eye view (at a distance). The worm's eye view is more likely to be legalistic and less likely to see the "big picture." The bird's eye view will include a consideration of the trajectory of history and governing biblical themes such as redemption and the Creator's plan for the renewal of all things.[40] Sadly, there has been a regrettable lack of respect of one "side" for the other: one side claiming the other is "unbiblical" and "liberal" and the other side grieved and angry because they perceive their rights have been denied them.[41]

---

39. See Davison, Hirst and Macintyre [ed.], *The Oxford Companion to Australian History*, 247–8; A O'Brien, "Women in the churches before 1992: 'No obtrusive womanhood.'" Chapter 2, in E Lindsay & J Scarfe [Ed.], *Preachers, Prophets and Heretics*; http://www.abs.gov.au Trends in Women's Employment; G Bolton, The Oxford History of Australia 5, 1942–1995, 201; Carey, *Believing in Australia*, Chapter 5.

40. France, *Women in the Church's Ministry*, 91–95.

41. Voysey, *By The Way*, 194–202.

That is the dilemma. More than any other single issue in the church's history since the Reformation, it has called the authority of the Bible into question. That is why it is so important, and partly why it is so deeply divisive. Sydney Anglicans claim as their identity a subjection to the supreme authority of Scripture in all matters of faith. Probably all Christians claim to try to obey the Scriptures, but Evangelicals claim it as a primary attribute. Unfortunately, those who maintain that they have the only right interpretation of Scripture in what is a disputable matter appear to be guilty of arrogance.[42] The women's ordination issue has accordingly driven Evangelical Sydney Anglicans further out into the cold.

Prophets, Preachers and Heretics, a collection of essays on the ministry of Anglican women, is a fascinating insight into the movement for the ordination of women.[43] The range of topics is wide as are the different kinds of men and women who contributed. It is scholarly and very readable, and as such, a fitting tribute to Dr Patricia Brennan OAM, founder of Movement for the Ordination of Women. There are nineteen essays in all. Curiously, none sets out to address two key issues. The first is, what is the *theological* underpinning of the drive to ordain women? The second, what is the *goal* of woman's ordination? Is it in obedience to Christ, to serve Christ? Does it build up the church?[44] Is it primarily an equal opportunity issue?

During Archbishop Loane's time in office, the question about the role of women in the church became steadily more pressing. In a very early Presidential Address Loane made his position clear. He was opposed to women's ordination on the grounds that it conflicted with the doctrine of Headship and Authority rooted in the Godhead. Subscribing to the doctrine of the Eternal Subordination of the Son, he linked this with the ordination issue.[45] Loane's theology regarding male headship and also the Subordination of the Son are two doctrinal matters which are the subject of robust debate among theologians. Here he probably rested on the theological conclusions of TC Hammond and DB Knox. He said nothing further about the subject of women's ordination in his annual addresses to the Sydney Synod, merely noting without comment that in 1977 the General Synod resolved that there were no theological objections to the ordination of women to the priesthood.[46] Perhaps he did not want to buy into the debate.

---

42. The apostle Paul on disputable matters: Romans 14.
43. Lindsay and Scarfe [ed.], *Preachers, Prophets and Heretics*.
44. See Avis, *The Identity of Anglicanism*, 119–129.
45. *The Anglican* 17.10.1968, 1; *Sydney Year Book 1969*, 206–7.
46. *Sydney Year Book 1978*, 213.

The Lambeth Conference of 1968 raised the subject of women's ordination. Donald Coggan, Archbishop of York stated, "I hope that the Church will declare itself as ready and eager to receive from women, duly qualified and licensed, the ministry of the Word and the consecrated elements." The *Anglican*, on the side of women's ordination, featured a long article, entitled "The Devil slates Dr Coggan and Sydney priests." The article began:

> In a special (and exclusive) interview with THE ANGLICAN, His Satanic Majesty has spoken approvingly of the Lambeth decision to defer for another ten years all consideration of the role of women in the sacred ministry... "I am very pleased on the whole," The Devil said last Monday. "The bishops and most of the Anglican clergy throughout the world have stayed firm. They have steadfastly refused to be influenced by reason, and have been guided by emotion and prejudice."

The article reported ML Loane's statement to the conference that "I believe that if the ministry of the Church of England is to be thrown open to women, it will be the death knell of the Church for men."

Deaconess Mary Andrews said she thought the Scriptural evidence "not altogether one-sided." She looked at the issue from the standpoint of women's ministry recorded in the Bible: the woman of Samaria, Priscilla, Lydia, the "central evidence" of Jesus's revelation of himself to women first, at his Resurrection. She concluded:

> The fact is, women are just not being used as they should be in the Church. I do not think many of us particularly want to be priests, and to administer the Sacraments. However, I find the attitude to women preaching very strange in some parts of Australia. In China, I was sent to one congregation where I preached as a matter of course, and I have done so in Bathurst and other dioceses in Australia. In other places the attitude towards deaconesses is less enlightened than it was in China.[47]

The General Synod Doctrine Commission published its report *The Ministry of Women* for the 1977 meeting of General Synod.[48] DB Knox,

---

47. *The Anglican* 15 August 1968, 1, 11; ED Cameron in an interview with MHC (28.5.2013) spoke of women church-planting, running churches, preaching and pastoring their congregations. He visited such women during his term of office as Federal Secretary of CMS in Australia (1965–1972).

48. It followed three papers published by the Doctrine Commission of the General Synod in 1976, under the title *A Woman's Place*. The authors were John Gaden, Leon Morris and Barbara Thiering. *A Woman's Place* "offered no clear guidelines or recommendations for decision or action," according to a review by Margaret Rodgers in *Southern Cross* 17.3.1976, 17.

a member of the Doctrine Commission, published a minority dissenting report and explanation. He argued that the headship of men and the subordination of women in the family and the congregation were part of the eternal order of creation. He rejected the argument that this subordination was the result of the Fall and had no place in Christ's New Creation.[49] Knox's arguments were quiet and measured in their tone. For example, about headship he wrote,

> The principle of relationship itself (i.e. headship and subordination) is not culturally orientated but it will be expressed according to the spirit of the age. The principle of relationship of men and women is unchanging, being part of the created order [I Corinthians 11:3] . . . it is of course marriage (which is the quintessence of the relationship between man and woman) that this relation of headship and subordination is most clearly expressed and experienced.
> What is involved in this headship may be gathered from the fact that it is modeled on the headship of Christ to his people, and of God to Christ.[50]

Authors of books on Anglicanism, which mention the Sydney position, generally give the headship argument as the reason for the Sydney opposition to women's ordination, but rarely attempt to explain it.[51] The Rev. Dr Michael Jensen is an exception. In *Sydney Anglicanism. An Apology* he explains headship and DB Knox's teaching on it in relation to the family: "a model of leadership-through-service, and submission as a response."[52] Broughton Knox and his theology of headship are responsible for the Sydney Diocesan position on women in ministry. But in actual fact, Knox was heard to say that he had no problem with women being ordained—as long as they were not rectors of parishes. He had strong reservations about women preaching but none about women being bishops or archbishops. He expressed the wish, at least on one occasion, that women could be as free as men to exercise ministry.[53] He was a more flexible thinker (sometimes alarmingly so) than his successors.

---

49. Grant, *Episcopally Led and Synodically Governed*, 313; ACR 28.4.1977, 3, DB Knox Minority Report, ACR 28.4.1977, 3.

50. Ibid.

51. See for example, Avis, *The Identity of Anglicanism*, 112; Kaye, *An Introduction to World Anglicanism*, 168.

52. Jensen, *Sydney Anglicanism. An Apology*, 128–9.

53. MHC personal recollections. Conversations with ED Cameron. Knox, *Selected Works Vol II*, "The ordination of women," 205. Women and ordination: Canon Law Commission 1979, Knox papers, Box 14 Folder 12. See Cameron, *An Enigmatic Life*,

Events moved relatively slowly after the 1977 Doctrine Commission Report on the ministry of women. Deaconess Margaret Rodgers was the first woman elected to the Sydney Standing Committee in 1977. She remained a member until 2011 by which time there were seven women members (out of a total of 55 members).[54]

In 1980 the Appellate Tribunal of the General Synod advised "that the ordination of women was not inconsistent with the Constitution and the passing of an enabling canon." This meant that the Constitution as it stood did not permit the ordination of women. At the 1981 General Synod, the constitutional amendments were passed by simple majorities but needed the consent of three quarters of the dioceses, including all the metropolitan dioceses. Neither Adelaide nor Sydney gave their consent.[55]

The *ACR* contains numerous articles, letters and book reviews on the subject, during the 1970s. Broughton Knox and Donald Robinson made contributions from time to time, both opposing women's ordination to the priesthood. The Rev. Kevin Giles, described as "a conservative Evangelical" published *Women and their Ministry*, espousing the view that there are no theological barriers to the full equality of women with men in the ministry of the church. Sold by a Roman Catholic publishing house, it stated three propositions:

- Equality before God
- Equality of worth
- Equality of opportunity to use God given gifts in the Church.[56]

Ironically, sitting next to her brother's article for the month in *ARC*, was a letter entitled "Christian Unity," by Constance Knox. She wrote supporting women's ministry. It shows how women of the time were thinking, how the conservatives running the *ACR* were willing to allow diversity of opinion, and how more than one member of the Knox family was a keen biblical thinker and held strong views. Her letter and the views expressed by Mary Andrews at the 1968 Lambeth Conference reveal a greater concern for women to be allowed to preach than for ordination to the priesthood, *per se*. This is the distinctive position of many Evangelical men and women who espouse active ministry of women to both women and men. There is less emphasis on administering the sacraments, and more on allowing

---

Chapter 10.

54. *Sydney Year Book* 2012, 53.
55. Grant, *Episcopally Led and Synodically Governed*, 314.
56. ACR 15.9.1977, 8.

women to exercise their teaching and pastoring gifts for the benefit of both men and women.

In a complex and well-reasoned letter Constance Knox wrote:

> In her letter, ACR 26.5.77, Mrs. P Creasey said: "I cannot verify this, but I have read that Paul was quoting from a letter received from the Corinthians, 'Let your women keep silence in the churches,' etc. and his comment, 'What! Came the word of God out from you or came it unto you only?'"[57]
>
> I think I can give her a clue as to where she may have read this. Mary S Wood ... in her book "A Christian Girl's Problems" has a chapter entitled, "Should women preach?" She points out that it was the Talmud or Jewish Rabbinical traditions, which St Paul was quoting from—the same traditions which our Lord attacked (Mark 7:8).
>
> She quotes the words: "It is a shame for a woman to let her voice be heard among men" and other such maxims. She says that it is significant that no apostle ever quoted from the Talmud except Paul, who only quoted it to refute it, as in these verses, I Cor. 14:13, 35.
>
> That the apostle had been answering questions from the Corinthians is clear from I Cor. 7:1, "Now for the questions about which you wrote," and the section of the epistle devoted to these replies goes on to the end of Chapter 14 which includes these verses.
>
> This explanation removes the apparent contradiction in the same epistle where St Paul gives instructions about how women are to dress when praying or preaching in public (I Cor. 11:1–15).
>
> Mrs. Wood goes on to ask how it could be a shame for women to speak in public when they are distinctly commanded to do so in Acts 2:17. (It is noteworthy that this command is first found in the Old Testament).
>
> May I also add to the debate the observation that we as Christians should be a lot poorer if Martha had not passed on to men what our Lord had told her about His being the Resurrection and the Life (John 11:25,26) and if the woman of Samaria had not passed on what our Lord told her about worship (John 4:23,24).
>
> And where would the Christian Church be without the testimony of Mary about the Virgin Birth? Joseph's dream is not

---

57. I Corinthians 14:34 and 36.

strong enough evidence to base such an important doctrine on, though it does support Mary's testimony.

These truths were committed to the minds of women for the benefit of the whole church. God might do the same again.

CONSTANCE S KNOX

Gordon[58]

In the same edition of *ACR* Neil Cameron wrote the first of two learned articles about the Appellate Tribunal and the legal situation regarding women's ordination. The obstacles to legal ordination of women to the priesthood were considerable, so in his opinion it would not happen for a long time: "until the proposal has much greater support than it has at present." He stated that the concept of ordination ought to be re-examined and he urged clergy to share ministry with lay people—using the gifts of laywomen in particular.[59]

Meanwhile, the Diocese of Sydney was growing robustly: in the decade spanning 1969–1980 the number of parishes increased from 188 to 238. Parishes, not the bishops and diocesan administration, are the action stations of the Diocese. This is where changes in individuals and communities happen, with each parish a vital part of the Diocese. It is impossible in the space of this book to describe the parishes in all their variety and vitality but there are quite a few published histories of Sydney parishes.[60] St Barnabas' Broadway, although not a typical parish in this era, or ever, provides some insight into parish life and parish initiatives in the early 1970s.

A century before, St Barnabas had been built for those living in the slum areas around Chippendale and Blackwattle Bay by the Evangelical Thomas Smith. Later it was the base from which the Rev. RBS Hammond (not to be confused with TC) managed his social services and evangelism ministry before and during the Great Depression of the 1930s. In the 1960s St Barnabas reinvented itself yet again, this time as a student church. The Rector was the Rev. Paul Barnett and his assistant, the Rev. Peter Jensen. Barnett was Rector from 1967 to 1973. The church was close to the University of Sydney and ran student hostels in terraces located in the neighboring suburb of Glebe. Foreign students, in particular Chinese, heard the good

---

58. *ACR* 15.9.1977, 4.

59. *ACR* 15.9.1977, 3.

60. For example, St Mark's Darling Point, St Paul's Chatswood, Christ Church St Ives, Christ Church Sydney (better known as Christ Church St Laurence), St Swithun's Pymble and St John's Gordon.

news of Christ, often for the first time in their lives, and many returned to their home countries as Christians.

Paul and Anita Barnett were very conscious that many students were living away from their families. They felt it important to create a genuine community among the church members. So they engaged in extensive hospitality for small groups as well in large-scale barbecues at the rambling old rectory with its substantial grounds—ideal for that purpose. They were keen that the Sunday-by-Sunday church teaching was translated into loving and caring relationships.

Bishop Paul Barnett

The parish did its best to connect with a congregation of great variety: the local residents who might best be described as "working class," the university students, and those who stayed on, having completed their university studies, now working in one of the professions, or as academics, or raising young families. Nearby, of course, was Moore College, and members of its Faculty, including Broughton and Ailsa Knox and their family, were members of the congregation.

At this time in its history, St Barnabas (known affectionately as "Barneys") was notable for its sermons. Paul Barnett organized the preaching by means of a published sermon series, each series working through a book of the Bible. Keen members of the congregation were able to read the relevant Bible passage ahead of time, and were encouraged to take notes during the sermon. The sermons were like lectures, and Paul and Peter aimed to educate their congregation in biblical theology. Barnett held the view that tertiary students should be well educated, not just developing intellectually through their university studies, but simultaneously growing in their understanding of the God of the Bible. To this end he wrestled with the Scriptures, always preparing from the Greek, and his delight in this engagement was evident. The Scriptures were an inexhaustible well, infinitely rewarding to those who used their intellect as well as their faith. This kind of preaching exegeted a passage, not a single verse, and in this it was a departure from an earlier style of preaching. John Stott and Donald Robinson were the main influences here. When Barney's people finally left and joined a new parish, they expected this kind of teaching, and they were like a diaspora into other parishes of the Diocese.

After Barnett left, the Rev. Allan Blanch succeeded him (1974–1982). In Blanch's time, there were two further momentous developments: a series of very successful university missions, organized by the Barney's staff, and Bible studies in homes. In Barnett's time, there was a weekly Bible study, led by the Rector in the Rectory. In Blanch's time small groups formed. The Rector did not initiate them, and it is probable that he (with other rectors in parishes where this was happening) was somewhat apprehensive about lay people running their own Bible studies. Some indeed referred to this activity as "pooled ignorance."[61] They provided a forum for mutual exploration of the Bible (with the aid of commentaries). This was a group of people with whom to share life's joys and problems, and with whom to pray. In a way that a whole congregation could never be, because of its size, these groups were like little families, caring, listening, helping and learning together. It is not entirely clear why they arose when they did, but they aided personal

---

61. My mother's term. Married to a clergyman, she saw through clergy eyes.

accountability and fostered maturity in the lives of numerous Christians.[62] Since the seventies these groups have become normative in most evangelical parishes in Sydney. Another consequence of the Bible study groups was to empower lay people to engage in active learning and not to be so reliant upon the Rector. This in turn led them to become much more active in Christian ministry. A further result was that many then went on to enroll in formal theological courses, such as the PTC (Preliminary Theological Course) offered by Moore College.

Another aspect of parish life was involvement with the community. St Barnabas, like many other parishes in the 1970s, sent Scripture teachers into their local state school, held Sunday School classes and rented a dilapidated terrace house where they ran a weekly youth drop-in center.

The Diocese was growing wealthier: Gough's Archbishop's Commission was finally bearing fruit. Glebe lands at Edgecliff were sold, as were some 700 terraces in the suburb of Glebe for a sum of $17,500,000. The proceeds were invested for the most part in commercial properties and by 1985 the assets of the Glebe Administration Board had risen to $150,000,000 (compared with $25,000,000 in 1970).

Charlotte Rivers, a long-standing diocesan staff member, recalled in an interview,

> When I came to Sydney in January 1965, the diocesan offices were in Church House, which was the Deanery. It was a small administration, but with the glebe land sale and the money becoming available for investment (there had been peppercorn rents on most of the housing in the Glebe on very long leases); it became over the next two decades much more efficient and businesslike.[63]

A sign of the diocesan reinvestment policy was the construction of St Andrew's House, finally opened in 1976. Built behind and between St Andrew's Cathedral and the Sydney Town Hall, it occupied a prestigious location in the heart of the city. It had six floors of offices, a car park, a shopping arcade and a school for 500 students. Its final cost was $21,000,000 and was the last of the diocesan construction projects for a time.[64] Geoffrey Moorehouse described St Andrew's House as "of an opulence normally encountered at the headquarters of international corporations."[65]

---

62. The house church movement of the 1970s may well have contributed to the rise of the small group Bible studies.

63. Charlotte Rivers telephone interview with MHC 23.5.2011.

64. Judd and Cable, *Sydney Anglicans*, 268–73.

65. Moorehouse, *Sydney*, 164.

Diocesan administration was streamlined with the establishment of a Secretariat in 1973, the servant of the Standing Committee. The Diocese was now able to fund its projects for ministry and evangelism, with 42% of its annual income ($2,358,364 in 1982) spent on education, evangelism, chaplaincy and social work; and 10% on training ordinands.[66] The authors of *Sydney Anglicans* comment: "This was the age of bureaucracy: the administration of governments, private business and universities were all expanding rapidly... This was the age of large head offices for private corporations..."[67]

A crisis with diocesan schools in the early 1970s shook the Diocese and changed its policy towards some church schools. Seven schools were in financial straits: The SCEGGS group of schools, The Illawarra Grammar School and the Blue Mountains Grammar School. The SCEGGS (Sydney Church of England Girls' Grammar School) group of schools comprised the Head School at Darlinghurst, and branch schools: *Redlands* at Cremorne, *Gleniffer Brae* at Wollongong, SCEGGS Moss Vale, and *Loquat Valley* school at Bayview. Financial misjudgement and inept governance by the SCEGGS School Council caused the closure of Moss Vale and *Gleniffer Brae*. SCEGGS *Redlands* and SCEGGS Darlinghurst became parent-controlled and *Loquat Valley* was purchased by the Council for the Promotion of Sydney Church of England Diocesan Schools. The Diocese contributed $1,000,000 towards repaying the $7.5 million debt, secured by mortgages on the schools.[68] The Illawarra Grammar School took the *Gleniffer Brae* girls in, and in time this newly constituted school began to grow vigorously.[69] The Blue Mountains Grammar School nearly closed. NM Cameron remembers that at his first Standing Committee meeting, the motion to close the school was defeated by one vote.[70] The King's School took over its management.[71]

The consequence of these school crises was that in the case of the SCEGGS schools the Diocese devolved financial management onto the parents, but with diocesan representation on the school board. In this way the Diocese was no longer liable for debts incurred by the schools, but could maintain a Christian presence in the schools. It was a major change in strategy for managing some Diocesan schools.

---

66. *Sydney Year Book 1982*, 37.
67. Judd and Cable, *Sydney Anglicans*, 275.
68. Cameron, *SCEGGS* Chapter 14, Cameron, *The School on the Hill*, Chapter 5; *Sydney Year Books* 1976, 343–4, 1977, 283, and 1978, 286–88.
69. Cameron, 'The SCEGGS Connection" 52–61.
70. NM Cameron interview with MHC, 25.5.2013.
71. *Sydney Year Book 1977*, 273.

Moore College under Broughton Knox was also continuing to grow. By 1979 there were 129 students, and the number of staff had increased. Broughton had introduced a fourth year in 1960 and the BD was now offered at the College. Now that the Faculty were encouraged to study overseas for their PhD, Broughton looked forward to having six members of staff with PhDs by 1977. He began a series of lectures with high-profile visiting speakers: among them FF Bruce, JJ Packer and Klaas Runia. His strenuous efforts to raise the academic quality of the College included expanding the library, which by 1985 had about 70,000 books. His drive to acquire property in the suburb of Newtown continued, staff houses were built, and the Glebe Board was regularly, but unsuccessfully, pressured to invest in rent-producing property for the College. Diocesan funding was generous, leaping by 50% in two years, from $164,758 in 1982, to $318,000 in 1984. Broughton's long tenure at the College (he resigned as Principal in 1985) gave him very great influence over students, Faculty and the Diocese. It seems that, at the College, his conservative theology was shared by the Faculty, almost without question. Those Faculty members who were unhappy tended to leave.[72]

The most obvious manifestation of the relationship of the Sydney Diocese with the rest of the Anglican Church in Australia and overseas, is at the level of the General Synod. It generally meets every three years and its chairman is the Primate. Views of the powers of the Primacy differ. Sydney holds a minimalist view, limiting the Primate's role to presiding over the General Synod and chairing the Standing Committee. The Constitution appears to support this.[73] A Committee appointed to investigate the Primacy submitted its report to the General Synod in 1969. While making some practical proposals, it did not attempt to define the role of the Primate. In his Foreword to Brian Porter's biography of Archbishop Sir Frank Woods, Archbishop Aspinall, Primate (2005–2014), called the Primate "titular head" of the Church.[74] Keith Rayner, a former Primate, holds a similar view.[75]

As we saw, Mowll was elected Primate a decade or so after his election as Archbishop of Sydney. His successor, Archbishop Gough, was elected Primate as successor to Mowll. When Gough departed Sydney, Archbishop Philip Strong of Brisbane was elected Primate. He retired in 1970 and two men stood for election: Archbishop Marcus Loane and Archbishop Frank

---

72. Cameron, *An Enigmatic Life*, Chapters 8–11.

73. Constitution of the Anglican Church of Australia, Chapter 3.10,11 and Chapter 4.20 and 23(c); A Committee to Investigate the Primacy, 240–250, *Proceedings of the Third General Synod. Official Report 1969*, Standing Committee of General Synod, 1969.

74. Porter, *Frank Woods*, i.

75. Rayner, "The Primacy: Past, Present and Future," 18.11.1998, 4 and 8.

Woods. Woods was elected Primate, after Loane withdrew his name. Woods later wrote to Loane,

> I have tried to say to you how I feel and I want to put it on paper, how very deeply I appreciate your magnanimity at the primatial election, so resolving the deadlock which could so easily have left us forced to call a special meeting of General Synod. We all, and I in particular, owe you a very great debt of gratitude.[76]

When Woods retired, Loane was elected Primate in 1978. He had gracious words for Woods:

> His life-long commitment to the ecumenical movement and the cause of Christian unity drew him into the inner counsels of the World Council of Churches and enabled him to cultivate personal contacts and friendships with leaders all around the world.
>
> Perhaps his main contribution was not in the way of major speeches or the cut-and-thrust of public debate, but in patient committee work where he could throw out ideas and express himself with a sense of ease and freedom . . .
>
> He has often stayed in our home and I always marvel at his resilience. No matter how late at night he goes to bed he is up at or before 6.00 am to make his own cup of tea and then sit in the garden to read and pray. And at the end of the day, he is just as ready to relax and talk over a cup of tea when one would think most people would only be ready to drop asleep.
>
> He keeps in touch with a wide circle of friends and writes countless letters by hand . . . His pastoral spirit has always been evident in the trouble he takes to visit those who are sick . . . He maintains a steady attempt at the reading of theology and related literature, and his life is characterized by undoubted piety in devotional worship and prayer.[77]

Kindly meant though this is, what is not stated is eloquent.

Brian Porter describes Woods as "even though less Anglo-Catholic than Philip Strong, [he] was definitely not an Evangelical of the Sydney ilk."[78] He was nervous when chairing the General Synod, "scared of certain factions in General Synod as he was of sharks in Sydney Harbour." Porter states:

---

76. Reid, *Marcus L Loane*, 130. No reference to source.
77. *ACR* 31.3.77, 3.
78 Porter, *Frank Woods*, 132.

He felt inadequate in his understanding of constitutional legalities and was more often than not wary of lawyers especially when they came from the Diocese of Sydney. He never really understood the forensic mindset of the Sydney Evangelicals who dominated sittings of the General Synod unless they themselves had broadened as had Bishops Delbridge and Donald Cameron. He found the seedbed of Sydney evangelicalism—Moore Theological College—and its Principal, Dr Broughton Knox, particularly adversarial.[79]

Rayner's estimate of Frank Woods was: "Though he might have seemed closer to the Sydney outlook than Philip Strong, he did not achieve the same rapport with Sydney, and he himself often felt frustrated at both the theological and political stance adopted in the largest diocese."[80]

As Metropolitan, Loane visited every diocese of the province of NSW, speaking at their synods and visiting regional centers. He concentrated on giving pastoral care rather than on churchmanship issues, and wherever he went, he was warmly received.[81] He saw a number of dioceses struggling financially and in 1977 persuaded the Sydney Standing Committee to grant $25,000 to each of the dioceses of Armidale, Bathurst, Grafton and Riverina. By 1981 the grants to the four dioceses had increased to $100,000 each. This Loane did, irrespective of churchmanship differences. Loane's biographer believes that this helped to create a more positive attitude to the Sydney Diocese and to Loane himself.[82]

Later, when he became Primate, Loane visited, as had Woods, every diocese of the Anglican Church of Australia.[83] These visits were a unifying presence throughout the width and depth of Australia in all its diversity and vast distances. Even before Loane's election as Primate, Woods wrote to Loane on the occasion of Loane's receiving a KBE,[84]

> Perhaps I may be allowed to use your KBE as an excuse to say how much I admire your leadership, in the management of your great diocese, and how I thank God for your fellowship in the

---

79. Ibid., 135.
80. Ibid., 139.
81. Reid, *Marcus L Loane*, 127.
82. Ibid., 128.
83. Presidential Address to the General Synod of Australia 1981, 5.
84. KBE stands for Knight Commander of the most Excellent Order of the British Empire, a grade within the British order of chivalry. The KBE was discontinued by the Queen on advice from the Hawke Labor government in 1986 and renewed in 2014 by Prime Minister Tony Abbott. After receiving his knighthood Marcus Loane was known as "Archbishop Sir Marcus Loane" and his wife Patricia as "Lady Loane."

Gospel both personally and on a national level. You will know that I have been deeply concerned for Anglican unity. But you have done more than any of us to heal these divisions and to bring the Diocese of Sydney into fellowship with the rest of the Anglican Church and, by your personal action and now by your aid to the country dioceses of your Province, you are bringing the Anglo-Catholic dioceses to understand and respect your own position and that of the Sydney Diocese.[85]

After Loane became Primate, the focus of his Presidential Addresses to the Sydney Synod widened. They were now concerned, at least in part, with issues concerning all Australian Anglicans, and with issues beyond Australia's shores. The recurring theme was that of unity. On what basis could there be real unity? What were the distinctives of Evangelical theology? And what of ecumenism? These were the years when there were talks between Methodists and Anglicans and Loane's response, theologically grounded as always, was that "a worthy but sentimental desire to leap over all difficulties and treat them as non-existent only meant that they would rear their thorny heads later."[86] ARCIC (Anglican-Roman Catholic International Commission) was established at the 1978 Lambeth Conference. At a plenary session of the Conference Loane moved that as an amendment to the words that ARCIC "should provide a basis for a changed relationship" be deleted and that the words "lead to further fruitful dialogue" should be inserted instead.[87] He did not succeed.

Having been assured by Professor Henry Chadwick that there was now no disagreement among ARCIC members on the doctrine of SOLA FIDE, Loane went on in his Presidential Address of 1979 to pinpoint the teaching of Justification by Faith alone as the crux of the Reformation, described by Martin Luther as "the article of a standing or falling church." Loane spoke with great passion and conviction of the necessity to stand firm in this doctrine and pointed out that the difference in approach to Justification by orthodox Roman theology and Reformed theology:

> Orthodox Roman theology asserts that to justify is to MAKE righteous; Reformed theology insists that to justify is to COUNT righteous . . . We are acquitted, justified, accepted, not on the ground of what we are, but on the ground of what God Who was

---

85. Quoted in Reid, *Marcus L Loane*, 129. No source reference given.
86. *The Anglican* 10.6.1969.
87. *Sydney Year Book 1980*, 231.

in Christ has done on our behalf . . . It is an act of grace . . . in Christ alone, by grace alone, by faith alone.[88]

Liberal theology was still in the air. Two examples of its influence are, first an incident in Melbourne at Easter in 1968, and second, in the changing nature of the WCC (World Council of Churches). The publication of JAT Robinson's book *Honest to God* in 1963[89] sparked a short-lived controversy in Melbourne in 1968. Two clergy had attempted to explain the new theology and queried the necessity for the bodily resurrection of Christ. The response of Melbourne's Archbishop Woods was to issue a letter to be read aloud in church on Sunday, 28 April 1968, in which he described the new theology as "a blast of vain doctrine" and "old heresies dressed up in new clothes." He wrote that a priest with such views should ask to be relieved of his priestly responsibilities and ended the letter with a quotation from I Corinthians 3 about fire testing what sort of work each one has done. Woods' letter was stern but waffly, as it did not deal with the specific matter which needed to be addressed: namely the Resurrection of Christ. The stern tone was so unlike Woods that it took people by surprise. Unfortunately, Woods appended the names of two assistant bishops, Sambell and Arnott, to the letter although they had not seen the letter to approve it.

Archdeacon Dann (Woods' successor as Archbishop) bristled at its "insensitive tone," Dr Robin Sharwood (Warden of Trinity College) and Dr Barry Marshall (Chaplain at Trinity College) were concerned that the letter stifled theological debate. Conservative Christians congratulated Woods and offered him their support; the two clergy wrote a letter to Woods which "seemed to mollify him," although the authors' theology was, to a conservative, deliberately vague and as solid as a blancmange. Brian Porter is critical of Woods' attempt to censure his clergy and noted that Woods later came to regret the stand he had taken. The two clergy, David Pope and Peter Lane, subsequently left the priesthood.[90] This "tempest in a teacup" shows a contrast in the leadership qualities of Woods and Loane, and also indicates the broader theological perspectives of Woods' team of bishops, with whom he had to work. Sambell, Arnott and possibly Dann were all strong-minded clergy: quite a daunting group, in fact. Loane had an aura of authority and an inner toughness, which made him a leader few dared oppose.

The WCC had been established in 1948 as part of the post war enthusiasm for ecumenism. Broughton Knox attended the a meeting in Evanston in 1954, reporting that he believed there were real benefits from the work

---

88. *Sydney Year Book 1980*, 234.
89. See Chapter 5.
90. Porter, *Frank Woods*, 199–205; J Grant, *Episcopally Led*, 254–55.

of the WCC, not least the opportunity to share their common faith, and so move closer together in spirit. He reported from Evanston "that it is indeed a remarkable thing that the churches which in the past have persecuted each other, have now met, for the second time, to study the teaching of the Bible together, in a common loyalty to Christ."[91] He and other conservatives became disillusioned over the following decades, although Donald Cameron reported that the 1975 assembly in Nairobi, while hosting a wide range of theological opinions, affirmed the Great Commission. The assembly affirmed "that the Great Commission which asks us to go into all the world to make disciples and baptise them in the Triune name should not be abandoned, betrayed, disobeyed or compromised."[92] Further, the conference stated "We are opposed to any form of syncretism, incipient nascent or developed, if by syncretism we mean a human attempt to create a new religion out of elements taken from different religions." Cameron thought that Nairobi, with its "concern for salvation in a supernatural sense" had recaptured the note of the early WCC assemblies.[93] Despite Cameron's optimism, it became increasingly difficult for Evangelicals to have any sort of meaningful or fruitful input at the WCC. In his monograph, *Evangelicals and the World Council of Churches,* published in 2000, Cameron noted that Nairobi had been the last WCC Assembly and that this Assembly "carried a very broad spectrum of Christian opinion." [94] Most Evangelicals thought that there were more strategic places for them to use their time and gifts.[95] The WCC has more recently been described as "a vast whale, beached."

The revision of the 1662 *Book of Common Prayer* was something of a triumph in relationships within the Anglican Church of Australia. It was an undertaking which showed that Sydney Evangelicals and the rest of the Anglican Church of Australia could be united despite potential division. The need for a prayer book in more modern language had long been recognized, and in England the preparation of a new one had dominated Archbishop Randall Davidson's tenure of the See of Canterbury from 1903 to 1928. Owing to theological differences, mostly over the Order of Holy Communion, the new Prayer Book was decisively rejected by the House of Commons twice: in 1927 and 1928.[96] In Australia, the tensions over the Red Book Case

91. *ACR* 16.9.1954, 5.

92. This, however, was a truncated version of the Great Commission, since it omitted the words, "teaching them to obey everything I have commanded you" (NIV).

93. *ACR* 22.1.1976, 3.

94. Cameron, *Evangelicals and the World Council of Churches,* 14.

95. *ACR* 20.9.73, 2; Cameron, *Evangelicals and the World Council of Churches,* 5.

96. *Sydney Year Book 1974,* 225. Influenced by Anglo-Catholic theology, it allowed prayers for the dead, reservation of the sacrament and "vestments"—Judd and Cable,

had exposed the need for *Prayer Book* revision, but possibly delayed it.[97] At the first meeting of the General Synod, after the Constitution came into effect 1962, a Commission of thirty-two people was formed to explore the possibilities of revision of, and addition to, the *BCP*.[98] Later, twelve men were appointed to a Liturgical Commission, of which Donald Robinson was a member. Robinson has written: "*AAPB* (*An Australian Prayer Book*) was still only—in the words of Bishop Grindrod of Brisbane—'an ordered means for experiment in liturgy' which 'may be expected to have a life of ten to fifteen years, as a step towards revision of *BCP* itself.'"[99] After a series of experimental services in booklet form, the Liturgical Commission put before the 1977 General Synod a Prayer Book, essentially a revision of *BCP*. It was intended that *BCP* and *AAPB* should exist side by side.[100] This is still happening, in at least one Sydney parish, in 2013.[101]

Loane regarded the vote in favour of *AAPB* "by far the most significant piece of legislation which has yet come into effect under the new Constitution." There was only one single dissenting voice in the whole of the General Synod to the adoption of the new Prayer Book. The reasons for the unanimity of the vote, and the successful drafting sessions were probably twofold. The twelve men on the Liturgical Commission respected each other and enjoyed working together.[102] They represented the whole spectrum of churchmanship, and produced from this "creative tension" two orders of service which satisfied the vast majority of Anglicans.[103] In addition, because the book was a revision of *BCP*, radical change lay in the future. The "green book" as it came to be called, was attractive in size and colour and was graced by several beautiful line drawings of Australian wildflowers. Donald Robinson later commented, "In 1962 I could not see how opposing views about *Prayer Book* revision could be reconciled. What finally happened in 1977 was not in the least what anyone had expected or predicted in 1962."[104]

Evangelicals in England had sought to strengthen themselves by various conferences held after the War. The National Evangelical Anglican

---

Sydney Anglicans, 210.

97. Cameron, *An Enigmatic Life*, 103.

98. Minute Book of General Synod 1902–1966, 9.5.1962.

99. DWB Robinson note to MHC.

100. *Sydney Year Book*, 219.

101. St Swithun's, Pymble uses *BCP* at their quarterly choral evensong services, and at monthly Thursday morning services.

102. DWB Robinson conversations with MHC. DWBR in Presidential Address 1985, *Sydney Year Book 1986*, 221.

103. Judd and Cable, *Sydney Anglicans*, 293.

104. *Sydney Year Book 1986*, 223.

Conference (NEAC), held in 1967, in Keele, was a new attempt to rally Evangelicals by gathering together to show their strength and affirm a common policy.[105] Another NEAC was held in Melbourne in 1971. Marcus Loane showed his support for this gathering of Anglican Evangelicals by consenting to be the final speaker. He took the opportunity to state clearly his kind of Anglicanism. He likened his position to a series of concentric circles: the innermost was allegiance to Christ; the next, Reformed Protestant; and the outermost Anglican.[106]

He said:

> I am a Christian; I am a Protestant; I am an Anglican.
> It is of of far greater significance to be the first rather than the second, or to be the second rather than the third.
> Nevertheless the order is vital if I am to define what constitutes the position of an Evangelical in the Church of England, because there are many who divide from me as the circles contract and who will stand outside each fresh category.
> They may be found in the widest circle, but not in the middle circle; they may belong to the middle circle but not to the smaller circle. Yet the smallest circle is where the true Evangelical in the Church of England is to be found.
> Does all this sort of thing really matter? It does indeed, because vague and careless thinking is the source of endless trouble. Men of little mind and little spirit beget men of narrow faith and restricted sympathy. But men of large mind and burning spirit beget men of strong faith and far-seeing vision.

Loane's statement is profoundly important for understanding Sydney Evangelicals. Their allegiance is not primarily to the Anglican Church, and that gives rise to decisions, plans and behaviour, which at times causes deep offence.[107]

Two assistant bishops from Sydney attended NEAC conferences: ED Cameron in 1977 and JR Reid in 1981. The conferences made orthodox conservative Evangelical statements, but, as an editorial in the *ACR* put it in 1971,

> The NEAC Statement is a significant document and can be commended for study. It reflects a clamour of change, flexibility and

---

105. Chapman, *Godly Ambition*, 91.
106. *ACR* 26.8.71, 6; see also *Sydney Year Book 1981*, 224.
107. See for example, Fletcher, *The Place of Anglicanism in Australia*, 186, "some of the more extreme evangelicals placed their own religious convictions above their Anglicanism."

> variety in Church life. It crystallises in a significant way what Evangelicals have been saying for a few years. The NEAC Statement ultimately achieves nothing. It is a significant document produced by those who were meeting outside the regular structures for debate and decision within our denomination.
>
> Change will only come as some of the vision is translated by painstaking care into the present structures of our congregations. Will there be the same enthusiasm for this travail as there was for the principle of change at Melbourne?[108]

Loane devoted a major part of his Presidential Address of 1980 to the NEAC Conference and it prompted him to reflect at some length on evangelical spiritual values. He summed them up in three words: VERITY, SANCTITY, UNITY. On VERITY, he spoke of the importance of engaging in relevant dialogue, based on intelligent study of the Scriptures. On SANCTITY he spoke of a "positive attitude," "men of robust conviction and front-line calibre who will think, write, speak, lead and dare to act; not to tear down but to build up; and to blow the trumpet of the everlasting Gospel with a note that is sweet and clear." Third, Evangelicals "must be willing to pursue a genuine UNITY."

> We all rejoice in the Right of Private Judgement as one of the doctrines which was re-discovered by the Masters of the English Reformation. Each man is free to form his own judgement and to follow the light of his own conscience on the basis of his understanding of and obedience to the Word of God. But the reckless pursuit of such independence means that Evangelicals have produced more ultra-individualists than any other school of thought in the church. As a result we have as much internal cohesion as the proverbial rope of sand . . . Each must learn to bow in continual obedience to the Word of God and the Lordship of Christ, and each needs the grace to discern which are the old paths they must not forsake and which are the new paths they are called to explore. This is why we need to consult with each other, to seek understanding, and to concert our plans for the furtherance of the Gospel.[109]

Under Loane's watch, visiting evangelists, as well as local men continued to hold out the Gospel of life. Before Billy Graham returned to Sydney in 1968, Loane wrote of the Graham Crusade in Seoul: "Never in Christian history have so many people stood to listen to the Gospel in one place at one

---

108. *ACR* 26.8.71, 2.
109. *Sydney Year Book 1981*, 220–22.

time."[110] Graham returned to Sydney again in 1979.[111] These visits did not have the same dramatic impact upon Sydney as the 1959 Crusade, but the Crusades were, even so, an unforgettable experience. Lesley Hicks, a regular feature writer for the *ACR*, wrote that 85,000 people attended on the last Sunday afternoon of the 1979 Crusade. She commented,

> Time will test both the obviously transformed and those making a quiet new beginning, learning to live in love to others and to God, and at peace with themselves. Over 20,000 were counseled, all told, and the churches now have the task, for which most have prepared carefully, of nurturing and assimilating these new Christians or newly awakened members.[112]

Other evangelists visiting Sydney and beyond were the Rev. Michael Green, whose presence in Melbourne drew a packed congregation in St Paul's Cathedral; also John Stott, and British journalist Malcolm Muggeridge.

Some five years into Loane's episcopate, *Move in for Action,* a report to the Sydney Synod on the state of Evangelism in the Diocese was published. Its conclusion was bleak: "Very little evangelism is going on."[113] The Report started with a well-researched survey of Sydney people ("Spying out the Land"), followed by theological reflections including the methods of evangelism of Jesus, and the apostles Paul and Peter (by Paul Barnett and the Rev. Bruce Smith); and a theology of evangelism by John Chapman. The ensuing sections surveyed the situation in the local churches and the wealth of opportunities for evangelism offered by the media. The synod received the Report with enthusiasm. As well as recommending greater use of the media, the Report laid obligations at the door of the local churches to look at new ways of engaging with the local community. Nothing much came of the Report in the short-term, but within five years evangelism in the universities and in Sydney's inner city was activated in new or revitalised forms.

The Rev. John Chapman's return to Sydney from the Armidale Diocese began twenty years' fruitful work first as Director of Christian Education, then Diocesan Missioner, and finally Director of the Department of Evangelism. As Youth Director in the Diocese of Armidale he had been the leader of a handful of evangelical clergy, and when the time to elect a new bishop arrived, Chapman masterminded the appointment of an Evangelical to the

---

110. *Sydney Year Book 1975,* 213.

111. *ACR* 7.5.1979, 1.

112. *ACR* 4, 6.79, 7.

113. *Move in For Action,* Commission of Evangelism, Board of Diocesan Missions, and Information and Public Relations Office, Church of England Diocese of Sydney, 114.

vacant see. The new bishop, Clive Kerle, set about appointing evangelical clergy who promoted Bible teaching. A rural diocese with an Anglo-Catholic core had been transformed, not without much difficulty, into a primarily Evangelical diocese by the time Kerle departed.[114] The transformation of the Diocese of Armidale still rankles with some Anglo-Catholics.[115]

John Chapman (known as "Chappo") began to conduct university missions, beginning with one at the University of Sydney in 1976, and with the Rev. Paul Barnett as a co-speaker.[116] Organized by the Evangelical Union, whose President at the time was Adrian Lane, and with the enthusiastic backing of the Rector of St Barnabas' Broadway, the Rev. Allan Blanch, the mission was a tremendous success, and the first of many. John went on to conduct missions at the University of New South Wales and Macquarie University, at first with Paul Barnett and later with the Rev. Phillip Jensen. As a result, thousands of students were touched by the Gospel of Christ.

Another form of mission was in the inner city area of Sydney. This had changed enormously in the post-war era. Abject, slum-like poverty had disappeared, multi storey home units had created a high-density population and European migrants were a new, permanent element of the population. At the same time, congregations in Anglican churches were shrinking, the income of these churches was dropping and church buildings were often in disrepair.[117] About fifteen parishes were within a two and a half mile radius of Sydney Central Station, and were seriously affected by these changes. In 1969 the Sydney Synod set up an Inner City Committee with the Rev. Paul Barnett as Director. The turning point for the Inner City Committee was the address Loane gave at St John's Darlinghurst on 15 July 1972. NM Cameron, a member of the Committee, recalled,

> The Inner City Committee had been set up by the synod to assist to revive church life of some 20 inner city parishes, which had previously been quite strong with viable congregations, but the movement of Australians out of inner city suburbs had decimated the congregations. Their places were taken by people from European nationalities—Italians, Greeks, Yugoslavs and so on. Many of them had a religious background but didn't attend church anywhere and arguably had no Christian commitment.

114. Loane, *These Happy Warriors* 47; M Orpwood, *Chappo.* 33–42; Cameron, *Living Stones,* 159.

115. Porter, *Sydney Anglicans,* 4.

116. Lake, *Proclaiming Jesus Christ as Lord.* 87–96; Orpwood, *Chappo,* 121–39.

117. Inner City Commission of Inquiry: Chairman's Correspondence, undated, unsigned memorandum, probably by Bishop Jack Dain, in 1967. Box 55, Sydney Diocesan Archives.

> The average Greek commitment was generally baptisms, weddings and funerals. Purely cultural. The Anglican Church had previously set up a Department of Immigration to assist to bring English people migrating to Australia into the Anglican Church here. The Department showed no interest in people coming from mainland European countries.
>
> Sir Marcus Loane gave an address on what he perceived to be the area of evangelism in the inner city areas. He took a radically different view from the one generally held previously. His view was, that all Australians should be evangelized, other than those who were active members of existing churches. That meant that nominal or cultural minorities were to be the subject of the same efforts to bring them into the Anglican Church as people of English or Australian origin.
>
> His views were surprising to many of the people there and to many of the people who were not there. But by a kind of osmosis they got through the Diocese and whilst there was never an official change in the sense of a synod resolution or the like, it has been the position of the Anglican Church in the Sydney Diocese ever since.[118]

All Australians, not just those of white Anglo-Saxon origin, needed to hear the Gospel of Jesus Christ. Loane's approach to inner-city ministry demonstrated a desire to exclude no one. In multicultural Australia, unless Anglicans included people of all religious and ethnic backgrounds, Anglicans would become a dying denomination.

The years under Loane's leadership were relatively quiet, compared with what happened before and after. Loane, a shy and reserved man, with a dramatic way of communicating in public, was respected and admired. He was a leader, but one who eschewed conflict where possible. In no way did he compromise his passion for communicating the Gospel and for equipping others to do so. A man with a phenomenal memory, he was also a good administrator and an excellent chairman. He leant on others for analysis of some new theological issues. Iron-willed where key Reformed doctrine was at stake, he was kind and pastorally very able with individuals. During his time as Archbishop of Sydney, and later as Primate, peace and goodwill mostly reigned.

He also operated through other people where he could, and sometimes others did the difficult things on his behalf. By the end of his time, there was

---

118. NM Cameron interview with MHC 25.5.2013.

an undercurrent of desire to be more adventuresome. According to Peter Jensen, "he put the lid on a social explosion that was inevitable."[119]

His parting words to his synod were:

> I have sometimes thought of the words of John Charles Ryle after his consecration as the first Bishop of Liverpool on 1880, "You know what are my opinions, I am a committed man. It would be vain for me to make any statement at all as to what I feel with regard to the duties of a Bishop . . . I come among you a Protestant and an Evangelical; but . . . I come with a desire to hold out the right hand to all loyal churchmen, by whatever name they are known." To the extent that I may be allowed to borrow that language, it represents the attitude which I hope has governed my going out and coming in since you elected me as the eighth Bishop of this Diocese a little more than fifteen years ago . . . dare I borrow the words of John Bunyan: "My sword I give to him that shall succeed me . . . and my courage and skill to him that can get it."[120]

---

119. PF Jensen interview with MHC 14.4.2015.
120. *Sydney Year Book* 1983, 232–33.

Chapter 7

Sound and Fury 1982–1992

Canon Sam Van Culin, Secretary-General of the Anglican Consultative Council (ACC), was a guest of at the Sydney Synod in 1986. His presence prompted Sydney's Archbishop Donald Robinson to describe the current state of the worldwide Anglican Communion. It had "uncertain frontiers," being "an entity without formal constitution or declared doctrinal basis."[1] The ACC had its own constitution and procedures for determining who were its members. Robinson thought that while that was reasonable, he was not so sure that the ACC was "entitled to declare which are the constituent churches of the Anglican Communion." Similar comments could be made concerning the Lambeth Conference, he continued. "Invitations to the Lambeth Conference issue from the Archbishop of Canterbury [but] . . . membership of the Lambeth Conference is not a necessary objective criterion to determine what churches may be in communion with one another."[2]

A recently published report of the Inter-Anglican Theological and Doctrinal Commission drew attention "to the need for a clarification of what Anglicanism means by the church once Anglicanism has been separated from its English context and from 'the vision of a certain symbiosis of church and nation.'" Such a clarification, according to the report, was a "necessary first step towards a theology of Anglican identity." Robinson concluded, "In this situation, consultation is desirable. Canon Van Culin has a difficult job keeping the member churches of the ACC in relationship with each other, and he has our support and sympathy."[3] These remarks

---

1. The Lambeth Quadrilateral of 1887 was the template for Anglican polity. See Appendix.
2. *Sydney Year Book 1987*, 211.
3. Ibid., 211.

were offered when Robinson was midway through his episcopate. By this time the noise of debate over the ministry of women, sometimes called "the women's wars" was rising to a crescendo, posing a real threat to the Anglican Communion.

Donald Robinson was Archbishop of Sydney from 1982 to 1992. These years marked renewed turmoil in Sydney's relationship with the rest of Anglican Australia, and with the Communion across the sea. Robinson and others since have looked back to the time of the publication of the *AAPB* as a high water mark in relationships between Sydney and other Australian Anglicans, and the manner in which dissension was handled on that occasion, as a guide to any future process of decision-making. Then, the near impossible had been achieved.[4] Referring to the vexed issue of the ordination of women to the priesthood, Robinson stated: "It seems to me essential that a process comparable to that which we adopted for the revision of our liturgy should be adopted," and he went on to outline the procedure adopted. He believed that it had been a far more complex issue than women's ordination, but the process had been slow and gradual with proposals "tested at every stage." What Robinson wanted was a law-abiding process, whereby no changes were made without a very significant majority. Otherwise, the church would be broken open. In the matter of the ordination of women, canon law would be broken, and changes thrust upon the Australian Church without a significant majority. The result has indeed been a fractured Anglican Church in Australia. After the completion of *AAPB* the level of trust was very high throughout the ACA. After the premature ordination of women in the ACA, there was no longer anything like the same level of trust. But in the mid 1980s this was still in the future.

Third child and only son of Archdeacon Richard Bradley Robinson and his wife Gertrude Marsden Ross, Donald William Bradley Robinson was born in 1922. His father was one of Howard Mowll's right-hand men.[5] As happens with clergy, the Robinson family lived in a variety of rectories: Lithgow, Leichardt and Chatswood. Donald recalled that while they were living at Chatswood,

> Mother and Dad, I think, would have liked me to have gone to Shore [Sydney Church of England Grammar School at North Sydney] when I was there but they couldn't afford it. In fact they couldn't afford to use the car! I remember when the car was up on bricks in the garage at St. Paul's Rectory. I had two years at

---

4. *Sydney Year Book 1986*, 222; NM Cameron comments to MHC re discussions relating to General Synod problems, May 2013.

5. Judd and Cable, *Sydney Anglicans,* photograph 32, 236.

the primary school in Chatswood and bumped into people like Alan Friend and so on but then I went to North Sydney High for a year. At the end of that year I got the Archbishop's of Sydney Exhibition for sons of clergy at Shore. I think I was the only one who sat for it. But anyhow I got it and that enabled me to go to Shore.

In 1938 Donald's family went to live at Moore College in the Vice-Principal's house, when Donald's father became Secretary to the Home Mission Society, also teaching Pastoralia to the College students.[6] Apart from the War years and two years in Cambridge, Donald was to live mostly at Moore College until appointed Bishop in Parramatta in 1973—some 30 years.

While at Shore, Donald began to learn Classical Greek. He remembered,

> There were three of us in the Greek class, and two dropped out. I was the only one by the time we got to the end of the year and I got the Greek prize. I wasn't very good at it. I am not a good scholar in language. I know that I never get high honours purely on the linguistic side, but the concepts, the inner meaning of it grasped me very much from the beginning.[7]

He was also musical, and while an undergraduate at the University of Sydney, learned to play the pipe organ under Christian Helleman, formerly an organist at Christ Church St Laurence.[8] Robinson's musical ear and love for language probably contributed to his great love for liturgy—used with such effect for the Anglican Church of Australia in *APBA*.

During the Second World War he served for a time in Newcastle where he worshipped with Anglicans and Baptists, and later, while working with the Central Bureau of Military Intelligence in "Traffic Analysis" in Brisbane, attended a Pentecostal church. He was impressed by the latter's "good order."[9] In 1943 he flew to New Guinea for a special code-breaking operation. He was stationed some 60 miles down river from Lae. He said,

> I remember it occurred to me when I was there that for the first time in my life I was not conscious of any fellow Christians around me. I realised there had never been any time in my life when I had been alone, or seemed to be alone. I couldn't believe I was actually alone but I didn't know anybody who were

---

6. DWB Robinson interview with MHC 2.9.2006.
7. DWB Robinson interview with MHC 8.5.2007.
8. Ibid., 15.12.2006.
9. Ibid., 24.10.2006 and 31.10.2006.

Christians of my kind. I remember praying for guidance that if there were any there I would find them and the first clue which came up, I happened to be looking at the mail and there was someone in the unit who was receiving the Christian newspaper *New Life*. Do you remember *New Life*? Well it was very well known in evangelical circles. I thought, well, if he is getting *New Life*, he may be a starter, so I dug him out. I didn't know him. His name was Godden and I asked him "Are you a Christian?" and he hesitatingly said yes he was. I told him exactly what had happened and I was actually looking for some fellow Christians and he volunteered, "I think possibly that so and so, and so and so, might be." So I dug them out, and they were, and within a fairly short time we had about six or seven and we met regularly just for prayer together and bible study together. The interesting thing is that this Godden boy I have only learnt in the last year or two was, I think a nephew of Charles Christopher Godden, whose martyrdom the Synod was celebrating.[10]

Robinson's postgraduate years in Cambridge (1947–8) were very significant ones. He was influenced by a whole range of people whom he would never have met in Sydney, including Evangelicals who were not necessarily from the same evangelical stable. He learned to recognise the value of what they were giving him, without putting labels on them. At Queen's College his two supervisors were Henry Hart, a Hebrew scholar, Dean and Fellow of Queen's for 68 years,[11] and Henry Chadwick, a distinguished scholar in New Testament, Church History and Doctrine.[12] In Great St Mary's he heard the Vice-Chancellor, Charles Raven, preach. One sermon influenced him for life. It was on the collect, "Grant that we may both perceive and know what things we ought to do and also have grace and power, faithfully to perform them." From that time onwards, Robinson prayed that collect every day.[13] This is a lens with which to view his episcopate, especially in the very troubled last year, when dealing with the 1991 crisis of the Women's Ordination debate.

10. Ibid., 31.10.2006.
11. From his obituary in *The Times*, 21.12.2004: "The office of dean at Queens' in that period involved running the chapel and being head of discipline. In those days of curfews and locked gates, Hart once caught an undergraduate climbing into college late at night. Poised on the top of the railings, and seeing the dean below, the student exclaimed, "O, God!" "No—just his earthly representative," replied Hart, a quip that has not only gone down in Cambridge folklore but also serves as a typical example of Hart's ready wit." The E-Sylum: Volume 7, Number 52, December 26, 2004, Article 5.
12. DWB Robinson interview with MHC 28.11.2006.
13. Ibid., 28.11.2006.

CH Dodd was another luminary whose lectures and books impressed Robinson greatly. He says of Dodd:

> I came in contact with some very considerable people, whom I didn't know, but people like Dodd—I went there particularly to hear and sit at their feet. It was very much a biblical approach to life and they were so anxious to find out what the Bible was really on about that although there were some lecturers there who had a reputation of being a bit more liberal, on the whole that didn't come out. They really threw so much light on the New Testament. Dodd's book on the parables of Jesus, what is a parable, how do they work and so on, and the apostolic preaching and its developments, the concept of the gospel within the New Testament. They were wonderful eye-openers to me... Oh, it was pretty original, I mean, they did have links with the Continentals but were not dominated by the Continentals. I found it so exciting.

One of Robinson's more famous former students thought that Robinson was able to enjoy the riches of Cambridge because he was not frightened of people with different ideas from his own. Robinson modelled an openness to others, which came from a deep confidence in the Bible, and this enabled him to be free. Later on, as a lecturer at Moore College, Robinson had a freshness of approach, which was radical, even revolutionary, because he was "on top of" his material. He did not write much, but he paved the way for real scholars in Sydney. Because of his erudition he was an intellectual leader.[14]

A most important contact was Gabriel Hebert, whom he heard preach in Cambridge. Hebert was a member of the Society of the Sacred Mission (SSM) and later came out to Adelaide to the SSM Institute at Crafers. He was a biblical theologian and of him Robinson has said,

> I think if anyone was my guide to the concept of Biblical Theology as a whole, the Bible as a whole and its pattern, it would be Gabriel Hebert and he has got two or three books in which he outlined his pattern and I have to admit that the concept of seeing the Bible as a whole in the way he did it, I would probably differ from him here and there, but I must admit I owe a great deal to the wholeness of his view and some of the people that he introduced me to.[15]

---

14. PF Jensen interview with MHC 19.5.2015.
15. DWB Robinson interview with MHC 28.11.2006.

The fact that Robinson was still in his twenties when he experienced Cambridge life almost certainly meant he was more open to its influence than he would have been had he been older. In due course, Robinson would invite Hebert to stay at Moore College, and at his holiday house in the Blue Mountains, and introduced him to the redoubtable TC Hammond, with whom they "had some very good discussions."

While at Cambridge Robinson also threw himself into the CICCU— "greatly attracted by that center of evangelical, Reformation melting pot." He found all the activities "very positive and constructive" but sometimes "a bit shallow." He attended daily prayer meetings, the weekly evangelistic services and he was a founding member of the International Fellowship of Evangelical Students (IFES), and "very much in touch" with the Inter-Varsity headquarters, including Douglas Johnson.[16]

Archbishop Donald William Bradley Robinson

16. Douglas Johnson: see Chapter 3; DWB Robinson interview with MHC 15.12.2006.

Returning to Sydney in 1949, he married Marie Taubmann, was ordained deacon in 1950 and although Mowll wanted him on the staff at Moore College, Robinson decided he needed some parish experience. He became a curate at Manly, and then moved to Moore College in 1952. In due time he became Senior Lecturer, then Vice-Principal (1959–1972). With Broughton Knox as Principal (1959–1985), Robinson was an intellectually stimulating influence on Knox, but also a moderating one. The years of this partnership were the best years of Knox's time as Principal. Many observers are of the opinion that these were also Robinson's best years: as lecturer and scholar he was in the right place.

One other aspect of Robinson is notable: his eirenic character. He did not like conflict and a good example of this characteristic is his relationship with the Sinless Perfectionists of the 1940s. Asked about this, he replied, "I can't remember anybody that I had a row with over this, I liked talking about things and I liked probing things and well *you* can decide what you think about things . . . "[17]

He also said, on another occasion,

I don't ever remember getting involved in conflict of a personal kind in Christian connections . . . I was quite good at stating differences of views but more to set out "some say this and some say that." I don't think I was polemic very much and I certainly did value maintaining as much personal relationship as possible . . . I must say that I often look for other ledges as it were to hang onto. [18]

Donald William Bradley Robinson was elected ninth Diocesan Bishop of the See of Sydney 1 April 1982. He was Marcus Loane's chosen successor.[19] Of the drawn-out election process he commented that it had been like "being roasted over a slow fire." In some ways, the analogy continued through his episcopate. He was also, and remains, Sydney's most scholarly Archbishop to date.

The question of the ordination of women to the priesthood dominated Robinson's episcopate and Sydney's rejection of the ordination of women to the priesthood has defined Sydney Diocese's identity for many people ever since. In his Presidential Address to the General Synod in 1966, Archbishop Strong had said,

> We must together make this General Synod an effective agent and medium for the triumph of the cause of Christ in this our

17. DWB Robinson interview with MHC 2.9.2006.

18. Ibid., 24.10.2006.

19. Ibid., 28.5.2007. That came as a surprise to ED Cameron, who thought JR Reid was his likely choice. ED Cameron interview with MHC 16.7.2013.

generation … The new constitution which bound our Dioceses together into one autonomous whole is not unlike marriage. The success of marriage depends not only on the initial act of union but on a lifetime of successive decisions in which two separate minds and wills must continually find their unity by mutual giving and receiving.[20]

The "marriage" was under greater strain than ever before.

As we shall see, Robinson placed a great deal of trust in law, both secular and church law, and this meant placing his trust in the Constitution, which he had criticized from before its adoption, and which, in this time of testing revealed great flaws.[21] He was a man of honor. Though he had been opposed to the Constitution, he believed that since it had been ratified, Australian Anglicans ought to stick to it. For him it was a matter of abiding by promises made, a covenant agreed upon. He could not sympathize with people who broke their promises, even in a greater cause.

His regard for the law had the effect at times of legalism. Sometimes the letter trumped the spirit of the law so that it was easy to lampoon a man who insisted on what younger clergy regarded as outdated regulations, such as the number of times the Athanasian Creed ought to be said annually, or the continuing use of the *Prayer Book* in services. In these situations younger clergy were deciding that the new evangelical situation in which they found themselves demanded an appeal to the spirit, rather than to the letter of the law. The *Prayer Book* they regarded as obsolete. It was too formal and non-technological in the new age of data projectors and screens and video clips.

The women's ministry issue represented an immense cultural clash. The problem was how to deal with it so that Sydney remained true to the Bible but evangelically savvy. Robinson's position was that of an honorable man who had shown that honor could work in the *Prayer Book* debate, but who was now placed in a situation where his method was not agreed to. According to others, his appeal to the law was not working any more. So, both within Sydney and beyond, Robinson's continued commitment to a kind of covenant put him in a most unenviable position.

Despite other initiatives of his episcopate, Robinson is remembered for his "tireless and implacable" opposition to the ordination of women, which Stuart Barton Babbage described as an "all consuming crusade during his entire occupancy of the See."[22]

---

20. Presidential Address 1966 by the Acting Primate, PNW Strong, Archbishop of Brisbane.
21. See Chapter 5; *Sydney Year Book 1993*, 261.
22. Babbage, *Memoirs of a Loose Canon*, 204.

A comment on Synod. This may be the work of Graham Wade (1931–2009). Southern Cross October 1965, 6.

There were two approaches, if not three, to the vexed question of whether women should be ordained to the priesthood. One approach was legal—did the Constitution allow it? The second was theological—what did the Bible say on the matter? The third was pragmatic. All three became mixed from time to time, especially when pressure for change increased. Australian Anglicans were, of course, not alone in grappling with the multi-dimensional problems of this most sensitive issue. The Salvation Army, founded by William and Catherin Booth in 1865, was possibly the first church to allow women to exercise ministry on the same level as men. From the beginning the work of women was a distinctive feature of the "Salvos."[23] The Congregational Church ordained women from 1929 onwards.[24] The first woman was ordained in the Methodist Church in 1969 and in the Presbyterian Church in 1974.[25] In the worldwide Anglican Communion the Anglicans in Hong Kong were the first to ordain women. Jane Hwang and Joyce Bennet were ordained priest there in 1971 and Florence Li Tim-Oi's priesthood was formally recognized.[26] In the Episcopal Church in the USA eleven women were ordained in 1974 in Philadelphia. The ordaining bishop had declined to wait until his church gave permission and it was not until the General Convention in Washington in 1976 that women were authorized to become priests. Those defending the bishop's action spoke of the guidance of the Holy Spirit:

The event was distressing to many because these women and their supporters had declined to wait for the Church's permission. Pamela Darling interprets their actions as following the model of the civil rights movement, appealing to the "higher" authority of conscience informed by the Holy Spirit, accountable to a community which valued the full humanity of women above the claims of ecclesiastical tradition.[27]

Appeals to the Holy Spirit's guidance were heard in Sydney not infrequently, as the debate raged in the 1980s and early 1990s. It was difficult to know how to evaluate them. It might well be a ploy of those under the influence of liberal theology. The best way was to look into the Scriptures the Spirit himself had inspired, but people read the words differently. Dorothy Lee, Dean of Trinity College Theological School, Melbourne, has written,

> For me, the Bible (like the tradition) remained fundamentally a friend to women, if read aright. The basic problem, as I saw it, was not the Bible itself. In its untidiness and diversity, with its plurality of voices, the Bible was a difficult text to grasp. Although it was not easily controlled or neatly pigeonholed, it was often manipulated by narrow interest groups in the Church, on the right and on the left. To my mind, the Bible needed to be

23. Lieut-Col Ayene Finger http://www.salvationarmy.org.au/

24. Lee, "An Anglo-Uniting Perspective. The journey taken," in Scarfe [ed.], *Preachers, Prophets and Heretics*, 254.

25. Shaw, "The ordination of Anglican women. Challenging tradition," in Scarfe [ed.], *Preachers, Prophets and Heretics*, 22–23.

26. Ibid. See also Chapter 3.

27. Ibid., 24.

read in its wholeness, within the context of the Church's life and liturgy. It was never a question of finding a solitary text to support a pre-determined point of view. Rather the text should be interpreted by the text, taking into account the multiple voices that made up the whole. Moreover, the Bible needed to be interpreted as it was written: from a distinct perspective, from a vantage point and context, and never neutrally or in isolation . . . From this viewpoint, I became deeply concerned by what I considered to be a growing trend in feminist biblical scholarship towards prejudicial readings of Scripture that drew the most hostile of interpretations from the text. It seemed often a form of "conspiracy theory."[28]

In Canada women were first ordained priest in 1975 and New Zealand in 1976. The United Kingdom waited for almost another 20 years. It was while George Carey was Archbishop of Canterbury that the Synod voted in favour of the ordination of women to the priesthood. The first women were ordained there in 1994. Archbishop Carey knew that this issue "had the capacity to split the Church down the middle" and needed careful handling. Nevertheless, he was committed to the ordination of women. In a letter to Cardinal Hume, he gave some of his reasons. They are enlightening as to his view of how the Spirit of God works, and some of his ideas are quite fresh, to some evangelical Sydney eyes, at least. Of the certainty of knowing God's will, he wrote,

> Where is that certainty to be found? Doctrinal definitions do not work like that—if we were to take the Early Church disputes for example, both sides considered they had truth on their side. Within the Anglican tradition we maintain that "very few decisions are ever made on the basis of certainty." Certainty often comes at the end of a process, rarely at the beginning . . . here are some of the arguments I find compelling for taking this step now:
>
> - The New Testament shows that the Spirit of God falls on women as well as men
>
> - Jesus gives women an unprecedented place in the context of His ministry—associating with them and counting them as valuable to his ministry
>
> - Even if women were not part of the apostolic group this certainly has something to do with the fact that that as women

---

28 Lee, "An Anglo-Uniting Perspective. The journey taken," in *Preachers, Prophets and Heretics*, edited by Lindsay and Scarfe, 259–60.

they did not have the freedom to move about in society which suggests that cultural factors should not be excluded

- All the first apostles were Jews; nobody would now argue that all priests should first be Jews.

He made further points to the Cardinal, but of his speech to the Synod he said:

> I reminded Synod that they had been debating this issue as far back as 1975, when they had concluded that there were no theological issues barring women from being ordained. I drew a parallel from Acts 10, where the early Church had to decide whether or not to baptize Gentiles. I contended that Peter was led to see that the inclusion of the Gentiles was not a departure from the tradition but a widening of it, as the first believers began to understand that the Christianity was about "God liberating, renewing and drawing out what has been there implicitly from the beginning." I concluded by appealing to Synod to be bold and to begin the process that would lead to full integration of women in the ministry of the Church.[29]

The Anglican Church of Australia began ordaining the first women priests in 1992, a little ahead of the Mother Church. Like the General Synod, the Sydney Synod is a kind of parliament, and therefore a law-making body. Major changes to church organization and polity require legislation, and this was the path which both the General Synod and the Sydney Synod took. Lawyers considered the terms of the Constitution and the powers of the Appellate Tribunal while theologians fine-combed the Scriptures. Both produced reports; synods debated and voted, and the situation became steadily more complicated.

The Movement for the Ordination of Women (MOW), established in 1983 by Dr Patricia Brennan, accelerated the pace. Anne O'Brien records,

> Patricia Brennan pinpointed the moment she became an activist to a sermon in her local church. Knowing her views on ordination, the curate dictated the "received theology on men's headship and women's subservience" with "the advantage of altitude, posture and no audience participation." For Brennan it was an abuse of power that catapulted her into the bullring."[30]

Brennan was highly articulate and a born leader. Deliberately activist and provocative, her style irritated and alienated many, both those pro

---

29. Carey, *Know the Truth*, 137–42.
30. O'Brien, "Women in the Churches Before 1992," 48.

ordination of women, and those against. Within two years, with national publications, considerable media coverage and well-timed conferences MOW had 800 members. Highly visible at General Synods, Brennan and MOW also visited the Lambeth Conference of Bishops in 1988. Joining with the "Women's Witnessing Community," with banners and press releases they made headlines in *Paris Soir*, the Australian press and television news.[31]

Stuart Piggin has commented on MOW:

> It was relatively dysfunctional and numerically weak. It is amazing that it achieved as much as it did . . . If MOW had been a movement for the training of women in the school of the prophets, rather than for the ordination of women to the priesthood, it would have been a runaway success.[32]

Even before MOW's birth, a bill to alter the Constitution went before the 1981 General Synod, to the effect that, "Nothing in this section prevents this church from authorising by canon the ordaining of women into the three orders of bishops, priests and deacons in the sacred ministry."[33] In his Presidential Address of 1985, Robinson rehearsed the events which had followed this bill. First, this bill failed in the General Synod because "anything like consensus was clearly lacking."[34] Then in 1985 the Appellate Tribunal gave an opinion that the ordination of women "was not inconsistent with the Constitution as it presently stands," except for obstacles presented by the wording of the ordinal and the Canons of 1603 relating to the ordination of ministers. On the strength of that opinion, a bill was introduced for the ordination of women to the priesthood. It failed.

Robinson said,

> I will not comment here on the opinion of the Appellate Tribunal as to its status or implications. The fact is that the unity of our church is at stake if we act without agreement on the matter of the acceptance and recognition of orders throughout the Church . . . In three successive General Synods more than one-third of the Synod has shown itself to be opposed to the principle of ordaining women. In 1977, 41% opposed the proposition "that the theological objections that have been raised do

---

31. Scarfe, "Movement for the Ordination of Women. Their hearts in their mouths," *Preachers, Prophets and Heretics*, 120–28.

32. Piggin, "The Diocese of Sydney. 'This terrible conflict,'" 178.

33. A Bill to Alter the Constitution of the Anglican Church of Australia with respect to the Ordination of Women, *The Constitution Canons and Rules of the Anglican Church of Australia 2010*, 331.

34. *Sydney Year Book 1986*, 222.

not constitute a barrier to the ordination of women to the priesthood;" in 1981 more than a third opposed the bill to change the Constitution; in 1985, 37½% opposed the second reading of a bill for a canon to permit women to be ordained priest. These are large minorities.[35]

The General Synod of 1985 voted to allow women to be ordained as deacons, but until the Sydney Synod agreed to ordain women to a new order of deacon—one which would never lead to priesthood—Robinson was not prepared to assent to the ordinance. This he did, once his requirements were accommodated, in 1987.

Also in 1987 a Special General Synod debated the question of the ordination of women to the priesthood. The necessary votes to pass the legislation were insufficient.[36] Primate Grindrod was in favour of women's ordination and in his Presidential Address, prior to the synod proceedings, stated,

> I believe there is a way forward which applies both to the Church in Australia, the Anglican Communion and the wider church.
>
> Is it not possible that when a key issue of doctrine and practice, such as the ordination of women, has people of the Church adhering to the same doctrine and practice but interpreting them in different ways, for the Church to allow both forms to co-exist, with the prayer that over the years it will become clear which, under God, is to be finally followed? There has to be that honest respect and openness, which lays the decision of the Synod before God, humbly recognising that either mind might in the course of time be proved to be the one God chooses to bless. It is for the Church a test of faith, patience, *koinonia* and love.
>
> Most of us have forgotten that it took years for the doctrines of the Church to be embodied in creeds, received and agreed to by the whole Church. It took time for the three-fold order of ministry to become the accepted norm. It is more difficult

---

35 *Sydney Year Book 1986*, 222–23.

36. Minute Book of General Synod 1977–1987, "A Bill for a Canon to provide for the ordination of Women to the Office of priest and for other purposes." Lost as a Special Bill in the third reading. The numbers were:

	Number present	Majority Required	For	Against
House of Laity	92	62	62	30
House of Clergy	96	64	60	36
House of Bishops	23	16	17	6

when the doctrines are embodied in people and being tested in people, but therein lies the challenge to our trust in God, sensitivity in love towards one another, acceptance of the fact that time will test whether what is taking place is for the good of the Church or not. Impaired communion there may be, but that is more tolerable than schism.[37]

In the years following the birth of MOW, the Sydney Diocesan Doctrine Commission wrote a number of reports re the theology of the place of women in the church. The first report of this kind had been the 1977 Report of the General Synod Commission on Doctrine, *The Ministry of Women*.[38] The Commission members represented a range of theological positions, and at least three were Evangelicals. The Report was quite detailed in its theological survey and shows the influence of Leon Morris, in particular.[39] It recommended that women be ordained to the three orders of ministry. DB Knox wrote a dissenting addendum in which he seems to have inferred that women are inferior to men.[40]

The Sydney Diocesan Doctrine Commission submitted reports in 1983, 1984, 1985, 1987 and 1988. They examined a theology of ordination, and theological arguments pro and con women's ordination.[41] Pat Brennan

---

37. Presidential Address General Synod, 1987.

38. Members of the Commission were: Archbishop Sir Frank Woods, Miss J Wyatt, Dr AM Bryson, the Rev. DR PF Carnley, the Rev. Canon IF Church, the Rev. Dr JR Gaden, Archbishop JBR Grindrod, the Rev. Canon DB Knox, the Rev. Canon LL Morris, the Rev. EL Randall, Archbishop K Rayner and Bishop MM Thomas.

39. The same arguments are to be found in a similar form in Morris' essay in *A Women's Place*, 1976.

40. See Chapter 6. Referring to I Corinthians 11: 3–12, the statement was: "In furtherance of its argument that there is complete equality and equivalence between man and woman the Report states that 'the headship of God to Christ is not to be understood in terms of superiority—inferiority' (Para. 32) but Christ himself explicitly affirmed this superiority—inferiority character of the relationship; e.g. 'The Father is greater than I' (Jn. 14:28). Similarly the Report says that Christ's relationship to man is not one of a superior to an inferior (par. 32) though Jesus affirmed this was the case: 'I am your Lord and teacher' (Jn. 13:14). It is not possible to set aside the natural meaning of the word 'head' in St Paul's statement 'the head of the woman is the man'. For there does not seem any doubt as to what St Paul meant. His words are: 'But I want you to understand that the head of every man is Christ, the head of the woman is the man, and the head of Christ is God.' He supports this by reference to two features of the creation narrative of Genesis 2: 'For the man was not of the woman but the woman is of man. For neither was the man created for the woman but the woman for the man.' These are theological statements enunciating a principle of relationship between men and women." For an alternative interpretation of this passage of Scripture, see Giles, *Created Woman*, 32–36.

41. One argument in the 1984 Committee Report was: "Women act as an erotic

was among those appointed by the Sydney Synod to the 1982 Committee to examine the question of the ordination of women.[42] While the Sydney Synod chose at least one member who was pro women's ordination for each committee, these people were always in a significant minority. It would have been very difficult for them to argue their case cogently and confidently in the context of such groups.[43] It would also have been helpful for the Commission to have co-opted people like the Rev. Dr Graham Cole and the Rev. Dr Tim Harris, scholars who interpreted the Scriptures differently from DB Knox.[44] Bishop Donald Cameron chaired at least one of these commissions.[45] He has subsequently moved from a position of opposition to the ordination of women to the priesthood, to a position of support. Cameron has stated that when he first became involved in the debate he was very much influenced by what DB Knox and DWB Robinson had said. This position was reinforced by the position of people he met during ARCIC discussions. But when he heard the views of FF Bruce and Leon Morris, he reconsidered his views. They opened up new ways to read and apply the Bible. There were other ways of reading the Bible from the way that those opposed to the ministry of women read it. In addition, during his time as Federal Secretary of CMS his contact with women missionaries, "who did everything under the sun," and very capably, made him decide that this was an issue "you cannot be certain on." He has ended up with the position that: "I am open-minded and I don't think Scripture is as clear-cut on this issue so as to exclude women doing anything in the church that any man could do."[46]

The 1985 Report was somewhat open-ended:

> We have not reached unanimity in our own minds on every detail of the ministry of women ... our theological work ... has not provided sufficient reason to change the existing practice of restricting to men, admission to the Priesthood as described in

---

stimulus to men whereas men do not so greatly affect women. Women taking the leadership role in public worship would be a distraction" *Sydney Year Book 1985*, 468, 4.

42. *Sydney Year Book*, Resolution 18/82, 236.

43 For example, the 1988 Report was produced by Bishop ED Cameron, Dr DB Knox, Dr PT O'Brien, Dr PW Barnett, Dss MA Rodgers, Dr PF Jensen, the Rev. RE Lamb, the Rev. JG Mason and the Rev. R Bowles. As far as is known, all the men were opposed to the ordination of women to the priesthood and four were "heavies" at Moore College. Dss E Mathieson and Dss Rodgers were largely absent from the discussions. *Sydney Year Book 1989*, 353. There is anecdotal evidence that Dss Mathieson found her role very stressful. Conversations with P Herbert and ED Cameron, June 2013.

44. These men all acquired doctorates and published their views on women in ministry.

45. *Sydney Year Books*: 1984, 386, 1986, 338; 1989, 353.

46. Interview with MHC 16.7.2013.

the formularies . . . It may be that further theological work could lead to modification of this point of view.[47]

The theological argument for restricting ordination to men was, in essence, about "headship" of the male, that there is an order in relationships, beginning at Creation and this includes "headship" with the implied meaning of responsibility and authority.[48]

Books and articles on the subject included *A Women's Place*, published in 1976. Three theologians examined the issues: JR Gaden, Leon Morris and Barbara Thiering. Margaret Rodgers reviewed the booklet for *Southern Cross* and found it rather disappointing for a way forward in the debate.

> These three papers . . . offer no clear guidelines or recommendations for decision or action . . . Leon Morris' contribution is an excellent collection of the relevant biblical material but it is irritating in its indefiniteness and in its tentative conclusions . . . I suppose we ladies should be glad that the gentlemen of the Doctrine Commission are at least considering the question of the role and status of women in the Church of England in Australia . . . We assume our present rightful position and sit with meekly folded hands waiting for them to tell us what "place" they are going to allow us to have.[49]

Leon Morris raised some important issues, such as that the Pauline directive to do "what is fitting in the Lord" might have different implications today from those in the early church, so "in these days it would be brought into disrepute by strict subjugation."[50] Morris also noted that women were to "rule their households" (*oikodespotein*)—a word normally associated with the function of a male. It is also notable that he did not buy into the argument that the subjection of the woman reflects the subordination of the Son to the Father. Referring to I Corinthians 11 he wrote,

> . . . there is mention of three headships, those of Christ to man, man to wife and God to Christ. The argument usually runs that as man is inferior to Christ, so the wife is inferior to the husband. But the headship of God to Christ does not involve this kind of superiority (cf. the Athanasian Creed, "in the Trinity none is afore or after other: none is greater, or less than another"). It is true that the New Testament sees a certain subordination of the

47. *Sydney Year Book 1986*, 338.
48. *Sydney Year Book 1986*, 323–38.
49. *Southern Cross* May 1976, 17.
50. Morris, Gaden and Thiering, *A Woman's Place*, 27, quoting Titus 2:5 and Colossians 3:18.

incarnate Son to the Father, but the question is whether at this point it is the incarnation or the essential nature that is in mind. In any case it can scarcely be denied that the three headships are all different.[51]

Morris' tentative conclusion was that considering the all but universal attitude of the first century AD that women must be in subjection, there are "as many examples of women being active in teaching and the like as we could reasonably expect."

Another evangelical theologian of international repute was FF Bruce. He argued for the ordination of women because "whatever in Paul's teaching promotes true freedom is of universal and permanent validity; whatever seems to impose restrictions on true freedom has regard to local and temporary conditions."[52]

The influential John Stott published a chapter on women in *Issues Facing Christians Today*. He concluded that "submission" was "of permanent and universal validity" because of "Paul's constant teaching about female submission to male headship" but that women ought to be free to teach men, with certain provisos.[53] These provisos were in terms of content, context and style. With regard to *content*, Stott argues that in in teaching, women might be numbered with men as those who expound the apostolic doctrine in the New Testament. They do not claim authority for themselves, but put themselves and their teaching under the authority of Scripture. With regard to *context*, Stott argues for team ministry, in which "members can capitalise the sum total of their gifts, and in it there should surely be a woman or women. He believed that the team leader should be a man "in keeping with biblical teaching on masculine headship." As to *style*, Stott urged humility for men and women as Christian teachers.

The Rev. Dr Kevin Giles, a Melbourne clergyman, has published a number of books on the church and women's place in ministry, including *Created Woman,* published in 1985. He noted that I Timothy 2:11-14 is the only prohibition to the ministry of women in the New Testament and the only place where the order of creation is made the ground for women's subordination to men.[54] He concluded:

> It is because majoring on one text always gives either distorted or erroneous theology that such an approach is described as "a

51. Ibid., 25.

52. *Sydney Year Book 1986,* 327, quoting "Women in the Church: A Biblical Survey," *Christian Brethren Review,* 23.

53. Stott, *Issues Facing Christians Today,* 252.

54. Giles, *Created Woman,* 40.

sectarian hermeneutic" to be contrasted with "a catholic hermeneutic" which draws on all of Scripture and has the power to convince all Christians . . . The overall drift of Scripture is in fact in favour of equality, with the only real exception being I Timothy 2:11-14. But as we have argued, one text cannot be the basis of sound biblical theology and especially so when it is interpreted to contradict the teaching and example of Jesus, the apostolic theology of ministry and the New Testament's insistence that in Christ there is "a new creation."[55]

Narelle Jarrett (Principal of Deaconess House and later Archdeacon for Women) reviewed Giles' book very favourably, although not uncritically. She found his arguments on key sections of Genesis, I Corinthians and Ephesians "exegetically reasonable" but unnecessarily brief on I Timothy 2:11-14. She recommended the book as valuable reading "irrespective of which side a person may take in the debate."[56]

Other notable contributors to the debate were the Rev. Dr John Woodhouse, Justice Keith Mason QC and the Archbishop of Sydney. In two articles in *Southern Cross* John Woodhouse discussed six reasons for women's ordination, as he understood them.[57] He set out his case in a clear and logical manner, but also in a way that admitted no alternative interpretations of the text. He stated that the pro-ordination argument that men and women are equal is properly expressed biblically as equality in status before God; the passages of the Bible usually quoted to "prove" the equality of man and woman are not about equality but *unity* as male and female; and the important question is what the Bible teaches about "difference" between men and women. Woodhouse wrote that a wrong view of equality (i.e. as interchangeability) leads to a wrong demand for ordination, and that secular feminism (like the humanism of the 19th Century) has proved to lead to delusion.

He understood Genesis 1 and 2 in terms of a hierarchical relationship: God, man, woman, animals, in that order. In his second article, Woodhouse examined the key New Testament texts, arriving at a different conclusion from Morris and Giles. Essentially, he stated the headship of the male from I Corinthians 11:1–16, noting that the three relationships (man—Christ, woman—man, Christ—God) are described "in identical terms."[58]

---

55. Ibid., 68–69.
56. *Southern Cross*, October 1985, 27.
57. Ibid., June 1985, 12–13 and July 1985, 16–17.
58. He also commented on I Corinthians 14:34–36, saying of it, "the point is already familiar to us," regarding the principle of order in the male/female relationship.

Of I Timothy 2:11–15 he stated:

> The passage is more straightforward than one might think from the extraordinary lengths to which some have gone to show that it does not mean what it appears to mean! We do not find any principle in this passage with which we are by now not familiar from the passages already discussed.

Woodhouse's view is very clearly in line with Sydney conservative theology on the place of women in the church. But it is important to note that W Ward Gasque, Professor of New Testament Studies at Regent College, Vancouver, wrote a response to Woodhouse's two articles, ending with the words,

> Dr Woodhouse has a right to his own opinions. But the readers of your magazine should be aware that the views he expresses cannot be regarded as *the* evangelical view, since many of the most respected evangelical scholars of our day come to quite different conclusions.[59]

In all the complexity of weighing arguments and striving for the right path in the women's ordination debate, one fact must be noted. According to Archbishop Jensen, there is unfortunately no compromise position for a diocese. Either it opts for ordination or it doesn't. It is either ON or OFF. This is the dilemma for the head of an institution. It must be remembered that in seeing no theological barriers to ordination, theologians like Ward Gasque and FF Bruce were Brethren, and the Brethren do not have ordination. They did not have to deal with the practical outcome of ordination, which made it simpler for them to come to a theological conclusion on the matter.[60]

Woodhouse also dismissed the position of the renowned Evangelical scholar FF Bruce with the words,

> Those arguing for the ordination of women to the priesthood on the same basis as men often cite respected New Testament scholars who support their point of view. This can be misleading. Professor FF Bruce is a case in point. What leads Professor Bruce to his views about the ordination of women is not so much his undoubtedly expert exegesis of the New Testament texts (with which I am largely in agreement), but his method of *applying* these texts.

---

59. *Southern Cross*, November 1985, 3.
60. Jensen interview with MHC, 19.5.2015.

Here Woodhouse quoted FF Bruce on Paul's teaching and true freedom.

> Let me emphasise that it is this statement which puts Professor Bruce on one side of the ordination of women debate, not his expert exegesis of the New Testament texts.
>
> But the principle he puts forward is, I suggest, untenable, or at least unworkable. Who decides what true freedom *is*? I do not think that Professor Bruce would argue that it is the absence of all restrictions. Certain restrictions actually promote true freedom [as] when Paul says in Colossians 3:9 "Do not lie to one another" . . . [61]

K Mason QC was Solicitor-General in New South Wales (1987–1997) and an active, vocal supporter of MOW. His articles and speeches appeared from time to time in *Southern Cross*. A copy of his speech to the synod in 1986 contains, with reference to Archbishop Robinson, the ominous phrase "with the greatest respect," several times. Mason took issue with the Archbishop's perception of his authority *vis-à-vis* his own synod, the General Synod and the Constitution.[62] Mason also had a view of the Appellate Tribunal which differed from that of other Sydney lawyers (see below). Despite a gentle and quiet bearing, he was a formidable presence, owing to his senior status as a prominent, brilliant lawyer and because he did not hesitate to confront the Archbishop himself.

Donald Robinson probably ended up pleasing almost nobody as he tried to pick his way through the minefield of the issues raised by the question of the ministry of women. In 1985 he withheld his assent to three ordinances, although they were passed by clergy and laity in the Sydney Synod.[63] To Keith Mason, this smacked of unconstitutional and authoritarian behaviour.[64] Robinson, despite Mason's jibes, was committed to the legal process. This was to cause him considerable difficulty, since lawyers like Mason interpreted the Constitution differently from Robinson and his legal advisors, who included his Chancellor Ken Handley QC and Neil Cameron, the Advocate of the Diocese.

---

61. *Southern Cross* July 1984, 17.

62. *Southern Cross* December 1986, 6–7. Another speech was printed in *Southern Cross*, December 1987.

63. The three bills concerned: the ordination of women as deacons, marriage of divorced persons and Lay Presidency.

64. *Southern Cross* December 1986, 6–7. Justice Peter Young wrote an article analyzing this unusual situation, leaving the conclusion open-ended. *Southern Cross* 1986 February, 10.

Robinson's reasons for opposing the ordination of women were articulated in his presidential addresses and the occasional Archbishop's letter in *Southern Cross*. Nowhere did he publish a reasoned exegesis of the Scriptures for his position. He appears, in public, at least, to have left that to DB Knox and other members of the Doctrine Commission. His main reasons were: apostolic tradition as contained in the New Testament and the unity of the worldwide Church. We can see this stated as clearly as anywhere, in the 1987 Presidential Address:

> I believe the ordination of women as presbyters has not only brought about an inevitable lessening of communion between churches, since we are unable to record recognition to all ministers in each other's churches, but is at variance with the fundamental faith and order we receive from the apostolic church, on which we rest our claim to apostolicity and to fidelity to scripture. So far, only four or five of the member churches of the Anglican Communion—out of some twenty-eight—have canonical authority for such ordinations in their churches, and even this canonical authority, being determined by individual churches rather than by a general council, is queried by many. Other bishops have acted without canonical authority. A proposal for canonical authority failed to get the necessary majority in our own General Synod in August. I understand the personal disappointment many feel about this, but the issue is far greater than the context in which many, both inside and outside the Church, generally view it. It has to do with authority: the authority of Christ, the authority of his apostle, consequently the authority of Scripture and the way in which Christ governs His Church . . .
>
> I should like to see women assisting in ministry in every parish. In fact there are, I think, more than eighty women who hold my licence or authority for one kind or another of parish ministry at present, not counting those authorised to assist at communion, and I should be glad to see this increased. There is probably more authorised women's ministry in Sydney than any other diocese in Australia.[65]

Robinson seemed utterly convinced of his position. He stated: "For my own part, I do not regard the ordination of women to the priesthood as a negotiable matter . . . "[66] Three women, signing themselves as "Convenors, MOW Sydney" responded with a letter. They would have been regarded as

---

65. *Sydney Year Book* 1988, 244–45.
66. *Southern Cross* March 1985, 7.

disturbers of the peace by Sydney conservatives, and indeed they were. But their argument was good. They wrote:

> As the Archbishop can, in his non-assent, reject legislation passed by the Synod, does his statement mean that even if both laity and clergy voted in favour of women's ordination to the priesthood, the Archbishop would not assent?
>
> Does it mean that any real debate on the issue is closed?
>
> Does it mean that the Rural Deanery meetings being organised to discuss the matter are a sham because the Archbishop has pre-empted the decision?
>
> Does it mean, in the event of all the other metropolitan dioceses in Australia being in favour, that Archbishop Robinson would prevent the assent of the Sydney Diocese? Would that result in a breaking of communion with other Anglican Dioceses in Australia?
>
> We would ask the Archbishop to declare clearly the implied consequences of such a strong statement, to his diocese.
>
> Marlene Cohen
> Eileen Diesendorf
> Colleen Stewart[67]

Alongside the reports from the Doctrine Commission were the legal issues. Essentially, they concerned two entities: the Constitution and the Appellate Tribunal. There were attempts to alter the Constitution so that ordination of women was legal under the Constitution. In 1983 the Sydney Synod passed NM Cameron's Resolution titled "'Bill' Procedure to alter the Constitution." The Resolution (21/83) stated:

> This Synod:
>
> a. Expresses its concern that provisions of the Constitution which protect the theological position and practices of sections of the Anglican Church of Australia are circumvented by the "bill" procedure and records its view that, in the long term, this will be divisive; and
>
> b. Is unwilling to entertain a measure to amend the Constitution which is not a canon duly made with relevant requirements of the Constitution.[68]

---

67. *Southern Cross* June 1985, 3.
68. *Sydney Year Book 1984*, 235.

The Bill referred to, "A Bill to Alter the Constitution of the Anglican Church of Australia with respect to the Ordination of Women 1981" did not come into effect because insufficient synods of the ACA assented to it.

Another legal way forward was to use the Appellate Tribunal. The Tribunal, according to a careful reading of the Constitution, has jurisdiction in four areas.[69] They are:

1. To determine whether an act or part thereof is contrary to the Fundamental Declarations or Ruling Principles.[70]
2. To hear and determine appeals from Diocesan Tribunals and the Special Tribunal.[71]
3. To give an opinion or determination re the Constitution. Note: under the Constitution only the canons and rules are binding.[72]
4. To determine a question relating to the good order and government of the Church within a diocese.[73]

Keith Mason took a different position. He has written that the Appellate Tribunal "is a mechanism for resolving constitutional and other disputes within the Church."[74] He continued,

> The Appellate Tribunal has a broad original jurisdiction to resolve constitutional disputes. It may determine the validity of canons or proposed canons of the General Synod. It may also provide what are described as determinations or opinions in all manner of constitutional issues if questions are referred to it by the Primate at his discretion or if requested to do so by 25 members of General Synod or a provincial synod affected thereby.[75] The decision of the Appellate Tribunal may extend to questions of doctrine, faith, ritual, ceremonial or discipline as well as the interpretation of the Constitution itself. Unless unanimous, the Tribunal is required to consult with the House of Bishops and a board of priestly assessors in matters of doctrine.[76]

---

69. Information from NM Cameron and also *The Constitution Canons and Rules of the Anglican Church of Australia*, 12–13.
70. Ibid., 12–13. This, according to NM Cameron, has never been used.
71. Ibid., 59:4, 26.
72. Ibid., 30.
73. Ibid., (c) (iii), 15.
74. Mason, *Believers in Court*, 13.
75. *The Constitution Canons and Rules of the Anglican Church of Australia*, 29, 63.
76. Mason, *Believers in Court*, 13.

From a lay perspective, the Appellate Tribunal has a number of defects, although Mason and others have wanted it to become a final authority. First, it must be almost impossible for its members to be impartial on an issue such as the ordination of women to the priesthood. Second, unless its members are unanimous in their verdict, there is a stalemate. Third, it is not in the least democratic, since only a tiny part of the General Synod is represented in its final decision. Over the years these defects have become obvious to Sydney members of the General Synod, as later events have demonstrated. Robinson certainly regarded the Tribunal, of which he was a member, as a body which had no further power other than to hand down *opinions*. He repeatedly voiced this view, which he stated, for example, in his Presidential Address of 1990.[77]

> The Appellate Tribunal has jurisdiction to "give its opinion" on questions which "arise under the Constitution" and which are referred to the Tribunal in a prescribed manner. The Tribunal will have to decide whether the questions now being referred to it "arise under this Constitution." If they do, the Tribunal can give its opinion on them. If they do not, it cannot.[78]

Meanwhile Bishop Owen Dowling of the Diocese of Canberra Goulburn, in August 1990 announced his intention to ordain some women in February 1991. Robinson was deeply unhappy about Dowling's move. Dowling, he reasoned, was "not supported by General Synod legislation or the Appellate Tribunal, legal opinion on the issue was divided, and a reference to the Appellate Tribunal relevant to the issue was pending."[79] Robinson's other concern was that Dowling was under oath of obedience to him as Metropolitan.[80]

What then happened is a matter for continuing debate. Robinson resorted to the secular courts. He sought a restraining injunction from the NSW Supreme Court and the Court of Appeal agreed to hear the case. There were nine questions of law to consider. The case is known as *Scandrett v Dowling* 1.01.1992.[81] The case took two days instead of the expected

77. *Sydney Year Book 1991*, 255.

78. General Synod Report, *Sydney Year Book 1989*, 334. The Appellate Tribunal waited until December 1991 to hand down their opinion. J Scarfe, "Movement for the Ordination of Women," in Lindsay and Scarfe [ed.], *Preachers, prophets and Heretics*, 133. Eleven questions had been referred to the Tribunal by the Acting Primate and other parties. *Sydney Year Book 1992*, 259.

79. *Sydney Year Book*, 255.

80. *Sydney Year Book*, 259.

81. The plaintiffs were: the Rev. Dalba Primmer (Diocese of Canberra Goulburn), the Rev. David Robarts (Diocese of Melbourne) and Dr Laurie Scandrett (Diocese of

one, and cost the Diocese of Sydney $100,000. The judgement was awarded against the plaintiffs. In effect, the judgement ruled that the court had power of jurisdiction over property alone. This in turn meant that the Constitution was not binding and this was good news for the Diocese of Sydney.

This was of immense importance. With the Court's Judgement came the sudden realisation that henceforth appealing to the Constitution no longer worked. The Constitution now lacked its former power and this freed Sydney to do what it wanted to do, unhindered. The Diocese was now free to begin more church planting, to refashion liturgy, and to engage in evangelism unfettered by the Constitution. By using unconstitutional means to achieve their ends, those who later went ahead and ordained women had caused an explosion which blew up in their face. The act fractured the Anglican Church of Australia and the Constitution of the Anglican Church of Australia was stripped of the authority it once had.

Many were outraged that Christians had taken fellow Christians to court. Letters to *Southern Cross* reveal that on the basis of Paul's teaching in I Corinthians 6, they believed this action was wrong. The Rev. Dr Peter O'Brien, Vice-Principal of Moore College, wrote a measured and probing article on the subject in April 1992. He asked

1. Whether there are any significant differences between the issue Paul is addressing and the events of recent months?
2. Did Paul heed his own advice?

O'Brien continued,

> The matter was not personal. It had nothing to do with material possessions, and none of the plaintiffs had been defrauded or wronged. Instead, a declaration was being sought from the Supreme Court that the Constitution of the Church precluded a bishop ordaining a woman to the priesthood unless a canon of the General Synod had been passed to authorise it. An interpretation of the Church's Constitution was being sought, not a settlement for damages or the like. Sadly, the Church itself had failed to clarify this point of law and the Court was being asked to interpret the Act of Parliament.
>
> Our 1962 Constitution was set up by Act of Parliament.
> . . . Did Paul follow his own advice? If the conclusion is drawn as it is by some, that I Corinthians 6 prohibits a Christian

---

Sydney). Scandrett was asked by the Rev. Bruce Ballantine-Jones to do this—*Southern Cross* March 1992, 11–12. According to Robinson, the initiative for the appeal came from a Melbourne layman and one of the three plaintiffs was "a prominent Melbourne clergyman." Robinson, *Selected Works* 2, 490.

> from initiating any court action, then Paul's own appeals as a Roman citizen to the magistrates at Philippi (Acts 16:37) and to Caesar (Acts 25:11) in his own defence and for the sake of mission seem to be inconsistent. In fact, he was not going to court against a fellow Christian, or because he had been defrauded and was seeking reparation. He therefore was not contradicting his own strong admonition of I Corinthians 6. But he does appeal on occasion to the civil courts . . .
>
> A Christian faced with circumstances different from those described in I Corinthians 6 will therefore need to exercise godly wisdom before deciding what to do. Sometimes restraint, possible suffering, and no further action may be the better course. On other occasions, it may be appropriate, even if unpleasant, to initiate proceedings. The events of recent days suggest that Christians do not always agree on how this godly wisdom is to be applied.[82]

O'Brien did not deal with the heart of the complaint: that Christians were taking fellow Christians to the secular courts. Sydney lawyers have defended the appeal on the grounds that they were seeking clarification of the law, as the Constitution of 1962 came into effect by Act of Parliament.

On 7 March 1992, Archbishop Peter Carnley of Perth pre-empted the legal process and ordained seven women. Now the genie was out of the bottle. Later in 1992 the General Synod voted for the ordination of women to the priesthood when the Law of the Church of England Clarification Canon 1992 was passed. It was a "provisional canon," because the voting fell below the required majority for it to become a canon in its own right. This meant that it would come into force in each diocese only when each diocese adopted it. No bishop could ordain women without its synod's consent.[83] By the end of 1992, according to Dr Janet Scarfe, there were 92 women priests in the Anglican Church of Australia.

Archbishop Rayner, the Acting Primate, believed that unless the General Synod of July 1992 found "a way forward" the ACA would face "an extremely serious threat to the order and unity of our Church." He continued, in a speech reproduced in *Southern Cross,*

> The heart of the problem for the Church is that on both sides there are people who conscientiously believe that they know the mind of God on the matter. We should begin by respecting the

---

82. *Southern Cross* April 1992, 25.

83. *Constitution, Canons and Rules of the Anglican Church of Australia,* 146–47; K Rayner, "The Decision-makers," in Lindsay and Scarfe, *Preachers, Prophets and Heretics,* 146.

conscientious convictions of those from whom we differ. They are not rogues or villains; they are people who, like us, care for the truth... We should not be daunted by the fact that the journey to common understanding is long and painful.[84]

Archbishop Robinson accused the pro-ordination Anglicans of not having properly examined the Scriptures, yet the 1977 Report on the Ministry of Women from General Synod ran to 27 pages of exegesis, interpretation and application.[85] He stated in the same Presidential Address that they had no concern for the pastoral consequences, yet Rayner's statement, and those of his predecessor Grindrod demonstrate a keen concern for the pastoral implications of change in this area. One of Robinson's arguments (quoted previously) was that there were so few who supported the ordination of women that it would cause unnecessary and great upheaval.[86] The numbers of dioceses supporting the ordination of women have steadily grown over the years. Even by 1992, the great majority of dioceses in Australia supported it. The Archbishop of Canterbury, George Carey, supported it, and the Synod of which he was President approved it, as we have seen, in 1994. This particular argument of Robinson's argument accordingly was not a convincing one, long term. But it does demonstrate his overriding concern for the Church beyond Sydney: for the Australia-wide Anglican Church and for the Church beyond. For him, the decision to ordain women was against holy writ and meant that the ACA was "no longer unequivocally apostolic, catholic and reformed. He believed it had lost its vocation.[87]

Sydney people who wanted to see women ordained tried a bit longer. The Rev. Tim Harris called for a Report on women to the priesthood for the 1992 Sydney Synod, and for a public conference "involving participants chosen as to fairly reflect the range of positions held on this issue." The conference was held and the Report issued in 1992. The Report was a presentation of alternate evangelical views and the committee was well balanced, in terms of the members' professional qualifications and views.[88] Sensible, practical questions as to the way forward for women in ministry in Sydney formed the conclusion.

Harris was one of many men and women who left the diocese for ministry elsewhere. Some people interviewed have commented that this has

84. *Southern Cross* February 1992, 5.
85. *Sydney Year Book 1978*, 232.
86. See *Sydney Year Book* 1988, 244–45.
87. *Sydney Year Book 1993*, 266.
88. Gerald R Christmas, Dr. Chris Forbes, Marion Gabbott, Bishop Harry Goodhew, Rev. Tim Harris, Canon Ray Heslehurst, Rev. Narelle Jarrett.

been a gift from Sydney to other dioceses: well-trained, able teachers and pastors who have contributed considerably to the ministry of another place. Two former Sydney women have even become bishops.[89] This diaspora, like that of Acts 8, has blessed countless people.[90]

Ranking far below the ordination issue, but nevertheless very important in Robinson's episcopate, were at least five other matters, all of which demonstrate some unusual characteristics of the Diocese of Sydney. They were: the question of the remarriage of divorced persons; Lay Presidency; the rise of a new attitude to practicing homosexuality; ARCIC; and the consecration of a Sydney clergyman to be Bishop of the Church of England in South Africa. All were weighty issues, but none dominated the Diocese of Sydney as did the women's ordination matter.

Following the no fault legislation of the 1970s, the number of divorces had increased to the point that remarriage of divorced people was a new pastoral problem to be addressed. The 1981 General Synod had passed a bill for remarriage of divorced persons as a provisional Canon, so the matter had been referred to the Sydney Synod of 1982. As was usual with the Sydney Diocese, very careful preparation preceded a bill before its appearance at the Synod. The Archbishop, on the advice of his Chancellor, requested Justice Peter Young for advice on the present law of the Church in the Diocese in this matter and the answer was that marriage of a divorced person was permitted only when a previous marriage had been terminated because of adultery, and the permission of the Archbishop or his surrogate obtained. The Diocesan Doctrine Commission prepared a paper for the Synod in 1983, and a Report was followed by a final Report the following year. The last two reports together ran to 30 pages. The Marriage of Divorced Persons Ordinance 1985 came before the Sydney Synod in 1986. The Synod passed the Ordinance but Robinson declined his assent. His main reason was that he "did not want to resign his role as the proper person to grant permission for such marriages as the church considers lawful."[91]

The idea of Sydney assenting to Lay Presidency has been the cause of major unease in many other dioceses of Australia, as well as in the worldwide Anglican Communion.[92] Many Sydney people have found this position hard to understand, and on many occasions Sydney people have unofficially conducted their own Holy Communion service, or Eucharist,

---

89. Barbara Darling and Genieve Blackwell.

90. Cornish interview with MHC 14.9.2011, Rodgers interview with MHC 23.5.11.

91. *Sydney Year Books: 1983*, 223–25; *1984*, 203–7; 376–86; *1985*, 421–50; and *1987*, 263.

92. Porter, *The New Puritans*, 50, 137–45.

without clergy presiding. As early as 1983, in a five-clause Resolution, "Towards a theology of ordination," John Chapman inserted as the fifth clause: "This Synod requests the Standing Committee to set up a committee to explore the desirability and constitutional aspects of Lay Presidency at the Holy Communion." The next year a Resolution from Bishop Harry Goodhew endorsed the principle of Lay Presidency and a report from a committee chaired by Goodhew endorsed Lay Presidency. Robinson indicated he would decline assent if Lay Presidency were put to Synod. Further work followed, and when in 1987 another Report was complete, the Archbishop again indicated that he would decline assent.[93]

Sydney's reasons for Lay Presidency are important: wrong motives have sometimes been attributed. The reasons given at the 1987 Synod were:

> Bearing in mind the preaching ministry of a large number of lay persons in our Diocese, the occasions when a clergyman can only be found with difficulty to take a Holy Communion Service, and the important principle that word and sacrament should be united . . . Lay Presidency is desirable under the following circumstances:
>
> a. Where the minister of the church is unable to conduct the Lord's Supper; or
>
> b. Where there is no minister of the church because of a vacancy in the cure; or
>
> c. For institutions such as Deaconess House, by a suitable member of the church or institution.[94]

What is termed "reserved sacrament," that is, the reservation, after consecration of the bread and wine, for use at another time and place, is repugnant to conservative Sydney Evangelicals. It is the *disuniting* of word and sacrament and smacks of superstition and unreformed theology where the Host, as it is called in the Roman Catholic Church, is reserved in a special container called a tabernacle, for later use. The issue underlines the Sydney perspective on ordained clergy: that they are not transformed into sacred beings who engage in special ministry after their ordination to the priesthood. Behind this lies the theology of "the priesthood of all believers," enunciated by Martin Luther, and found in the letter of I Peter chapter 2.[95]

---

93. Lay Presidency is when a layperson says the words of consecration over the bread and wine during the service of Holy Communion. *Sydney Year Books 1984*, 238; *1986*, 244 and 314–16; *1987*, 258; and *1988*, 325–34.

94. *Sydney Year Book 1988*, 326; Porter, *The New Puritans*, 144.

95. I Peter 2:9. A classic statement of this position is seen in Griffith Thomas's *The*

With regard to another vexed issue, that of homosexual practice, two external events caused Anglicans in Sydney to make definitive statements about the issue.[96] This was to be the beginning of a long and divisive argument in the ACA, with the real possibility that the eventual outcome would be schism. The first event was the Report on Discrimination and Homosexuality issued by the NSW Anti-Discrimination Board in 1982. According to Robinson, the Report ranged from "qualified support to unqualified rejection" of the "Christian view of homosexuality."[97] The second event was an assembly of the Episcopal Church of the USA (ECUSA) in 1991. The assembly was dominated by a debate on homosexuality, at which two motions were defeated. One motion was "that it is expected that the clergy abstain from sexual relations outside marriage" and the other asked for "a moratorium on the ordination of sexually active homosexuals."[98] In response to such views, Archbishop Robinson wrote:

> For the Christian, the Bible must be the decisive norm. In the Bible, homosexual love is never approved and where named, it is condemned. But at the same time we must remember to distinguish between the "sin" and the "sinner." The act of homosexuality is condemned. The non-practising homosexual person desirous of living a life acceptable to God is not. Christians have responsibilities of love, acceptance, concern and compassion but the offering of these qualities is not an endorsement of an unacceptable lifestyle."[99]

ARCIC (Anglican-Roman Catholic International Commission) had been established, as we have seen at Lambeth 1978. Dialogue between Anglicans and Roman Catholics had been continuing since 1969: the Pope visited England in 1982 and later the Archbishop of Canterbury visited Rome.[100] ARCIC discussions and reports gave those involved a better understanding of both Churches, fresh insights and the affirmation of common areas of agreement. But this was as far as it went. In his autobiography, Archbishop George Carey states that as Archbishop of Canterbury he was committed to

---

Principles of Theology: "There is no function of the Christian priesthood which cannot be exercised by every individual believer at all times. Differences of function exist in the ministry exist, but none in the priesthood." 318.

96. *Sydney Year Book 1986*, Resolution 29/85, 245; *1993*, Resolution 32/92, 290.
97. *Southern Cross* September 1982, 2.
98. *Sydney Year Book 1992*, 260.
99. *Southern Cross* December 1982, 2.
100. Ibid., July 1982, *Sydney Year Book 1990*, 232.

dialogue and eventual union with Rome.[101] But he relinquished this hope when he realised another goal was realised: the ordination of women to the priesthood—unacceptable to the Roman Catholic Church. The two intractable problems, "that of authority and particularly the Bishop of Rome, and the place of women within the ordained ministry of the church," remained unsolved according to ED Cameron, who was the ACA delegate to ARCIC.[102]

Robinson gave short shrift to an ARCIC resolution at Lambeth 1988:

> I voted against the whole ARCIC Resolution at Lambeth, as I do not consider the Agreed Statements are consonant in substance with our Anglican faith in some important respects; and in relation to the Authority statement I think the quest for a universal primacy is on the wrong track. I can only add that I do not think it will get very far if it continues to explore the basis of such a universal primacy in Scripture, as the Lambeth resolution proposed![103]

The consecration of a new bishop for the Church of England in South Africa (CESA) was potentially divisive. The CESA was still not recognised by the Archbishop of Canterbury and was estranged from the other Anglican Church in South Africa, the Church of the Province (CPSA).[104] Robinson, like Loane and Mowll before him, warmly supported the CESA, and when the Rev. Dr Dudley Foord, a senior Sydney clergyman, was elected to be the new bishop of the CESA, Robinson was asked to consecrate Foord. Robinson would only do so if he had the goodwill of CPSA, the Primate of the ACA and "a reasonable number of bishops."[105] The Primate agreed, as did the majority of the Australian bishops.[106] There had been censure that the consecration of earlier CESA bishops Morris and Bradley had been irregular. There was no question as to the authenticity of Foord's consecration: twelve bishops, including the Primate Sir John Grindrod, Archbishop Sir Marcus Loane, Archbishop Robinson, and at least one CPSA representative, took part in the ceremony in St Andrew's Cathedral. Foord was in South Africa for only a short time (1984–1987), but he made a most significant contribution by working hard to establish a theological college for CESA

---

101. Carey, *Tell the Truth*, 139.

102. *Southern Cross* 1991 March, 9; Archbishop J Grindrod, General Synod Presidential Address, 1985.

103. *Sydney Year Book 1990*, 234.

104. See Chapter 3.

105. *Sydney Year Book 1985*, 218–19.

106. General Synod Presidential Address, J Grindrod 1984; *Southern Cross* March 1984, 5.

clergy.[107] Before Foord left South Africa, Broughton Knox accepted the invitation to found a theological college there. Its name is George Whitefield College: Knox established the solid foundations of what is today a thriving evangelical college.[108]

The population of Sydney continued to spread and further growth was predicted. Robinson launched his "Vision for Growth" in 1985, its aim to establish or consolidate nineteen new churches and centers of ministry in the six years till 1990.[109] It was the initiative of former missionary Bishop Ken Short.[110] The Rev. Stuart Abrahams and his team raised funds, purchased land, and supported the appointment of staff to work in the new areas. His tireless work achieved a great deal: by 1988, 29 of the 46 projects had been completed and Vision for Growth was assisting in 22 different communities. The initiative cost $7,000,000 and was funded by parishes and individuals.[111] Places like Menai, Doonside, Cranebrook, Minchinbury and St Clair saw gradual but steady growth in numbers. The emphasis in reports from these developing churches was upon teaching and learning from the Bible: in children's groups, youth groups, and different kinds of adult group ministry, including prayer meetings and Sunday morning and evening services. Some held special clubs and occasional luncheons to reach out into the community.[112] Vision 2001 replaced Vision for Growth in 1990.[113]

Concomitant with population growth was diocesan growth. The Diocese still stretched from Nowra to the Hawkesbury and west beyond Lithgow. It was huge. In 1986 Robinson pointed out to his Synod that 20 years previously, Loane had addressed himself, in his first speech to the Synod, to the possible division of the Diocese. He pointed out that no new See had been carved out of Sydney since 1869.[114] Robinson was very keen to create two new dioceses: Wollongong and Parramatta.[115] St Michael's Wollongong and St John's Parramatta were already "Provisional-Cathedrals." Robinsons' reasons were largely about the problem, as he saw it, that assistant bishops did

---

107. Foord left South Africa in 1989.
108. Cameron, *An Enigmatic* Life, Chapter 12.
109. *Sydney Year Book 1986*, 213.
110. Interview with ED Cameron.
111. *Sydney Year Book 1989*, 227.
112. *Southern Cross* March 1988.
113. *Sydney Year Book 1991*, 258.
114. *Sydney Year Book 1987*, 219–20.
115. *Sydney Year Books*, *1990*, 240 and *1992*, 263.

not have sufficient independent jurisdiction.[116] There were better reasons, as the Synod saw it, to remain undivided, so Sydney has remained huge.

During the Robinson era Moore College continued to expand. DB Knox retired and the Rev. Dr Peter Jensen succeeded him as Principal in 1985. Moore College influenced many external students through its Preliminary Theological Course; and members of its Faculty, notably Bill Dumbrell, Graham Goldsworthy, Peter O'Brien and Paul Barnett, published a significant number of books, including commentaries.

Within Sydney parishes, the home bible study group, a new phenomenon of Evangelicals, was now firmly established. In many places this replaced the Rector's weekly bible study group. Some scoffed at first, but lay men and women were becoming theologically informed as they listened to sermons (sometimes taking notes), owned and read commentaries, and were availing themselves of the PTC courses, or even studying theology for the BD or the ThL by correspondence, at a Bible College, at Moore College, or at the newly established School for Christian Studies (SOCS)—the latter having been born in the Rev. Dr Paul Barnett's lounge-room at Robert Menzies College. The home groups, as they were often called, became the backbone of the local church: fostering a sense of "belonging," giving members ownership of Scriptural studies, giving opportunities to teach, and providing regular times for corporate prayer. These groups were places of encouragement, comfort, shared meals and friendship. They were a taste of the new Christian communities described in the Book of Acts.

Archbishop Donald Robinson was an eirenic man and foremost a scholar. He was also regarded by many as inflexibly legalistic. Toward individuals he was unfailingly kind and non-judgemental. It was his unhappy lot to lead the Diocese of Sydney through very rough seas and under his determined helmsmanship the ship charted its course by a particular reading of the map of the Scriptures, that is, a traditional and Catholic one, which is still the majority position around the Christian world. The crew and the passengers were far from unanimous about the way the map should be read, although as the decade progressed, Robinson and his team of bishops and the Moore College Faculty spoke with authority and with a single voice—any differences of opinion remained hidden below the surface. Once part of a fleet, Sydney and a few other little ships were now tacking in a different direction.

---

116. *Sydney Year Book 1992*, 263–64.

Rev. Dr David Broughton Knox

With the benefit of some 40 years' hindsight, it would seem that the Knox opinion on the General Synod Report on the ordination of women of 1977 had a profound effect upon the way Sydney leaders viewed the Scriptures. Knox by then had guru status, and his conclusions were accepted by the majority. The Knox-Robinson partnership from Moore College days became the authority, via the Moore College Faculty and thence the diocesan clergy, by which the Scriptures in all their complexity were interpreted.

Special mention must be made of those men, who could gain nothing except opprobrium by supporting women's ministry. They were labelled "liberals" and others who agreed with them dared not join them publicly. Among them were Keith Mason, Tim Harris, Stuart Piggin and Gerald Christmas. A number of key clergy stayed publicly silent on the issue, but moved, seemingly with ease, to another diocese where ordained women were accepted and affirmed.[117] There have also been the "daughters of the diocese:" those who continued to minister in the Diocese, did not join MOW, but secretly waited and hoped for change; others waited and hoped, but finally departed for a place where they might be paid to work, using their gifts, full-time.[118]

Rev. Dr Evonne Paddison

117. Such outstanding MTC lecturers as Graham Cole (Principal of Ridley College, Melbourne, then Anglican Professor of Divinity, Beeson Divinity School, Samford University, USA; presently Dean of Trinity Evangelical Divinity School) and Brian Rosner (Principal of Ridley College, Melbourne).

118. The Rev. Di Nicolios, formerly Archdeacon of Women in Sydney, Rector of the large evangelical parish of Diamond Creek 2002–12 (Melbourne Diocese); and the Rev. Dr Evonne Paddison, formerly employed in the Diocese of Sydney, then lecturer at Ridley College, Melbourne, and CEO of Access Ministries, Victoria (2006–2013).

Part of the phenomenon of evangelical Sydney women and men is their focus on ministry rather than upon ordination, sacraments and tradition. This focus upon ministry has ensured that women, even if regarded as subservient to men, and not allowed to be ordained, or even preach, have immense informal influence to their family and to other women. This in turn is a powerful influence upon men. Some call it operating under the radar. Women have simply got on with the task of teaching, writing and pastoring wherever they have seen opportunities. The church is larger, much larger, than the Sunday service inside the consecrated building. Some would say that the real work mostly occurs outside that space. But there is a big "but:" for all the women who seek paid employment in ministry, there are sadly very limited avenues in Sydney. As a consequence, many have gone out to serve as missionaries, and many have left Sydney for paid work in other dioceses.

Chapter 8

The Cost of Relationship 1993–2001

HARRY GOODHEW WAS ARCHBISHOP of Sydney for a relatively short time: eight years. Only two of his predecessors, Bishop Barry and Archbishop Gough, had a similarly brief tenure.[1] During the Goodhew era Sydney turned in upon itself, as though eating its vitals. The election was fiercely contested and the upheavals during his episcopate considerable. Goodhew was out of step with diocesan leaders to a degree perhaps never experienced in Sydney before. This was, on the face of it, remarkable, since Harry Goodhew was a man of particular grace. The length of his term of office was a consequence of his age: he was 62 when elected Archbishop.

It was a particularly painful time for the Diocese. Goodhew came to office at the height of the turmoil over the women's ordination issue, which was proving increasingly divisive over the decade. Not long after this was the notorious Pymble matter, where a congregation sought to divest itself of its rector. Towards the end of his term, the Standing Committee conducted their inquiry into the Anglican Counseling Center and was censured by the Diocesan Synod. These were internal earthquakes. Externally, the Diocese continued to be at loggerheads with the Anglican Church of Australia on a number of matters including the ordination of women to the priesthood. The vexed issue of Lay and Diaconal Presidency at the Holy Communion not only drove a wedge between Goodhew and his synod, but also between Sydney and the ACA; and the publication of a new prayer book exacerbated the ill feeling. In addition Goodhew incurred opprobrium outside the Diocese when, as Metropolitan, he had the unpleasant task of dealing with

---

1. Bishop Barry's term of office was 1884–9 and Archbishop Gough's was 1959–1966. Archbishop Goodhew's was 1 April 1993–19 March 2001—thirteen days short of eight years.

the case of an adulterous bishop of another diocese. As Archbishop, Harry Goodhew never gained the trust of key diocesan men.

Born in 1931, in Sydney, Goodhew has said of himself,

> I'm a son of the diocese. I was converted in the diocese, I was nurtured in the diocese, I worked as a youth worker in the diocese, I was trained at Moore College, I was deputy senior student, I was a member of YECL [Young Evangelical Churchman's League], I read papers at YECL with Peter O'Brien. One of the formative influences in my life was Broughton as a teacher, Donald Robinson, Marcus Loane. I spoke for Marcus Loane when he refused to go to a joint service with the Pope. . . So I always thought of myself as a son of the diocese. I think, in a sense, that those who have assumed leadership have a different understanding of what that meant. And different agendas.[2]

As a young man in the capacity of a youth worker he attended conferences outside Sydney where he saw aspects of the Anglican Church which were different from what he had been used to. Later, working with the BCA (Bush Church Aid Society) in the Adelaide Diocese, he came to appreciate the strengths and weaknesses he saw there. Above all, he became convinced that ministry was based on relationships: "if you didn't build relationships, you didn't have a ministry." For him, the term "diocese" is primarily the parishes: the people in them and those who minister to them.

Ordained priest in 1958, he was Curate at St Matthew's Bondi, then Curate-in-Charge at Beverley Hills 1959–63, then with BCA Ceduna 1963–66. From 1966–71 he was Rector of St Paul's Carlingford. He then went to the Brisbane Diocese where he was Rector of the evangelical St Stephen's Coorparoo. In 1976 he returned to the Sydney Diocese to be Rector of St Michael's Wollongong and Rural Dean of Wollongong. From 1979 to 1982 he was Archdeacon of Wollongong and Camden. He was Bishop of Wollongong from 1982 until elected Archbishop Sydney in April 1993. His parish experience was probably greater than that of any of his predecessors. This ought to have been a huge asset for the new shepherd of God's flock in Sydney but there were a few potential drawbacks from the Sydney leaders' perspective. He was relatively unknown, since his work had been mostly outside the Sydney Diocese or in Wollongong, to the south of the city of Sydney. This meant fewer links forged with the key Sydney men and, when he made his key appointments, he relied on the Wollongong people, rather than key Sydney men. In addition, he had not come via Moore College as a revered teacher and mentor there, as both Marcus

2. Harry Goodhew interview with MHC 15.2.10.

Loane and Donald Robinson had done (and Peter Jensen, his successor). Moore College and the Diocese are so welded together, that the Rev. Dr John Woodhouse has said,

> Some people have talked to me about the relationship between the College and the Diocese, and I say, "Well that's a really funny thing to ask about. The Diocese created this College, and this College created the Diocese." They're not separate. They are inseparable. The teaching here, particularly from Broughton, that was the most powerful thing in our generation, that has permeated the Diocese. The Diocese is distinctive. Why? Because of the teaching that happened here. But how did it happen here? The relationship is inseparable.[3]

In terms of academic achievement, Harry had gained his university degree quite late. He was awarded an MA (Hons) from Wollongong University in 1990, and an honorary doctorate from the same university in 1993. These things matter to some Sydney people: did it mean he was an "intellectual lightweight"? Furthermore, his academic mentor had been Dr Stuart Piggin, a member of the Standing Committee, but regarded as "liberal" for his forthright support of the ordination of women to the priesthood. There were those who thought Harry Goodhew was inclined to be "weak," not strong enough to hold the Sydney line when it counted. His considerable gifts for relationship might well weaken his ability to be a tough and uncompromising leader.

Donald Robinson retired in early 1993. In the lead-up to electing his successor and even before his retirement, two new groups sprang up in the Diocese. REPA (Reformed Evangelical Protestant Association), later known as The Grim Reaper by its critics; and Anglicans Together.[4] REPA began as an informal gathering of Sydney's younger and more accomplished clergy to discuss "how the Anglican church could change for the better." Its foundation statement read:

> We are a group of Reformed evangelical protestant pastors of churches in Sydney, who are dissatisfied with our Association of churches [that is, the Anglican Church of Australia] because of its failure to: stimulate growth, develop resources, maintain evangelicalism, handle controversy, and spread and establish the gospel. Therefore we are meeting to try to rectify the weaknesses in our Association, whose place in our society is diminishing and whose integrity to our theological position is compromised . . .

---

3. Woodhouse interview with MHC 30.5.2011.
4. REPA began in February 1992 and Anglicans Together in July 1992.

> The essential change that we need to make is to put our reformed evangelical theology (with its characteristic evangelical style of ministry) ahead of any denominational, institutional or vested interest at every level of our Association. It is not a grand stroke but a thousand changes that need to be made. However, all the changes run in the same direction, so that our Association will reinforce, assist and spread our pastoral ministries. It is a grass roots rather than centrally organized change in direction based in theology and evangelism rather than in liturgy and structuralism.[5]

Members of REPA included the Rev. Phillip Jensen, the Rev. Dr John Woodhouse, the Rev. Robert Forsyth and the Rev. Bruce Ballantine-Jones. The group had a certain revolutionary fervor and according to Harry Goodhew, damaged a lot of friendships as people felt they ought to take sides.[6] By the beginning of 1993, REPA claimed to represent almost half of the 400 clergy in the diocese.[7] Phillip Jensen was chairman of REPA when he, with nine other men, was nominated to be Archbishop of Sydney. This deflected REPA from its initial aims, as many of its members threw their weight behind Phillip Jensen.

Anglicans Together had a membership of about 250 by the beginning of 1993. By contrast with REPA, most of its members were lay. According to John Cornish, later the President of Anglicans Together, the group was formed to "arrange for a moderate person to be elected archbishop."[8]

Of the seven nominations, the final names were those of Bishop Paul Barnett, Bishop Harry Goodhew, Bishop John Reid and Phillip Jensen. Jensen had multiple nominations (some 44 proposers and another 44 seconders), far more than the others. There was a strong lay vote against Jensen, and two epithets used of him in the synod debate hit their mark. Jensen was described "as a bull in a china shop" and having a "polarising personality."[9] Hearing this, the scales fell from the eyes of some of Phillip's supporters. Reid, though immensely capable and experienced, was thought to be "weak" on the women's issue, and he was already 64. At the time the retiring age for an archbishop was 70.[10] In the Final List of 30 March, Jensen and Reid were

---

5. Quoted from McGillion, *The Chosen Ones*, 8–9.
6. McGillion, *The Chosen Ones*, 10.
7. "War in the Cloisters," *Sydney Morning Herald*, 13.3.1993, 39.
8. McGillion, *The Chosen Ones*, 10.
9. McGillion, *The Chosen Ones*, 14; MHC recollection..
10. This was changed in 1993 when the retirement age was retained at 70 years for Robinson's successor, but with a 65-year limit to take effect after that. The Synod had the power to extend the retirement age to 70 under the Retirements Ordinance 1993

dropped, leaving Barnett and Goodhew. Barnett was a moderate, a scholar, a fine pastor, and the author of excellent commentaries and books on New Testament theology and history. He had been a member of the Faculty of Moore College, or a visiting lecturer there, since 1963. The voting, in each of the two houses of clergy and lay, was close. The clergy vote for Goodhew was 137 and for Barnett 122. It was, as Chris McGillion has written, "an ominously weak mandate" for Goodhew.[11] Ironically, according to Dr Stephen Judd, Harry Goodhew was most people's *second choice*. The situation ensured that the second choice of a number of people became the first choice.[12]

Archbishop Harry Goodhew

—*Sydney Year Book* 1994, 721–28.
11. McGillion, *The Chosen Ones*, 16.
12. Stephen Judd interview with MHC 4.5.11.

Bishop Donald Cameron presided at the Election Synod, and Bishop John Reid, the Administrator of the Diocese, gave the Presidential Address. Reid began his address by defining the "unique" ethos of the Diocese of Sydney. He noted seven significant influences. The first was the influence of Holy Scripture. He said,

> Leaving aside the teaching of the place of Holy Scripture at Moore College and serious debates on Scripture in Synod, I can say that throughout the life of the Diocese there has been a conspicuous emphasis on parishioners reading and obeying the Scripture in their daily lives. For generations through sermons, Sunday School classes and confirmation classes, Anglican Christians have been vigorously encouraged to read the Bible daily and to live by its truth. From the beginning of this century it was not always so elsewhere. The Bible was recommended in many places to be read with caution and its historicity was questioned. By the grace of God, in Sydney men and women had the strong encouragement over many generations to read the Scripture and to tremble at its truth. The widespread daily reading of Scripture and its exposition in the churches has entered into the soul of this Diocese and is at the center of its life.[13]

The second was the proclamation of a need for a spiritual birth: "the first chaplains in the colony had this clearly before them and it has been so ever since." Third, the Convention movement, replaced more recently by the CMS Summer School at Katoomba where there was "a balance between exposition, godly and missionary obedience." Fourth, the widespread endorsement of the voluntary society principle: Reid stated "there was not another diocese in Australia which has so committed itself to this principle so that the support of bodies not under the control of the Synod or the bishop has been considered normal." Fifth, the active and powerful involvement of the laity: theologically literate, spiritually aware people who have exercised influence and the result was "a great independence in the diocese." Sixth, an involvement in social justice. For example, the Home Mission Society (HMS) was one of the largest welfare organisations in the country.[14] Seventh, a learned group of clergy, because of the strong emphasis on academic enhancement of its ministers.

Reid's masterly analysis is an insider's perspective of the Diocese. Outsiders would note key issues which divided Sydney from most of the rest of the ACA: for example, attitude to clerical dress, to the sacraments, to

---

13. Presidential Address *Sydney Year Book 1994*, 252–53.
14. HMS was re-named "Anglicare" in 1997, *Southern Cross* September, 1.

the Prayer Book and liturgy, and to the role of women. What Reid noted are fundamental to Sydney's ethos, while what outsiders perceive is a result of Sydney Diocese's unique compound personality. His emphasis upon the centrality of Scripture as the primary influence is correct. It explains much of Sydney's ethos. It has created great tension within and without the Diocese when different people have read the same words and arrived at a different answer—especially when no room is allowed for the validity of another's interpretation. In the matters arising during Goodhew's episcopate, each of the differing parties would claim Scripture as their guide. It is unthinkable not to do so, in the Diocese of Sydney.

Further on in his address Reid gave some NCLS (National Church Life Survey) statistics for religion in Australia. The Diocese of Sydney was ahead of other Protestant churches in its *growth*: 15% as against the national average of 6%. Congregation sizes were larger than in other Anglican dioceses: 75% had congregations of fewer than 100 people, while Sydney had 56%. More young people were attending church in Sydney: there 41% were under the age of 40, while elsewhere only 34% of Anglicans were under the age of 40. Reid noted in passing that "if certain large congregations had cooperated in the Survey, I am advised that the rate could have been higher." This could only be a reference to St Matthias: Phillip Jensen's hugely successful parish with its seven congregations.[15]

Reid's final words were devoted to the question of the unity of the ACA: and whether Sydney should secede or remain within the fold. He noted that Sydney had decided to support the Constitution "at a time when theological liberalism and ritualism were more pronounced and vocal than probably they are now." He noted that since then more than 60 Moore College graduates had been licensed to an appointment in another diocese: some of which had not previously opened their doors to Sydney-trained men. Unity grew after the acceptance of the *AAPB* (the Green Prayer Book of 1978), but more recently there were signs in some elections for the national church "that there is a prejudice against Sydney from other dioceses." He then quoted from the letter from Archbishop Woods, in which the Archbishop had written that the response to the new Prayer Book, grants made to the endowments of some country dioceses and the influence of its Archbishop visiting many dioceses had done more for Anglican unity than any other section

---

15. McGillion, *The Chosen Ones*, 12: well over 1000 people were meeting weekly in seven congregations linked to the parish.

of the Church.[16] Reid concluded: "Frankly, I want to see Sydney regain its sphere of influence and not to retreat into a ghetto."[17]

One of the problems for Harry Goodhew, as Sydney's new Archbishop, was how to foster good relations with the rest of Australian Anglicans, without forgoing the trust of his own diocesan leaders. In his first Presidential Address he spoke of being "dynamically Anglican" and proposed a strategy of growth, which began with prayer. He was clearly a prayerful man, speaking of the church living *Coram Deo*—in the presence of God. He said:

> Those who pray well, listen well. We must listen to God as he addresses us in and through his word. The Scriptures are our guide, as Christ, by his Spirit, causes new light to shine from them for our direction. God must be allowed to speak in our midst and we must continually learn to listen and obey. The humility and preparedness to engage with one another in understanding God's purpose for us now is a major priority. God "opposes the proud, but gives grace to the humble." Therefore in humility of spirit we must seek to be taught afresh to listen to God in his Word and follow Him with courage and devotion.[18]

Various people in interviews have volunteered that in Sydney there should be more "waiting on God" in prayer. It seems that Harry Goodhew thought so too. Too many "how to vote" tickets, too much caucusing before meetings, too much politicking.[19]

During Goodhew's first year in office he developed a five-point focus for the Diocese. He visited every area deanery to explain it, and encouraged his team of bishops and archdeacons to promote it.[20] It was: To be more and more Observably God's People, Pastorally Effective, Evangelistically Enterprising, Genuinely Caring and Dynamically Anglican. He promoted it throughout his episcopate, but it didn't seem to percolate through. It did not inspire. This was the era of mission statements and often it was only the CEO who could recite them. Later, Mrs. Pam Goodhew said of them,

> Harry had five points that were quite brilliant but some people said "I don't know what he means by that." Things like "Observably God's People." I'm thinking "Why can't they understand what that means?"

16. See Chapter 6.
17. Presidential Address *Sydney Year Book 1994*, 263.
18. Presidential Address *Sydney Year Book 1994*, 303 and 323.
19. Robinson interview with MHC 8.5.2013, Rodgers interview with MHC 9.5.2011.
20. Rodgers conversation with MHC 9.5.2011, Alicia Watson interview with MHC 2.5.2011.

> I thought they summed up what we hoped to see happen. Harry really felt that the place for things to happen was in the parish—a lot more than in the Standing Committee or those institutions, because he was a parish man for 20-odd years and felt that was really where the strength lay.[21]

Whether the parish is the right place for an archbishop's focus is a moot point. On the one hand, the parish is where the pastoring and teaching and evangelism are largely done. The REPA people would have agreed with this, and it harks back to the Knox-Robinson view of the congregation as the gathered people of God. But the problem with this, is that every congregation would be "doing its own thing" without reference to the bishops, archbishop or wider Anglican Church. Harry himself, by 1994, was saying, in his Presidential Address, "We are more than just a conglomerate of otherwise autonomous units."[22] His predecessor had found that the parishes with their rectors were indeed almost completely a law unto themselves: the rectors were like mini popes.

Harry Goodhew's first months in office were very challenging. He had a Standing Committee, which, in Stephen Judd's words, were "playing hard ball."[23] Harry's wife Pam remembers that some members of the Standing Committee made life very difficult for him. She stated:

> Never once did he malign them. He used to say, "They've got a point of view, they've got a right to say what they want to say" and he would absorb all their anger and pray for them. I saw that all the time. And I've got to say that I wasn't so godly. I had some very unkind thoughts about the behaviour of some people because of the treatment through Standing Committee that Harry had to go through.[24]

Elections for a new Standing Committee came up in the Synod of October 1993. Stephen Judd, with a number of others, was of the view that the elected archbishop ought to be given a free rein to succeed or fail. With this in view, he and a handful of others devised what came to be called the "Blue Ticket:" an alternative list of people from the ACL list, as a how to vote ticket, for Standing Committee. He recalled:

---

21. Goodhew interview with MHC 15.2.2010.
22. *Sydney Year Book 1996*, 321.
23. Judd interview with MHC 4.5.11. Dr. Judd was a member of the Sydney Standing Committee 1994–1995 and is co-author of the official Sydney Diocesan history, *Sydney Anglicans*.
24. Goodhew interview with MHC 15.2.2010.

When the election came up in the October, it was the only time that the ACL was dented. If you were on both the ACL ticket and the Blue Ticket, you were elected, and eight others from the ACL ticket were elected and eight from the Blue Ticket. It evened it up a bit. Two of the notable non-elected, and I remember sitting in the Synod next to them, when it was going on, were Laurie Scandrett and Bruce Ballantine-Jones.[25]

The "Blue Ticket" people faded into the background in the next few years. They had been, quite deliberately, a very small group of people, with "no organization, no bank account, no office bearers." They were "quite deliberately a non-organization."[26] They achieved very little: Bruce Ballantine-Jones used his considerable energy and acumen to pump new life into the ACL, in the next seven years doubling its membership to 400.[27] In the 1996 elections for Standing Committee, Ballantine-Jones did a deal with the Blue Ticket people, and by 1999 the ACL had recovered complete ascendancy.[28] Phillip Jensen became a member of the Standing Committee in 1993. Before this time, and before the run-up to the archbishop's election Synod, he had kept quite aloof from diocesan polity. The election had politicised him, but already he was a very considerable influence in Sydney. In the decade of the nineties and the one following, he was without question the most powerful man in the Diocese, and his huge influence has stamped the diocese with its present character. But before we look at Phillip, we must turn to the Pymble matter.

In early 1993 a new rector took up his duties in the leafy North Shore parish of Pymble. But within months of his arrival he fell out with parishioners and staff, to the point where he was encouraged to find another place to minister, because he was a "square peg in a round hole" as one prominent parishioner put it. Usually, when a congregation and its rector disagree, the unhappy parishioners depart. On this occasion, the parishioners did not follow that precedent but decided that it was their parish, the rector was the most recent arrival and they did not want to go. The parish's corporate unity had been built up over the previous decade by bible study groups, which met weekly, where genuine friendships were fostered. Public meetings, by invitation only, to discuss the situation and find a solution, were held in the Kur-ring-gai Town Hall. By November, the Parish Council, noting that the Rector had lost the confidence of the majority of the congregation and had declined the unanimous request by the wardens and the advice of the

25. Judd interview with MHC 4.5.11.
26. Judd interview with MHC 4.5.11.
27. McGillion, *The Chosen Ones*, 25.
28. NM Cameron interview with MHC March 2014.

regional Bishop and the Archbishop to resign, directed the wardens to secure the Rector's resignation.[29]

Finally, an enquiry under the Incapacity and Inefficiency Ordinance 1906 investigated the events which had occurred in Pymble parish and reported to the Archbishop that there were circumstances "that raised the question of the removal of the Rector on the grounds of incapacity and inefficiency." In March 1994 three Commissioners were appointed to investigate the case.[30]

In all, the Commissioners interviewed 58 people and costs ran to some $201,353. The Commissioners (who performed their duties unpaid) handed their report to the Archbishop in September 1994, recommending the Rector's removal from Pymble. The Pymble Matter was extremely divisive in the parish itself, the youth work dissolved, and congregational numbers dropped. It was divisive in the Diocese, with people taking sides and the Synod of October 1994 was memorably acrimonious. Archbishop Goodhew took the brunt of the great anger of the many people supporting the Rector. It was an issue which revealed a clergy/lay split: the clergy expected their archbishop to back one of their number, revealing a certain "clergy club" mentality. The matter was notorious throughout Australia and as far away as England. Synod wrestled for the next 20 years with the issues arising. Bills and ordinances attempted solutions: the Parish Disputes Ordinance, finally passed in 1999, was the fruit of the work of a Select Committee dating back to 1994.[31] This ordinance legislated "for a disputes resolution procedure between a minister and his parish." Despite this, the issue remained unsolved, and the ordinance was never implemented. Clergy resistance to it was the main reason for the impasse. It has been described as "a hollow piece of legislation."[32] The 1999 Synod Report on Clerical Tenure arose out of the Pymble Matter, as did the Parish Relationships Bill. This aimed "to provide the appropriate structure for certain parishes to have licensing reviews carried out by godly and competent people." Synod did not assent to it.[33]

29. St Swithun's Pymble Parish Council Minutes 9.11.1993.

30. Presidential Address, *Sydney Year Book* 1995, 393-94, *Southern Cross* February 1994, 9.

31. *Sydney Year Book* 2000, 601-17.

32. Bellenger interview with MHC 29.7.2013. The 1999 Synod Report on Clerical Tenure arose out of the Pymble Matter: *Sydney Year Book* 2000, 450.

33. *Sydney Year Book* 2000, 462-69. Bruce Ballantine-Jones analyzed the Pymble Matter in his PhD thesis, "Changes in policy and practises in the Anglican Diocese of Sydney 1966-2013: the political factor," 2013, 207-212. Ballantine-Jones concluded: "The safeguards of ministerial independence had been overturned by a novel interpretation of a little used ordinance which was assumed to relate to matters of mental or physical incapacity. It was a very unpopular decision among clergy."

Harry Goodhew's struggles with the Standing Committee continued throughout his episcopate. By 1995 he stated:

> People who push the edges are both a blessing and a bane. They can force the wider constituency out of lethargy and acceptance of the status quo. In that role they are the saviors of an organization, and deliver it from death by atrophy. They can be a sign of the future. On the other hand, they can be iconoclastic and unnecessarily destructive, eliminating and uprooting structures which serve a beneficial and enduring purpose. In times such as ours, radicals and conservatives must find constructive common cause in charting the future.[34]

There can be little doubt that he was addressing the REPA elements of the Standing Committee. He spoke more bluntly towards the end of the same Presidential Address. He said,

> I am greatly disturbed by an opinion I saw expressed in a recent ACL publication. It said, "The synodical process is not based on truth but on numbers. Decisions in Synod are made on the basis of majority opinion. Furthermore, Synod members are not always elected on the basis of their godly discernment and wisdom."
>
> Do many here share that opinion? If that view of Synod is widely held we should stop meeting now . . . .
>
> . . . my remarks spring from concern for the church in this diocese, not lack of it . . . I want to preside over an assembly of God's people where participants wait on God for guidance, look for truth from anyone who speaks it, and offer respect to those with whom they differ. If the group and the party rule, liberty of thought and freedom of conscience will go.[35]

These were prophetic words.

He also struggled with Moore College, of which Peter Jensen was now Principal. Harry sought involvement with the selection process for ordination. He appointed Archdeacon Paul Perini Ordination Chaplain and Archdeacon for Ordination and Ministry Development. Perini had a panel to assist him to select people who were suitable according to such criteria as ability to lead a congregation of at least 100–150 people, personal and spiritual life and psychological health. Goodhew remembers:

> The College leadership was not happy about the move and raised questions about it . . . One major concern for them was

---

34. Presidential Address *Sydney Year Book 1997*, 321.
35. Presidential Address *Sydney Year Book 1997*, 336.

the possibility of a conflict arising where the Diocesan Selectors might accept someone whom the College might not want to accept. This remained a tension.

Phillip Jensen is a phenomenon in the phenomenal Diocese of Sydney. In some ways an enigma like his hero Broughton Knox, he is, on any view, enormously gifted, influential and successful. As with Broughton Knox, his name evokes extreme reactions, from adulation to loathing. His perceived public and private personae are quite different: publicly he can be insensitive and provocative; privately he is kind, gracious and charming. A further layer of complexity is that people regularly confuse him with his very able brother Peter who had succeeded Broughton Knox as Principal of Moore College and who became Sydney's 11th Archbishop in 2001.

Rev. Phillip Jensen

Tall, well built and handsome, Phillip is quintessentially a leader. He has a charismatic personality. His greatest success has been with university students and his ministry there has borne amazing fruit. According to his website CV, he made his public profession of faith at the 1959 Billy Graham Crusade. He attended Moore College and was ordained in 1970. From 1973–4 he worked with John Chapman for Evangelism Ministries (then called the Department of Evangelism). His website states:

> From that time to today, Phillip's main work has been his regular exposition of the Scriptures. Be it at the university at lunch times, on the weekend in church, or more lately at the Cathedral lunchtime ministry and weekend preaching, Phillip has devoted himself to preaching Christ by consistently expounding the Bible. His pastoral counselling, evangelistic ministries, polemical and apologetic forays, itinerant preaching, and initiatives in founding new ministries, organizations and media have all taken place in the context of this basic work of teaching the Scriptures week by week.[36]

He was Chaplain at the University of NSW from 1975 to 2005. By 1993 his 50 minute long Bible lectures attracted some 850 students each week, who also met in 35 Bible study groups, led by a team of 39 pastors. According to a Herald journalist, it was "part of a highly organised, well-oiled machine."[37] His time at UNSW was immensely influential: many students went on to train at Moore College for ordination. A survey of clergy in the 2006 Sydney *Year Book* reveals some 76 clergy had graduated from UNSW during Phillip's time there: almost certainly most of these people had been influenced by him.

That in itself would have been a considerable achievement. But there is more: much more. He went as Rector to the parish of St Matthias' Centennial Park, in 1978, and remained there until 2003. While he was Rector, the congregation grew from about 30 to well over a 1000 by the mid 1990s. By 1993 the church had seven congregations and ran 103 home Bible study groups.[38] From 1996 to 2001 a total of 54 St Matthias men and women went to Moore College to study theology; in 1993 20–30% of the first year intake at Moore College were Matthias men and women.[39] This was a big proportion of candidates from one parish out of Sydney's 270 parishes. In the years

---

36. http://phillipjensen.com/about/#sthash.8ZAntEgh.dpuf.
37. "War in the Cloisters" *Sydney Morning Herald* 13.3.1993, 39.
38. Ibid.
39. MTC Registrar data; "War in the Cloisters" *Sydney Morning Herald* 13.3.1993, p39

to come, a considerable proportion of Sydney clergy would be Phillip Jensen protégés: some have estimated it to be as much as 25% by 2013.[40] A large number of Phillip Jensen men have also become clergy in the Presbyterian Church of Australia.[41]

Phillip speaks with great authority. When he speaks it is as though there is no other truth, no other alternative. Like Jesus his master, he uses hyperbole, which his disciples have not always borne in mind. Some of them have the reputation of being less nuanced, more extreme, than Phillip himself.

His drive and vision were recognised by Bishop John Reid, Chairman of the Katoomba Christian Convention Council, and Phillip Jensen joined the Council in 1974. At this time the Convention was in the doldrums. The first Katoomba Youth Convention (KYC), of which Phillip was Chairman, was held in 1974 and displayed a fundamental change from the Keswick pietism which had marked the Convention's previous 40 years.[42] About 600 hundred attended, considerably more than at the previous convention. By 1982 numbers had swelled to 1,500, and 3,000–4,000 were expected the following year. Phillip Jensen became Chairman Katoomba Christian Convention Council in 1983, having by this time set his stamp on the Convention. By 1988 6,000 attended the Convention: the largest number in its history. Stuart Braga, in *A Century Preaching Christ*, stated,

> When Phillip Jensen concluded his eight years as Chairman in 1991, the transformation of the Convention was complete. It was again becoming the spiritual powerhouse for the Christian community of Sydney that it had been for so many years, and was once more focussed on the needs of Christian people, especially Christian youth.[43]

Phillip's influence extended widely through his publishing company, Matthias Media. This began as an activity under the name of "St Matthias Press and Tapes." Tony Payne became editor of the new publishing venture in 1988. By 1994 the name was changed to Matthias Media. *The Briefing*, a monthly journal, publishes articles on conservative evangelical theology, book reviews and bible studies. According to Ian Carmichael of St Matthias

---

40. Huntly Gordon to MHC, March 2014.

41. Ibid.

42. He was KYC Chairman 1974–1991 and Chairman of the Convention Council 1983-1991.

43. Braga, *A Century Preaching Christ*, 131–44. See also *Southern Cross* April 1998 re inaugural Men's Katoomba Event where "almost 4,000 men gathered." By 2000, 7,000 men attended the Katoomba Men's Convention.

Press, in 2013 it had a "strong readership in print and online around the world." The Press has produced many books, including many bible study guides. St Matthias Press developed The Good Book Company in the United Kingdom, "a very successful publishing company in its own right."[44] Matthias Media's two best-known printed resources would be *Two Ways to Live* and *The Trellis and the Vine*. Intervarsity Press (IVP) UK, has distributed the Matthias Media resources throughout the world since 2005. The publisher also has had a branch office in the United States since 2005. Phillip is the author of a number of these publications: some thirteen bible study guides, seven books and some tracts. He is a fine communicator: such titles as *Pure Sex, Prayer and the Voice of God* and *Free for All* provide a sound bite of his skill[45]. The result of Matthias Media and its offspring is that Phillip's influence has extended far beyond Sydney.

In addition, Phillip has undertaken many speaking engagements including university missions, student training conferences, church planting conferences and clergy conferences, in Australia and in the UK. He was involved in the establishment of the Evangelical Ministers Assembly, the Proclamation Trust and the London Men's Convention. His influence on Evangelicals in England has been considerable, particularly through his association with St Helen's Bishopsgate, where the Rev. Dick Lucas was the Rector for almost 40 years (1961 to 1998).

Phillip Jensen has arguably been the most powerful influence in Sydney from the 1980s. This has not been via the well-established pathways to Anglican power: he has been a parish clergyman, a university chaplain until the end of the Goodhew era, and a failed contender for the position of Archbishop of Sydney. He has not been consecrated as a bishop and until 1993 was not even a member of the Standing Committee of the Sydney Synod. But it is his influence over thousands of young men and women students, on the threshold of adulthood, who in their turn have exercised great influence as parish clergy, that is possibly the greatest measure of his influence in Sydney. Add to that his written work and his speaking engagements elsewhere: countless lay people have been indelibly changed by him.

Phillip has also exercised considerable influence over clergy training, through the MT&D, the Sydney Diocesan Ministry Training and Development, as Director from 2003–2012. According to some who have worked in this sphere with him, his method is didactic: telling people how to think rather than giving them a toolkit to use to think out issues for themselves.

---

44. Ian Carmichael email to MHC 18.6.2013.

45. 1,500 copies of *Pure Sex* were sold in two hours at Katoomba Men's Convention in February 1999—*Southern Cross* April 1999, 5.

His greatest achievement is as an evangelist. He is passionate for people to hear the gospel of Christ and to respond by lifelong commitment to Him.[46] Countless people owe their new life in Christ to hearing him preach, and to be built up in the faith by his sound biblical teaching. This is Phillip's great strength.[47]

But there is a "but." There are several, in fact. They go some way to explain Sydney Diocese as it has developed in the last two decades. The first is Phillip's apparent lack of interest in being traditionally Anglican. This has manifested itself in a number of ways and was not peculiar to Phillip. Harry Goodhew recollected,

> I recall the occasion when Donald Robinson required of Phillip Jensen certain conformity to clerical undertakings. Donald was forced, in the light of Phillip's unwillingness to comply, to announce that he was a clergyman in whom he could no longer have confidence. As one of Donald's assistant bishops I shared in a small committee that was appointed to look into the matter . . . The outcome was from memory, far from satisfactory. I do not think it was ever resolved. However, it provided an example of how the situation with regard to episcopal regulation was tending. No one was going to back an Archbishop who insisted on the use of Prayer Book services or distinctive dress. It was not improving in my time. I certainly had no desire just to let illegal things progress but there was in actuality no functioning and supported mechanism to curb them.

Goodhew also said,

> A new mindset was taking hold of the clergy and leading laypeople that would not accept the discipline that a bishop might wish to exercise. It was, in my estimation, a case of the governed not wishing to be governed.[48]

Bishop Peter Watson, later Archbishop of Melbourne (2001–6) stated:

> The irony of Sydney is that it spends hours debating legislation, then the clergy go and do precisely what they want. But we dot i's and cross t's in the debate, you know, phrases and whatevers. It is certainly regarded as legalistic but I don't know that the

---

46. Braga, *A Century Preaching Christ*, 132.
47. Bellenger interview with MHC 29.7.2013.
48. Goodhew letter to MHC. Undated but around April 2010.

archbishops have held the clergy to account or breathed down their necks! It was certainly not my experience.[49]

Phillip was the front man for what John Reid called "extreme congregationalism" —the view that the local congregation is the only valid expression of the church, ignoring the concept of the wider church. Reid went on to say,

> This concept—first promoted by Dr Broughton Knox—would make the diocese a mere service appendage to the local congregation. It also disregards any concept of the larger Anglican Community.
>
> This movement has been accompanied by denigration of the office of bishop in the diocese which would make bishops servants of the local church and mere administrative functionaries.[50]

Of course, Phillip and iconoclasts like him were not new in the Diocese: Broughton Knox had made no secret of his dismissive views on the episcopacy.[51] Apart from taking a leading role in the re-Anglicanising of Sydney, there were other aspects of Phillip which were controversial, and remain so. There was his hardline approach to able young men entering the professions: he strenuously encouraged them to enter the ministry. It was perceived as a devaluing of the professions *vis-à-vis* ministry. It has possibly caused a diminution of able Christian professionals at the top of their tree.[52] This attitude caused a rather public disagreement between John Stott and Phillip.

Phillip's passion for evangelism seemed to overwhelm sensitivity to social issues. John Reid alluded to this in his comments on REPA when he stated that he was strongly opposed to the view that proclamation of the Gospel message and personal salvation were paramount, while social welfare efforts were not essential to the church's mission. It was a veiled reference to Phillip.[53] In addition, according to the Rev. Dr Greg Anderson, personal evangelism was extremely important, to the point that "in some people's thinking, the main mark of Christian maturity is evangelistic courage and evangelistic practice."[54] Others see this kind of focus on evangelism

---

49. Peter Watson interview with MHC 28.10.2008.
50. "War in the Cloisters," *Sydney Morning Herald* 13.3.1993, 39.
51. Cameron, *An Enigmatic Life*, 193.
52. Conversation with Bellenger January 2014.
53. "War in the Cloisters" *Sydney Morning Herald* 13.3.1993.
54. Greg Anderson interview with MHC 12.7.2013. Anderson was Head of the Department of Mission at Moore College 2007–2014 and elected Bishop of the Northern Territory in June 2014. See also Giles, "An outsider's response to an insider's defence of the Anglican Diocese of Sydney," Michael Jensen, *Sydney Anglicanism*," 8.

as unbalanced: there was too little emphasis on living *in Coram Deo*, as Goodhew put it.

Finally we come to Phillip's theology on women in ministry. In May 2013, I sent him a letter.

> Dear Phillip,
>
> Just so that I have an accurate understanding of your position on women in the church, would you mind answering the following questions?
>
> 1. What do you understand as the biblical role of women in the church? Please include the following:
>   - Leading services,
>   - Reading the Bible,
>   - Preaching,
>   - Teaching in a mixed Bible study group,
>   - Ordination to the priesthood
> 2. What is your understanding of the Bible's teaching on the above?
> 3. What do you understand by "headship"?
> 4. Do you see any anomalies in this position (e.g. women missionaries planting churches)?
> 5. Have you published anything on the above?
>
> Please be assured I do not want to "set you up" in any way, but I do want clear statements as to your position.
>
> Many thanks,
>
> Marcia

Phillip finally granted me an interview in April 2014. It was very amicable. He stated that he was not prepared to answer the questions I had put to him in my letter. He said,

> That is a topic so massive that every sentence has to be put in the right context. Because my assumptions, and philosophies about ministry, ordination, work and things like that are so different from other people's, when they hear my comment on women they don't put it in this framework.

Asked about what he allowed women to do in public, to mixed congregations, he replied, "I'm not going to answer because that's legalism." He spoke of three views of professional ministry: a governmental view (coming from our English heritage), a business view ("from our American brethren") and the family view (the one which he holds). The family view is that

> The congregation is a family and my staff our families. I don't employ them, I live with them. I don't treat members of my family by rules and regulations, authorities or structures. I'll let them do anything that is helpful and beneficial to them. And when I see something they're no good at, I'll say "Oh, how about we get someone else to do that and you do this." My colleagues are my brothers and my sisters and I want to treat them as a family man in a family . . . Now in families men are men and women are women. So equal and different is the shorthand thing that I am committed to. I don't treat my sisters as brothers and I don't treat my brothers as sisters. I treat them as equals but I treat them differently.

Phillip would not be drawn into articulating exactly what this meant in practice. He has written very little on the subject of women in the church. In an article entitled *The Ordination of Women as Presbyters*, he wrote,

> At the climax of the ordination of presbyters the bishop places a Bible into the hands of the ordinand and says "Take thou authority to preach the Word of God . . ." In the Bible God says "I do not permit a woman to teach or have authority over a man . . . ." (1 Tim 2:12). We have little option but to follow God's command on this matter.
>
> The public media do not understand this way of thinking. They never will. We must not be bullied by public debate conducted by people who do not come to church and have no intention of ever coming. Church people need to make the decision based upon the Word of God. The Church is to speak God's message to the world rather than have the world speak its message to the church.[55]

Anecdotal evidence is that women in Phillip's church are not to lead mixed gender Bible studies, nor lead services, nor preach. He is most definitely opposed to the ordination of women to the priesthood.

Back in 1995 the *Briefing* devoted an entire double edition to the subject of women preaching to mixed congregations. It contained articles by Gary Nelson, Kirsty Birkett, Peter Bolt, Lesley Ramsay, Mark Thompson, Claire Smith, Marion Gabbott, Glenn Davies, and Greg Clarke, some of

---

55. http://phillipjensen.com/articles/the-ordination-of-women-as-presbyters.

whom were influential Diocesan clergy. It also offered a collection of taped sermons by Phillip Jensen advertised as "six addresses from I Timothy 2." The *Briefing* edition runs to 27 pages of well-argued, well-written text promoting the view that women should not preach to mixed congregations. A keen Sydney Christian person who read this would be very much disposed to be persuaded by what is really a barrage offensive.[56]

A female who attended one of Phillip's conferences while a medical student has written about Phillip's interpretation of I Corinthians 14:35. She recalled:

> I went to the MYC (mid year conference) when I was at UNSW in 1995. The only thing I really remember from that conference is a Q & A session at the end of one evening with Phillip Jensen. There were a lot of people there—hundreds. Someone asked him what he would do if a woman asked him a question privately e.g. after church. He replied that if the woman was married, he would tell her to go and ask her husband. If her husband was not able to answer the question, then he could come and ask Phillip, Phillip would tell him the answer, and then the husband would be able to go and reply to the wife. However, if the woman was not married, then Phillip would answer her question himself. I was quite astonished, but everyone else there was nodding and he was obviously held in such high regard by the group. I didn't hear anyone comment on it.[57]

Greg Anderson believes that a revolution has occurred in the Diocese of Sydney since the 1970s. He said:

> I don't know how many years from 1980 to 1990 were the big years of the move towards *informal* liturgy in the Sydney Diocese, and I think Phillip was a leader in that, so things that had been regarded as mainstream evangelical Anglicanism were more and more pushed to the margins. I don't know how that happened on a parish by parish basis, but now, as you know, the default setting around Sydney is that if a book is used at all, it is only used for the traditional 8.00 am service for the oldies, and everything else is family service or contemporary service, and there are many flagship churches in the Diocese whose meeting on a Sunday bears no relation to historical evangelical Anglicanism. So a whole lot of things that were just mainstream evangelical were just pushed aside. And that's what I call the revolution in the Sydney Diocese . . .

---

56. *The Briefing*, June 20 1995.
57. Alice Cunningham email to MHC, 16.3.2014.

He noted the language "shibboleths" of the revolution: church services were now church "meetings" or "gatherings;" music was now mostly pop music; the church service was primarily for being taught and the "vertical connection with God" no longer sought. The sermon was paramount.[58] Another shibboleth was the arts: "anything that looks artistic is out." As for work: it was simply a means of raising money for ministry: it had no intrinsic value. He thought it was disseminated through Phillip's influence at UNSW and through the Katoomba Convention movements.

Re women in ministry, Greg recalled:

> When I was at Sydney Uni in the early 80s, we had women doing the talks at the public meetings! Narelle Jarrett: she gave three talks on, I think, the Lord's Prayer. As late as 1983 or 84, Narelle Jarrett gave the talks at the public meetings of the AFES. Nobody batted an eyelid. It was a complete non issue. . . Also, in 1988 Elizabeth Elliot Gren gave talks at the AFES (Australian Fellowship of Evangelical Students) National Conference in January 1984. Helen Roseveare spoke at the Katoomba Youth Convention in, I think, 1985: she gave Bible talks from the platform. [59]

He noted that the word "staff" for the ministry team was part of the revolutionary rhetoric. "Staff" used to be the teachers at school. The professionalizing of the ministry team has been part of the revolution. While there is rampant anti-clericalism, the irony is that lay people's roles have been diminished.

Greg concluded:

> It's all about tribal law. I wonder if my own experience with aboriginal people sensitized me to issues of tribal loyalty. We use tribe as a metaphor because people in a natural tribe are related by blood, and ours aren't. But the loyalty is no less. Even to point it out is in a sense disloyalty because you don't believe it because it's the tribal line. You think you believe it because you've read the Scriptures and you've been convinced about it and been convinced and so to suggest that someone will believe something because they are loyal to the party is to impugn their motives. The reality is that people don't have enough time to think through all of the issues so they do take intellectual short cuts and go with influential people.[60]

Archbishop Goodhew appointed the Rev. Di Nicolios to be the first woman Archdeacon in 1994. Her title was Archdeacon for the Promotion of

---

58. See Jensen *Sydney Anglicanism. An Apology*, 57.
59. PF Jensen states that Phillip Jensen invited Helen Roseveare twice.
60. Greg Anderson interview with MHC 12.7.2013.

Women's Ministry.[61] Although the title "Archdeacon" was new, Goodhew claimed that Nicolios was succeeding the Rev. Maureen Cripps, appointed by Archbishop Robinson. As such, it was not a contentious appointment, but the fact that Sydney now had an archdeacon who was not ordained priest may have been a world first. Di Nicolios was a fine pastor: sane and steady, and focused on her work rather than flaunting her new position. While she held office, the women's ordination issue had never been hotter. In fact, the 1996 Synod voted to oppose it. The lay vote was split: 210 to 200, while the clergy vote was 151 to 79. Such voting demonstrated a strong groundswell of support for women's ordination to the priesthood, especially by laymen and women, and a significant division between lay and clergy. At this stage, ordination of women to the priesthood was not an option, given the strength of the opposition.

Rev. Di Nicolios

61. *Southern Cross* February 1994,8.

In the lead-up to a conference on women's ministry, called by the Archbishop, Archdeacon Nicolios outlined what women were permitted to do by ordinance in the diocese. She noted that since 1922 deaconesses and "duly qualified and approved laywomen" had been permitted, by licence of the Archbishop and with the approval of the minister, to address the congregation, read Morning and Evening Prayer and the Litany.[62] An ordinance of 1981 authorized laypersons, both men and women, to preach.[63] Then in 1987, Synod passed an ordinance authorizing women to be ordained deacon.[64] This carried with it the authority to preach, if granted a licence. In 1998 all Sydney deacons held a licence to preach, but no rector was under compulsion to invite a deacon to preach. Nicolios' article was notable for its cool tone and useful factual information. She remained Archdeacon until 2002, when she was appointed Rector of Diamond Creek, a sizeable evangelical Melbourne parish. In an interview with *SMH* journalist Julia Baird, she said that Sydney's opposition to women priests was "a fact of life." She stressed she was sad to leave, and was doing so on good terms: "I don't have an axe to grind . . . People might not appreciate that I have not been an activist, but that's me. I haven't pursued the ordination of women to the priesthood—that's not been a priority."[65]

Back in 1994 the Scottish Episcopal Church had ordained 42 women deacons to the priesthood, and Canada Episcopal Church had ordained its first woman bishop. The year following the *Briefing* issue against women preaching, Nicolios produced the Women's Ministry Report, which showed strong support for women preaching. Some 73% of clergy surveyed in 227 parishes (85% of the diocese) supported the appointment of women as assistant ministers and agreed that they could preach and lead services. Significantly, the strongest support came from parishes where women were already serving on the staff.[66]

Letters about women's ministry bounced back and forth in *Southern Cross*. The President of MOW claimed that the Bible was being used as an instrument of oppression and that Sydney leaders changed the ground of their argument when it suited them. The people who argued against women priests were now using the same arguments *for* Lay Presidency. She chose two examples: on the issue of one Diocese going it alone, Sydney leaders

62. *Southern Cross* May 1998, 9. *Women's Work in the Church 1922 Ordinance.*

63. 1981 Deaconesses, Readers and Other Lay Persons Ordinance.

64. General Synod Ordination of Women to the Office of Deacon Canon 1988 Adopting Ordinance.

65. Julia Baird, "As the brothers huddle, the sisters are splintered in a demoralizing dame drain," *Sydney Morning Herald*, 27.5.2002.

66. *Southern Cross* Sept. 1996,1.

opposed this for ordination of women, but supported it for Lay Presidency. Some Sydney leaders also opposed ordination on the grounds of tradition, but then said, "Just because church tradition has always been against Lay Presidency, doesn't make it right."[67]

Justice Keith Mason took Claire Smith, a strong opponent of women's ordination, to task for making a distinction between teaching "in church" and in the media or Synod. He wrote:

> What is the problem? Is there some difference about expounding Scripture "in church" as distinct from "in the media" or in Synod? I cannot see it. Perhaps Claire might like to opportunity to explain.[68]

Claire did. Her answer was that it was the *context* of the teaching that was vital: exposition of God's Word in church carried different authoritative weight from teaching in synod or in the media. She wrote:

> I am grateful for the opportunity to respond to Keith Mason's question: Is there is some difference about [women] expounding Scripture "in church" as distinct from "in the media" or in Synod?
>
> My answer is "yes."
>
> The New Testament discussions of the ministry of women are given in the context of the church. When we think of "church" we may think in universal and institutional terms, however in the New Testament the word refers to the gathered Christian community, brought together for the purpose of fellowship with each other and with God, through the ministry of his Word.
>
> The instructions for women's participation in prayer and prophecy (I Cor.11: 3–16; I Cor. 14:26ff; cf. Col. 3:16), and the restrictions for women from the roles of teaching elder (I Tim. 2:11–15; I Cor. 14:33–36) rise in the context of the gathered community, which Paul describes as the "household of God." This household includes the oversight, authority and instruction of male teaching elders, whose responsibilities resemble that of father and husband (I Tim. 3:5). Their ministry of teaching, discipline and care occurs in ongoing relationships, where their instruction and authority are responded to with respect and submission (I Cor. 16:16; I Thess. 5:12–13), within a framework of mutual love and service.

---

67. Patricia Hayward, *Southern Cross* December 1994, 5.
68. *Southern Cross* April 2000, 8.

> These relationships in God's household provide the reason and context of Paul's prohibition of women teaching and exercising authority.
>
> On this understanding, the media and Synod are an abstraction from the relationships of the gathered Christian community.
>
> Synod is a "legislative" assembly, gathered not primarily for relationships of fellowship and instruction, but to debate and decide the practicalities and parameters of our association as many churches, or gathered communities. Speeches in Synod are explicitly and deliberately contributions to *debates*, rather than teaching. As such they do not carry the same authoritative weight as the exposition of God's Word in church.
>
> Similarly the media by its very nature (the wide dissemination of news and opinion) is not characterised by the fellowship and instruction that mark the relationships of the gathered Christian community. Furthermore authority in the media rests with the editorial team and the reader. Readers are not called upon to submit to what they read (as we are to Scripture or to our church elders); instead varying opinions are presented for the reader's consideration, with the opportunity for debate.[69]

Canon James McPherson weighed in the following month.

> Claire Smith has performed a valuable service in responding to Keith Mason's question about women expounding Scripture "in church."
>
> In differentiating biblically between "church" and "the media" and "the Synod," she describes "Church" as the gathered community, and concludes that therefore different rules apply—namely that women should neither expound Scripture nor exercise any authority in such a context.
>
> Dr Woodhouse, in his 1996 submission to the Appellate Tribunal regarding Lay Presidency, argued that administration of the Lord's Supper might be delegated, by analogy with the president of an organisation who "does not forfeit his office if a particular meeting is chaired, at his request, by another member of the organisation." This suggests that the "church," whose unique distinctiveness Claire Smith argues for, operates as a club and by commonplace and secular club rules.
>
> Who is right?
>
> If Dr Woodhouse is right, then a woman can expound Scripture in church just as she can in Synod or the media.

---

69. *Southern Cross* May 2000,8.

If Claire Smith is right, then arguing for Lay Presidency on the grounds of "delegation" cannot be justified by simple analogy with meeting of a local interest group.[70]

A group, calling itself "Equal but Different" sprang into life in 1992. The brainchild of Patricia Judge, it aimed to counter MOW and the women's ordination movement.[71] By August 1994 it began producing a newsletter two, later three times a year. The forthcoming vote in the Synod on women's ordination in 1996 was the catalyst.[72] The group also ran seminars, circulated book lists and engaged overseas speakers such as Don Carson and Mary Kassian. There was little attempt to understand or explain the pro ordination position, and only one of the books reviewed was one which examined the views of "the other side." [73]

There were regular articles on the worth of quiet ministry by women. A refreshing article by Marion Gabbott, a member of its Steering Committee, struck a different note. Marion was by 1999 working with her husband as a missionary in Thailand and observed the tragic lives of women driven to work in the sex trade, and many others in prison for drug-related crimes. She wrote:

> As I sit in the quiet of the late tropical afternoon, men and women are meeting in Sydney in the Synod of the Diocese. One question keeps being discussed: women's ordination to the priesthood. Questions will be raised about the authority of Scripture, the unity of the church, the pain of some women prevented from ministry by selfish men, security of employment and income, of rights and spiritual gifts unused, obedience and disobedience, of status, value and right ordering of services of the denomination . . .
>
> In my isolation from the heat of the debate I keep thinking the Synod has voted on this again and again and the mind of the Synod has been plain. The Synod has not wanted women ordained to the priesthood but it has wanted women used as fully as possible in ministry. Please, please stop raising the issue, listen to the voice of the Synod and spare a thought—even a prayer—for the women of Thailand who need to hear the good news of Jesus which will give true life and liberate them from the chains of their present lives. Who will come and help us? Only

70. *Southern Cross* June 2000, 8.
71. Edwin Judge interview with MHC, 22.8.2011.
72. *Equal but Different*, August 1994.
73. France, *Women in the Church's Ministry* was reviewed by Rev. Rob Smith, receiving short shrift.

1% of Thailand's population is reckoned to be Christian. What is true of Thailand is just as true of Afghanistan, India, Pakistan, Malaysia, Cambodia, Burma . . .[74]

Underneath the words lies the view that there are more important issues than women's ordination. The latter seemed to have consumed some people to the point where it had the burning importance of a gospel imperative. The women on the Steering Committee included Christine Jensen, wife of Peter, Helen Jensen wife of Phillip, Claire Smith and five others.[75] Equal But Different must have influenced the Synod voting on the women's issue, to an appreciable extent.

Rev. Jacinth Myles

74. *Equal but Different* April 1999, 6.
75. Patricia Judge, Lesley Ramsay, Marion Gabbott, Lesley Hicks, Di Warren.

Meanwhile, an ordained woman was quietly leading a parish, with support from fellow (male) clergy, including bishops. Her name is the Rev. Jacinth Myles. By the time she was ordained Deacon in 1989, she had already been in ministry for seventeen years. She trained as a primary school teacher and her plan was to go to Africa with CMS.[76] CMS required her to attend Deaconess House for a year, and when, at the end of the year, CMS decided against accepting her as a candidate, because of a back problem, she was delighted. She had found a new avenue by then for ministry: parish work. After a further three years at Deaconess House, and work in the parishes of Lane Cove and Lawson (where she did not preach), Bishop Clive Kerle invited her to the Cathedral at Armidale, where she was to share half the work: leading services, preaching, and taking baptisms, weddings and funerals.

She has written,

> At this stage I was aware that godly and evangelical, Bible believing Christians had examined the Scriptures and that several had opinions that differed from each other. I went to Armidale, praying that if I and those who had invited me (the Bishop, Clive Kerle, the Dean, Peter Newell and the Curate, Michael Hill) had misunderstood the Scriptures on the issue of whether it was Biblical for a woman to preach, teach and lead when men were present, that God would make this clear to me. If he did, I said that I would resign immediately.[77]

For almost seven years she was the assistant at the Cathedral.

She did not think she was a very good preacher, so she tried to withdraw from preaching, but the Dean, the Archdeacon and the Bishop would not let her. They suggested she attend the Sydney School of Preaching. This was only open to men, to clergymen in their tenth year or more of ministry. She was allowed to go, the small group of men who attended with her treated her "as an equal" and warmly affirmed her preaching.

After Armidale, while Marcus Loane was Archbishop, Bishop John Reid invited her to the parish of Haberfield, to share the preaching and services. She led the parish's only bible study with the Rector as a group member. When the Rector went on sick leave for three months, she was *Locum Tenens*. After Haberfield she went to South Canterbury and Clemton Park for seven years, and for half of that time was effectively the Rector. By this time Donald Robinson was the Archbishop.

---

76. Jacinth Myles interview with MHC 5.8.2013.
77. Jacinth Myles memo to MHC.

In 1993 she went to Abbotsford where there were only a few parishioners left. She ran Christianity Explained courses and saw many people come to know Christ and continue to follow him. The Sydney Diocesan *Year Books* speak for themselves: in 1992 the income for Abbotsford parish was $39,375; in 2006 it was $108,537. Jacinth speaks very highly of the full support she received from Bishop Robert Forsyth, and noted that Archbishops Harry Goodhew and Peter Jensen allowed her to carry on her ministry. She said, "I just put down my head and got on with it."[78] And, I am completely mystified as to why God would provide me with all these unusual ministry opportunities and why he would gift me to fulfil them, including the preaching and teaching and the leadership of two parishes, if he is against women performing these ministries.[79]

She has also written,

> God has done the unusual in placing me in positions where I have been given ministry opportunities that didn't seem to have been possible for women at that particular time and place. I have never sought any of them but I am eternally grateful to the Lord for them, especially because of the type of person I am normally. For example, during my school years, I always managed to avoid all debating, acting, public speaking and discussions because I was so quiet and shy and lacking in self-confidence in these areas.

Jacinth Myles: the quiet exception.

The debate about women extended into another area of theology: the nature of the Trinity. The question raised is, "Is it ever proper to use the word 'subordination' of the relationship of the Father and the Son?" The church's classic statement of belief, the Athenasian Creed, states that Jesus is "inferior to the Father, *as touching his manhood."*[80] According to Millard J Erickson, in *Who's Tampering with the Trinity? An Assessment of the Subordination Debate*, the theology of hierarchy in the Trinity is an evangelical doctrine of fairly recent origin and proposed by Charles Hodge of Princeton Seminary in the latter 19th Century.[81] Erickson relied heavily at points on Kevin Giles,

78. She was not the incumbent. Technically the Rev. John Griffiths was acting Curate in Charge. He came to take Holy Communion from time to time. R Forsyth to MHC 14.4.2014.

79. J Myles memo to MHC.

80. Piggin, "Kevin Giles, *The Father and the Son: modern evangelicals reinvent the doctrine of the Trinity,* Zondervan, 2006." Address given at the launch of Kevin Giles's book in Sydney, 21.6.2006.

81. Erickson, *Who's Tampering with the Trinity?* 27–28. Erickson quotes Hodge,

whose book *The Trinity and Subordinationism: The Doctrine of God and the Contemporary Gender Debate* was published in 2002. Close examination of Giles's work raises its own questions about the reliability of his quotations from and interpretation of the Church Fathers and other writers.

In Sydney we see a statement about the eternal subordination of the Son stated quite baldly in TC Hammond's *In Understanding Be Men*, first published in 1936, where he wrote that the Son and the Spirit are subordinate to the Father.[82] The matter seems to have been dormant, at least in Sydney, until the rise of the debate about the place of women in the church. In 1977 DB Knox, in his Minority Report to the Doctrine Commission of General Synod on the Ordination of Women to the Priesthood, endorsed the theology of the eternal subordination of the Son, as did Archbishop Loane. DB Knox had written: [83]

> In the spiritual realm there are angels and archangels, and in our world humanity has been given headship and dominion over the lower creation and within humanity the Bible makes clear, what nature teaches us, that man is the head of the woman.
>
> This principle of order, of headship and subordination, is clearly seen in I Corinthians 15:23-28 where Christ is head over all things and *yet himself is subordinate to the Father*.[84]

Here, possibly for the first time, Knox linked a theology of the Trinity with a theology of women's ministry in the church. In response to a request from the Sydney Synod, in 1999 the Sydney Doctrine Commission published a Report whose title stated the link: "The Doctrine of the Trinity and its bearing on the relationship of Men and Women." It concluded:

> That the concept of "functional subordination," of equality of essence with order in relation, represents the long-held teaching of the church ... This teaching should determine ... appropriately biblical expressions of the functional difference between men and women in home and church."[85]

Sometimes called the Sydney Heresy, it continued into the episcopate of Peter Jensen (2001-2013) and attracted the attention of Archbishop Peter Carnley of Perth, who had been elected Primate in 2000.[86] Carnley claimed

---

Systematic Theology (Grand Rapids: Eerdmans, 1952, 1:445, 460 and 462.
  82. Hammond, *In Understanding Be Men*, 56.
  83. See Chapter 6.
  84. *ACR* 28.4.1977, 3.
  85. *Sydney Year Book 2000*, 549.
  86. Ibid., 541.

that to teach "functional subordination" was "to fall into the ancient heresy of Arianism. Arius (d.336) championed subordinationist teaching about the person of Christ, by holding that the Son was inferior to the Father."[87] For Sydney theologians to be charged with Arianism was a terrible accusation, especially as Carnley was rightly regarded as a theological liberal.[88] Peter Jensen responded, in a defence of TC Hammond,

> Let me hasten to say that the Sydney Doctrine Commission gave careful consideration to these charges, and rejected them decisively. The use of the word "subordination," carefully nuanced, although unusual in recent theology is one easy enough to establish in classical theology over the years, as, more importantly, is the doctrine of the eternal obedience of the Son, or the asymmetrical relationship of Son and Father. It is the egalitarian theologians who are more prone to innovation, and in greater danger of error.[89]

Rev. Dr Graham Cole, previously a member of the Moore College Faculty, later Principal of Ridley College, Melbourne, and currently Dean of Trinity Evangelical Divinity School in the US, stated in an interview:[90]

> There's a big debate going on about the eternal subordination of the Son. From my perspective, some people are reading patristic texts and maybe even some of the medieval ones anachronistically as though these writers were talking about roles, and functions. I don't think it was going through their heads at all. If you read the Fathers in context, it's instead a question of origin and relation—that's what this sort of language of "Father" and "Son"

---

87. Carnley, *Reflections in the Glass* 232–3; Carnley, "TC Hammond and the Theological Roots of Sydney Arianism," St Mark's Review 198, 2005, 5–10.

88. Rodgers' perceptive article in *Southern Cross* March 2000, 5. See Appendix.

89. "Caleb in the Antipodes." The TC Hammond lecture presented by Archbishop Peter Jensen during his trip to Ireland in June 2005, Posted on 14.09.2005.(www.sydneyanglicans.net/indepth/caleb_in_the_antipodes_peter_jensen)

90. Graham Cole joined the Beeson Divinity School faculty in 2011; and was appointed Dean of Trinity Evangelical Divinity School from mid 2015. Before coming to Beeson Divinity School, he taught at Trinity Evangelical Divinity School. He has also served as an administrator in the New South Wales Department of Education, lecturer in Christian Thought at Moore Theological College and in Philosophy of Religion at the University of Sydney, and from 1992 to 2001 he was the Principal of Ridley College, University of Melbourne. He is the author of *Engaging With the Holy Spirit: Real Questions, Practical Answers*; *He Who Gives Life: The Doctrine Of The Holy Spirit*; *God the Peacemaker: How Atonement Brings Shalom*, and *The God Who Became Human: A Biblical Theology of Incarnation*. He is an ordained Anglican minister.

was about—the idea of roles and functions I think comes much later in the history of ideas.

For example, think of a medieval theologian like Peter Lombard, whose *Sentences*—propositions in theology—was standard in theology until the late 16th Century. In Book 3 of Lombard's *Sentences* he argues that any one of the Godhead could have become incarnate. Aquinas restates that, but at more length. So the argument of some today that "only the Son could be incarnate because he was the subordinate One eternally and therefore . . ." would, I think, have puzzled them. The problem with that argument is that if the Son can do something the Father can't do, then the Son is omnipotent and the Father isn't. Likewise, the Spirit is not omnipotent. And you have problems with the doctrine of God. So these are some of the subtleties that I think get missed these days because of our not knowing medieval theology well enough, and before that, Patristic theology.[91]

Numerous leading theologians, from all ages, and shades of churchmanship, have used the language of subordination with regard to the relationship of Father and Son: William Perkins, Jonathan Edwards, AA Hodge, Handley CG Moule, Karl Barth, Louis Berkhof, Emil Brunner, JI Packer, Gordon Fee, and Rowan Williams, to name a few.

Wolfhart Pannenberg stated the doctrine thus:

> . . . *By their work the Son and Spirit serve the monarchy of the Father* [MHC italics]. Yet the Father does not have his kingdom or monarchy without the Son and Spirit, but only through them. This is true not merely of the event of revelation. On the basis of the historical relation of Jesus to the Father we may say this of the inner life of the triune God as well. Normative again in this regard is the aspect of self-distinction in the relation of the Son to the Father. *The Son is not subordinate to the Father in the sense of ontological inferiority, but he subjects himself to the Father* [MHC italics]. In this regard he is himself in eternity the locus of the monarchy of the Father. Herein he is one with the Father by the Holy Spirit. The monarchy of the Father is not the presupposition but the result of the common operation of the three persons. It is thus the seal of their unity.[92]

The debate had continued into Peter Jensen's episcopate. Jensen read a paper to the Australian bishops entitled "The Charge of Arianism." In an opening paragraph he stated:

91. Graham Cole interview with MHC 5.6.2009.
92. Pannenberg, *Systematic Theology* I: 324–25.

The accusation of heresy however, brings us to a new stage in the relationships of the Australian church. To say that we are wrong about the ministry of women and homosexuality and stem cell research; to say that our behaviour is deplorable and our religion is rationalistic—this is one thing. But to say that we are both Docetic and Arian, is another...

Dr Carnley has confirmed to both Glenn Davies and me that he considers the Report [of the Sydney Doctrine Commission] Arian...

The Sydney Doctrine Commission was chaired by Paul Barnett. Its members were Bishop Forsyth, former Archbishop Robinson, the present Principal of Moore College, the present Dean of Armidale Cathedral, the then Rector of Christ Church St Lawrence, the former vice Principal of Moore College, the Principal of Mary Andrews College, Dr Robert Doyle and the present Archbishop of Sydney. It is hard to imagine a more representative group of Sydney Anglican theologians or a more authoritative Report as far as the Diocese of Sydney is concerned. The Primate's remarks are aimed at the very center of our Diocese. We cannot evade them or dismiss them as lacking in seriousness...

Arianism and Docetism are without doubt two of the most deadly heresies ever to afflict the Christian church. "Docetism," of course, teaches that the incarnation is only an apparent one; it denies the real humanity of Jesus. Arianism denies Christ's full divinity.

Having explained the difference between functional subordination and ontological subordination, Jensen concluded:

The accusation of Arianism is the theological equivalent of a charge of Nazism. This Report is not Arian (or Docetic for that matter) either in its intention or in its plain teaching. I believe furthermore that it rightly appeals to the Scriptures and to the mainstream Nicene tradition of our Church. *Allow me to say with all my heart that the Diocese of Sydney through its official teachers utterly repudiates either Docetism or Arianism.* If by any chance we have unwittingly strayed into heretical ways of thought or modes of expression we wish to amend that as soon as possible and to announce to the world that we have done so, so that this stain will be expunged. If, on the other hand, the Primate now concedes that his words were ill considered, I call upon him to take such public action as will achieve the same result as soon as possible. I suggest that, even if a withdrawal of his book is too much to hope for, an agreed statement to be posted on our web site would be a sound beginning.[93]

Before we turn to other aspects of Sydney's relationship with the ACA during Goodhew's time, there is one further matter, a crisis, which has occasioned long-term division and extreme pain in the Diocese. Because of it Christian brothers and sisters have been divided from one another by terrible suspicion and it is as if they are separated by a deep, unbridgeable, subterranean chasm. Families have been chopped in two.

The crisis concerned the Anglican Counseling Center. It probably arose from increasing awareness of the evils of sexual misconduct during the 1990s. The Wood Royal Commission, originally set up in 1994 to determine the existence and extent of corruption within the NSW Police Force, by 1995 had its terms of reference widened to investigate the activities of organised paedophile networks in New South Wales, the suitability of care arrangements for at-risk minors and the effectiveness of police guidelines for the investigation of sex-offences against minors.[94] The Diocese responded by drawing up a protocol for dealing with sexual misconduct.[95]

The Counselling Center had grown out of a Marriage Guidance Center, constituted by ordinance in 1963. Since then it had widened its work well beyond the terms of the original ordinance. At issue was use of a therapy called "recovered memory" and the lack of adequate qualifications of counsellors using this therapy.

Problems within the Anglican Counselling Center prompted the Standing Committee to appoint a committee to enquire into the operations of the Center. There were allegations, generated by "recovered memory" of sexual abuse in families. The report concluded

> The sincerity with which "recovered memories" can be believed to be true was not disputed. However in the absence of corroboration one way or the other, it is impossible to know whether such "recovered memories" are related to real historical events or not.[96]

The committee's brief was to review the qualifications of the staff, the counselling guidelines and how they were monitored, and the range and nature of the counselling practices and techniques used. John Woodhouse,

---

93. Jensen, "The Charge of Arianism," undated.
94. http://en.wikipedia.org/wiki/Royal_Commission_into_the_New_South_Wales_Police_Service
95. *Southern Cross* July/Aug. 1995; *Sydney Year Book 1994*, 312.
96. *Sydney Year Book 2000*, 24, 435.

Rector of Christ Church St Ives was appointed Chairman and the committee comprised health professionals and a lawyer. Each member of the committee endorsed the finished report.[97]

The Report contained 22 recommendations, of which seven were disputed by the staff and council of the Center. The disputed recommendations sought to: have the Center major on General Counselling; require professional registration for those engaged in Clinical Counselling; require that the Center not practice Specialised Psychotherapy and not be involved in cases using "recovered memory." The Standing Committee adopted the Disputed Recommendations.[98]

John Woodhouse recalls:

> There really was something rotten in the Counseling Centre. Terribly rotten. I sat with a man I'd never met before, never met since, and on this recovered memory thing, he said, "John, you cannot know whether I am telling you the truth or not." I said, "That's right." But he said, "I want you to understand that if I am, that is, I haven't done these things that my adult children now believe I did, the counsellor that led them to believe that I did those things has done to my children what I would have done if I'd done them." That got to me, and I thought we were not in a position to set up a judicial enquiry as to where the truth lay, but we did have the capacity to investigate whether the practices were professional and had proper safeguards and they didn't. They were shonky. There's every reason to think that terrible, terrible harm was done to people.[99]

The 1999 Synod censured the Standing Committee for its handling of the Counseling Center issue.[100] This was probably unique in the history of the Diocese. John Woodhouse resigned from the Standing Committee.

The Australian Psychological Society Ltd has published "Guidelines for psychological practice with clients with previously unreported traumatic memories."[101] It concluded:

> 7.1. Psychologists are aware of the complex nature of human memory. When working with clients who refer to previously unreported traumatic memories, psychologists acknowledge

---

97. Ibid., 432.
98. ibid., 30, 436.
99. Woodhouse interview with MHC 30.5.2011.
100. *Sydney Year Book 2001*, 15/00, 425.
101. The Australian Psychological Society, "Guidelines for psychological practise [sic] with clients with previously unreported traumatic memories." March 2010.

that the welfare and interests of their clients are their primary concerns. They understand that currently, in the absence of corroborating evidence, it is not possible to distinguish a valid retrieved memory from a false one.

7.2. Psychologists do not have as a goal of treatment the "recovery" of currently unreported memories of prior trauma where the client previously had no recollection of any trauma. They avoid drawing premature conclusions about the accuracy of any previously unreported memory, and assist their clients to tolerate uncertainty and ambiguity regarding their experience. The psychologist and client may both have to accept that the nature of past events cannot be known with certainty, which means the goals of therapy may include working towards acceptance of incomplete reported memories and treatment of current symptoms.[102]

The Counseling Center was integrated with HMS the following year.[103]

Another result of the Wood Royal Commission was that a National Register was created for the ACA. Originally conceived as a database of clergy and lay people in the ACA, it became a register of sexual offenders.[104] While the Register had its merits, it did not necessarily achieve its purpose. The architect of the Register tended to regard anyone charged as guilty until proven innocent; there were huge problems with privacy issues and the potential to ruin an individual's reputation. It was not necessarily an effective instrument to protect the Christian community against sexual predators, and it strained out gnats while letting camels go free.

And so we come to Sydney's relationship with the other Australian dioceses, and the Anglican Communion. Apart from the issue of whether women might be bishops, the four big matters were: church planting, another prayer book, Lay and Diaconal Presidency, and an adulterous bishop.

Sydney's legislation for "church planting" was first promoted in 1995, by Phillip Jensen. Five years later Synod passed the Recognised Churches Ordinance. This gave recognition to independent churches after they had been planted and proved viable. Many planted churches did not seek registration under the Ordinance.[105] Phillip's own church had multiplied its congregations, and they met in various places. Church planting was, of

---

102. Ibid., 7.

103. *Sydney Year Book 2001*, 482–83.

104. By April 2014 there were over 200 names on the Register, according to Garth Blake.

105. NM Cameron to MHC 17.4.2014.

course, mission work. But when it occurred in another man's parish, or diocese, there was friction. Bishop Herft of the Newcastle Diocese called church planters ideologues with an agenda "which amounts to the deconstruction of the Anglican Church as it is presently constituted." He likened the strategy to a political coup, representing an "anarchical deconstruction of duly constituted forms of governance." Archbishop Hollingworth of Brisbane called upon his diocese to pray for the Sydney Diocese to "overcome movements within it which could tend to cause schism within the national church."[106] The church plants were often immensely successful and a threat to parishes where little growth occurred and where little evangelism was attempted. The first, by the Rev. Andrew Heard, was on the Central Coast, north of Sydney, in the Diocese of Newcastle, in 1999.

Heard had visited the Central Coast on many occasions and over many years of familiarity with the area and discussions with leaders of various churches in the region, he was encouraged by them to see that there was a significant need for new churches to be established. Locals assured him that there were not many evangelical churches, of whatever denomination. Heard has stated: "I had a real burden for the area but the thing that tipped me over to actually do it was the expression of need from the locals. They were the ones saying there was a need."[107]

Conversations with local clergy confirmed his concerns. They insisted that they were evangelistically minded, telling him of all the weddings and funerals they did. Heard perceived a lack of Bible teaching and was determined to "do more than wait for people to come to us for occasional services." He wanted to build a group of people who would be on mission.[108] He resigned from his position at Gladesville, where he was assistant rector, but Christians at Gladesville decided to support the venture for a time to ensure that he and his wife had enough money to live on.

---

106. *Southern Cross* August 2000, 5.
107. Heard email to MHC 11.2.2015.
108. Ibid.

Rev. Andrew Heard

Erina is in the Anglican diocese of Newcastle. Heard's venture reached the attention of the Bishop of Newcastle of the day, who went ballistic. He expressed his views in the local newspapers, describing the church plant in strong and critical terms. The newspapers approached Heard for his response and published his views. The result was to the advantage of the Independent Evangelical Church that Heard was trying to found, as Heard could not have afforded to pay for the publicity, which the Bishop provided for him in the local press. The church grew very quickly and moved from the house to a local school and it continued to meet in local schools. It grew bigger. Heard was able to engage assistants. From the start, Heard and his assistants were engaging in public ministry in a way which the Anglican churches were not doing in the area. Also, he was a very effective preacher.

He followed the Moore College example in preaching in a thoroughly exegetical way, not bouncing from a particular verse to another.[109] By 2015 the average attendance was about 2,000 people, which means about 3,500 people were regularly part of this church. The annual budget was $3.5 million dollars and the church owned nine acres of land in the heart of Erina with a 1,100-seat auditorium, a 400-seat hall and numbers of classrooms for their thriving children's ministry (there were 380 at their services). They have seen around 100 people become Christians each year.[110] Heard concluded: "It has been a wonderful journey and testimony to the faithfulness of God to bless the ministry of his word."

In December 2000, with some reluctance, Archbishop Goodhew assented to the Recognised Churches Ordinance. "I had to ask, 'With signing this, am I dumping on my successor?'" he said.[111]

The General Synod of 1995 produced *A Prayer Book for Australia* (*APBA*). Sometimes called "the Red Brick," some of it had an Anglo-Catholic flavour. Phillip Jensen and a number of REPA colleagues were strongly opposed to it—Phillip calling it "a disaster for Anglicans."[112] Robert Tong recalls that "Harry let us down badly at about Day Three" of the General Synod in Melbourne. Sydney had held rounds of discussions on the new prayer book and agreement on certain positions had been reached. But once down in Melbourne, Harry was persuaded by Melbourne Evangelicals to change his mind. "They did him over," said Tong. He did not consult with any of the Sydney people before he changed his mind. He agreed to add the words on the title page: "Liturgical Resources authorised by the General Synod." By agreeing to the *APBA* as a *resource*, he enabled the book to be passed by the General Synod, and not as a provisional canon, where it would have perforce gone the rounds of the dioceses. Each synod would have looked at the book and it would have come back three years later, with "some working over." According to Tong, the word "resource" counts for little: in reality, *APBA* has the same status as the *BCP* and the *AAPB* of 1978. Tong remembered that Harry's handling of the issue of the new prayer book generated "a lot of heat." Harry had been "conned."[113] The Diocesan Doctrine Commission's report on *APBA* concluded that there were significant departures from *BCP*: "This is not to say that of necessity *APBA* explicitly teaches false doctrines. The *APBA* inadequately expresses the doctrine

---

109. NM Cameron interview with MHC 23.1.2015.
110. A Heard email to MHC 11.2.2015.
111. *Southern Cross* Dec. 2000, 1.
112. McGillion, *The Chosen Ones*, 31.
113. Tong interview with MHC 7.6.2010.

found in *BCP* at certain points and is capable of being interpreted at other points in ways that are contrary to the doctrine of *BCP*."[114] Sydney did not adopt *APBA*. This was another mark of its separation from the rest of the Anglican Church in Australia. In a sense, this was not greatly important, since fewer and fewer churches in Sydney used any sort of prayer book.

In the 1996 Synod, Harry spoke with some passion and at length about Sydney's abandonment of a common liturgy. He said:

> It is possible that some who take a strong line against *APBA* in the Synod will be those who themselves rarely use the authorised forms already in existence. A section of *APBA* has been very closely scrutinised by our Doctrine Commission. In some sections it has been line by line word by word. It will probably receive the same sort of review in this house. It will be evaluated for what it omits as well as for what it includes. Prayers in other parts of the book will no doubt be similarly considered. That is appropriate. My question is, if that is appropriate for a new prayer book, is it not also appropriate for what's done week by week in parish churches which construct their own services? If the doctrine committee spends long hours of meeting over words and phrases and nuanced meanings in the thanksgiving prayers of *APBA*, and they should, (I requested them to do that work even before the Synod made a similar request), what about those prayers which, it is asserted, are being created and used in some of their churches? Who evaluates them with the same rigour?[115]

Lay and Diaconal Presidency is yet another divisive issue dividing Sydney from the rest of the Anglican Communion. Most Sydney Anglicans find it difficult to understand why this is so. They understand Lay and Diaconal Presidency to be biblical (for example, in terms of the priesthood of all believers)[116] and it deals with situations where there is no ordained priest to preside at Holy Communion. But it is red rag to a bull for non-Sydney people. To the point that the Rev. David Short, an ex-Sydney clergyman based in Vancouver, pleaded with Sydney to consider the consequences of Lay Presidency, on the grounds that it would be schismatic and would "render Sydney clergy unemployable."[117]

---

114. *Sydney Year Book 1997*, 450-73.
115. Ibid., 329-30.
116. For example, I Peter 2:9 "You are . . . a royal priesthood."
117. *Southern Cross* August 2000, 3.

Harry Goodhew's handling of this matter lost him a great deal of credibility with the Sydney Synod. There were such questions as: Was Lay and Diaconal Presidency desirable? And was it legal under the Constitution? Sydney had first raised the issue in 1977. But it was in 1993 that the first of a number of weighty reports addressed the question. The Doctrine Commission, chaired by Bishop Paul Barnett, concluded that "there would appear to be no theological objection to legislation which would enable deacons to preside at the Holy Communion."[118] Similarly, another report the same year examined the case for Lay Presidency at the Lord's Supper. Its conclusion was even more strongly expressed:

> There are no sound doctrinal objections to, and there are significant doctrinal reasons for, Lay Presidency at the Lord's Supper. There are also sound reasons based on our received Anglican order for allowing Lay Presidency. In the light of this the continued prohibition of Lay Presidency at the Lord's Supper does not seem justifiable theologically. Since church practice ought to conform to sound doctrine, practical problems related to the introduction of Lay Presidency ought to be dealt with, but should not constitute an obstacle to reform motivated by theological truth.[119]

John Woodhouse and Dr Barry Newman's report the following year proposed various ways forward to implement what was now called Lay and Diaconal Administration of the Lord's Supper. Lay Presidency is the alternative to Anglo-Catholic practices such as reserving the sacraments and ordaining so-called local priests, practices which are illegal.[120]

Was it legal under the Constitution? In 1996 Donald Robinson wrote a minority report that this was "not consistent with the doctrine and principles of *BCP* and the Articles."[121] Neil Cameron, a former member of the Canon Law Commission, wrote in *Southern Cross* that much of what happened in Anglican churches at the time was illegal: Good Friday services, Carol services and family services, for example.[122] Church law had simply

---

118. *Sydney Year Book 1994*, 418.

119. *Sydney Year Book 1994*, 469.

120. The situation arises when there is no priest present. Reservation of the sacraments is the practice of consecrating the elements then keeping them for later use. Local priests are men and women without formal theological training, being ordained for the purpose of consecrating the elements.

121. *Sydney Year Book 1996*, 430.

122. *Southern Cross* July 1999, 1.

not kept pace with contemporary church practice.[123] Archbishop Rayner referred the matter to the Appellate Tribunal in 1996. John Woodhouse pointed out that the Tribunal "only gives an opinion to be evaluated, not a judgement to be obeyed."[124] In 1998 the Tribunal finally handed down its opinion, which was "yes" and "no." By a four to three majority the Tribunal said that there was nothing in the Constitution to prevent lay people and deacons presiding at Communion. But a second ruling was (six to one) that any move to allow Lay and Diaconal Presidency must be approved by the General Synod.

Later that year Harry Goodhew told his Synod that if they voted for Lay Presidency, he would withhold his assent. But if the Synod were to vote for women to be ordained priest, he would not withhold his assent.[125] When the Synod voted for Lay Presidency he indeed withheld his assent, on the grounds of the impact on the Australian Church and the wider Communion. He wrote:

> If I was not aware of it before, correspondence and phone conversations over the last few weeks have convinced me that whatever we do will have a significant impact. I am particularly sensitive on this point because I have been engaged since Lambeth with other parts of the Communion arguing against unilateral action over crucial moral issues and attendant theological norms. To act unilaterally myself and without wide consultation would undermine my credibility in these ongoing debates.[126]

According to Robert Tong, there was enormous pressure on Goodhew. George Carey, the Archbishop of Canterbury, wrote to him saying "Don't do it." There was the threat of court action.[127] However, he may not have anticipated the Sydney response to his stand. Synod members noted that the Archbishop was not prepared to assent to a change which they considered to be consistent with Scripture (Lay and Diaconal Presidency), but was prepared to assent to a change which a majority believed to be inconsistent with Scripture (Women's Ordination). Harry's statements about giving and withholding assent on the two matters where he was at odds with his Synod completed his estrangement from Sydney diocesan leaders, especially since

---

123. Ibid., September 1999, 18–19. The old law has been extensively revised since.
124. Ibid., April 1996.
125. *Sydney Year Book 1999*, 347 and 350.
126. *Sydney Year Book 2000*, 646.
127. *Southern Cross* Dec. 1999–Jan 2000, 1.

he had stated before his election that he opposed women's ordination to the priesthood.[128]

Harry Goodhew's dealings with a bishop who had committed adultery, whilst a priest, added to his unpopularity. This time it was with another diocese in the Province of NSW. The woman in the affair complained to the Primate, Keith Rayner, and he decided he could not handle her complaint in case the matter was referred to the Special Tribunal of which he was Chairman. The Primate persuaded Harry Goodhew to prefer a charge against the man. The result was that the Bishop of Canberra and Goulburn, the man in question, was very angry with Harry and he and his diocese "have been angry with the diocese ever since." It was thought that the Diocese of Sydney was "having a go" at the Diocese of Canberra and Goulburn, whereas Harry Goodhew as Metropolitan had been saddled with the problem. Thereafter, the bishop, who continued in his see, was a destabilizing center against the Diocese of Sydney.[129] The problem of how to discipline errant bishops surfaced in a series of canons in the General Synod over the next fifteen years and still remains unsolved.

Sydney's relationship with the wider Anglican Communion can be viewed through the Lambeth Conferences, which occur every decade. Lambeth 1998 marked the end of an era: that of a united Anglican Communion. It was the largest number of Anglican bishops ever to gather together for mutual consultation and prayer.[130] Sydney men and women at Lambeth 1998 had little or no place in the limelight. But their presence was significant in their support for those opposing homosexual practice. Archbishop Carey made his position quite clear: "I have long been persuaded that the entire Bible and Christian tradition give us no permission to condone sexual practices of any sort outside the relationship of husband and wife in holy matrimony. Therefore, so far as I can see, physical homosexual acts fall within that restriction."[131] Motion 1.10, which included the words: "While rejecting homosexual practice as incompatible with Scripture . . . calls on everyone in the Communion to minister pastorally to all," was strongly supported with 526 votes, 70 opposing and 45 abstaining.[132] This was something of a surprise.

Within two years the fabric began to tear. Declaring that ECUSA (The Episcopal Church of America) was in a state of emergency, Archbishop

---

128. The Rev. Neil Flower conversation with MHC 6.5.2015.
129. Margaret Rodgers interview with MHC 9.5.2011.
130. Carey, *Know the Truth*, 319 and 331: there were 750 bishops.
131. Carey, *Know the Truth*, 328–29.
132. Ibid.

Moses Tay and Archbishop Emmanuel Kolini of Rwanda consecrated two missionary bishops: John Rodgers and Chuck Murphy in January, 2000. Their episcopal authority was not recognized by ECUSA or the Archbishop of Canterbury.[133] Carey has written,

> It has often struck me as profoundly ironic that Bishops who profess themselves anxious to maintain scriptural purity against the departure from Scripture which they perceived to be the direction of the American Church, were quite prepared to ignore the same Scripture's insistence on unity and walking together in love.

Sydney sided with AMiA (Anglican Mission in America) and the dissident bishops. Archbishop Harry Goodhew went on a fact-finding mission to the USA and reported very negatively about ECUSA.

In 2002 Michael Ingham, Bishop of the Diocese of New Westminster in Canada gave the green light for the blessing of same-sex marriage, and in August 2003, Canon Gene Robinson, a practicing homosexual, was nominated Bishop of New Hampshire. Evangelical and conservative churches in the USA severed their ties with ECUSA to join the growing AMiA.[134]

Despite its internal upheavals and clashes with the ACA and the wider Anglican communion, Sydney was growing faster than any of the other Australian dioceses: much faster. NCLS figures are only one of the indicators. Essentially, the figures indicated that Sydney churches were younger and demonstrated more growth in congregation sizes than the national average.[135] In Sydney the average congregational size was 126 compared with a national average of 71 and an Anglican average of 57. A quarter of churches in Sydney had congregations of fewer than 50 compared with over half in the national church.[136] Moore College was big and growing steadily bigger. Total undergraduate enrollments for 1997 were 208 and the number grew annually until in 2001 there were 287 undergraduates, of whom about one quarter were women.[137]

In 1998 7,000 people attended the CMS Summer School at Katoomba.[138] Peter Jensen has commented,

---

133. *Southern Cross* Nov 2000, 6 and Carey, *Know the Truth*, 333.

134. Ibid.

135. "Church Finds Way Ahead," *Southern Cross* March 1998, 18.

136. Presidential Address *Sydney Year Book 1998*, 296.

137. Rhonda Barry, Moore College Registrar: Statistics for Undergraduate Commencing Enrolments.

138. *Southern Cross* 1998 February, 1.

> Well, my hope is that every clergyman goes to Summer School because that begins the year by reminding them of the big world. And sets a standard for Bible exposition, to remind you of what you should be aspiring to, informs lay people and inspires people to get involved with mission. If the Summer School didn't exist, we'd have to invent it. It's a brilliant contributor to the Diocese.
>
> You can't understand Sydney Diocese without Summer School, and CMS and the contribution made through Don Cameron, Geoff Fletcher—leading guys, Peter Tasker. We generally make the General Secretary of CMS a Canon of the Cathedral, and they are generally a member of Synod. So although there's no formal connection, it's generally very significant. Even more than the Katoomba Convention, in my opinion, is CMS Summer School.[139]

In 2000 Youthworks was established at Loftus, with the aim of training for youth and children's ministry. Beginning with 28 students, and affiliated with the Australian College of Theology, numbers have grown steadily.[140]

Then there are the university colleges, the established schools and more recently, the Anglican Schools Corporation. The Corporation had started with five schools in 1995, which grew to sixteen by 2010. The aim was to establish one new school each year. They have sprung from Archbishop Goodhew's initiative to establish Low Fee Anglican Schools in the developing areas of the Diocese, particularly Western Sydney. They have, as has been their aim, "provided an important link with the local community to enhance gospel outreach and church growth in these new areas."[141]

That significant growth had taken place in one of the most difficult decades for the Diocese is amazing: despite fighting within and without, and on a number of fronts; despite suspicion, enmity and great disappointment; despite questions about interpretation of Scripture and about right leadership; despite questions about the future of the Anglican Church and about Sydney's membership of it, God had granted healthy growth. Harry Goodhew's parting words to his Synod were a quotation from Richard Baxter: "In essentials unity; in non-essentials liberty; and in all things charity."[142]

---

139. Peter Jensen interview with MHC 23.11.2010.
140. By April 2014 there were 130 full time students and about 80 part time students.
141. Anglican Schools Corporation. http://www.sasc.nsw.edu.au.
142. *Sydney Year Book* 2001 Presidential Address, 411.

Chapter 9

The Jensen Ascendancy 2001–2013

MASSIVE CHANGE HAS SWEPT across the western world, Australia, NSW and Sydney in the course of half a century. During this time the Christian church has been marginalized. The refashioning of various rites of passage is a good indicator of this phenomenon: such rites as baptism, confirmation, marriage and funerals. Fifty years ago, anyone with any sort of connection with a church would have had their baby baptised. The problem at that time was to help them understand what baptism was about. At that time, numbers of confirmees were so large that often two confirmation services on the one day would be held in some North Shore parishes. Whereas two generations years ago people married in a church, now the majority opt simply to live together or to avail themselves of a civil celebrant. In the case of exequies, a glance at the classified death notices in today's *Sydney Morning Herald* indicates the great number of secular funerals, whereas once they would have been conducted in a church.

Donald Cameron, a former Bishop of North Sydney has said,

> Let's look at the wider world. These are only straws in the wind, but it always struck me as very interesting that when Queen Elizabeth arrived in Sydney in 1954, she was greeted, to my best recollection, by three people as representing Australia, as she set foot on Australian soil. They were the Governor, the Premier, and the Anglican Archbishop of Sydney. Marcus Loane's biography of HWK Mowll records how the Archbishop was much involved in the ceremonies which attended the English Queen's visit.[1]

---

1. ED Cameron interview with MHC 8.12.2014.

Cameron also pointed to the change in the media. Using the ABC (Australian Broadcasting Commission) as an example, he listed the great number of religious programs it produced in the 1950s: daily morning Bible readings, Sunday service broadcasts, and a religious program on Sunday nights called *Plain Christianity*. In addition, every Monday the *Sydney Morning Herald* published a report on a sermon preached the previous day in one of the city churches. Viewed from the vantage point of today, such endorsement by the media seems little short of astounding.

Back in 1934, TS Eliot spoke prophetically of the new age of godless secularism, of which he saw the signs:

> But it seems that something has happened that has never
>
> happened before: though we know not just when, or
>
> why, or how, or where.
>
> Men have left GOD not for other gods, they say, but for no
>
> god; and this has never happened before
>
> That men both deny both gods and worship gods, professing
>
> first Reason,
>
> And then Money, and Power, and what they call Life, or
>
> Race or Dialectic.[2]

Donald Cameron has said,

> If a society excludes God from its thinking, does it leave itself open to credulity and amorality? If a society excludes God from its thinking, to what extent does it exclude morality from its thinking? And to what extent does morality—right and wrong, fidelity between people—provide a foundation for ordered society? There is an old rabbinical saying which goes: "men must pray for rulers, even though they be evil, for without them men would consume each other." In other words, order is necessary for the maintenance of any kind of society. What does that tell us about humankind? And the secular atheistic society? Where does a Christian church as an institution in decline fit into a society which has marginalized or ignored God and in so doing has unconsciously abandoned certain principles of order and morality which are holding that very society together?[3]

---

2. TS Eliot, Chorus VII from The Rock, *Collected Poems*, 177.
3. ED Cameron interview with MHC 8.12.2014.

The Diocese of Sydney's God-given commission has been to connect a post-Christian era with the gospel of Christ. To effect this, huge energy has been directed to mission at parish and diocesan level, in schools, colleges and universities, and on beaches at Christmastime. There have numerous imaginative programs for young people, which have included camps and widespread Scripture teaching in schools. Top of the agenda is always to teach from the Bible, to encourage daily Bible reading and prayer and daily obedience in a life committed to follow Christ, who is Saviour and Lord. To this end church services have changed dramatically: they have been indigenized musically and liturgically, with songs and instruments that suit the taste of Australians raised on pop music; with informal liturgy, bookless services and casual dress. One rector maintained that he chose assistants at youth Holy Communion services on the basis of their footwear. Those wearing something on their feet, even if it were only thongs, were eligible.[4] In addition, new land has been purchased for new churches in new suburbs, and church-planting initiatives have been given strong support.

The events of the Jensen episcopate (2001–2013) are still too close to recount in any kind of detail for this history of the Diocese of Sydney. All that can be done here is to draw some outlines and crosshatch here and there. Many people generously granted me interviews for this book but since the great bulk of their recollections and views falls into the eras of the Goodhew and Jensen episcopates, it has been impossible to do justice to the wealth of their fascinating contributions. I had not foreseen such a situation. Each person I interviewed has either helped me to form my conclusions or has given invaluable insights into the Diocese of Sydney, or both.

Many were asked how they would define the Diocese in a few words. Responses included views of non-Sydney people, of those who now live outside Sydney but were once natives of the Diocese, and of Sydney people who are either its admirers or its critics. Their responses mostly describe the Diocese during Peter Jensen's time as Archbishop of Sydney.

Bishop James Grant and Rowena Armstrong, church leaders from Melbourne, used the words: "impressive, efficient, definite, confident and wealthy." Archdeacon PJ Newman of Melbourne added that there is rivalry and behind the rivalry, fear—at least from Melbourne's perspective. He added that Sydney's great wealth was the cause of some disquiet, since the original estates gifted to Sydney when it was the sole Diocese in Australia ought to have been divided up among the whole of the Anglican church of

---

4. MHC conversation with Rev. Boak Jobbins, former Rector of St Swithun's Pymble.

Australia because the resource "was gifted to the whole church."[5] But Archdeacon Newman's assertion that the grants of land by the NSW government were "given to the whole church" is not supported by any evidence. Most of the grants were to particular churches in Sydney. The NSW Parliament enacted that the Bishop of Sydney was the successor to the Bishop of Australia.[6] In a subsequent court case in 1895 and 1896 concerning gifts by an individual, the NSW Supreme Court again found that the Bishop of Sydney was the successor to the Bishop of Australia.

Some critics from the United Kingdom and from Sydney have identified poor preaching.[7] In 1997 Jim Bates conducted a survey of 145 Sydney clergy's sermons. His conclusion was scathing:

> There were really only two doctrines that were taught. The first was the need and means of salvation/redemption . . . without exception it was only about justification . . . There was not one allusion to the fact that it is not just the status of the person that is changed, but also his/her nature; nothing about regeneration which Paul talked about as "the renewing of the mind" . . .
>
> In about April 1997 I sent a letter to all the clergy who had sent me sermons. In that I asked them to send or refer me to any material which suggested or showed that anything I had written to them was false. About twenty contacted me, but they, including the archbishop and a bishop, agreed with me. Nobody tried to convince me I was wrong.[8]

Jim's conclusion was that John Chapman and before him, Keswick theology, had influenced this kind of preaching.[9]

Many would disagree with Bates' analysis and it comes as a surprise. For example, Paul Barnett has noted the salutary effect John Stott, whom many regard as the father of modern expository preaching, has had upon the Sydney sermon: "Stott was to the point, very well organised, very rooted in the text, and yet interesting. And as good on paper as he was as a speaker. Very gifted."[10]

---

5. Newman OAM interview with MHC, 24.10.2008.

6. The Bishopric and Church Property Act 1887.

7. Fletcher interview with MHC 12.8.2008; Lucas letter to MHC 31.7.2007; Bates email to MHC 31.7.2013; Tong interview with MHC 7.6.2010.

8. Jim Bates email to MHC 29.7.2013.

9. See full email in Appendix.

10. Barnett interview with MHC 17.11.2010; Phillip Heath also noted the quality of the preaching, Heath interview with MHC 20.2.2009.

My own experience is of sermons from a host of gifted preachers (male and female) who have prepared carefully and whose sermons not only teach the biblical passages before them with insight and good scholarship, but also give delight to their hearers because of the preacher's excellent communication skills.[11]

Other criticisms of Sydney are that it is insular, clubbish, that "the church's life and social action are not as clearly connected as in some other Dioceses," and that we don't always draw on our best talent.[12] Another called the Diocese "punitive, adversarial, controlling and sectarian." Paul Barnett noted that although there was a strong intellectual tradition within Moore College and the Diocese, there was not sufficient effort made to understand other peoples' positions. During the years of the Jensen Episcopate (2001–2013) there was an unhappy minority who felt they were neither respected nor heard. "Anglicans Together" was a gathering of such people, who published a newsletter three times a year. Their President, the Rev. John Cornish, spoke of being "driven to the margins . . . last on the list for funding . . . never offered appointments."[13] Michael Horsburgh stated: "The arrival of the Jensens has removed the possibility of loyal opposition in the Diocese."[14] Most of the unhappy minority shared a common view in their support for women in public ministry to men as well as women. Ann Young described the Diocese as "Power hungry. Non-Anglican. And self-righteous."[15]

---

11. The two churches of which I have been a member for over 40 years have been St Barnabas' Broadway, and St Swithun's Pymble.

12. "Insular:" Ross Weaver and Peter Watson; "clubbish:" Stuart Piggin; social action: Phillip Heath (formerly Headmaster of St Andrew's Cathedral School, currently Headmaster of Barker College); re talent: Stuart Piggin.

13. McGillion, *The Chosen Ones*, 188.

14. McGillion, *The Chosen Ones*, 188. Professor Michael Horsburgh is a former member of Standing Committee.

15. Ann Young interview with MHC 29.2.2012. Dr Young is a former member of the Standing Committee and a former Sydney delegate to General Synod.

Wilcox cartoon of the Diocese of Sydney[16]

Many of those interviewed have lamented the loss of Anglican liturgy. Paul Barnett stated:

> I am concerned that what I will call the postmodern direction of church life in which the unifying realities of *Prayer Book*, *Articles* and *Ordinal* are at a discount. And ministers and congregations are basically doing their own designer thing. Clergy sign up to certain commitments that place them within certain boundaries. I'm not advocating, of course, a return to 1662, or some other Seventeenth Century prayer book expression. That would be ridiculous, in my opinion. But those liturgies have effectively been revised and modernized over the years. Not perfectly, but adequately. I think that they do represent our boundaries that we ought to proudly own and seek to understand better. Seek to teach people their value. So that we have, in terms of the Cranmer vision, we have gatherings of Christians where the Bible is central in terms of reading Old and New Testaments, Psalms, where the creeds are fundamental, where the collects are used. Prudent use of the church calendar is employed to continue to shape the direction of Christian life. It is a great shame, I think, where it all may depend on the preaching and on the "music."
>
> I think in effect what we will have is just a series of undifferentiated Protestant community churches—they might be Baptist or Church of Christ or whatever, so far as we can see. We criticize people outside of Sydney for departing theologically. Well, I think we have departed significantly liturgically. I think

16. Cathy Wilcox cartoon in *Southern Cross*, July 2000.

we ought to rethink this whole thing very carefully. Church leaders ought to ensure it happens.[17]

Charlotte Rivers, formerly Director of the AIO (Anglican Information Office) enunciated three qualities with which there has been general agreement: Sydney is "conservative, orthodox and evangelical."[18] Other adjectives were: "diverse," "Bible-centered," "robust," "male-oriented," "strong," "proudly orthodox."[19] Others saw a "larrikin element" in Sydney. Wendy Colquhoun succinctly summed up a prevailing view about Sydney and the Bible: that Sydney people believed in the Bible as God's message to us. It has authority over us.[20] Bishop Peter Tasker pointed out that because the Diocese has remained very large, it has the unusual advantage of its own theological college, which comes under the Synod and its Trustees and committees. A consequence is the opportunity for teamwork: "Now there are lots of different personalities, lots of different ways of doing things, but at least with the simple basics of theology there is an agreement which allows you to get on and do things together—to know and understand each other better."

Professor Edwin Judge used one word: "didactic." By this he meant "not hagiological:"

> A hagiological Diocese would be one such as Marcus Loane embodied, or Howard Guinness. Or Principal Jones of 100 years ago. A hagiological Diocese would be a Keswick inspired Diocese. I was brought up on Keswick hymns. I miss them. I don't want them also. I mean by "didactic" that the *tone* of what passes through our pulpits now, so far as I see them in the parish I go to. There's quite a big turnover of young men, who are being brought through all the time, with a very concentrated didactic drive.
>
> Now I'm not saying anything about preaching the gospel: the gospel is preached either way. I'm polarising the possibilities into two extremes if you like, and there seems to be a profound difference between the way—the spirituality, if you like—of Marcus Loane, and the very intellectual, analytical, work of Broughton Knox. But they were presumably in agreement on most things at any rate and their credal position would have been the same and so on, so it is a matter of by what style of experience of style and tradition, or whatever it is, is communicated. That's what I am talking about.

17. Barnett interview with MHC 17.11.2010.
18. Charlotte Rivers telephone interview with MHC 23.5.2011.
19. "Diverse," "Bible centered:" Margaret Rodgers interview with MHC 9.5.2011; "robust," "male-oriented," "strong," "larrikin element:" Rod and Janet West interview with MHC 12.9.2011; "proudly orthodox:" Stephen Judd interview with MHC 4.5.2011
20. Wendy Colquhoun interview with MHC 2.6.2011.

> I don't want to imply that the didactic people are less zealous. They are intensely zealous and they are of course dedicated. Half the ones who come to our parish are on their way to Mongolia, for example, it seems to me. They're just as missionary-minded. It is quite clear that the didacticism is mediated through Moore College. But not only Moore College but through the Ministry Training Scheme of Phillip Jensen.[21]

Evangelicals living outside Sydney have spoken with deep gratitude of Sydney's support. David Mulready, Bishop of the Diocese of Northwest Australia (2004–2011) recalled Sydney's biblical stance, strong leadership, generosity and hospitality. He concluded, "I cannot speak highly enough of the Diocese and its leadership."[22] The Rev. Jonathan Fletcher, Vicar of Emmanuel Church Wimbledon noted the huge contribution of John Chapman (Chappo) to English Evangelicals, by his friendship with the Rev. Dick Lucas of St Helen's Bishopsgate, and by his coupling of evangelism with Reformed theology. Henceforth Fletcher and others like him could be "Reformed in our theology and flat out in evangelism."[23]

Three other leaders in Dioceses remote from Sydney have added their appreciation. Bishop Yong Chen Fah, Bishop of Sabah (1998–2007) was grateful for the faithful way in which mentors from his Moore College days kept in touch for the next 30 or so years: in particular Bishop Paul Barnett and Peter Jensen, Principal of Moore College, later Archbishop of Sydney.[24] Kanishka Raffel, Rector of Shenton Park, Perth, Western Australia, had many appreciative comments.[25] This is one:

> The Sydney Diocese has been setting a kind of benchmark—whether it is out of flattery or envy, I think the truth is, there are a lot of things about Sydney that other people would like to imitate. People would like to know how it is that there are so many ordination candidates; how Sydney approaches youth and children's ministry. Many Dioceses have practically no youth! So whether it's through gritted teeth or whether it's through a sense of thanksgiving to God, people would like to know how Sydney is doing this and I think—you talk about it as a phenomenon. It's not uncommon for people to say, "This is the situation for the whole church throughout Australia, with the exception of Sydney, where it's different." Inevitably it raises the question: why is it different?

---

21. Edwin Judge interview with MHC, 22.8.2011.
22. David Mulready interview with MHC 23.6.2008.
23. J Fletcher interview with MHC 12.8.2008.
24. Yong Chen Fah interview with MHC 28.6.2008.
25. He became Dean of Sydney in 2016.

> [Re the Mission] I think the Sydney Diocese is showing that it is willing to upset its structures and its bureaucracy and to continually review them to see whether they are really serving the Mission.[26] And that's a difficult and rare thing in any denomination.[27]

Further afield, the Rev. David Short, who trained at Moore College and at the time of the interview was Rector of Canada's largest Anglican church, St John's Shaughnessy, Vancouver, spoke of the "enormous energy in overseas commitment" by CMS missionaries who have come predominantly from the Sydney Diocese.[28] He noted five generations of Moore College principals who had been "trained in a robust intellectual, forward-looking, mission-focussed, Reformed Evangelical tradition."

He liked the Knox-Robinson view of *ecclesia*:

> . . . [it] gave very helpful expression to the weakness of trusting structure, which is of course the constant danger for Anglicans. Neglect the gospel, and into the vacuum flows the institutional view of the church. So the Sydney view of the church, which I think is unique in a way, has had a remarkable effect on the ecclesiology of the clergy and their congregations.[29]

He liked the unique form of biblical theology developed in Sydney:

> This is one of the most remarkable and unique gifts which I think it offers the Communion. A number of names are identified with that. Bill Dumbrell was pivotal in this, but he is not alone. By Biblical Theology I don't mean the old German framework, but I mean seeing the Bible as one story, and understanding that we preach Christ from the whole of Scripture and that Scripture itself is gospel-shaped. So that prevents us from the kind of devotional silliness that so many fall into. When pieces of the Christian faith are attacked, Sydney people are uniquely equipped to be able to look at the forest and to see where it fits. How to assess the theological importance or unimportance of some issues.

Like Yong Chen Fah, he expressed gratitude for the kind personal support he regularly received from busy Sydney leaders, men like Paul Barnett and Peter Jensen.

---

26. A Peter Jensen initiative.
27. Kanishka Raffel interview with MHC 26.6.2008.
28. Canon David Short is now Rector of St John's Anglican Church, Vancouver, after he and most of his congregation left the Shaughnessy church site, having lost a court case after a theological dispute with the bishop of the diocese.
29. Short interview with MHC 25.6.2008.

With the election of Peter Frederick Jensen as eleventh Archbishop of Sydney in June 2001, the Diocese of Sydney moved into a new phase. Its watchword was "Mission." He and his brother Phillip had attended school at Scots College in Sydney's Eastern Suburbs. Both were converted at the 1959 Billy Graham Crusade. Peter initially enrolled in Law at the University of Sydney, but found it did not suit. He became a teacher until he entered Moore College to train for ordination. He began lecturing at Moore College in 1973, then, encouraged by Broughton Knox the College Principal, he went to Oxford for three years to read for a DPhil. Broughton Knox retired in 1985 and Peter became Principal of Moore College at the comparatively young age of 42. Under him the College continued to thrive and he remained there until elected Archbishop. With an Oxford DPhil Peter Jensen was the first Archbishop of Sydney to possess an earned doctorate. His parish experience was minimal: he first served as a curate at St Barnabas' Broadway (a student church close to the University of Sydney), then in North Oxford. Like Mowll, Loane and Robinson he was never rector of a parish. He was consecrated bishop on the same evening that he was consecrated Archbishop of Sydney, so his ascent to the See of Sydney was not via the customary ladder.

Archbishop Peter Frederick Jensen

He was very well liked, and the Standing Committee and the Synod during his term of office were strongly supportive. Muriel Porter, no friend of Sydney Evangelicals, wrote perceptively of him in 2006:

> Jensen's authority is unchallenged and his personal influence considerable. Whether this equates with authoritarianism I do not know, but I suspect that this archbishop does not need to be authoritarian. It seems to outsiders at least that his Diocese is, in the main, eating out of his hands . . . There is also every indication that his leadership charisma is being magnified by an astonishingly effective public relations exercise, which casts him as something of a celebrity.[30]

He had an energetic, almost boyish air, with his crop of thick hair, ready smile, sense of humour and engaging personality. He could be also tough and dismissive, a confident leader who had a well thought-out position on the issues of the day. His leadership style was consciously different from that of previous archbishops, in Sydney and elsewhere. The Diocese had a taste of the future when "Deep Impact," the official diocesan welcome for Archbishop Jensen and his wife Christine, was held at the State Sports Center at Homebush. Four thousand people attended, there were performances from children's entertainer Colin Buchanan, a multicultural choir of over 250 people, and an impromptu "rap" rendition of Isaiah 53:6 "All we have gone astray . . . " in which the Archbishop, wearing dark glasses, joined Buchanan. In his address, the Archbishop stated "What our nation needs above all is the Gospel of Jesus Christ to be at the center of her life."[31] These were exciting times for Sydney Anglicans.

His first Synod Charge was radically different from those of his predecessors. Despite his background of scholarship in history, he chose not to reflect on the past, but to energise and exhort the synod about mission.[32] In nearly every subsequent address to the Synod the Diocesan Mission was his main theme. In 2001 he quoted from his speech at the Deep Impact rally:

> Church-going Anglicans in Sydney are about 1% of the population. We are becoming invisible. It is almost as unusual to have a friend who is a church-going Anglican as it is to have one who is an animal-keeper in the zoo. We are poised to become exotic. Most people will never meet or know one of us: it is hard for our

30. Porter, *The New Puritans*, 30–31.
31. *Southern Cross* September 2001, 1.
32. His MA Hons thesis: "Calvinism and the Persecution of Witches in England (1563–1604)," supervised by Professor Patrick Collinson; D Phil thesis: "The Life of Faith in the Teaching of Elizabethan Protestants" supervised by Dr Barrie White.

children to have sufficient friends to support them. How will our neighbours hear the gospel from us?

If we wish to have a deep impact on our society—humanly speaking—we need to aim in the next decade to have at least 10% of the population who are committed, equipped and bold to speak in the name of Christ. Whether God will so bless us, is in his hands . . .

I do not believe that I have been brought to this position of Archbishop in order to acquiesce silently in the passing away of Anglican Christianity in this region.[33]

He had a mission statement:

> To glorify God by proclaiming Christ our Saviour the Lord Jesus in prayerful dependence on the Holy Spirit, so that everyone will hear his call to repent, trust and serve Christ in love, and be established in the fellowship of his disciples while they await his return.[34]

It was rather clumsy, with its multiple dependent clauses, but if one thought about it carefully, the aim of the Mission was clear: to tell people the good news of Jesus' Christ as Saviour and Lord. No doubt an American televangelist would have thought of something more snappy.

In an interview in 2014, Peter said,

> I think at the heart of the Mission . . . I think it helped churches to have permission . . . to look at what was going on in their own parishes. We were not just trying to attract people to our churches, good though that may be. But were also trying to get the churches situated well into the actual suburb in which they are found. Make connections in the suburb in which they are found. Connections for good.
>
> . . . If we'd done ESL (English as a Second Language) in 1960 when all the migrants came in, I think we'd be looking at a different church. Talk about us reaching the working classes—well the working classes *were* the migrants![35]

The strategy for the Mission was fourfold:

1. To pray and preach

---

33. *Sydney Year Book 2002*, 376.
34. Ibid., 377.
35. Peter Jensen interview with MHC 9.5.2014.

2. To evangelise, particularly through planting new churches
3. To raise up new workers and to train lay people
4. To reform[36]

It might be said that Sydney Diocese, being evangelical, had always been mission-minded—especially during and since Mowll's episcopate. This was true, and Peter Jensen's Mission was not his brainchild. It was the idea of the Diocesan Executive Board (DEB) in Harry Goodhew's time.[37] Evangelists, missioners, youth workers and parish missions had been a characteristic of Sydney since World War II. What made this Mission different was that it was the first Diocese-wide mission in half a century, and it was a mission undertaken primarily by the parishes. Peter Tasker, one of Peter Jensen's assistant bishops, explained,

> Within Sydney it is quite amazing that we have a diocesan mission. There are other dioceses in the world that have a diocesan mission, but nine times out of ten it's the bishop's mission, not the peoples' mission. And I think it's unique that we have a mission that Synod has worked through for two years, and Synod looks at every year.[38]

There were at least two other areas in which Peter was an innovator. He was accessible to the media, which resulted in fairly frequent media coverage, at least in the *Sydney Morning Herald*. It was mostly positive. He was invited to give the prestigious Boyer lectures in 2005. He spoke on the topic "The Future of Jesus" and the lectures were later published as a paperback.[39] His other initiative was to align Anglicare with the Diocesan Mission.

Anglicare had a long and distinguished history. Established in 1856 as the Church Society, its main purpose was to plant churches: it looked after "mission" in the Diocese. During the 1930s its name changed to the Home Mission Society (HMS) and over the next fifty years it became more concerned with social welfare and with supporting new churches. Renamed for the third time in 1997, as Anglicare, it moved out of its previous parish support and development function, and further into welfare: nursing homes, "Op shops," disability services, migrant services, counseling, emergency relief centers—to name a few of its widespread operations.[40] Neither

---

36. Ibid.
37. Ibid.
38. Tasker interview with MHC 29.6.2008.
39. Jensen, *The Future of Jesus*.
40. *Southern Cross*, August 2005, 10.

Archbishop Donald Robinson nor Archbishop Harry Goodhew chaired the Council of Anglicare during their episcopates.[41] But Archbishop Peter Jensen became Chairman of Anglicare in 2005. For him, Anglicare and Moore College were the two key organisations of the Diocese.[42] He said,

> I spent a fair bit of time on Anglicare. I don't want to criticize Anglicare before I took over. On the contrary, it was a good ship that was floating independently of the Diocese in a sense, for various reasons. We needed to say to Anglicare, " you are one of us" and to the Diocese, "Anglicare is ours." And we needed to bring the two together in a way which meant that Anglicare was an authentic expression of the Diocese.[43]

Anglicare is a hugely significant welfare provider. In 2004 its expenditure was $61,000,000 and it had a staff of 1,200 with a further 2,000 volunteers.[44] In 2013 its expenditure had climbed to $100,000,000. Some idea of its scale can be understood by comparing the 2013 expenditure of Anglicare in Sydney with that of the high-profile Salvation Army in the same year. Australia-wide, the Salvos' *national* expenditure was $362,350,000, while Anglicare *Sydney* was $100,000,000.[45]

In his paper, "A Christian Philosophy of Care," Peter Jensen wrote:

> On any account Anglicare Sydney is one of the most significant caring organisations in the Sydney-Wollongong area and hence one of the most significant in Australia. I am told that is impressive in terms of what is available elsewhere in world Anglicanism. It is curious, stimulating and frightening to have some responsibility for its affairs . . .
>
> . . . The best care comes through persons in relationship. Thus our care may be a child's Christmas gift for those who have nothing; but our care cannot stop there; it needs to be the transforming care of a love which draws people into relationship with those who care, and offers the possibility of a relationship with God to persons, who after all—however poor and destitute they may be outwardly—are destined for immortality in the age to come.[46]

---

41. Jensen, Paper 2: Positioning Anglicare. Where we are. Emailed to MHC by PFJ.
42. Ibid.
43. Jensen interview with MHC 9.5.2014.
44. *Southern Cross* August 2005, 10.
45. *Anglicare Diocese of Sydney Financial Report for the year ended 30 June 2013; The Salvation Army Annual Report 2013.*
46. Jensen, "A Christian Philosophy of Care." Emailed to MHC by Jensen.

The new CEO of Anglicare, Peter Kell, had a number of challenges before him. The first was financial. Kell has written:

> For a number of years there had been heavy deficits which had been covered by using reserves. The Council was anxious that this trend be reversed as soon as possible . . . Tough decisions were needed but had not been taken.[47]

There was a justified suspicion that Christian people were not always in leadership positions. Anglicare Sydney adopted a policy of "only appointing to leadership positions all the way through the organisations 'Christian people who displayed an active involvement with their local bible-believing churches.'" Kell also developed a Parish Partnership team whose brief was to visit each parish, ascertain their strategies and needs and to explore ways Anglicare could work with the parishes. This had not been attempted before. Kell commented "The growing number of fine Christian leaders in Anglicare and the effort we took to get alongside the parishes led to a 'reblossoming' of the relationship."[48]

Kell also embarked on a leadership-training program. He has written,

> It was designed to encourage our people to understand Christian leadership better particularly in the context of their professional areas. The program had several layers including one which counted towards a Master's degree. During my time there several hundred managers across the organisation completed training in this way. This deepened the spiritual and professional life of the organisation.[49]

The parishes were "the shop windows" of Anglicare, so Anglicare strove to work where possible out of the parishes. Some parishes, for example, provided space for an Anglican counsellor.[50] Jensen's strategy with parishes and with the institutions of the church, which were like "ships in the ocean," was to "get them to sail in convoy." The Mission shaped the strategy, and as most parishes and institutions began to embrace the concept of the Mission, it enabled "a conceptual flotilla to form."[51]

The question remains: how successful was the Diocesan Mission by the end of Peter's term as Archbishop? Financially, in terms of parish offertories, there was quite dramatic expansion. Between 2002 and 2013

---

47. Peter Kell email to MHC 25.6.2015.
48. Ibid.
49. Ibid.
50. St Swithun's Pymble was one parish which did this.
51. Jensen interview with MHC 9.5.2014.

offertories increased from $38,000,000 to $96,042,894.[52] Even after the Global Financial Crisis and the Diocesan loss of some $160,000,000 the trend continued.[53]

An analysis of the Mission and its results used the NCLS figures of 2011, and also responses to questionnaires sent to wardens and synod representatives. The analysis indicated that weekly church attendance had increased roughly in line with population growth over the previous 20 years. Since the beginning of the Mission in 2002, there was a 26% increase in the number of ordained clergy; over 100 new congregations were started; over 100 other new ministries commenced; and approximately 40 new ethnic congregations commenced. These results represented considerable growth. One negative finding was that the flow of newcomers into church life had declined.[54] The Diocese as a whole had benefited most, the report concluded. No doubt the changes to Anglicare and like organisations were in mind.[55] But the goal of 10% of the population who were committed, equipped and bold to speak in the name of Christ was not attained.

Compared with most of the rest of the Anglican Church of Australia, Sydney was unique in its positive growth. The NCLS statistics for 2001 showed that Sydney had grown in church attendance whereas most other Diocese had falling attendances, with the exception of the 70+ age group.[56]

Category	Under 15	15–19 yrs	20–29 yrs	30–39 yrs	40–49 yrs	50–59 yrs	60–69 yrs	70+ yrs	Total
1996 Sydney	7,200	3,410	6,049	6,131	6,780	6,090	5,400	6,780	47,000
2001 Sydney	8,800	3,586	6,480	6,134	7,171	6,523	65,573	7,690	52,000
Change Sydney (1996-2001)	1,600	176	431	3	391	433	173	910	4,200

---

52. *Annual Report of the Standing Committee to the 2014 Session of the Synod*, 86. This figure represents the total parish receipts less money given to missionary societies and other deductible expenditure.

53. *Southern Cross* November 2009, 6; PF Jensen interview with MHC 9.5.2014.

54. Diocesan Mission Indicators. Prepared by the *What's Next?* Committee, June 2013. See Ballantine-Jones, "Changes in Policies and Practices," 275; PF Jensen Synod Address 2012.

55. ARV (Anglican Retirement Villages), another huge Sydney Diocesan organization with an income of $191.4 million and assets valued at $1011.7 million in 2013 had also undergone major renovations in its leadership structure. PF Jensen interview with MHC 9.5.2014; *ARV Annual Review*, 34–35.

56. The NCLS figures of 2011 were not available to the general public in 2013.

Category	Under 15	15-19 yrs	20-29 yrs	30-39 yrs	40-49 yrs	50-59 yrs	60-69 yrs	70+ yrs	Total
% change Sydney (1996-2001)	22%	5%	7%	0%	6%	7%	3%	13%	9%
1996 All Anglican wo Sydney	21,300	3,822	6,182	11,015	17,310	20,682	23,267	30,123	133,700
2001 All Anglican wo Sydney	18,600	3,320	4,820	8,568	13,602	19,920	22,705	34,165	125,700
Change All Anglican wo Sydney	-2,700	-502	-1,362	-2,447	-3,708	-762	-562	4,042	-8,000
% Change All Anglican wo Sydney	-13%	-13%	-22%	-22%	-21%	-4%	-2%	13%	-6%

Note: "wo" stands for "without Sydney"

Table 9.1 Comparisons of Estimated Weekly Attendance: Sydney and All Anglicans

In other words, by 2001, while Sydney attendances *grew* by 9% since 1996, attendances in the rest of the Anglican Church of Australia in the same period *fell* by 6%. These trends have continued since.[57] In terms of those who call themselves Anglican, a different trend has been noted by the ABS in the period 1991-2011.[58] By this measure, the percentage of people in Sydney identifying as Anglican has fallen by 20.6% while Anglicans' numbers have grown in such places as Brisbane (9.9%), Bunbury (25.2%), Canberra-Goulburn (10.5%), Newcastle (5%) and North Queensland (31.2%). Overall, the total number of Australians who call themselves Anglicans has fallen by 7.7% in the two decades 1991-2011.

It is a grim picture for all Australian Anglicans, especially when the situation of the whole nation is considered. Evangelicals are strongly mission-minded and this drove some of them, rightly or not, to cross boundaries in their desire to plant new churches. Several things should be noted: first, people who called themselves Anglican were not necessarily church

---

57. Anglican Church of Australia, *Report of the Viability and Structures Taskforce*, 8-031 to 8-032.

58. Anglican Church of Australia, *Report of the Viability and Structures Taskforce*, Appendix 1.1, Number of people identifying as Anglican.

attenders.[59] Second, for Sydney Diocese, the statistics indicate that while an identity of being "Anglican" was becoming less important here, church attendance had risen, and was keeping pace with population. This was no cause for complacency, and that is where the vexed issue of church planting was relevant.

"Church planting," the creation of independent evangelical churches by Sydney Anglicans outside the Sydney Diocese, has been outside of the structures of The Anglican Church of Australia. It has not been popular with Anglican bishops. However, the jurisdiction of the bishops is limited to the Anglican churches and institutions in their dioceses and, for this reason, "official" ties between Sydney and these churches is limited to recognition by Sydney of their existence. Some have sought and have been granted a degree of affiliation with the Sydney Diocese.

The first Independent Evangelical Church was so successful that others have been and continue to be set up by Moore College trained clergy. Initially, the churches were mostly in the Newcastle diocese but since then they have spread elsewhere. At present there are almost 30 such churches mostly spread across the Eastern States of Australia. Each is independent of the others and of the Sydney Diocese and each has its own constitution. Each is a member of an unincorporated association called the Fellowship of Independent Evangelical Churches (FIEC).

Not at all Evangelical independent churches have been as successful as the church founded in Erina by Andrew Heard (See Chapter 8). It seems that very few people have joined the independent churches from other denominations, Anglican or otherwise—not surprising as, in many of the Anglican churches in country areas, the congregations are elderly, insular, resistant to change and unlikely to be enthusiastic about the more informal church service which is held in these independent churches. Only two independent churches have been a breakaway from Anglican churches. One is in Brisbane where the people left their Anglican church because they tired of the liberal clergymen the bishop insisted on appointing for them. Another, in Sale in Victoria, was a group of Anglicans who broke away because the bishop accepted practicing homosexual clergy. Most cities in New South Wales have an Independent Evangelical Church. For example, they are to be found in Albury, Bathurst, Maitland, and Orange. The Orange church has purchased a disused cinema in Lord Street, Orange, costing well over $1 million, as its center and meeting place.

---

59. This is picked up in Anglican Church of Australia, *Report of the Viability and Structures Taskforce*, 8-029.

Many members of Sydney Anglican Churches have privately supported FIEC churches with prayer, advice and funds. The Sydney Synod has not financially supported any FIEC church but has helped FIEC members who want advice on matters such as workers' compensation, superannuation and child legislation. The Anglican standard of ministry, *Faithfulness in Service*, is the standard for FIEC members.

The Anglican Church of Australia is at a crossroads. Most of the dioceses have not grown in the past 50 years. The only dioceses which have grown in number of clergy are Brisbane, Sydney, Canberra and Goulburn, Melbourne, and Perth, and the growth has not been even. Since the first General Synod in 1962, Sydney has doubled its numbers at General Synod. That is a reflection of the number of clergy holding positions in the diocese. No other diocese has expanded to this extent.[60]

The future of Anglicanism in rural areas is questionable. The rural areas themselves are in a state of decline, apart from a small number of country cities. Only three dioceses in Australia are able to replace their clergy at the moment. The three dioceses, in alphabetical order, are Armidale, Northwest Australia and Sydney.[61] The Sydney Synod has supported country dioceses for many years. At the 2014 Synod, appropriation assessment monies were allocated to the dioceses of Armidale, Northwest Australia, Northern Territory and Tasmania. Sydney is likely to continue to make these grants to these dioceses because while Moore College-trained clergy are not welcome in many of the other dioceses they are welcome as clergy in these dioceses.

All of this means that the movement amongst the FIEC members is expanding and the expectation is that there will be more Moore College-trained graduates taking independent churches, members of FIEC, across all of Australia.

At the time when affiliation of independent evangelical churches was mooted, there were clergy and laity in Sydney who were opposed, but they were unable to persuade the Synod not to pass the legislation. Archbishop Goodhew assented to it. The legislation was drafted so that no future Archbishop could prevent affiliation.[62]

---

60. Diocesan Representation at General Synods 1962–2014. Table compiled by Robert Tong 27.6.2014. See Appendix.

61. Anglican Church of Australia, *Report of the Viability and Structures Taskforce*, Book 8 015 states: "In only three dioceses (Armidale, North West Australia and Sydney) are sufficient numbers of clergy being ordained to replace those in current active ministry."

62. MHC interview with NM Cameron 23.1.2015.

Archbishop Peter Jensen and his brother Phillip strongly supported church planting as an evangelistic strategy.[63] According to NCLS data in 2003, church plants were the most effective mission strategy. They ranged from starting a new congregation, for example a Chinese congregation at an existing church, to starting a whole new church somewhere. This "somewhere" might be in an existing parish in the Diocese, or in another diocese, as we have seen. In 2004 the Archbishop told the Synod that to develop ten new church sites would cost "something in the order of $100 million." This money was not available and he spoke of a New Capital Project to raise the money. This project, he said, "Is going to test the spiritual life of the Diocese to its limits."[64] Also in 2004, he signed the Recognised Churches Ordinance 2000: an ordinance "to recognize and govern established churches in the Diocese." Such a church qualified only if it had at least 80 members.[65] The following year the Synod passed the Affiliated Churches Ordinance 2005, which provided for the affiliation of non-Anglican churches with the Anglican Church of Australia in the Diocese of Sydney.[66]

The 2014 Report from the General Synod Taskforce for Viability and Structures emphasized the importance of mission. Here Sydney Diocese, with its mission focus, was in accord with the General Synod Taskforce (the members of which, for some reason, did not include Sydney representatives).[67] The Report stated:

> When mission becomes a priority in the Diocese, a bishop may make use of a whole variety of educational opportunities to further that mission. Retreats, conferences, seminars and other regular occasions in diocesan life may all contribute to a deepening awareness of and equipping for mission. A bishop will have myriad opportunities to identify ministry activity which is already happening, to relate it to broader mission directions and to encourage celebration of those endeavours. Naming and celebrating mission in this way contributes to a sense of cohesiveness and confidence in the church's mission. Fostering the notion that every baptised person is called to participate in the

---

63. For example, *Sydney Year Book* 2004 Resolution 3/03, 334.
64. *Sydney Year Book* 2004, 380–1.
65. *Sydney Year Book* 2004, 570–84.
66. *Sydney Year Book* 2006, 615–624 but not assented to by Archbishop Jensen. He assented to Associated Congregations (Amendment) Ordinance 2005, *Sydney Year Book* 2006, 621–631.
67. Anglican Church of Australia, *Report of the Viability and Structures Taskforce*, 8-004.

mission of God will be a constant emphasis in the teaching role of a bishop leading the church into mission.[68]

There seems to be little agreement in the ACA as to what *mission* really is. It remains undefined and therefore amorphous in the General Synod's Taskforce Report. By contrast, Jensen's words about mission are clear and focussed: "What our nation needs above all is the Gospel of Jesus Christ to be at the center of her life." The Sydney Diocese Mission Statement likewise defines mission : "To glorify God by proclaiming Christ our Saviour the Lord Jesus in prayerful dependence on the Holy Spirit, so that everyone will hear his call to repent, trust and serve Christ in love, and be established in the fellowship of his disciples while they await his return."[69]

When asked what was the most significant issue of his episcopate, Peter Jensen answered "the Mission." In his Presidential Address in 2004 he stated that the Synod's vote to support the Diocesan Mission was the high point of the 46th Synod.[70] He was utterly committed to driving it and was himself a model evangelist. He led by example, occasionally relating to the Synod how he spoke to taxi drivers or neighbours about Jesus. Phillip, his evangelist brother, has said that Peter is a better evangelist than he.[71]

The divisive issue of Lay and Diaconal Administration continued to simmer. In his Pastoral Address to the Synod of the Diocese of Ballarat, Bishop Michael Hough stated:

> In a matter closer to home, we are also going to face some quite serious difficulties in our relationship with the Diocese of Sydney if they were to proceed with their plans to allow lay people to preside at the Eucharist. Such a move would prove to be a major break with both the traditions and practice of the universal Church as well as our own Anglican traditions. If they were to go ahead with this radical and unprecedented move, we in the Diocese of Ballarat would need to make a most painful decision. If they proceed, how are we to understand the nature of our relationship in the future? While there would be occasions at which we might be able to vote together on certain issues, Sydney would in many ways be a new branch of Anglicanism. Their decision will place unnecessary obstacles between us and create further insurmountable problems on an ecumenical level ... What Sydney would be doing is forcing one more division

---

68. Ibid. 8-045—8-046.
69. *Sydney Year Book* 2002, 377.
70. *Sydney Year Book* 2005, 389.
71. Phillip Jensen interview with MHC 30.4.2014.

on a Church that is already sinfully divided. What is equally important is that we need Sydney as an active part of our Church if there is going to be any kind of national renewal of our national identity.[72]

These moving words were printed in Sydney's Year Book as an appendix to a report on Lay and Diaconal Administration. The report quoted Archbishop Jensen, who had stated, "Lay Administration, should it be legal, would be a contribution to the common task of bringing the Gospel to Australia."[73] Since 2008 Sydney had also been implementing a permanent diaconate and by 2010 there were 215 permanent deacons, both men and women, actively ministering in the Sydney Diocese.[74] In the Sydney Synod, Bishop Glenn Davies moved a resolution stating that Lay and Diaconal Administration of the Lord's Supper is consistent with the teaching of Scripture and the Resolution was passed. In 2010 the Appellate Tribunal opined against Diaconal Administration. So Sydney by a Resolution authorized the administration of Holy Communion by deacons and lay men and women, legitimizing a practice that had been widespread for many years.

The Permanent Diaconate was an innovation insofar as those belonging to this order of deacons remained permanently within it. Since they were part of a team, there would henceforth be a new flexibility for ministry and mission. Team ministry has become an important new trend in the Diocese: the old model of the Rector of a parish doing everything, and having a curate if the parish could afford one, has been replaced in many Sydney parishes with a team. The Permanent Diaconate also gave women greater opportunity of portability and security, and, as we have seen, enabled deacons, both men and women, to celebrate Holy Communion. Another aspect of the Permanent Diaconate was that not all were trained henceforth at Moore College. Peter Jensen, as a former Principal of Moore College, has called that one of the most breathtaking decisions he made in his episcopate. Here again, was evidence of flexibility of thinking for the sake of effective mission.[75]

The years of the Jensen episcopate were widely viewed as the ascendancy of the Jensen family. Phillip Jensen became Dean in October 2002. It was thought that Peter had unilaterally appointed his brother to the position, although this was not the case. The position had been vacant for some time,

---

72. *Sydney Year Book 2005*, 458.

73. Ibid., 456.

74. Jeremy Halcrow, *Sydney resolute on deacons celebrating Lord's Supper*, 15.10.2010, www./ Sydney Anglican Gateway to the Anglican Church in Sydney.

75. PF Jensen interview with MHC 19.5.2015.

and it had proved exceedingly difficult to find a new Dean. The Cathedral Chapter voted unanimously for Phillip by secret ballot. Peter Jensen was Chairman of the Chapter but not present.[76] Phillip's subsequent controversial management of the Cathedral provoked widespread opposition to him: a man who was at home with the informality characteristic of university students could not import such informality to a cathedral with impunity. Michael Jensen, Peter's eldest son, was appointed to the Faculty of Moore College, where Peter was Chairman of the Council, although the appointment was not at his instigation. Peter's wife Christine was *de facto* the head of the clergy wives, an unpaid role. Narelle Jarrett, the newly-appointed Archdeacon for Women's Ministry, and Principal of Mary Andrew's College (formerly known as Deaconess House), at a commissioning service in St Andrew's Cathedral, asked Christine Jensen to join her and her team at the front of the Cathedral. It was no more than a gesture of respect. A *Sydney Morning Herald* reporter assumed that Christine had been given a new position of leadership, which was in fact not so. These appointments seemed to the many who were misinformed, to be a Jensen take-over.

A question is: to what extent did Phillip influence Peter? Both men acknowledge they are close; both have stated that they rarely discuss diocesan matters together. Phillip is an "ideas man" and almost certainly Peter took up some of his ideas. Peter is an "ideas man" in his own right and an excellent strategist. In Sydney, as Peter has pointed out, the Archbishop does not have much real power. His task is to persuade rather than coerce. Both were members of some of the same committees: the Cathedral Chapter and the Mission Executive, for example. The latter was the DEB (Diocesan Executive Board), a kind of inner ring think-tank dating from the Goodhew era, re-branded. Those who have worked with the brothers do not see any undue influence over Peter by Phillip.[77]

Further appointments also proved controversial. Of the four men Peter appointed assistant bishop, only one, Glenn Davies, stood for the position of Archbishop when Peter retired. One of Peter's appointments, Al Stewart, actually retired from being Bishop of Wollongong after three years.[78] But the situation regarding potential leadership at the end of Peter's episcopate was little different from that at the end of Harry Goodhew's. As the Goodhew era drew to a close, Peter was not a bishop and the only serious contender

---

76. NM Cameron conversation with MHC 2014.

77. NM Cameron conversation with MHC 2014 and R Tong interview with MHC 7.6.2010.

78. He was Bishop of Wollongong from 30.3.2007 to 2010.

for the position, apart from Peter, was the Rev. Robert Forsyth, a parish clergyman who was consecrated bishop late in the Goodhew era.

Meanwhile Moore College was booming under the new Principal, John Woodhouse. By now it defined the Diocese: to have been trained there was almost always a prerequisite for employment as rector of a Sydney parish. This gave the College Faculty extraordinary influence over the shape of the Diocese. Between 2001 and 2011, annual undergraduate enrollments rose from 287 to 401 and a third of the undergraduate students were women.[79] The College received glowing approval from the AUQA (Australian Universities Quality Agency) accreditation process. John Woodhouse commented: "On virtually every matrix they use to assess an institution we are way ahead of the game. A lot of that has to do with the kind of student body we have. And the Faculty we have. For no one is it just a job."[80]

About the commonly expressed view that the College was ingrown, Woodhouse stated,

> We have folk who did not study at Moore College: Paul Williamson, the Irishman, Philip Kern the American, Brian Rosner, [an Australian] . . . If you put it in purely academic terms rather than Christian terms, we represent a school of thought, just as you might have a history department at a university that has a school of thought that is developing . . . You've got to be very careful that you're open to outside scrutiny . . . one of our policies is that a potential faculty member who has done their first degree here, almost always is sent off overseas to do their doctoral work where they're exposed to a wider world of thought and ideas, have things tested, and come back with a fresh objectivity. We have a programme of study leave where faculty members regularly go and work in another institution.
>
> There is a danger of becoming completely inward looking, and it is for others to look at us, for I don't think we are. That itself might not be an objective view of things, but it's not for people who don't know, just to assume that because many of the Faculty have trained at the same place, that they are not open to other ideas. My general experience is that our students are exposed to a wider range of ideas than I encounter in other places . . .
>
> But our students are forced to read the range of literature. We do have guests come and give lectures, who are not "toeing

---

79. From Rhonda Barry, Registrar at MTC: Statistics for Undergraduate Commencing Enrolments.

80. J Woodhouse interview with MHC 30.5.2011.

the line." There is, as you would expect, a range of opinion on the Faculty, about a number of controversial issues.[81]

Moore College has an External Studies Department. It began humbly enough, during TC Hammond's time as Principal. In 1941 he gave a new series of evening lectures for a two-year course known as SPTC (Sydney Preliminary Theological Certificate). At the end of the first year 24 students sat for the May examination.[82] Gradually the course was offered by correspondence to those not able to attend the lectures. The course has been offered ever since, under different names. By 2008 the Certificate in Theology had students from a variety of denominations in 50 countries around the world. It was used to train and equip pastors, lay missionaries and church leaders in places like Africa, India, Fiji and South America.[83] By 2013 5,000 students in 100 countries were enrolled in the course.[84] The influence of Moore College through its correspondence course, in Australia and overseas has been immense.

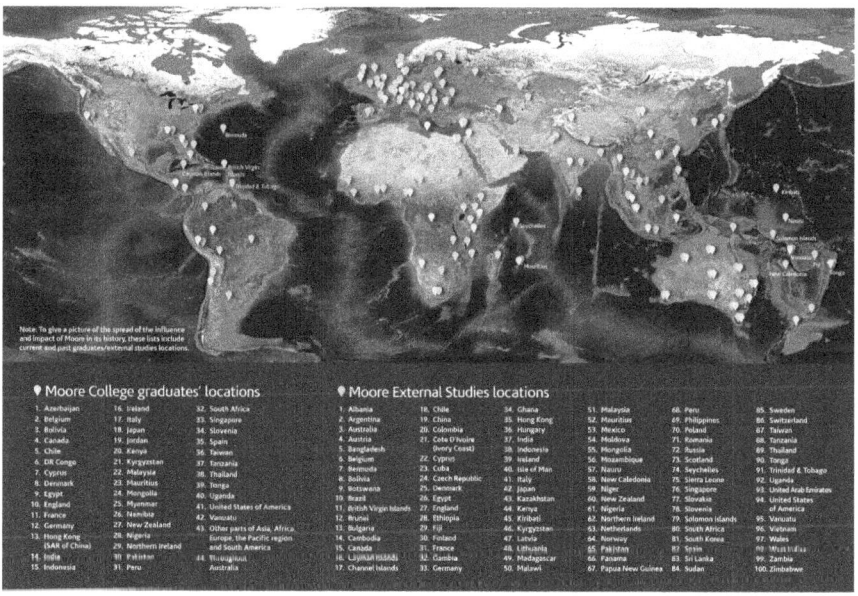

Moore College External Studies worldwide

81. J Woodhouse interview with MHC 30.5.2011.
82. Loane, *A Centenary History of Moore Theological College*, 144.
83. *Reaching the World*, Moore College External Studies, 4.
84. Conversation with Elizabeth Smith 31.7.2013.

John Woodhouse while Principal founded the Priscilla and Aquila Center. This has been established "to encourage and promote further thinking about the practice of Christian ministry by women, in partnership with men."[85] To date the Center has held four conferences, at the second of which, John Woodhouse delivered the keynote address on I Timothy 2. The conference registered 250 people, one person even travelling from New Zealand. John Woodhouse has said,

> One of the key things is to work out the practical implications of our understanding of men and women in ministry. The battles of the 80s and 90s have been fought. We'd like to settle down and in a less combative mood. So we've come to this position. What are its implications? That's, I think, a context in which a lot of this sort of thing will be worked out. When you're in the trenches you tend to draw the lines more sharply than they need to be drawn. If you give an inch and someone's going to take a mile, you don't give an inch. But in a more peaceful environment that I think we're in now, I think we can think through the greys of this, the areas where there ought to be more flexibility, and that's what we're trying to do.[86]

Jane Tooher, the Director of the Center, is also a member of the Faculty of Moore College. She lectures in Ministry, New Testament and Church History. She has stated:

> I lecture to men and women in New Testament lectures, but basically don't do exegetical lectures in New Testament . . . I don't preach to mixed congregations. I preach at women's chapel and I have given what we call sermon sidebars in mixed chapel, which I think come under the topic of prophecy (I Corinthians 11). They are normally a topic coming out of the sermon passage.[87]

Re the Priscilla and Aquila Center, she wrote:

> I understand completely that people have different views on the ministries of women, that there's a range of views, but what I find frustrating and discouraging is that some people assume things, and don't try and understand what we are doing at Moore, which is that we are coming from a complementarian understanding, but what I'm doing with the Priscilla & Aquila Center is wanting us to think much more seriously and creatively

---

85. www.vimeo.com: Priscilla and Aquila Center.
86. Woodhouse interview with MHC 30.5.2011.
87. Jane Tooher email to MHC 1.7.2015.

about what really is the application end of complementarianism, hence, doing things like combined male and female team teaching (though there are times when female lecturers will lecture alone), and do sermon side bars in mixed chapel (as well as encouraging women in writing projects, post-graduate study at Moore, and other things). [88]

Jane Tooher

While John Woodhouse and others maintain that the battles over women's ministry are now over in the Sydney Diocese, many would not

88. Ibid.

agree. Ken Handley QC, a former Chancellor of the Diocese, calls the issue "a sleeper." He has said, "It does require some obvious leader but sooner or later it will re-emerge."[89] Meanwhile the issue of whether the Anglican Church of Australia might have women bishops had been debated by the General Synod in Fremantle (2004) and the conservatives won the day. Keen promoters of women bishops then took the matter to the Appellate Tribunal. It gave an opinion that there was no canonical barrier to women being consecrated bishops. Its advice was highly controversial, as can be seen from Robert Tong's letter to *Southern Cross* in 2008.[90]

He wrote:

> ... the pronouncement is an advisory opinion given under a constitutional provision where questions concerning the constitution (the 1961 constitution of the Anglican Church of Australia) can be posed to the Appellate Tribunal for an answer. The opinion is neither binding or final, such is the nature of advisory opinions. Only a civil court can make final decisions.
>
> Second, the advisory opinion had the support of only four of its seven members. The four members in the majority are all known public supporters of female ordination.
>
> Thirdly, the result swung on whether a change to a constitutional definition of "canonical fitness" affected a change in the substantive law. Up to now the General Synod and the Australian Anglican Church at large, took the view that a General Synod canon was necessary to change the law concerning female ordination. The Canon Law Commission supported this view.
>
> According to the Tribunal a canon is not necessary. But this raises a fundamental issue. Who should initiate such a change to episcopal ministry in the Australian church: the General Synod or the Appellate Tribunal? Surely foundational policy questions which go to the heart of one of the orders of ministry must be decided in the representative legislative forum of the General Synod.
>
> Robert Tong
>
> Sydney, NSW

---

89. Quoted in McGillion, *The Chosen Ones*, 136.

90. NM Cameron wrote an article for *Southern Cross, Women as Bishops: Change by judicial sleight of hand,* which examined the issue in greater detail than R Tong's succinct letter. Dec.2007/Feb. 2008, 15.

While it seemed to many that, following the ordination of women in the ACA, consecration of women as bishops would only be a matter of time, the *process* was quite wrong, as Tong pointed out. It was a marker that the General Synod was sliding away from democratic, legal processes: that there were those within the General Synod who regarded themselves as above the law and who would use questionable means to achieve their end. The hard work of legislating and debating seemed a hollow endeavor if this were to be the way of the future. It also rang warning bells about the Primate's desire for more power, for himself and for the General Synod, at the expense of the dioceses.

Relationships between Sydney Diocese and the other metropolitan sees seemed to become more difficult during the Jensen years. John Reid had noted such a trend as far back as 1993.[91] In the Dioceses of Brisbane, Perth, and Adelaide, Sydney-trained clergy were rarely admitted as rectors or assistant clergy, notwithstanding the desire of the relevant parishes, to have such a person ministering in the parish. In each case the Archbishop was committed to maintaining the Liberal Catholic nature of his diocese and did not want to upset the balance. One evangelical rector in a Liberal Catholic diocese has written, "The great sadness is that generally speaking, only the evangelical parishes are growing and typically only the evangelical parishes have any youth or children's ministry."[92]

During the Jensen years, the "paddock became smaller," as Karin Sowada has put it, for women in ministry. The new criterion for orthodoxy was whether a woman *preached* or not. This had not been the case in the 1970s and 1980s. There is considerable evidence of women preaching in public to men and women: not just Jacinth Myles (see Chapter 8), but Rosie Pidgeon who trained men and women and led mixed Bible studies, Narelle Jarrett, Helen Roseveare, and Margaret Rodgers are just some of the women who preached in church, at the university public EU meetings and at least one CMS convention.[93] The *ground* of the debate had also shifted, from the argument about "headship" of the male, to I Timothy 2: 12 "I do not permit a woman to teach or to have authority over a man; she must be silent." The ground for the prohibition of preaching was now a *single verse*! Nevertheless, Archbishop Jensen continued to issue licences to women to preach, and women deacons, by virtue of their office, could preach.[94]

91. See Chapter 8.
92. Name withheld.
93. Rosie Pidgeon email to MHC 18.7.2013, Greg Anderson interview with MHC 12.7.2013. K Mascord, "Open Letter to the Anglican Diocese of Sydney," in *A Restless Faith*, 235–40.
94. For example, the author has been licensed to preach in her local church since

People began to write books about the Diocese, or for the Diocese. Chris McGillion's *The Chosen Ones* (2005) is a fascinated and perceptive look at the Sydney Diocese, although its subtitle, *The Politics of Salvation in the Anglican Church*, suggests it was to be about the whole Anglican Church of Australia. It examined the turmoil of the Goodhew years and the first years of Peter Jensen's episcopate. Comments from Sydney leaders were that "Chris McGillion doesn't understand us because he doesn't understand evangelism."

Dr Claire Smith wrote *God's Good Design. What the Bible really says about MEN and WOMEN*, published by Matthias Media in 2012. It was a conservative look at a number of key passages of Scripture dealing with women, their relationship with men, and their ministry roles. The problem for this position is that there are inherent anomalies for those who seek to abide by it in the 21st Century: anomalies for women who write articles, books and theses or use the electronic media to teach men and women the Scriptures. There is a sense in which conservatives on the women question have to draw lines in the sand, as to what women may or may not do.

The Rev. Keith Mascord's *A Restless Faith. Leaving Fundamentalism in a Quest for God* (2012) relates his journey of faith from fundamentalism to theological liberalism. At one time a member of the Moore College Faculty, he moved, in a metaphorical sense, to a far country. His Open Letter to the Diocese of Sydney (2007) was included at the end of book. In this he accused the Diocese of Sydney of being unloving and arrogant and of exhibiting a disturbing trend towards censorship of thought. There was some truth in his assertions, although they were tangled in personal disappointment and theological waywardness. His book makes for painful reading and is certainly a stimulus for self-examination.

The Rev. Dr Michael Jensen wrote *Sydney Anglicanism. An Apology* (2012), examining some of Sydney's distinctive philosophy and theology. He kept his cards close to his chest on the issue of women in ministry. The Rev. Dr John Dickson's beautifully titled book *Hearing Her Voice* was published first as an e-Book in 2013. It raised a question of semantics as it examined the meaning of one key word in I Timothy 2:12. The argument about this word, *didaskō*, was not new: the Report of the Diocesan Doctrine Commission of 1988 spelt this out clearly.[95] Dickson received some negative reactions from some Sydney leaders. Matthias Media's response was a book of essays, *Women, Sermons and the Bible*, edited by Tony Payne and the Rev. Dr Peter Bolt.

1994.

95. *Sydney Year Book 1989*, 4.3 352. See Appendix.

We come finally to what would generally be regarded as the two major issues of Peter Jensen's episcopate: the Global Financial Crisis and the Jerusalem GAFCON. Both occurred in 2008. Sydney Diocese lost $160,000,000 in the maelstrom of the Global Financial Crisis. Sydney had lost money before, but not on a scale such as this.[96] Something similar had occurred to the Church of England in England some sixteen years earlier. In 1992 it lost the huge sum of £800,000,000! The Archbishop of Canterbury of the day, George Carey, explained in his autobiography that the losses were caused by "ambitious targets in order to meet the strong wishes of the Synod to fuel the mission of the church."[97] But he has written that the day the *Financial Times* broke the story of the losses "may in time come to be seen as the day the church grew up."[98]

The CEO of the Glebe Administration Board (GAB), Steve McKerihan explained the Sydney Diocesan losses: "In hindsight . . . we would acknowledge that we had too much risk in our asset profile relative to the level of debt we were carrying. And when we experienced the greatest stockmarket fall in 100 years in Australia, we had a severe problem."[99] In his apology to the Sydney Synod, Phil Shirriff, Chairman of the GAB, presented evidence that the Diocese would have only been $10,000,000 better off without the gearing strategy.[100] The outcome was a severe cut in annual expenditure: from $10,000,000 to $4,000,000.

Peter Jensen has stated:

> It seemed to me that . . . we needed to know what actually happened. Some people rushed to conclusions and of course were very very alarmed and terribly critical. The losses, though immensely serious, were not as serious as it seemed. If we had just put the money in the bank, and left it there, our losses would have only been a certain amount, if you follow me. Because you'd done more with the money, your losses were comparatively more. If you took the advice of the people who are complaining loudest, then you wouldn't have paid any money, you would have been so conservative, full stop. So that's life. So you've got to analyse what's happened.

---

96. PF Jensen interview with MHC 9.5.2014. A Diocesan venture into real estate in Chatswood in 1992 lost a lot of money.

97. Carey, *Know the Truth* pp161, 167.

98. Ibid.,172.

99. *Southern Cross* July 2009, 14.

100. *Southern Cross* November 2009, 6; "Gearing" is taking on debt in order to increase the size of investments.

> Secondly in my opinion, is offering leadership. There would be little point in all the passengers on the ship hitting each other with their oars and so on. Clearly, things were done that in retrospect—it's always in retrospect that you wouldn't do again. And there were one or two people on the Glebe Board who were truly concerned before it happened.
>
> There were questions, very serious questions, but the synodical response was a mark of maturity. Peter Kell had an enormous part to play in the good things that were achieved at that time, because people trusted him and he worked very very hard indeed to make this happen. As did Peter Tasker and others. That leadership was crucial.
>
> At the same time, the parishes were giving more and more generously. And that never faltered.
>
> My next point is: trust God. He removed $6 million *per annum* from us—it may be that generosity will come in other ways. I think it was a test for us to trust in God's sovereignty and provision for us to do the work he is calling us to do. That how I see it. I don't think it's a cause for panic or bewailing, people fighting each other, but rather a test to see if we could trust him.[101]

Like George Carey, Peter Jensen found huge financial losses thrust the Diocese back upon trusting God, and watching for him to work out his hidden purposes.[102]

In his Presidential Address of 2009, Jensen stated:

> Let me be quite personal about my experience of the year since last Synod. It was in November that I got the first inkling of the magnitude of what had happened to our investments. Each successive month seemed to bring worse news. It has taken a long time to grasp and begin to see the implications of it. I can tell you some of the things I have felt:
>
> I felt *disbelief*—I have been schooled to believe that this could not happen because we have been so careful and professional in our handling of the Endowment.
>
> I felt both *let down* and yet *responsible* since this has occurred on my watch and in part within funds in which I have a special interest.
>
> I felt *doubt* about whether we had engaged in ethically dubious practices by gearing the Endowment.

---

101. PF Jensen interview with MHC 9.5.2014.
102. Presidential Address *Sydney Year Book 2010*, 376.

> I felt deep *uncertainty* about what we should now do and how we could carry on.
>
> Above all, I felt *grief*—and this I have continued to feel—as the impact of these losses on many fine ministries and on the jobs and personal lives of friends and colleagues has become clear. It is not easy to see the dismantling of so much of the Anglican Media for example; the loss of our Archdeacons; the impact on the Cathedral; the inability to fund local ministries through regions and through the Archbishop; the decline in resources available to Youthworks—I could go on and on.
>
> Are there signs here? Yes, as always, there are signs of our human weaknesses; signs which have rightly brought forth words of sorrow and apology; but there are also signs which say that God is our only hope and our true resource; signs which summon us again to persistent, active faith.[103]

GAFCON stands for Global Anglican Future Conference. The first GAFCON was held in Jerusalem, in June 2008. At Lambeth 1998, Motion 1.10, rejecting homosexual practice as incompatible with Scripture, was passed with a huge majority. But by 2003, several Dioceses in the Episcopal Church (ECUSA) were legitimizing same-sex unions. In 2003 Gene Robinson, a man in an active homosexual relationship, was elected, and later consecrated, Bishop of New Hampshire. Attempts to mediate some kind of compromise solution by Rowan Williams, the successor to George Carey as Archbishop of Canterbury, were fruitless.

Since 2003 there had been many attempts to call the offending North Americans back to biblical standards. At the same time, there was condemnation for those bishops from the Global South who were providing ministry for orthodox Christians still wishing to be Anglican but unable to do so in the fellowship of the American churches.[104] In a *Southern Cross* article titled "Why I am going to Israel," Peter Jensen wrote: "Individuals, parishes and even dioceses have left the original church, becoming associated with other parts of the world, and with new bishops being appointed from overseas to care for the disaffected."[105] He continued,

> The next Lambeth Conference has been summoned for July-August 2008. The Archbishop of Canterbury is responsible for the guest list, and he has invited all except for the Bishop of New Hampshire on the one hand and some of the new

---

103. Presidential Address *Sydney Year Book 2010*, 374.
104. Archbishop Peter Akinola's Address to GAFCON.
105. *Southern Cross* February 2008, 10.

bishops appointed to care for the dissidents on the other. Thus, for example, the Bishop of New Westminster has been invited although his actions have caused the Reverend David Short and his congregation (which includes Dr Jim Packer) to withdraw as far as they can from the Diocese. An invitation to share the conference under these circumstances has posed a real difficulty for many of us.

Several African provinces have indicated that they will not be attending Lambeth, because to do so would be to acquiesce with the North American actions. They are not ending the Communion, or even dividing it. They are simply indicating that the nature of the Communion has now been altered by what has occurred.[106]

One thousand people came from all over the world to GAFCON. The bishops attending made up about one third of the total number invited to Lambeth, their provinces representing 75% of the world's Anglicans.[107] Peter Jensen designed the week's program, which included excellent Bible teaching each morning. Small groups and workshops met daily. On the last day the Jerusalem Declaration was crafted. This listed fourteen tenets of orthodoxy, which underpinned their Anglican identity. Peter Jensen's part in GAFCON was pivotal, not least because, as an Australian and with a DPhil from Oxford, his scholarship was respected and he did not treat the very large African contingent as "colonials."

Peter Jensen was asked by the Anglican Primates who met in Nairobi in 2007 to be the Chair of the Program Committee of GAFCON. The Rev. Chris Sugden, who organized the practical side of GAFCON, has written,

> Archbishop Jensen had a vision and concern to be able to lay out through the GAFCON programme the whole vista of Scripture focused from beginning to end on the love of God in Jesus Christ our Lord. So the decision was taken not to expound one book, but a series of passages throughout the Bible, which developed this theme.
>
> His decision proved wise. Those Bible expositions were so good and such a rounded whole that they have been gathered into a collection suitable for Home Group Study and published by Latimer Press as *The Way of the Cross*.
>
> Archbishop Peter called those giving leadership to the programme for a breakfast meeting every day in his hotel rooms. These meetings were most important for continuing the energy of the programme through the conference and ensuring that proper thought was given to each contribution . . . As the week

---

106. *Southern Cross* Feb. 2008, 10.
107. Ibid., June 2008, 27.

progressed Peter's stage presence giving shape and confidence to the day's programme was one of the feel-good factors of the conference.[108]

Rev. Prof Stephen Noll evaluated Peter Jensen's stepping forward to spearhead the process that led to GAFCON as "critical." Noll also thought that the move by Sydney Diocese "from a place of relative lack of involvement in the Anglican Communion and Global South affairs to a much more active involvement may be of historic significance." Most importantly, he stated,

> I think many people at GAFCON only knew of Peter by reputation as being part of an "evangelical bastion" were surprised at his willingness to work across "party" lines, at least, among those at GAFCON. He is clearly a godly man with a peaceable spirit. There were some "ecumenical" gestures in the Statement and Declaration which he and others from Sydney signed onto. It was helpful to have a theologian-bishop involved who could weigh the different issues involved.[109]

Since Peter was not a Primate, he was ineligible to join the Primates' Council as the supreme governing body of GAFCON. He has continued his leadership in GAFCON in the role of Secretary to the Primates' Council. A second GAFCON was held in Nairobi in 2013. So far GAFCON has served to strengthen Anglicans of different churchmanship who strive to stand true to Biblical and Anglican principles: its ongoing significance, possibly very great, lies in the future.

Wally Behan the Rector of St John's Latimer Square, Christchurch, New Zealand, attended GAFCON 2008. He stated,

> I'm at GAFCON because I feel that, probably next to America and Canada, New Zealand is probably the most liberal church. And I think that the Anglican Church in New Zealand wants to go the way of America. We have got to find a way as Evangelicals of stopping that while still remaining Anglicans. We won't stop it, but we have got to find a way of remaining Anglicans but not go the same way as America, from an Evangelical point of view. I've come to GAFCON to try, when we get back, to try hopefully, to encourage us to stay together more, but it's also got us other contacts, from which we can get help. In the law, for example, we have found experts who can teach us about where we can get advice about our own canon law... I'd hoped, coming to GAFCON, that I could go back to New Zealand and have

---

108. C Sugden email to MHC 18.2.2009.
109. S Noll email to MHC 1.8.2008.

some spiritual muscle to at least stop the flow of the liberal flow towards TEC.[110] It's not going to stop, because eventually it will go through. Same-sex blessings in New Zealand will eventually go through. What I hope GAFCON will do, is to give us some muscle to stop it, and to make the church realize the consequences of going down that track. That is huge for me. And I can now go back with that, as well as not feeling intimidated, and take the message to the other Evangelicals, not to feel intimidated, because they will remain Anglicans. If they get licences taken away, or they have to step aside, or whatever it is, there is a greater part of the Anglican Church in the world which will look after them and care for them.[111]

David Short, former Rector of St John Shaughnessy, Vancouver, described Sydney Diocese's involvement in GAFCON as "an act of pure grace:"

One of the marvelous things about GAFCON is the face-to-face relationships. I've seen Peter Jensen preach publicly in the North American context and people will shake their heads when they see the Archbishop of Sydney and he's not a monster. He's a lovely guy. Funny and loves Jesus and so I think it is very helpful to have so many people from Sydney. There's no reason for Sydney to be involved in this, in a way. It's an act of pure grace. The same with the Nigerians. The Nigerians don't need to be involved. From the point of view of the very small orthodox branch in North America, we just feel blown away by it.[112]

The present leaders of the Diocese of Sydney have been called "Biblical radicals," an apt description of the years of the Jensen ascendancy.[113] The Diocesan Mission, driven by the brothers Peter and Phillip focused on evangelizing Sydney, Australia and the world in a new dynamic way. In its commitment to Biblical Christianity, it established strong ties with Evangelicals around the world, inspired more young men and women to enter ministry and missionary work and engaged in creative and flexible, though sometimes controversial, ways of expressing its Anglicanism. Its conservatism on the issue of women's ministry grew more pronounced. While the latter created a sizeable minority of estranged dissidents, it is also true that the years of the Jensen ascendancy saw Sydney Anglicans sailing like a flotilla towards a common goal. With the first GAFCON, Peter's leadership assumed an international dimension which may well prove to be his most significant legacy.

110. TEC is the other name for ECUSA.
111. Wally Behan interview with MHC 29.6.2008.
112. Short interview with MHC 25.6.2008.
113. Stuart Piggin interview with MHC 27.4.2010.

Phenomenon

THE EVANGELICAL DIOCESE OF Sydney is a phenomenon in the Anglican Church of Australia and possibly in the entire Anglican Communion. Why Evangelicalism has been preserved in Sydney, while elsewhere it has faltered, is of prime concern. The key to the preservation of Evangelicalism has been the subject of an investigation by a Melbourne Evangelical, Jonathan Wei-Han Kuan. In his PhD thesis he argues that a confluence of four vital contributors is required for evangelical continuity and health in a setting such as an Anglican Diocese. These contributors are:

1. Healthy evangelical parishes
2. Healthy evangelical societies
3. A healthy evangelical training college and
4. A supportive diocesan bishop

Kuan concluded: "Melbourne has never had all four factors in place at the same time and hence, unlike Sydney, has not developed a more robust and rigorously uniform evangelical character." [1]

A brief review of Sydney's history shows that the four contributors were largely met over the history of the Diocese of Sydney. Healthy evangelical parishes existed from the time of Bishop Barker onward, especially because of his firm policy in appointing evangelical clergy. The foundation of the Church Society at the beginning of Barker's episcopate was the first of a number of healthy voluntary evangelical societies. The establishment of Moore College, also at the beginning of Barker's episcopate, over the next

---

1. J W-H Kuan, "The history of Evangelicalism in the Anglican Diocese of Melbourne, 1847–1937," 1.

150 years produced a stream of evangelical clergy. Finally, most of the archbishops of Sydney have been strongly supportive of evangelical work.

The eras of Barker, Mowll, Loane and Loane's successors have been times of evangelical growth as evangelical parishes proliferated; voluntary societies, especially those with mission and welfare goals, blossomed; and Moore College, under the Barker-appointed principals, followed by Nathaniel Jones, TC Hammond and all Hammond's successors, became the diocesan powerhouse.

Kuan's thesis admirably explains why the Diocese of Sydney has expanded and maintained its evangelical identity.

Sydney has had its ups and downs, ranging from an immoral archbishop to financial disasters such as the SCEGGS problems of the 1970s, and more recent losses as a consequence of the Global Financial Crash. But it has survived and may be said to be more focussed than it has ever been. Sydney is diverse in its parishes and liturgical practice but has largely adhered to Biblical truth and the need to tell about God's love for the lost and his offer of eternal life to those who repent and commit themselves to follow Christ.

Now that the worldwide Anglican Church is on the brink of fragmentation over the issue of homosexual practice, the Diocese of Sydney has taken up leadership of a global significance. With a key role since 2008 in the establishment and leadership of GAFCON, it is has provided a way forward for a diverse group of Anglicans including Anglo-Catholic, Pentecostal and Evangelical. It has provided a lifeline for hundreds of churches that found themselves out in the cold because they could no longer belong to a church that departed from Biblical practice. By gathering under the umbrella of the Fellowship of Confessing Anglicans (FCA), which has provided them with oversight and support, they have moved on, from uncertainty and insecurity, to hope. The ACNA (Anglican Church in North America), since its foundation in 2009, has created 500 new churches, has 1,000 congregations and 29 dioceses with 100,000 worshippers.[2]

To quote the Rev. Dr John Yates III, a leading American Anglican, "GAFCON is an essential good for the global church." He has recently made two pleas to Sydney Anglicans: first, to own our global significance because we have strength and stability to share with fellow Anglicans in the FCA. Second, to support GAFCON.[3] In the providence of God, two men have made GAFCON into an instrument of global Anglican rescue, reconstruc-

---

2. John Yates III, EFAC Address, 7.1.2015.

3. Ibid. ECUSA stands for Episcopal Church of the USA; ACNA stands for Anglican Church in North America.

tion and growth. One is Archbishop Peter Akinola of Nigeria. The other is Archbishop Peter Jensen.

Sydney's unique personality can be summed up in its serious commitment to the centrality of the Bible and the behaviour which flows from this: namely evangelism and missionary activity. The radical nature of the mandate to "go and make disciples . . . " trumps Anglican tradition whether it be liturgy, dress, architectural style or music. Another outcome of Sydney's biblicism is a particular perspective on such issues as the role of women in public ministry, lay and diaconal administration of the Lord's Supper, homosexual behaviour and church planting. Together with its size and wealth, all of the above traits mark Sydney out as different from the rest of Anglican Australia, and most of the rest of the Anglican Church, worldwide.

Healthy evangelical parishes, healthy evangelical societies, the excellent education provided by Moore College, and a succession, for the most part, of evangelical bishops have stamped the Diocese with its evangelical character. While it is a phenomenon in worldwide Anglican terms, its evangelical character is by no means unusual in other denominations of the Christian church. Composed of ordinary human beings with the usual human faults, the Diocese has, under God's hand, maintained its unswerving commitment to Reformed, Biblical theology and to continuing to obey the Great Commission of Christ:

Go and make disciples of all nations,

Baptizing them in the name of the Father and of the Son and of the Holy Spirit, and

Teaching them to obey everything that I have commanded you.[4]

---

4. Matthew 28:19–20.

Interviews, Emails and Letters Listed

Winifred Sharland October 1984
Archbishop Sir Marcus Loane 5.2.1996
Bishop Frank Retief 9.7.2004
Bishop Donald William Bradley Robinson 13 .6. 2006
Bishop DWB Robinson 20.9.2006
Bishop DWB Robinson 2.10.2006
Bishop DWB Robinson 24.10.2006
Bishop DWB Robinson 31.10.2006
Bishop Ewen Donald Cameron 15.11.2006
Bishop DWB Robinson 28.11.2006
Bishop DWB Robinson 15.11.2006
Bishop DWB Robinson 7.2.2007
Bishop DWB Robinson 8.5.2007
Anne Judd 9.5.2007
Bishop DWB Robinson 16.5.2007
Bishop DWB Robinson 28.5.2007
Bishop DWB Robinson 12.6.2007
Bishop DWB Robinson 27.6.2007
Rev. Dick Lucas *letter* 31.7.2007
Rev. Philip Newman OAM 24.10.2007
Marie Robinson 11.3.2008

Bishop James Grant and Rowena Armstrong 7.6.2008
Bishop Robert Forsyth 21.6.2008
Bishop R Forsyth 22.6.2008
Margaret Forsyth 21.6.2008
Rev. Dr Samuel Kefa Kamya 22.6.2008
Bishop David Mulready 23.6.2008
Rev. David Short 25.6.2008
Rev. Caesar Guzman 25.6.2008
Rev. Kanishka Raffel 26.6.2008
Cheryl Chang, Chancellor of the Anglican Network in Canada 27.6.2008
Bishop Marcus Ibrahim 27.6.2008
Bishop Yong Chen Fah 28.6.2008
Rev. Wally Behan 29.6.2008
Bishop Peter Tasker 29.6.2008
Archdeacon David Powys 1.8.2008
Rev. Prof. Stephen Noll *email* 1.8.2008
Rev. Allan Blanch: Notes from an address: 'Some Reflections on 40 years of Christian Ministry.' 27.7.2008

266   Interviews, Emails and Letters Listed

Rev. Jonathan Fletcher 12.8.2008
Bishop Peter Watson 28.10.2008
Dr Phillip Heath 20.2.2009
Rev. Dr Graham Cole 5.6.2009
Pam Goodhew 15.2.2010
Archbishop Harry Goodhew 15.2.2010
Dr Neil Cameron 30.3.2010
Professor Stuart Piggin 27.4.2010
Dr Robert Tong 7.6.2010
Rev. Dr Mark Harding 9.8.2010
Dr Paul and Dr Gabrielle Oslington 30.8.2010
Bishop Paul Barnett 17.11.10
Archbishop Peter Jensen 23.11.10
Alicia Watson 2.5.11
Dr Stephen Judd 4.5.11
Dss Margaret Rodgers 9.5.11
Dss M. Rodgers 23.5.11
Rev. Dr John Woodhouse 30.5.11
Wendy Colquhoun 2.6.11
Professor Edwin Judge 22.8.11
Rod and Dr Janet West 12.9.11
Rev. John Cornish 14.9.11
Dr Ann Young 29.2.2012
Rev. J Cornish 8.3.12
Rev. Ross Weaver 27.11.12
Archdeacon Kara Gilbert (Hartley) 26.2.2013

Rev. Peter Robinson 8.5.13
Bishop ED Cameron 16.5.13
Bishop Greg Anderson 12.7.2013
Dr Karin Sowada 17.7.2013
Prof. David MW Powers *email* 17.7.2013
Margaret Hall *email* 11.8.2013
Professor Christopher Bellenger 29.7.13
Rev. Jacinth Myles 5.8.2013
Dr Alice Cunningham *email* 16.3.2014
Ian Carmichael *email* 18.6.2013
Jim Bates *email* 31.7.2013
Rev. Phillip Jensen 30.4.2014
Archbishop P Jensen 9.5.2014
Dr NM Cameron 3.9.2014
Rev. Bruce Pass 8.9.2014
Bishop ED Cameron 8.12.2014
Dr N Cameron 23.1.2015
Rev. Andrew Heard *email* 11.2.2015
Archbishop P Jensen 4.2.2015
Archbishop P Jensen 6.5.2015
Archbishop P Jensen 19.5.2015
Peter Kell *email* 25.6.2015
Jane Tooher *emails* 28.6.2015-1.7.2015

Appendix

The Lambeth Quadrilateral of 1887

That, in the opinion of the Conference, the following Articles supply a basis on which approach may be by God's blessing made offer towards Home Reunion:

a. The Holy Scriptures of the Old and New Testaments, as 'containing all things necessary to salvation', and as being the rule and ultimate standard of faith.

b. The Apostles' Creed, as the Baptismal Symbol; and the Nicene Creed, as the sufficient statement of the Christian faith.

c. The two Sacraments ordained by Christ Himself—Baptism and the Supper of the Lord—administered with unfailing use of Christ's words of Institution, and of the elements ordained by Him.

d. The Historic Episcopate, locally adapted in the methods of its administration to the varying needs of the nations and peoples called of God into the Unity of His Church.[1]

Margaret Rodger's Article in Southern Cross March 2000, p5

Sydney sure to take issue with the new Primate

Comment by Margaret Rodgers

Rejecting 'liberal individualism', Archbishop Carnley prefers to call himself a 'progressive or dynamic orthodox'. The day after his election he indicated his

---

1. K Ward, *A History of Global Anglicanism* pp298-89.

opposition to 'lay presidency' but said he believed that the views of Sydney Synod members should be heard and understood in the Anglican Communion. He also said he hoped that the Diocese of Sydney would not become more isolationist as a result of his election. Sydney 'has an important contribution to make and needs to be involved rather than withdrawing' he said.

But Sydney Anglicans will note that it was Archbishop Carnley who ordained the first women priests in Perth in 1992, and he did so prior to the General Synod passing a Canon to allow the ordination of women to the priesthood.

In spite of this he relies on General Synod processes to decide the issue of lay presidency in the Diocese of Sydney. He told the media that no diocese could proceed until its legality had been thoroughly tested, so it might be some time before an Australian diocese could go ahead.

Though he emphasized that the Bible is 'the foundation of all Faith and theology' and that 'Scriptural texts have to be taken with huge seriousness', Archbishop Carnley may find that it is in the area of foundational Christian doctrine that Sydney Diocese will take issue with his views. When asked to comment on the phrase 'Christ died in our place' he told *Southern Cross* that a substitutionary view of the atonement, based on a theory of Justice contains some difficulties, since 'Jesus was an innocent victim and when an innocent person is punished for the crime of another, that is hardly justice'.

Asked to comment, Dr Paul Barnett wrote, 'The only satisfactory explanation is that this teaching derived from Jesus himself. He taught that his death was to be 'a ransom in place of many' and his blood was to be shed 'for many'.'

Add in the Primate's printed views on the resurrection and it's certain there will be more debate.

Jim Bates' email to MHC

In 1997 I wrote a letter/report to each of the clergy who had sent me sermons. I have it on disc, but it's not a disc that my computer can read any more so, rather than finding a computer that can read it I am now writing you a letter/report whose content will be the same as the 1997 letter, but not exactly the same form/language and obviously more historical than current. I've also added a few bits and pieces that I didn't include in the original.

In early 1995 I decided that I wanted to discover just what the message of Sydney Diocese was. Ever since I was a teenager I had heard that Sydney was rock-solid Bible based but I had rarely heard a sermon here that could be described as that. They had almost all started with a Biblical text but after that they could go off to anywhere. They did not seem to have the concept that the text had a theological meaning rather than being a trigger that fired the preacher at whatever he was interested in at the time. T.S.Eliot had spoken of poetry as a 'springboard into the stream of consciousness of the reader' and that's what many of the sermons I had heard sounded like; we were in the stream of consciousness of the preacher. I realised that I hadn't heard that many different preachers, certainly not enough to constitute a definitive sample, and that maybe I had just been unlucky.

Rather than go to a different church every week for two or three years I decided to ask clergy to send me a recently preached sermon. I talked to a number of people of my intention: a few, both lay and clergy, friends including Chris, a bishop and Peter Jensen who was still at Moore College. Most of them told me the same thing: that there was no way that clergy would send me sermons if they knew I was going to critique them. I decided to go ahead anyway and then spent a couple of weeks writing what I hoped was a non-threatening, politically acceptable letter which would produce a reasonably positive response. I used the 1994 Diocesan Handbook and selected all churches who had at least an average of 100 people attending each Sunday, and they became my target sample. In the letter I explained that I was trying to find out just what the message of Sydney Diocese was and how much it conformed to the way I had heard it so often described and to do that I would like them to send me a sermon that they had preached in March that year. I told them that I didn't want them to do anything immediately because I planned to phone them within the following three weeks or so mainly to answer any questions that they might have. I then spent three weeks on the phone, usually about ten hours a day, six days a week. Some I had to phone seven or eight times before I made contact. I reached all but two of them, one who was overseas and the other in hospital. Only one refused outright to give me a sermon, plus there were a few who apologetically said they preached from brief notes which would not be of much use to me. I agreed. After about a month I sent reminders to those who had said they would send me a sermon, but hadn't. More sermons came in.

The sermons started pouring in and I realised that I had something much bigger on my hands than I had anticipated and felt I should improve my sample by taking a further random sample of twenty of the smaller churches that I had not previously contacted, together with the archbishop, bishops, archdeacons and the senior staff at Moore College.

The end result of all of this was that I was sent a sermon by 145 different Sydney clergy, 72 on audio tape, the rest as transcripts or notes. I went through all the written material but decided to concentrate on the audio tapes because they were a more reliable record of what had actually been preached. I also thought that it gave me a sufficiently large sample. I felt I needed to know more about what was taught about preaching at Moore College. Peter Jensen had told me that the person who had had the greatest influence on preaching in the Diocese over the previous twenty years was John Chapman, but rather than talk to him I found out what textbooks on preaching/homiletics were used at the College, bought them and read them. During that time I didn't do any real work on the sermons but always had some tapes in my car which I listened to as I drove around, just trying to get a feel for what was going on.

By now it was getting close to the end of the year and my wife and I were preparing to go on her last sabbatical for the whole of 1996. She had taught in French studies at Sydney for over thirty years so in early January we, plus the tapes, headed for Paris where we stayed for about five months during which time I spent five or six hours on most week days listening to the tapes on a Walkman and writing full transcripts of every sermon. I listened to every sermon at least three times and parts of some sermons a lot more than that.

I had told the clergy that I wasn't interested in their rhetorical skills, just in the content and that is what I concentrated on. Statistically, on the basis of frequency, there were really only two doctrines that were taught: the first was the need and means of salvation/redemption. Obviously, that is what any conservative Christian would want and expect to be preached, at least some of the time, but there was a problem with how redemption was conceptualized; without exception it was only about justification, only forensic, our legal status before God. There was not one allusion to the fact that it is not just the status of the person that is changed, but also his/her nature; nothing about regeneration which Paul talked about as 'the renewing of the mind', or of the ongoing renewing and growth which is the essence of sanctification, growing in grace and knowledge. It is not just that the words weren't used, the ideas were not there, not once. Although I didn't mention it in the report, I wondered to what extent, if at all, this was an overreaction to the 'sinless perfection' controversies of the 1940s and early 50s.

It is very difficult to come up with a theology of the Christian life if redemption is only about justification. That could be why there were only two sermons which focused on morality/ethics and they were both about sexual impropriety and were, incidentally, mutually contradictory. It could also be why the whole New Testament ethical teaching, the very stipulations of the New Covenant, were ignored and replaced with a demand for 'personal evangelism' which was the responsibility of every Christian. This was the other doctrine that was most frequently taught. One preacher actually proclaimed that it was the **only** obligation that we have. That is not only a false teaching; it is insane.

I also think that the whole idea of 'personal evangelism' as a universal Christian obligation is a false teaching. I have only ever heard two attempts to justify it as a Christian teaching. The first was a little over thirty years ago when John Chapman argued in his book 'Know and Tell The Gospel' that we have to teach it otherwise not enough people will do it. The theological methodology of that is dreadful. The second was much more recently in a sermon where the preacher conceded that there was very little about personal evangelism as a Christian obligation in the Scriptures [I actually think there is nothing], but he said that there didn't need to be because it was so obvious. I sat there wondering what other basic doctrines of the Christian life were so obvious that they didn't need to be included in the New Testament and at the same time I thought I heard a gurgling sound and I knew it was the sound of 'sola Scriptura' being flushed down the theological toilet. Neither of these arguments is Bible based, let alone rock solid Bible based. Therefore, they are not theological statements, they are ideological statements which have no authority at all, but the teaching is one which is very common in this diocese. You might have read a book, 'The Trellis and the Vine', which came out of Matthias Press about three or so years ago and takes this teaching, which they assume to be true, to the top of the mountain in a way which is both exegetically and theologically disgraceful.

I'm sure you realise that saying something is not an obligation is not the same thing as saying it is forbidden. Rather it raised the question of who should be doing the evangelising, a question which Paul answers very clearly more than once.

The way this teaching was proclaimed in 1995 was common to all who taught it. They all started with a narrative text which was put into some kind of context, sometimes very well, but never into a biblical theological context, and the story was told. After that it didn't matter where the text came from nor what it was about. *Without exception* it was reduced to an example of either obedience or disobedience; it didn't matter which. Then again, without exception, the application was the same: 'you know that God is asking you to talk to your family, friends, neighbours, fellow workers, fellow students about the Gospel. Are you willing to obey or will you disobey?'

As I said above I believe this teaching to be false, but more than that; all of these preachers not only taught their people something that wasn't true, and certainly wasn't in the text, they didn't teach what was in the text.

Still in Paris, I phoned my old friend from Westminster, George Marsden, in the US and asked him how widespread this teaching was. He told me that it was taught in some smaller evangelical churches, but not in the big ones, and certainly not in the reformed churches. I also asked him did he know where it came from and he was fairly sure it had come to the US from Keswick in the second half of the nineteenth century. Not long afterwards we moved to Dublin . . . for a couple of months or so. During that time my wife and I both spent most weekdays in Trinity College library where I found the complete proceedings of Keswick and went to work looking for the personal evangelism obligation, and there it was. Of course, the fact that it was there didn't mean that it started there so I decided to look at the much earlier anti-clerical groups: Anabaptists, Mennonites and a couple of others but I can't remember which ones. Anyway, I couldn't find [anything] it so I still don't know where it came from.

We then moved to the Reformed Seminary in Jackson Mississippi where John McIntosh who was teaching there had arranged for us to have an apartment on campus as well as access to their library and any lectures we wanted to attend. In the library I came across the John Chapman book I mentioned earlier so I read that and found all the things that I was complaining about so I guess that Peter Jensen had been right in his assessment of Chapman's influence.

We arrived home for Christmas and then I spent some time over about three months tidying some sermon study loose ends. In about April 1997 I sent a letter to all the clergy who had sent me sermons. In that I asked them to send or refer me to any material which suggested or showed that anything I had written to them was false. About twenty contacted me, but they, including the archbishop and a bishop, agreed with me. Nobody tried to convince me I was wrong.

Regards,

Jim.

Report of the Diocesan Doctrine Commission, re 8/87 The Ministry of Women

> 4.3 Contemporary preaching is not identical with teaching in the NT. Preaching covers a wide range of activities, including teaching, evangelism, encouragement, exhortation, prophecy and testimony. Teaching in the New Testament refers to the faithful transmission and defence of apostolic doctrine or passing on the fundamental structures of the faith. Admonition, prophecy, exhortation and encouragement are derived from this teaching ministry.
>
> —*Year Book of the Diocese of Sydney* 1988, p352.

Diocesan Representation at General Synods 1962–2014[1] (under new constitution 1 Jan 1962)

Table complied by Robert Tong 27.06.2014

In addition there are 23 Diocesan bishops and 2 Indigenous bishops

[for GS2014, four dioceses are vacant, Gippsland/NT/Riverina/Rockhampton, and one indigenous position is not filled]

1. The table annexed to the Constitution gives the formula for the number of representatives from each diocese. The number of diocesan clergy (incumbents plus other full time clergy) divided by 20 gives the number of clergy representatives which are then matched by the same number of lay representatives.

2. Carpentaria and North Queensland amalgamate in 1996, see 1995 Proceeding p 12

3. Merged with Perth 1973 by Canon 4 of 1973

4. New diocese formed by Canon 6 of 1966

5. Resolution 40 of 1973

6. Merged with Bendigo 1976

7. Created out of Adelaide.

8. By sec 17(8) of the Constitution one Aboriginal and one Torres Strait Islander clergy and two corresponding lay persons are members of the synod. Canon 16 of 1998 came into effect 1 March 2000.

Diocese/year	'62	'66	'69	'73	'77	'81	'85	'89	'92	'95	'98	'01	'04	'07	'10	'14
Adelaide	14	14	14	10	10	12	12	12	12	12	12	14	10	10	12	12
Armidale	4	4	4	4	4	4	4	4	4	4	4	4	4	4	4	6
Ballarat	6	4	6	4	6	6	6	6	6	4	4	4	4	4	4	4
Bathurst	6	6	6	4	6	6	6	6	4	4	4	4	4	6	6	4
Bendigo	2	2	2	2	4	4	4	4	4	4	4	4	4	4	4	4
Brisbane	14	16	16	16	16	18	18	18	18	18	20	20	22	20	20	20
Bunbury	4	2	2	2	2	2	4	2	4	4	4	2	2	4	4	4
Can/Goulburn	6	8	8	8	8	8	8	8	8	10	10	10	10	10	12	14
Carpentaria[2]	2	4	2	2	2	2	2	2	2	2						
Gippsland	4	4	4	4	4	4	4	4	4	4	4	4	4	4	4	4
Grafton	4	4	4	4	4	4	4	4	4	4	4	4	4	4	4	4
Kalgoorlie[3]	2	2	2	2												
Melbourne	28	30	32	30	32	32	34	34	36	38	36	34	36	36	36	32
Newcastle	8	8	8	8	8	8	8	8	8	10	10	10	10	10	10	8
NT[4]			2	2	2	2	2	2	2	2	2	2	2	2	2	2
North Qld	6	4	4	4	4	6	4	4	4	4	6	6	6	6	6	4
NW Aust	2	2	2	2	2	2	2	2	2	2	2	2	2	2	2	2
PNG[5]	4	6	4	8												
Perth	10	10	10	12	12	12	12	12	14	16	16	18	18	18	18	18
Riverina	2	2	2	2	2	2	2	2	2	2	2	2	2	2	2	2
Rockhampton	2	2	2	2	2	2	2	2	2	2	2	2	2	2	2	2
St Arnaud[6]	2	2	2	2												
Sydney	32	36	36	36	36	38	38	38	40	42	48	48	52	56	60	66
Tasmania	4	4	8	6	6	6	6	6	8	6	6	6	6	6	6	6
The Murray[7]				2	2	2	2	2	2	2	2	2	2	2	2	2
Wangaratta	2	4	4	4	4	4	4	4	4	4	4	4	4	4	2	4
Willochra	2	2	2	2	2	2	2	2	2	2	2	2	2	2	2	2
Indigenous[8]												4	4	4	4	4
TOTALS	172	182	188	184	180	188	190	188	196	202	208	212	216	222	228	230

Bibliography

Allen, Laura. *A History of Christ Church S. Laurence Sydney.* Sydney: Finn, 1939.
Anglicare Diocese of Sydney. "Financial Report For the Year Ended 30 June 2013." https://www.anglicare.org.au/sites/default/files/public/ANGLICARE%20 2013%20Annual%20Financial%20Report%20(2).pdf.
The Anglican. The independent and unofficial newspaper of the Church of England in Australia, and the official organ of the Church of England Information Trust. Incorporating the Church Standard. Archbishop of Canterbury Speaks on Viet Nam, 1, April 6 1967; *U.S. Policy Criticized more at Home than Here, 1,000 Civilians Killed a Month by* Bombing, 1, April 27 1967; *The Devil Slates Dr Coggan and Sydney Priests,*1, August 15 1968; and *Ordination of Women a Theological Issue* 1, October 17 1968.
Anglican Church of Australia. *The Constitution Canons and Rules of the Anglican Church of Australia 2010.* Sydney: The Anglican Church of Australia Trust Corporation, 2011.
———. "Report of the Viability and Structures Taskforce and Other Materials Impinging on the Small Groups Discussion Programme." The Sixteenth General Synod, Book 8. Adelaide, June/July 2014. http://www.anglican.org.au/general-synods/2014/documents/books/book%208_for%20website.pdf
Anglican Schools Corporation. http://www.sasc.nsw.edu.au.
Angus, Samuel. *Essential Christianity.* Sydney: Angus and Robertson, 1939.
The Argus, Melbourne, November 4 1936.
Australian Church Record. Sydney.
Australian Psychological Society Ltd. *Guidelines for Psychological Practice with Clients with Previously Unreported Traumatic Memories.* March 2010.
Avis, Paul. *The Identity of Anglicanism: Essentials of Anglican Ecclesiology,* 2nd ed. London: T. & T. Clark, 2008.
Babbage, Stuart. "Flotsam and Jetsam. A Sequel to *Memoirs of a Loose Canon.*" Unpublished manuscript, 2011.
———. *Memoirs of a Loose Canon.* Melbourne: Acorn Press, 2004.
Baird, Julia. "As the Brothers Huddle, the Sisters are Splintered in a Demoralizing Dame Drain." *Sydney Morning Herald.* May 27 2002. http://www.smh.com.au/articles/2002/05/26/1022243291108.html.

Ballantine-Jones, Bruce. "Changes in Policy and Practices in the Anglican Diocese of Sydney 1966-2013: The Political Factor." PhD diss., Macquarie University, 2013.
Barcan, Alan. *A History of Australian Education*. Melbourne: Oxford University Press, 1980.
Barker, Jane. "Journal 1855-1856." In *Australian Christian Life from 1788. An Introduction and Anthology*. Edited by I H Murray, 219-48. Edinburgh: Banner of Truth Trust, 1988.
Barry, Rhonda. Moore College Statistics for Undergraduate Commencing Enrolments.
Bebbington, David. *Evangelicalism in Modern Britain. A History from the 1730s to the 1980s*. London: Routledge, 1995.
Birmingham, John. *Leviathan, The Unauthorised Biography of Sydney*. Sydney: Vintage, 2000.
Blanch, Alan. *From Strength to Strength: A Life of Marcus Loane*. Melbourne: Australian Scholarly, 2015.
Bolton, Geoffrey. *The Oxford History of Australia, Vol 5: The Middle Way 1942-1995*, 2nd ed. Melbourne: Oxford University Press, 1999.
Boyd, Tony, "Geared to High Heaven: How Anglicans lost $160m." *Australian Financial Review* (2009).
Braga, Stuart. *A Century Preaching Christ. Katoomba Christian Convention 1903-2003*. Sydney: Katoomba Christian Convention Ltd., 2003.
———. "William Macquarie Cowper." In *ADEB*, edited by Brian Dickey, 80-81. Sydney: Evangelical History Association, 1994.
Bray, Gerald, ed. *The Anglican Canons 1529-1947*. Suffolk: Boydell, 1998.
Breward, Ian. *A History of the Churches in Australasia*. Oxford: Clarendon, 2001.
Broughton Knox Papers. Boxes 1-17, 80a. Moore College Library.
Brown, Callum. *The Death of Christian Britain. Understanding Secularisation 1800-2000*, 2nd ed. Oxford: Routledge, 2009.
Bull, Melissa, Susan Pinto, and Paul Wilson. "Homosexual Law Reform in Australia." 1991. www.aic.gov.au/publications/current%20series/tandi/21.../tandi29.html.
Cable, Kenneth. "John Woolley." *ADB* 6, edited by Bede Nairn, 435-37. Australia: Melbourne University Press, 1988.
———. "Robert Cartwright." In *ADB* 1, edited by Douglas Pike, 211-12. Australia: Melbourne University Press, 1983.
———. "Robert Lethbridge King." In *ADEB*, edited by Brian Dickey, 200-201. Sydney: Evangelical History Association, 1994.
———. "William Cowper." In *ADEB*, edited by Brian Dickey, 79-80. Sydney: Evangelical History Association, 1994.
Cable, Kenneth and Leonie. Clergy Register 1788-1952.
Cakebread, WJ. "Address at the Memorial Service for DJ Davies in St Andrew's Cathedral." *Societas*, Michaelmas Term, 1935.
Cameron, Ewen Donald. *Evangelicals and the World Council of Churches*. Sydney: Anglican Information Office, 2000.
Cameron, Marcia. *S.C.E.G.G.S.: A Centenary History of Sydney Church of England Girls' Grammar School*. Sydney: Allen and Unwin, 1994.
———. "Aspects of Anglican Theological Education in Australia, 1900-1940, with Particular Reference to Four Colleges." PhD diss., Macquarie University, 1999.
———. "Moore College Under Nathaniel Jones 1897-1911. *Lucas: An Evangelical History Review*, 19/20 (1995-1996) 96-123.

---. *Living Stones: St Swithun's Pymble 1901-2001*. Sydney: Helicon, 2001.

---. *An Enigmatic Life: David Broughton Knox, Father of Contemporary Sydney Anglicanism*. Brunswick East: Acorn Press, 2006.

---. "The SCEGGS Connection." In *TIGS: 50 Years. From Strength to Strength*. Edited by J. Hales. Figtree: The Illawarra Grammar School, 2009.

---. *The School on the Hill. SCEGGS Gleniffer Brae 1955-1975*. Sydney: Eliot and Company, 2010.

Cameron, Neil. *Women as Bishops: Change by Judicial Sleight of Hand*. Southern Cross Dec. 2007/Feb. 2008.

Carnley, P. *Reflections in Glass. Trends and Tensions in the Contemporary Anglican Church*. Australia: HarperCollins, 2004.

---. "TC Hammond and the Theological Roots of Sydney Arianism." *St Mark's Review* 198 (2005) 5–10.

Carey, George. *Know the Truth. A Memoir*, 2nd ed. London: Harper Perennial, 2005.

Carey, Hilary. *Believing in Australia: A Cultural History of Religions*. Sydney: Allen and Unwin, 1996.

Chadwick, Owen. *The Victorian Church, Part I*, 3rd ed. London: Adam and Charles Black, 1971.

---. *The Victorian Church, Part II: 1860-1901*. London: SCM Press, 1992.

Chang, Jung, and Jon Halliday. *Mao: The Unknown Story*. London: Jonathan Cape, 2005.

Chester, Tim. *Delighting in the Trinity: Why Father, Son, and Spirit are Good News*, 2nd ed. UK: The Good Book Company, 2010.

Cole, Keith. *A History of the Church Missionary Society of Australia*. Melbourne: Church Missionary Historical, 1971.

Commission of Evangelism, Board of Diocesan Missions, and Information and Public Relations Office, Church of England Diocese of Sydney. *Move in For Action*. Sydney: ANZEA, 1971.

Cornish, FW. *A History of the English Church: VIII The English Church in the Nineteenth Century, Part II*. London: Macmillan, 1910.

The Courier-Mail. Brisbane, November 2 1953.

Davison, Graeme, John Hirst, and Stuart Macintyre, eds. *The Oxford Companion to Australian History*. Melbourne: Oxford University Press: 1998.

Davies, DJ. *The Church and the Plain Man. The Moorhouse Lectures 1917*. Sydney: Angus and Robertson, 1919.

Davis, John. *Australian Anglicans and their Constitution*. Canberra: Acorn Press, 1993.

Davis, PD. "Bishop Barker and the Decline of the Denominational System." In *Pioneers of Australian Education*, edited by Clifford Turney. Sydney: Sydney University Press, 1969.

Dickey, Brian. "Howard West Kilvinton Mowll." In *Biographical Dictionary of Evangelicals*, edited by Timothy Larsen, 455–56. Leicester: InterVarsity, 2003.

---. "Williams." *ADEB*, edited by Brian Dickey, 407. Sydney: Evangelical History Association, 1994.

Dickson, John. *Hearing Her Voice: A Case for Women Giving Sermons*. Grand Rapids: Zondervan, 2014.

Diocesan Digest. Church of England Diocese of Sydney, 1956, 1958, and 1961.

Driver, Jeffrey. *A Polity of Persuasion: Gift and Grief of Anglicanism*. Eugene, OR: Cascade Books, 2014.

Dudley-Smith, Timothy. *John Stott: The Making of a Leader*. Leicester: InterVarsity, 1999.

———. *John Stott: A Global Ministry*. Leicester: InterVarsity, 2001.

Eliot, TS. *Collected Poems 1909–1962:* London, Faber and Faber, 1963.

Emilson, Susan. *A Whiff of Heresy. Samuel Angus and the Presbyterian Church in New South Wales,* Sydney. University of New South Wales Press, 1991.

Equal but Different. Promoting Biblical Relationships for Women and Men. 1992–2013. Sydney.

Erickson, Millard. *Who's Tampering with the Trinity? An Assessment of the Subordination Dispute*. Grand Rapids: Kregel, 2009.

Fisher, Geoffrey. *The Fisher Papers*, 327 volumes, unpublished. Lambeth Palace Library.

Fletcher, Brian. "Memory and the Shaping of Australian Anglicanism." In *Agendas for Australian Anglicanism: Essays in Honour of Bruce Kaye,* edited by Tom Frame and Geoff Treloar, chapter 1. Adelaide: ATF, 2006.

———. *The Place of Anglicanism in Australia: Church, Society and Nation*. Mulgrave: Broughton Publishing, 2008.

Frame, Tom. *A House Divided? The Quest for Unity Within Anglicanism*. Brunswick East: Acorn Press, 2010.

———. *Anglicans in Australia*. Sydney: University of New South Wales Press, 2007.

———. "Recapturing the Vision Splendid: The 1933 Anglican Inter-diocesan Oxford Movement Centenary Celebrations held in Wagga Wagga." In *From Oxford to the Bush. Essays on Catholic Anglicanism in Australia,* edited by John Moses, 146–71. Canberra: Broughton, 1997.

Frame, Tom, and Geoff Treloar, eds. *Agendas for Australian Anglicanism. Essays in Honour of Bruce Kaye*. Adelaide: ATF, 2006.

Frappell, Ruth, et al., eds. *Anglicans in the Antipodes. An Indexed Calendar of the Papers and Correspondence of the Archbishops of Canterbury, 1788–1961: Relating to Australia, New Zealand, and the Pacific*. London: Greenwood, 1999.

Frappell, Ruth. "1933 and All That: The Oxford Movement Centenary in Australia." In *From Oxford to the Bush. Essays on Catholic Anglicanism in Australia,* edited by John Moses, 126–45. Canberra: Broughton, 1997.

GAFCON. "The Way, The Truth and the Life. Theological Resources for a Pilgrimage to a Global Anglican Future Prepared by the Theological Resource Team of the Global Anglican Future Conference (GAFCON)." 2008.

Galbraith, D. "Just Enough Religion to Make us Hate: An Historico-legal Study of the Red Book Case." PhD diss., University of New South Wales, 1998.

Giles, Kevin. *Jesus and the Father: Modern Evangelicals Reinvent the Doctrine of the Trinity*. Grand Rapids: Zondervan, 2006.

———. *The Trinity and Subordinationism: The Doctrine of God and the Contemporary Gender Debate*. Downers Grove, IL: InterVarsity Press, 2002.

———. *Created Woman: A Fresh Study of the Biblical Teaching*. Canberra: Acorn, 1985.

———. "An Outsider's Response to an Insider's Defence of the Anglican Diocese of Sydney Given by Michael P. Jensen in his book, *Sydney Anglicanism: An Apology*." http://sjks.org.au/wp-content/uploads/2015/12/Giles-Looking-at-Sydney-from-the-inside.pdf

Gorham, Suzanne. "Bound and Gagged? The Silence and Submission of Women in Public Meetings Within the Sydney Anglican Diocese." London School of Theology, An Associated College of Middlesex University, 2014.

Gough, H, to DB Knox. November 8 1960, 1993/10/2 Archbishop's Office-Correspondence Diocesan-Constitution 1955–1960, Sydney Diocesan Archives.
Grant, James. *Episcopally and Synodically Governed: Anglicans in Victoria 1803–1997*. Melbourne: Scholarly, 2010.
Hafemann, Scott, ed. *Biblical Theology. Retrospect and Prospect*. Leicester: InterVarsity, 2002.
Halcrow, Jeremy. "Sydney Resolute on Deacons Celebrating Lord's Supper. October 15 2010. http://sydneyanglicans.net/news/deacons/.
Hammond, TC. *In Understanding Be Men. A Handbook of Christian Doctrine*. Revised and edited by DF Wright, 6th ed. London: IVF, 1967.
Harris, Tim. *Synod of the Diocese of Sydney Committee Report, Biblical Perspectives on the Place of Women and Women's Ministry in the Church: a Presentation of Alternate Evangelical Views*. 1992. In *Year Book of the Diocese of Sydney* 1994, 476–517 as "10/91 Ordination of Women to the Priesthood: A Report to Synod."
Harrison, G, "A Consideration of Some of the Changes Occurring during the Episcopate of the Most Rev. Hugh Rowland Gough, Seventh Archbishop of the See of Sydney, being an Important Watershed in the History of that Diocese within the Anglican Church of Australia." MTh, Sydney, 1988.
Hart, Henry, in The E-Sylum: 7, Number 52, December 26, 2004, Article 5.
Hayward, Peter. *Review of Diocesan Mission*. What's Next? Committee, Diocesan Mission Indicators Anglican Diocese of Sydney, June 2013.
Hodgson Register. Moore College Library.
The Independent, Saturday 29 November, 1997.
Inner City Commission of Inquiry: Chairman's Correspondence, undated, unsigned "Memorandum", probably by Bishop Jack Dain, in 1967. Box 55, Sydney Diocesan Archives.
Inventors.about.com http://www.australianhistory.org/technology-timeline.
Jensen, M. *Sydney Anglicanism. An Apology*, Eugene, OR: Wipf and Stock, 2012.
Jensen, Peter Frederick. Address to the ACL Synod Dinner 2000, www. acl.asn.au.
———. *The Future of Jesus*. Sydney: ABC Books, 2005.
———. "The Role of an Evangelical Missionary Society." Address to CMS Summer School, Katoomba, January 2011.
———. "Positioning Anglicare. 1 Why We Are." Unpublished.
———. "Positioning Anglicare. 2 Who We Are." Unpublished.
———. "Positioning Anglicare. 3 What We Are." Unpublished.
———. "A Christian Philosophy of Care." Unpublished.
———. "Inaccurate by Habit." A Review-Article of Dr Kevin Giles' Book *Trinity and Subordinationism*." Unpublished.
———. "The Charge of Arianism " Unpublished.
———. "Caleb in the Antipodes" The TC Hammond Lecture presented by Archbishop Peter Jensen during his trip to Ireland in June 2005. Unpublished.
Jensen, Phillip. "About Phillip." http://phillipjensen.com/about/#sthash.8ZAntEgh.dpuf.
Johnson, Alan, ed. *How I Changed my Mind about Women in Leadership: Compelling Stories from Prominent Evangelicals*. Michigan: Zondervan, 2010.
Jones, Lang, Wootton & Sons, Sydney NSW: Report upon some Aspects of the Lands of the Church of England–Diocese of Sydney New South Wales, Australia September 1959. Sydney Diocesan Archives, Anglican Diocese of Sydney.

Judd, Stephen, and Kenneth Cable. *Sydney Anglicans: A History of the Diocese.* Sydney: Anglican Information Office, 1987.

Judd, Stephen, and Brian Dickey. "John Charles Wright." In *ADEB*, edited by Brian Dickey, 412–13. Sydney: Evangelical History Association, 1994.

Kaye, Bruce. *An Introduction to World Anglicanism.* Cambridge: Cambridge University Press, 2008.

———, ed. *Anglicanism in Australia: A History.* Melbourne: Melbourne University Press, 2002.

———. *A Church without Walls: Being Anglican in Australia.* Melbourne: Dove, 1995.

Kaye, Bruce, S Macneil, and H Thomson, eds. *'Wonderful and Confessedly Strange:' Australian Essays in Anglican Ecclesiology.* Adelaide: ATF, 2006.

Kelly, JND. *Early Christian Doctrines.* London. A & C Black, 1958.

Keane, John. *The Life and Death of Democracy.* London: Simon and Schuster, 2009.

Knox, David Broughton. *The Doctrine of Faith in the Reign of Henry VIII.* United Kingdom: Garden City, 1961.

———. "The Christian Doctrine of Sex," July 9 1972, and "The Last Tango," March 4 1973. In *The Protestant Faith*, Box 80a. Moore College Library.

———. "Minority Report in General Synod Report." *The Ministry of Women, ACR* April 28 1977, 3.

Kuan, Jonathan Wei-Han. "The History of Evangelicalism in the Diocese of Melbourne, 1837–1947." PhD diss., Ridley College Melbourne, 2010.

Lake, Meredith. *Proclaiming Jesus Christ as Lord. A History of the Sydney University Evangelical Union.* Sydney: Evangelical Union, 2005.

Larsen, Timothy, ed. *Biographical Dictionary of Evangelicals.* Leicester: InterVarsity, 2003.

Lawton, William. "Australian Anglican Theology." In *Anglicanism in Australia: A History*, edited by Bruce Kaye, 177–99. Melbourne: Melbourne University Press, 2002.

———. *The Better Time to Be; Utopian Attitudes to Society among Sydney Anglicans, 1885 to 1914.* Sydney: University of New South Wales Press, 1990.

Lee, Dorothy. "An Anglo-Uniting Perspective. The Journey Taken." In *Preachers, Prophets and Heretics,* edited by Elaine Lindsay and Janet Scarfe, 253–68. Sydney: University of NSW Press, 2012.

Loane, Marcus. *A Centenary History of Moore Theological College.* Sydney: Angus and Robertson, 1955.

———. *Archbishop Mowll: The Biography of Howard West Kilvinton Mowll, Archbishop of Sydney and Primate of Australia.* London: Hodder and Stoughton, 1960.

———. *Hewn from the Rock: Origins and Tradition of the Church in Sydney.* Sydney: Anglican Information Office, 1976.

———. "Howard West Kilvinton Mowll." In *ADEB*, edited by Brian Dickey, 272–74. Sydney: Evangelical History Association, 1994.

———. *Mark These Men: A Brief Account of some Evangelical Clergy in the Diocese of Sydney who were Associated with Archbishop Mowll.* Canberra: Acorn Press, 1985.

———. *Men to Remember.* Canberra: Acorn Press, 1967.

———. Presidential Address to General Synod 1981 by the Most Reverend ML Loane KBE, MA, DD, Primate of Australia. General Synod Archives.

———. *These Happy Warriors. Friends and Contemporaries.* Sydney: New Creation, 1988.

LUCAS. An Evangelical History Review.

Lyttleton, Arthur, "The Atonement." In *Lux Mundi*, edited by Charles Gore, 10th ed. London: John Murray, 1890.
MacCulloch, Diarmaid. *Reformation. Europe's House Divided 1490-1700*. London: Penguin, 2003.
———. *Thomas Cranmer: A Life*. New Haven and London: Yale University Press, 1996.
McGrath, Alister. *A Christian Theology: An Introduction*, Oxford: Blackwell, 1994.
McGillion, Chris. *The Chosen Ones: The Politics of Salvation in the Anglican Church*. Sydney: Allen and Unwin, 2005.
McIntosh, John, "Anglican Evangelicalism in Sydney 1897-1953: The Thought and Influence of Three Moore College Principals—Nathaniel Jones, DJ Davies, and TC Hammond." PhD Diss, University of New South Wales, 2014.
Manchester Guardian, October 4 1955, Fisher Papers, 154: Lambeth Palace Archives.
Maple, KJ. "Frederic Barker." In *ADEB*, edited by Brian Dickey, 21-26. Sydney: Evangelical History Association, 1994.
Mascord, Keith. *A Restless Faith. Leaving Fundamentalism in a Quest for God*. Sydney: Xlibris, 2012.
Mason, Keith. "The Cable Lecture." *Believers in Court: Sydney Anglicans going to Law*. The Cable Lecture Series. King Street, Sydney: The Anglican Church of Australia, Diocese of Sydney, St James', 2005.
The Mercury, Hobart, November 5 1936.
Miley, Caroline. *The Suicidal Church: Can the Anglican Church be Saved?* Annandale: Pluto Press, 2002.
Milliken, David. *Imperfect Company*. Australia: William Heinemann, 2000.
Minute Books of General Synod 1902-1966. General Synod Archives.
Moore College External Studies. *Reaching the World*. Undated.
Moorehouse, Geoffrey. *Sydney*. London: Weidenfield and Nicholson, 1999.
Morning Bulletin, Rockhampton, May 5 1945.
Morris, Leon, John Gaden, and Barbara Thiering. *A Woman's Place*. Anglican Doctrine Commission Papers on the Role of Women in the Church. Sydney: Anglican Information Office, 1976.
Morris, Leon. *The Apostolic Preaching of the Cross*. London: Tyndale Press, 1955.
Moses, John, ed. *From Oxford to the Bush. Catholic Anglicanism in Australia: The Centenary Essays from The Church Chronicle 1932-33*. ACT: Broughton Press, 1997.
Mowll, Howard. *Seeing all the World: Moorehouse Lectures*. Melbourne: Ruskin Press, 1947.
Murray, Iain. *Australian Christian Life from 1788: An Introduction and an Anthology*. Edinburgh: Banner of Truth, 1988.
———. *Nambour Chronicle and North Coast Advertiser*. November 4 1938.
Nelson, Warren. *TC Hammond: His Life and Legacy in Ireland and Australia*. Edinburgh: Banner of Truth, 1994.
———. "Thomas Chatterton Hammond." In *ADEB*, edited by Brian Dickey, 150-53. Sydney: Evangelical History Association, 1994.
Nichols, Anthony. *The Bible and Women's Ministry: An Australian Dialogue*. Melbourne: Acorn Press, 1990.
Noll, Mark, David Bebbington, and George Rawlyk, eds. *Evangelicalism: Comparative Studies of Popular Protestantism in North America, the British Isles, and Beyond 1700-1990*. Oxford: Oxford University Press, 1994.
Null, Ashley. "Thomas Cranmer and the Anglican Way of Reading Scripture." *Anglican and Episcopal History*: LXXV, Number 4, December 2006.

O'Brien, Anne, "Women in the Churches before 1992: 'No Obtrusive Womanhood.'" In *Preachers, Prophets, and Heretics*, edited by Elaine Lindsay and Janet Scarfe, 30–54. Sydney: University of New South Wales Press, 2012.

Orpwood, Michael. *Chappo: For the Sake of the Gospel*. Sydney: Eagleswift, 1995.

Packer, JI. *Keep in Step with the Spirit*. Grand Rapids: IVP, 1984.

Parish Council Minutes. St Swithun's Anglican Church Pymble.

Parsons, Vivienne. "Thomas Alison Scott." In *ADB* 2, edited by Douglas Pike, 430–31. Australia: Melbourne University Press, 1989.

Pannenberg, Wolfhart. *Systematic Theology* I. Edinburgh: T. & T. Clark, 1991.

Pelikan, Jaroslav. *The Christian Tradition: A History of the Development of Doctrine 1: The Emergence of the Catholic Tradition (100–600)*. Chicago: University of Chicago Press, 1971.

Piggin, Stuart. Address given at the launch of Kevin Giles' book *The Father and the Son. Modern Evangelicals Reinvent the Doctrine of the Trinity*. Sydney, June 21 2006.

———. *Evangelical Christianity in Australia. Spirit, Word, and World*. Oxford: Oxford University Press, 1996.

———. *Spirit of a Nation: The Story of Australia's Christian Heritage*. Sydney: Strand Publishing, 2004.

———. "Sydney Anglicanism: An Analysis of the Properties of Concrete." *Meanjin* 65.4 (2006) 184–93.

———. "The Diocese of Sydney. 'This Terrible Conflict'" in *Preachers, Prophets and Heretics*, edited by Elaine Lindsay and Janet Scarfe, 178–204. Sydney: University of NSW Press, 2012.

Porter, Brian. *Frank Woods. Archbishop of Melbourne 1957–1977*. Melbourne: Trinity College, 2007.

——— ed. *Melbourne Anglicans. The Diocese of Melbourne 1847-1997*, Melbourne: Mitre, 1997.

Porter, Muriel. *Women in the Church: The Great Ordination Debate*. Ringwood Victoria: Penguin, 1989.

———. *The New Puritans: The Rise of Fundamentalism in the Anglican Church* Melbourne: Melbourne University Press, 2006.

———. *Sydney Anglicans and the Threat to World Anglicanism: The Sydney Experiment*. Farnham: Ashgate, 2011.

Priscilla and Aquila Centee. www.vimeo.com.

Ramsey, Arthur. *From Gore to Temple: The Development of Anglican Theology Between Lux Mundi and the Second World War 1889–1939. The Hale Memorial Lectures of Seabury-Western Theological Seminary, 1959*. London: Longmans, 1960.

Rayner, Keith. "The Primacy: Past, Present and Future." Sydney Smith Memorial Lecture. November 18, 1998.

Reid, John. *Marcus L Loane: A Biography*. Melbourne: Acorn Press, 2004.

Report of the Commission Appointed by The Archbishop of Sydney 1964. Sydney: Wm Andrews, 1964.

Robinson, DWB. "Some Personal Reminiscences of Archbishop Mowll." *The Anglican Historical Society Journal* 48.1 (2003) 6–15.

———. "The Origins of the Anglican Church League." *Lucas* 21 and 22 (1996) 137–65.

———. *Donald Robinson: Selected Works 1: Assembling God's People*, edited by Peter Bolt and Mark Thompson. Sydney: Australian Church Record/Moore College, 2000.

———. *Donald Robinson: Selected Works 2: Preaching God's Word*, edited by Peter Bolt and Mark Thompson. Sydney: Australian Church Record/Moore College, 2008.

BIBLIOGRAPHY

———. *Donald Robinson: Selected Works: Appreciation*, edited by Peter Bolt and Mark Thompson. Sydney: Australian Church Record/Moore College, 2008.
Robinson, Martin. Anglicare: Personal File.
"Royal Commission into the New South Wales Police Service." Royal_Commission_into_the_New_South_Wales_Police_Service http://en.wikipedia.org/wiki/.
Salvation Army Australia Southern Territory. *2013 Salvation Army Annual Report*.
Salvation Army. www.salvationarmy.org.au/Ayene Finger.
Scarfe, Janet. "Movement for the Ordination of Women. Their Hearts in their Mouths." In *Preachers, Prophets and Heretics*, edited by Elaine Lindsay and Janet Scarfe, 117–45. Sydney: University of NSW Press, 2012.
Shaw, GP. *William Grant Broughton 1788-1853: Patriarch and Patriot*. Melbourne: Melbourne University Press, 1978.
Shaw, FAS. "David John Davies, an Appreciation." In *Societas*. Michaelmas Term, 1935.
Shevill, Ian. *Women Priests? A Survey of the Present Situation in the Anglican Communion Relating to the Ordination of Women*. Newcastle: The Australian Church Union, 1977.
Smith, Claire. *God's Good Design. What the Bible Really Says about Men and Women*. Kingsford: Matthias Media, 2012.
Smith, SH, and GT Spaull. *History of Education in New South Wales 1788-1925*, Sydney: George B Philip, 1925.
Societas. The Annual Moore College student magazine.
Southern Cross. Church of England Diocese of Sydney, 1961–2013.
Standing Committee of General Synod. "A Committee to Investigate the Primacy." *Proceedings of the Third General Synod. Official Report 1969*.
Steven, Margaret. "John MacArthur." In *ADB* 2, edited by Douglas Pike, 153–59. Australia: Melbourne University Press, 1989.
Stott, John, *Issues Facing Christians Today. A Major Appraisal of Contemporary Social and Moral Questions*. UK: Marshall Morgan and Scott, 1984.
———. verticallivingministries.com./John Stott.
Strong, Philip. Presidential Address 1966 by the Acting Primate, PNW Strong, Archbishop of Brisbane. General Synod Archives.
———. Notes from his diary in possession of Miss Elsie Manley, Wangaratta, Victoria.
Sydney Diocesan Magazine: The Official Organ of the Lord Archbishop Month by Month. 1945–1958.
Synod of the Diocese of Sydney Committee Report. "Biblical Perspectives on the Place of Women and Women's Ministry in the Church: A Presentation of Alternate Evangelical Views," 1992.
Synod of the Diocese of Sydney Committee Report, Ordination: Its Meaning, Value and Theology. Sydney: Anglican Information Office, 2000.
Teale, Ruth. "The 'Red Book' Case." *Journal of Religious History XII* (June 1982) 74–89.
Thomas, Griffith. *The Principles of Theology*. London: Longmans, 1930.
Thompson, Roger C. *Religion in Australia: A History*. New York: Oxford University Press, 1994.
Townsville Daily Bulletin. October 30 1943.
Treloar, Geoff, and Robert Linder, eds. *Making History for God: Essays on Evangelicalism, Revival and Mission. In Honour of Stuart Piggin Master of Robert Menzies College 1990-2004*. Sydney: Robert Menzies College, 2004.
Treloar, Geoffrey. "TC Hammond the Controversialist." *Journal of the Anglican Historical Society* 51.1 (June 2006) 20–35.

——— ed. *The Furtherance of Religious Beliefs. Essays on the History of Theological Education in Australia*, a Special Combined edition of *LUCAS: An Evangelical History Review* 19/20 (1995-96), Centre for the Studies of Australian Christianity (CSAC) for the Evangelical History Association of Australia.

———. "William Saumarez Smith." In *ADEB*, edited by Brian Dickey, 345–47. Sydney: Evangelical History Association, 1994.

"Trends in Religious Affiliation." Australian Bureau of Statistics. http://www.abs.gov.au/.

"Trends in Women's Employment." http://www.abs.gov.au.

Turney, Clifford, Ursula Bygott, and Peter Chippendale. *Australia's First: A History of the University of Sydney 1: 1850–1939,* Sydney: University of Sydney, 1991.

Turney, Clifford, ed. *Pioneers of Australian Education,* Sydney: Sydney University Press, 1969.

Voysey, Irene. *By the Way: Know the Joy of the Journey.* India: Glory Graphics, 2010.

Ward, Kevin. *A History of Global Anglicanism.* Cambridge: Cambridge University Press, 2006.

Ward, WR. "The Making of an Evangelical Mind." In *Making History for God, Essays on Evangelicalism, Revival and Mission: In Honour of Stuart Piggin, Master of Robert Menzies College 1990–2004,* edited by Geoffrey Treloar and Robert Linder, 309–28. Sydney: Robert Menzies College, 2004.

Warren, Riley. "Instructing Them in 'The Things of God:' The Response of the Bishop and the Synod of the Church of England in the Diocese of Sydney to the *Public Instruction Act 1880* (NSW) Regarding Education for its Children and Young People, 1880–1889." MEd Thesis, University of Sydney, 2014.

West, Janet. "A Principal Embattled." Moore College Library Lecture, 1988.

———. *Gilbulla 1899–1999: A History by Janet West.* Glebe: Australia, 2000.

Williams, Graham, and Judy Robinson, "War in the Cloisters." *Sydney Morning Herald,* 13.3.1993.

Williams, Rowan. *Tokens of Trust. An Introduction to Christian Belief.* Louisville Kentucky: Westminster John Knox, 2010.

Whitlam, Gough. http://www.themonthly.com.au/gough-whitlam-95-years-comment-lindsay-tanner-3477.

"Women and Ordination: Canon Law Commission 1979." Knox Papers, Box 14 Folder 12, Moore College Library.

Wylde, Arnold. *The Bathurst Ritual Case.* Sydney: GM Dash, 1948.

Yarwood, AT. "Samuel Marsden." In *ADEB*, edited by Brian Dickey, 250–53. Sydney: Evangelical History Association, 1994.

Yarwood-Lamb, Margaret. "'Out of All Proportion:' Christian Brethren Influence in Australian Evangelicalism, 1850–2000." In *Making History for God. Essays on Evangelicalism, Revival and Mission. In honour of Stuart Piggin, Master of Robert Menzies College 1990–2004,* edited by Geoffrey Treloar and Robert Linder, 87–110. Sydney: Robert Menzies College, 2004.

Yates, John. "Last One Out, Vacuum the Office. A Journey of Pain and Purpose from ECUSA to ACNA." EFAC Address, CMS Summer School, Katoomba, 7.1.2015.

Year Books of the Diocese of Sydney. New South Wales Australia. Sydney: Diocesan Registry, 1944–2014.

Index

Abbotsford parish, 208
Aboriginal people, 45, 45n40, 200, 274
Abrahams, Stuart, 174
Acts 10, 153
Acts 18, 51
adultery, marital infidelity, 12, 105n105, 106, 170, 222
Affiliated Churches Ordinance 2005, 244, 244n66
Akinola, Peter, 263
Albery, F.J., 24
Anderson, Greg, 196–97, 196n54, 199–200
Andrewes, Lancelot, 55
Andrews, Mary, 103–4, 120, 122
Anglican identity, efforts to clarify, 3–4n1, 56–57, 142–43
Anglican Church (England). See Church of England
Anglican Church Communion (ACC)
    growing disunity, 222–23
    issues related to Lay Presidency, 171
    and the Lambeth Conference of 1998, 222
    and the ordination of women, 151–52
    Robinson's critiques, 142
    uniqueness of Sydney Diocese in, 3–4, 259
Anglican Church in North America (ACNA), 262
Anglican Church League (ACL)
    Blue Ticket candidates, 1993, 187–88
    Gough's efforts to disband, 80
    growth during the 1990s, 188
    Knox's leadership, 83, 86
    opposition to Pentecostalism, 101
    power within Sydney Diocese, 28–29
    Talbot's and Davies' leadership, 29
Anglican Church of Australia (ACA). See also Constitution, Anglican Church of Australia
    ambivalence about Graham's crusades, 91
    and autonomy from the Church of England, 53–57, 59
    challenges faced by, 243, 243n61
    debates about Lay and Diaconal Presidency, 43, 170–71, 219–20
    debates about unity and a centrally governed Australian church, 54, 56
    Diocesan representation at General Synods, 1962–2014, 274–75
    discussions of homosexuality, 115, 172
    establishment of, 13–15, 54–55
    General Synod Taskforce for Viability and Structures, 244–45
    impact of the Pymble Matter, 189
    liturgy, debates about, 230–31

287

Anglican Church of Australia (ACA) (cont.)
  the National Register, and sexual predators, 215, 215n104
  and the ordination of women, 143, 153, 168, 252–53
  and *Prayer Book* revision, 49–51, 134–35, 218–19
  and persons identifying as Anglican, 96n73m 114, 241–42
  and relationships with the Sydney Diocese, 38, 54, 179, 210–13, 184–86, 215, 219, 242
  and responses to the Recognised Churches Ordinance, 216
  and the wealth of the Sydney Diocese, 228–29
Anglican Counseling Center investigation, 213–14, 179
Anglican Mission in America (AMiA), 223
Anglican National Emergency Fund (CENEF), 34
Anglican Retirement Villages (ARV), 10, 240n52
Anglican-Roman Catholic International Commission (ARCIC), 132, 172
Anglican Schools Corporation, 224
Anglicans Together, 181–82, 229
Anglicare Sydney, 10, 237–39. See also Home Mission Society (HMS)
Anglo-Catholic movement/Anglo-Catholicism
  and the Australian Anglican Constitution, 56–57
  and the chasuble controversy, 25–26
  criticisms of in *ACR*, 84–85
  Evangelical views of, 15–16, 15–16n14, 16n15, 22, 49n54, 64
  Lyndhurst theological college, 15
  and the 1928 Revised Prayer Book, 99
  rituals reintroduced by, 22
  teachings and challenges associated with, 8, 13, 39, 56
Angus, Samuel, 26–27
"Another English Archbishop" (*ACR*), 85–86

Anti-Discrimination Act, NSW, 1977, 115
anti-war activism, 113, 113n22
Apostle's Creed, 57, 267
Aquinas, Thomas, 211
Archbishop's Appeal Fund, 10
Archbishop's Commission, 1959, 88, 94–96, 127
Archbishop's Winter Appeal, 38
Archdall, Mervyn, 22, 43
Arianism, Arius, 210
Arminianism, 55
Armstrong, Rowena, 227
Aspinall, Phillip, 129
Associated Congregations (Amendment) Ordinance 2005, 244n66
Athanasian Creed, 101, 149, 158, 208
Atonement, redemption, 8, 26–28
"Auricular confession," defined, 16n15
Australia
  changes in during the 1950s, 64–65
  dual system of education, 18
  numbers of clergy by diocese, 41–42
  secularization of, 8
  turbulence/technological change, 113–14
  women priests, 1992, 168
  and women's equality, 117–18
Australian Anglicans and their Constitution (Davis), 53
Australian Broadcasting Commission (ABC), religious programming, 226
Australian Church Record (*ACR*)
  "Another English Archbishop," 85–86
  "Archbishop Warns Sydney: Don't Be Splinter Group," 97–98
  "Australian Evangelicals address Islington Conference," 85
  on Billy Graham Crusade, 1979, 138
  contributors and focus of articles in, 84, 88–89
  discussions of homosexuality in, 115–16
  on expansion of mission to new housing areas, 69

on Loane's election, 111
on NEAC Statement, 136
on the Pentecostal movement, 101
response to threats from
  ecumenism, 98
on serving residents of new housing
  areas, 65–66
"Should women be priests?," 72–73
strengthening of by Knox, 83–84
tracking of the constitutional debate,
  61–62
writings related to women's ministry
  in, 42–43, 104, 122
Australian Council of Churches, 70
"Australian Evangelicals address
  Islington Conference" (ACR), 85
An Australian Prayer Book (AAPB), 135,
  135n101, 143
Australian Psychological Society, Ltd.,
  guidelines for clients with
  unreported memories, 214–15
Australian Universities Quality Agency
  (AUQA) accreditation, 248
Avis, Paul (*The Identity of Anglicanism*),
  85

Babbage, Stuart Barton, 40, 78,
  105n105, 149
Ballantine-Jones, Bruce, 167n81, 182,
  188, 189n33
baptism, 49n54, 54, 57, 207, 225, 267
Barker, Frederic
  Barry as successor to, 19–20
  bishopric, 16
  community welfare activities, 19
  and diocesanism, 54
  educational emphasis, 17–19
  influence and legacy, 16–17, 19
  physical characteristics, 17
  relationship with Wooley, 12–13
  Sydney Church Society, 18–19
Barker, Jane
  and the education of women, 18, 21
  emphasis on a personal faith, 13
  on husband's recruitment skills, 16
  letters to sister, 12
Barnett, Anita, 125

Barnett, Paul W., 125f
  on Anglican liturgy and practice,
    230–31
  background, 183f
  criticisms of, 229
  election as Archbishop of Sydney,
    182–83
  as head of Inner City Committee,
    139
  on Lay and Diaconal Presidency,
    220
  and the *Move in for Action* report,
    138
  and the ordination of women,
    157n43
  preaching style, 126
  The Quest for Power, 101
  as Rector of St. Barnabas, 124–26
  School for Christian Studies, 175
  on Stott's importance, 229
  university missions, 139
Barry, Alfred, 19–21, 179n1
Basic Christianity (Stott), 93
Bates, Jim, 229, 268–72
Batty, Francis de W., 51, 57–61
Baxter, Richard, 224
beach missions, 67–68
Bebbington, David W./Bebbington
  Quadrilateral, 13
Begbie, Herbert S., 22
Behan, Wally, 259–60
Bell, R., 101
Bennet, Joyce, 151
the Bible, Holy Scripture. *See also*
  church planting; Evangelicalism,
  Evangelicals; Moore College
  in the Bebbington Quadrilateral, 13
  biblicism/biblical theology, 40 41,
    87n33, 146–47
  and church planting, 216
  condemnation of homosexuality in,
    115, 115n32
  Davies' teachings on, 27–28
  disuniting with sacrament, 171
  Hammond's teachings on, 28
  historical interpretations, 8
  home study groups, 126–27, 175

the Bible, Holy Scripture *(cont.)*
   interpretations related to the ordination of women, 74, 103–4, 117–20, 151–52, 156–62, 156n40, 203–4
   as the Word of God/absolute authority, 4, 6–7, 9, 12, 27, 56, 101, 137, 184, 227, 231, 233
Bible Colleges, 42
Biblical Research Committee, 40
Bigge, John Thomas, 14
"A Bill to Alter the Constitution of the Anglican Church of Australia with respect to the Ordination of Women 1981," 165
Billy Graham Crusade, 1954, 79, 90–91
Billy Graham Crusade, 1959
   goals and impacts, 86, 88–92
   as high point in Gough's episcopy, 106–7, 107n114
   Peter Jensen's profession of faith at, 234
   Phillip Jensen's profession of faith at, 192, 234
Billy Graham Crusade, 1968, 137
Billy Graham Crusade, 1979, 138
Bishop Kirkby Memorial Hospital, Cook, South Australia, 39
Blanch, Allan, 126, 139
Bligh, William, 14
Blue Ticket, 1993 Standing Committee election, 187–88
Book of Common Prayer (BCP)
   Cranmer version, 3, 4–5, 9
   departures from in the *APBA*, 218
   as manifestation of Reformed church, 55
   and the Red Book Case, 49–51, 49n54
   revising, challenges and controversies, 49–51, 59, 99, 134–35, 218–19
   rights to deviate from, 51
   and use of alternate texts for, 230
   view of as outdated, by younger clergy, 149
Border, J. T. Ross (*Church and State in Australia 1788–1872*), 54

Bosanquet, Richard, 41n28
Bowles, R., 157n43
Boyce, Francis "Bertie," 28
Braga, Stuart (*A Century Preaching Christ*), 193
Brennan, Patricia, 119, 153–54, 156–57
Brethrenism, 34
The Briefing, 193, 198–99, 202
British and Foreign Bible Society, 19
Broughton, William Grant
   as Bishop of Sydney, 14–15
   conference of Australian and New Zealand bishops, 54
   "High Church" strategies, 16
   and the University of Sydney, 20
Brown, Callum (*The Death of Christian Britain*), 65
Brown, Ross, 100
Bruce, Frederick Fyvie, 157, 159, 161–62
Buchanan, Colin, 235
Burgmann, Ernest H., 91
Bush Church Aid Society (BCA), 39, 180

Cable, Ken, 14–15, 17
Cambridge University
   Mowll's years at, 36
   Robinson's years at, 145–47, 145n11
Cameron, Ewen Donald
   on the Anglican-Roman Catholic International Commission, 173
   Evangelicals and the World Council of Churches, 134
   at NEAC conferences, 136
   on the 1975 WCC assembly, 134
   at the 1993 Election Synod, 184
   and the ordination of women, 157, 157n43
   on Queen Elizabeth's 1954 visit, 225
   on secularization of society, 226
   on women's role in the Anglican Church, 120n47
Cameron, Neil M.
   "'Bill' Procedure to alter the Constitution," 164–65

Index

on financial crisis and
   reorganization of SCEGGS
   during the 1970s, 128
on the Inner City Committee,
   139–40
as legal advisor to Robinson, 162
on legality of Lay and Diaconal
   Presidency, 220–21
on the legality of women's
   ordination, 124
Canada Episcopal Church, ordination of
   women, 152, 202
Canon Law, and the chasuble, 25–26,
   25n40
Cape Town, South Africa, Mowll's 1948
   trip to, 47–48
Carey, George
   authority as Archbishop of
      Canterbury, 172–73, 221
   on CPSA as the recognized Anglican
      Church in South Africa, 49, 223
   Evangelical theology, 49
   on homosexual practice, 222
   letter to Cardinal Hume, 152–53
   on 1992 Church of England
      financial losses, 255–56
   on the ordination of women, 152–
      53, 169, 173
Carey, Hilary M., 44
Carmichael, Ian, 193–94
Carnley, Peter
   criticisms of the Sydney Diocese, 4
   election as Primate of Australia, 209
   on "functional subordination"
      doctrine, 209–12
   on the ordination of women, 168
Carson, Don, 205
Cartwright, Robert, 14
A Century Preaching Christ (Braga), 193
ceremonial practices, 5
Chadwick, Henry, 132, 145
"Chaldercot," purchase of, 66
Chapman, John (Chappo)
   impact on the Sydney Diocese, 228
   on Lay and Diaconal
      Administration, 171
   Phillip Jensen's work with, 192
   theology of evangelism, 138–39, 232

"The Charge of Arianism" (Peter
   Jensen), 212
Charles I (king of England), 55
Charles II (king of England), 55
chasuble controversy, 24–26
Children's Court, 38, 44
Children's Special Service Mission
   (CSSM), 37, 67–68
China, Mowlls' missionary work in, 37,
   40, 46, 71
*The Chosen Ones: The Politics of
   Salvation in the Anglican Church*
   (McGillion), 4, 254
Christ Church, St. Laurence, 24
"A Christian Philosophy of Care" (Peter
   Jensen), 238
"Christian Unity" (Knox), 122–24
Chung Hua Sheng Kung Hui, 71
Church Act, 14–15
Church and State in Australia 1788–1872
   (Border), 54
Church Missionary Society (CMS),
   39, 102, 107, 184. *See also*
   Katoomba CMS Summer School
church music, 99–100, 144
Church of England Boys' Society
   (CEBS), 47
Church of England in England. *See also*
   Anglican Communion
   binding of the Australian Anglican
      church, 53–54
   changes in following World War
      II, 59
   committee to examine role of
      women, 102
   establishment of, 3–4n1
   fears about among Sydney
      Evangelicals, 99
   financial losses, 1992, 255
   "High Church," defined, 15n13
   Order of Deaconesses, 72
   ordination of women in, 152
Church of England in South Africa
   (CESA)
   Mowll's support for, 33–34, 76
   rift with the Church of England in
      England, 49
   Robinson's support for, 173

Church of England National Emergency
    Fund (CENEF), 34, 46, 74
Church of England Training School, 18
Church of Sweden, ordination of
    women, 72
Church of the Province in South Africa
    (CPSA), 33–34, 49, 173
church planting
    disapproval of by Anglican bishops,
        215, 242
    and expanding building needs, 68,
        96
    focus on, 228
    Jensens' support for, 244
    and Moore College-trained clergy,
        194, 243
    and remote diocese, 42
    types of activities, 244
The Church Record (ACL), 28–29
Clapham Sect, 13
Clark, Mrs. (letter writer), 104
Clergy Daughters School, 21
Coggan, Donald
    election as Archbishop of
        Canterbury, 114
    on the ordination of women, 120
    visit to Sydney, 1977, 114
Cohen, Marlene, 164
Cole, Graham
    background and academic work,
        177n117, 210n90
    interpretation of Scripture, 157
    on relationships within the Trinity,
        210–11
Colossians 3:9, 161–62
Colossians 3:16, 203
Colossians 3:18, 158n50
Colquhoun, Wendy, 231
Congregational Church, ordination of
    women, 151
conservative Reformed church, 58
Constitution, Anglican Church of
    Australia
    ACR editorials related to, 61–62
    and autonomy from England, 56, 59
    criticisms of, 81–82
    drafts and revisions, 57–61
    final passage, 64

goals, 99
and impacts of *Scandrett v Dowling*,
    167
and issues of unity, 58
Knox's opposition to, 81–83, 86
and legality of Lay and Diaconal
    Presidency, 220–21
and the ordination of women, 154,
    162, 164–65
Convention movement, 184
conversionism, 13
I Corinthians 6, 167–68
I Corinthians 11, 158–59
I Corinthians 11:3–12, 156n40
I Corinthians 11:3–16, 203
I Corinthians 14:26ff, 203
I Corinthians 14:33ff, 72–73
I Corinthians 14:33–36, 203
I Corinthians 14:34–36, 160n58
I Corinthians 14:35, 199
I Corinthians 15:23–28, 209
I Corinthians 16:16, 203
Cornish, John, 182, 229
Council of Churches, New South Wales,
    91–92
Cowper, William, 14–15
Cranmer, Thomas, 3, 71, 99
Created Woman (Giles), 159–60
Cripps, Maureen, 201
Crockford's Clerical Directory 1975–6,
    116
Cromwell, Oliver, 55
crucicentrism, 13

Danish Church, ordination of women,
    72
Dann, Robert, 133
Darling, Pamela, 151
Darwin, Charles, Darwinism, 8
Davidson, Randall, 134
Davies, David John
    clergy trained under, 31
    and curriculum at Moore College,
        27
    death and funeral remembrances,
        30–31
    as Principal of Moore College, 24
    theology of, 26–27

Index

as Vice President of the ACL, 29
Davies, Glenn, 246
Davis, John (*Australian Anglicans and their Constitution*), 53
deaconesses
    role and regulations, 43–44
    training, 43
Deaconess House (Mary Andrew's College), 102–3, 160, 171, 207
Deaconess Institution (Bethany House), 43
deacons, permanent, 246. *See also* Lay and Diaconal Administration
The Death of Christian Britain (Brown), 65
"Deep Impact" welcoming event for Peter Jensen, 235–36
Delbridge, Graham, 46–47, 66, 131
Democratic Labor Party (DLP), 64
Diaconal Presidency. *See* Lay and Diaconal Administration
Diamond Creek parish, Melbourne, 202
Dickson, John (*Hearing Her Voice*), 254
Diesendorf, Eileen, 164
Diocesan Doctrine Commission, 1988, 254
Diocesan Executive Board (DEB), 237, 247
Diocesan Mission, 1951, 66–67
Diocesan Theological College in Foochow (Fuzhou), China, 37
Diocese of Bathurst, complaint against, 49–50
Diocese of Canberra and Goulburn
    conflicts with the Diocese of Sydney, 222
    ordination of women in, 166
Diocese of Melbourne
    and the absence of factors needed for evangelical continuity, 261
    and controversy over *Honest to God*, 133
    creation of, 15
    early evangelicalism in, 15, 19
    and homosexual practice, 115
    mixed churchmanship in, 19
    and the Red Book Case, 218
    Scandrett v Dowlling 1.01 1992, 166–67n81
    sense of rivalry with Sydney, 228–29
Diocese of Newcastle, Heard's Evangelical church in Erina, 216
Diocese of Sydney. *See also* Evangelicalism, Evangelicals; homosexual practice; Lay and Diaconal Administration; Moore College; ordination of women *and specific church leaders*
    and the Anglican Church League, 28–29
    Anglican Counseling Center controversy, 179, 213–14
    assets/financial condition at time of Gough's arrival, 94–95
    and the Australian Anglican Constitution, 57, 58
    avoidance of centralism, 10
    and the Billy Graham Crusade, 1959, 89–91
    books about, 254
    characteristics, shared views of, 231
    commitment to the centrality of the Bible, 263
    common criticisms, 4–5, 7, 9, 106, 229–30
    conservative Evangelical faith/theology, 6, 7, 11, 13, 16, 22, 34–35, 58, 92, 136–37, 231
    Constitution, debates about, 54, 56
    defining, current views, 228
    didactic focus, 231–32
    and discussion of separation from the Anglican Church, 185, 242
    educational emphasis, 17–21, 41–42, 95–96, 102, 139, 184, 234, 248
    emphasis on social justice, social welfare, 10, 14, 184, 196–97
    emphasis on strict adherence to Reformation principles and practices, 59
    factions, politicization, 22
    finances, 95–96, 127–29, 167, 228–29, 240n52, 255
    focus on ministry and mission, 10, 178, 231–32, 263

Diocese of Sydney *(cont.)*
  growth, 64–66, 68s, 124, 174, 185, 223, 239–41, 240n52
  and the holiness movement, 34
  indigenizing efforts, 11
  Mission strategy, 66, 227, 234–37, 245
  non-Anglican identity, 9
  participation in GAFCON, 260
  and prayer book revisions, 50, 99, 134, 219
  primacy of parishes in, 9
  Provisional-Cathedrals, 174
  the Pymble Matter, 188–89
  and questions of sexual propriety, 106
  Recognised Churches Ordinance, 215–16
  relationships with non-Anglican Evangelicals, 23, 232–33
  relationship with other Anglican dioceses, 88, 129–40, 143, 185, 222, 253
  and remarriage of divorced people, 170
  representation at the Lambeth Conference, 1998, 222
  and the role of women in the ministry, 10, 42–43, 51, 151, 169–70, 251–52
  Secretariat and administrative streamlining, 128
  social justice concerns and activities, 10
  Stott's visits to, 93
  support for Independent Evangelical Churches, 243
  unique identity, ethos, 61–64, 184–85, 261–62
  "Vision for Growth" initiative, 174
  visits of evangelists to following Graham Crusade, 92
  wealth and finances, 5
  WWII chaplains from, 34
  youth work, 10, 46–47, 66
Diocese of Westminster, Canada, approval of same-sex marriage, 223
discipline, church, approaches to, as source of conflict, 222
Dissenters
  alignment of Anglican Evangelicals with, 12
  Evangelicals' links with, 34–35
  labeling of by Charles II and separation from the Church of England, 55–56
divorce, remarriage following, discussions in the Sydney Synod, 170
Docetism, Jensen's condemnation of, 210–12
Doctrine Commission, on the legitimacy of Lay and Diaconal Presidency, 220
Doctrine Commission (Diocese of Sydney)
  on the *APBA*, 218–19
  "The Doctrine of the Trinity and its bearing on the relationship of Men and Women," 209–13
  on remarriage of divorced persons, 170
  on women in the ministry, 156–58, 156n40, 157n43, 254, 272
Doctrine Commission (General Synod)
  The Ministry of Women, 120–21, 156, 156n38
  A Woman's Place, 120n48
Dodd, Charles H., 146
Dowling, Owen, 166
Dowling, Roy R., 81
Dykes, Owen, 100

ecclesia, Knox-Robinson view, 233
ecumenism, ecumenical integration, 98, 132–33
Election Synod, 1958, 78
Election Synod, 1993, 184
Eliot, T.S., 226
Elizabethan Settlement of 1559, 54–55
Elizabeth II (queen of England), visits to Australia, 64, 114, 225
Episcopal Church of the USA (ECUSA) declaration of state of emergency, 222–23

Goodhew's condemnation of, 223
homosexuality debate, 172
ordination of women, 151
and same-sex marriages, 257
"Equal but Different" group, 205–6
Equity Court, New South Wales, 49–50
Erickson, Millard J. (*Who's Tampering with the Trinity*), 208–9
Erina, Newcastle, Australia, Evangelical church in, 217–18, 242
Essential Christianity (Angus), 26
Eucharist. *See also* chasuble controversy; Holy Communion, Lord's Supper; Lay and Diaconal Administration
Evangelicalism, Evangelicals. *See also* Anglo-Catholics, Anglo-Catholicism; Diocese of Sydney; mission
    challenges facing, 7–8
    criticisms of Charismatic movement, 100–102
    early response to in Sydney, 16
    and justification by faith, 7–8, 12–13, 132–33
    mission, definition, 66
    Phillip Jensen's influence on, 192, 194
    proliferation in Australia, 262–63
    roots of, 13–16
    Short's appreciation for, 233
    social justice, social welfare activities, 10, 14, 184, 196–97
    Stott's role in promoting, 92
    theology and identity, 4–5, 12, 15–16n14, 23, 61–64, 136–37, 140, 195–96
Evangelicals and the World Council of Churches (Cameron), 134
Every Member Canvass, 69
expository preaching, 92
External Studies Department (Moore College), 249, 249f
"extreme congregationalism," 196

Faithfulness in Service, 243
Family Law Act of 1975, 115

Fellowship of Confessing Anglicans (FCA), 263
Fellowship of Independent Evangelical Churches (FIEC), 242–43
feminism, second wave, and the ordination of women, 117–18
Field, E.P., 22
First World War (WW I), as Holy War, 29
Fisher, Geoffrey Francis
    correspondence about Sydney Evangelicals, 81–82
    draft Constitution for the Anglican Church of Australia, 60–61
    election as Archbishop of Canterbury, 45
    on Gough as successor to Mowll, 80
    Mowll's relationship with, 47–49, 75
    opposition to Li's ordination, 42–43
    preference for strong central government, 59–60
    Red Book Case, 49–50
    responses to the Billy Graham Crusade, 1954, 90–91
    visit to Australia, 1950, 59–60
Fisher, Leonard, 47–48
Fletcher, Brian (*The Place of Anglicanism in Australia*), 4, 136n107
Fletcher, Geoff, 102
Fletcher, Jonathan, 232
Fliedner, Theodor, 43n34
Foord, Dudley, 173–74
Forsyth, Robert, 182, 208, 212, 248
Frame, Tom, 4
funerals, secular, 225
"The Future of Jesus" (Peter Jensen), 237

Gabbott, Marion, 205–6
Gaden, John R., 120n48, 156n38, 158
Gasque, W. Ward, 161
gearing, 255n100
General Synod (Anglican Church of Australia). *See also* Anglican Church of Australia; Constitution, Anglican Church of Australia
    Appellate Tribunal, jurisdiction and authority, 165–66

General Synod (Anglican Church of Australia) *(cont.)*
   and the Australian Anglican Constitution, 57
   and differing views about the Primacy, 129–30
   Diocesan representation at, 1962–2014, 274–75
   discussion of *Book of Common Prayer* revision, 135
   focus on mission, 244–45
   The Ministry of Women, 120–21, 156, 156n38
   Mowll's role with, 59, 75
   numbers from the Diocese of Sydney in, 243
   and the ordination of women, 122, 155–56, 155n36, 168, 252–53
   A Prayer Book for Australia, 218
   and provisional Canon governing remarriage of divorced people, 170
   role of the Diocese of Sydney in, 129, 243, 274–75
   A Woman's Place, 120n48
George Whitefield College, 174
"Gilbulla," Mowll's purchase of, 46, 46n44
Giles, Kevin
   theological arguments related to women's ordination, 159–160
   The Trinity and Subordinationism: The Doctrine of God and the Contemporary Gender Debate, 208–9
   Women and their Ministry, 122
Glebe Administration Board (GAB), 127, 255
Global Anglican Future Conference (GAFCON), 2008, 257–260, 263
Global Financial Crisis, 2008, 255
God, as supreme authority
   Evangelical understandings, 7–8
   spreading the news about, as cornerstone of Evangelical theology, 137
   and strict adherence to Scripture, 6, 12, 137, 231
   theological perspective on women's ordination, 119
God's Good Design. What the Bible really says about MEN and WOMEN (Smith), 254
The Good Book Company, 194
Goodhew, Harry, 183f
   on the abandonment of common liturgy in the Diocese of Sydney, 219
   academic studies, 181
   appointment of Nicholios, 200–201
   background, early parish experience, 180
   church planting legislation, 243
   departure from the Sydney Diocese, 224
   election as Archbishop of Sydney, 179, 182, 183
   five-point plan for the Sydney Diocese, 186–87
   handling of bishop accused of adultery, 222
   importance of prayer to, 186
   on independence of parish practice, 9, 195
   internal and external issues during episcopate of, 179
   and Lay and Diaconal Administration, 171, 220
   and Myles' ministry, 208
   negative report on the ECUSA, 223
   as an outsider, 180–81
   Piggins' mentorship of, 181
   and the *A Prayer Book for Australia*, 218
   proposed strategy for growth, 186
   relationships with Australian Anglicans, 179, 186, 187
   relationships with other Sydney Diocese leaders, 190–91, 221–22
   and response to the Pymble Matter, 189
   struggles with the Standing Committee, 190
   succession, 247–48
   withholding of consent for Lay Presidency, implications, 221–22

Goodhew, Pam, 186–87
Gook, Bernard, 67
Gorham vs. the Bishop of Exeter, 49n54
Gough, Hugh Rowlands, 79f
  Archbishop's Commission, 1959, 93
  arrival in Sydney, 93
  background, evangelical credentials, 79
  on the Bible over the Church, 84
  clashes with Sydney clergy, 81, 108
  and the Constitution Act, 83
  early visit to Sydney, 80
  election as Archbishop of Sydney, 78
  election as Primate of Australia, 93, 129
  episcopate, outside events during, 80–81, 83, 88, 96–97, 179n1
  leadership style, behavior, 80–81
  legacy, 106–7
  and *Prayer Book* revision efforts, 99
  resignation, 104–5, 105n105
  and Sydney's Evangelical identity, 97–98
Graham, Billy, 91–92. *See also* Billy Graham Crusade
Grant, James, 227
Grant, Lindsay, 34
Gray, Robert, 33
Great Commission of Christ, 134, 263, 263n4
Greaves, Talbot, 112–13
Green, Bryan, 67
Green, Michael, 138
"the green book." *See An Australian Prayer Book*
Griffiths, John, 208n78
Grindrod, John
  on the *Australian Prayer Book*, 135
  and Foord's consecration, 173
  and the ordination of women, 155–56, 156n38, 169
Grose, Francis, 14
Group Brotherhood, 24, 29
Grubb, George C.; Grubb mission, 22–23
"Guidelines for psychological practice with clients with previously unreported traumatic memories" (Australian Psychological Society, Ltd.), 214–15
Guinness, Howard, 67, 231

Hammond, Robert B., 22
Hammond, Thomas Chatterton
  areas of influence, 32–33
  and the Australian Anglican Constitution, 58–59, 99
  and autonomy for the Australian Anglican Church, 59
  background, leadership style, 32, 32n63
  charges of Arianism against, 210
  contributions to the *ACR*, 84
  criticisms of, 81–82
  influence on the Diocese of Sydney, 32
  relationship with Loane, 113, 113n20, 119
  relationship with Mowll, 40
  and the "Sinless Perfectionism" movement, 34
  tenure as Principal at Moore College, 28, 31–32
  In Understanding Be Men, 209
  and the Wylde case, 49–50
Hammondcare, 10
Handley, Ken, 162, 211, 252
Hannah, Horace John, 112–13
Harris, Tim, 157, 169, 176
Hart, Henry, 145
Hart, John Stephen, 57
headship of the male
  as argument against ordination of women, 119, 121, 153, 158
  Knox's view, 121, 156n40
  and Loane's theology, 119
  and the ordering of relationships, 158–60
  and the subordination of the Son, 209–10
Heard, Andrew, 216–17, 217f
Hearing Her Voice (Dickson), 254
Hebert, Gabriel, 146–47
Helleman, Christian, 144
Herft, Roger, 216

Hicks, Lesley, 138
"High Church," 15n13, 16, 21
Hill, Thomas Ernest, 17, 21
Historic Episcopate, local adaptation, 57, 267
historiography of recent events, challenges, 1–2
History of Global Anglicanism (Ward), 4
Hodge, Charles, 208
Hodgson, William, 13, 16
Hollingworth, Peter, 216
Holt, Harold, 114
Holy Communion, Lord's Supper
   Lay and Diaconal Administration, 8, 22, 171, 179, 204, 220, 246, 263
   Order of, disagreements about, 134
   and the Red Book Case, 49
   as Sacrament ordained by Christ, 57
   women's administration of, 42–43
Home Mission Society (HMS). *See also* Anglicare
   importance, population served, 10, 66, 184
   integration of the Counseling Center with, 215
   Mowlls' revitalizing, 38
   Service Bureau, 47, 214–15
   social welfare focus, 237
Home of Peace, 44
Home Visiting and Relief Society, 19
homosexual practice
   and anti-discrimination legislation, 115
   discussion of within the ACA, 172
   and homosexual clergy, 223, 242
   Lambeth Conference discussions, 222, 257
   and same-sex marriage, 223, 257
   Scriptural condemnation of, 115, 115n32, 117, 257
   Sydney Diocese stand against, 5, 212, 262–63
Honest to God (Robinson), 101–2, 133
Hooker, Richard (*The Laws of Ecclesiastical Polity*), 54–55
Horsburgh, Michael, 229, 229n14
Horton, Silas, 89–90
Hough, Michael, 245–46

Hunkin, Joseph, 29
Hunter, John, 14
Hwang, Jane, 102, 151

Independent Evangelical Church, 217, 242
Ingham, Michael, 223
Inner City Committee, Sydney Synod, 139
Inter-Anglican Theological and Doctrinal Commission, 142
International Federation of Evangelical Student (IFES), 46, 147
Inter Varsity Fellowship (IVF), 34
InterVarsity Press (IVP), 40, 194
An Introduction to World Anglicanism (Kaye), 85
Irish Church Missions (ICM), 32
Isaiah 53:6, 235
Issues Facing Christians Today (Stott), 159
ius liturgicum, Wylde's focus on, 50–51

Jarrett, Narelle, 160, 200, 247, 253
Jenkyn, Norman, 71
Jensen, Christine, 206, 235, 247
Jensen, Helen, 206
Jensen, Michael, 121, 247, 254
Jensen, Peter Frederick, 234f
   appointment by, 247–48
   as Assistant Rector of St. Barnabas, 124
   church planting efforts, 244
   criticisms of, 229, 247
   "Deep Impact" welcoming event for, 235
   education and early mission experience, 139, 234
   election as Archbishop of Sydney, 234
   emphasis on Mission, 234, 235–36
   flexibility regarding the training of deacons, 246
   and "functional subordination," 209–10
   at GAFCON, 2008, 257, 263
   handling of financial crises, 255–57
   honors thesis, 236n32

on the importance of Anglicare, 237–38
on the importance of the CMS Summer School, 223–24
influence of brother, Phillip, on, 191, 247
international impact, 260
and Lay and Diaconal Administration, 245–46
licensing of women to preach, 253, 253–54n94
as member of the Standing Committee, 188
Mission strategy, 236–37, 245
and Myles' ministry, 208
and the ordination of women, 157n43
parish focus, 9–10, 35
personality, leadership style, 235, 237
as principal of Moore College, 175
The Quest for Power, 101
relationships with other dioceses, 253
relationship with Knox, 88
responses to charges of Arianism, 210–12
and St. Matthias parish, 192–93
theology, 74
Jensen, Phillip, 191f
appointment as Dean of St. Andrew's Cathedral, 246–47
background and ministry, 192
books authored by, 194
as chair of REPA, 182
and church planting, 215, 244
Evangelical theology, 32, 195–96
influence, 193–94, 199–200, 247
and the Katoomba Christian Convention, 193, 193n42
Katoomba Youth Convention (KYC), 193–94
nomination as Archbishop of Sydney, 182
personality, leadership style, 191–93
on *A Prayer Book for Australia*, 218
promotion of informal liturgy, 199

publishing activities, 193
relationship with Knox, 88
speaking engagements, 194
St. Matthias parish, 185, 185n15
and traditional Anglicanism, 195
views on selection process for ordination, 190–91
on women in ministry, 197–99
Jerusalem Declaration (GAFCON), 258
John 4:23, 24, 123
John 11:25, 26, 123
John 13:14, 156n40
John 14:6, 7
John 14:28, 156n40
Johnson, Douglas ("DJ"), 32n65, 40, 147
Johnson, Richard, 14, 34
Johnson, William H., 58
Johnstone, J.R.L., 81
Jones, Lang, Wooton & Sons, 95
Jones, Nathaniel, 23–24, 34–35, 262
Judd, Stephen
on Goodhew's election, 183
on the Memorialists, 33
and the Standing Committee, 1993, 187–88, 187n23
Judge, Edwin, 231–32
Judge, Patricia, 205
Justification by Faith
emphasis on by Sydney clergy, 228–29, 270
Loane's emphasis on, 132–33

Kaiserwerth, Germany, deaconess movement, 43n34
Kassian, Mary, 205
Katoomba Christian Convention, 184, 193, 224
Katoomba CMS Summer School
attendance, 102, 223
importance, 107, 184, 224
Stott's addresses to, 92
Katoomba Men's Convention, 193n42
Katoomba Youth Convention (KYC), 193
Kaye, Bruce (*An Introduction to World Anglicanism*), 85
Kell, Peter, 239, 256

Kerle, Clive
  and the 1959 Billy Graham Crusade, 88–89, 91
  as candidate for Archbishop of Sydney, 78
  and Myles' ministry, 207
  university missions, 139
Kern, Philip, 248
Keswick Convention/theology, influence, 22–23, 34, 37, 229
The King's School, Sydney, 21
Kite, Dean, 24
Kitto, R.W., 50
Knox, Constance ("Christian Unity"), 122–24
Knox, David Broughton, 176f
  and the Anglican Church League, 86
  anti-episcopal stance, 87
  and the Australian Anglican Constitution, 61, 81, 83, 86
  changing views on the WCC, 133–34
  contributions to the *Australian Church Record*, 47
  criticisms of, 82–83
  Evangelical theology, 32
  on homosexuality, 117
  ideological confluence with Robinson, 176
  influence on Loane's theology, 119
  influence on the Sydney Diocese, 87–88, 176
  mentorship of Jensen, 191
  and the ordination of women, 120–21, 156–57, 157n43, 209
  participation with the Biblical Research Committee, 40
  personality, leadership style, 83, 88
  as Principal of Moore College, 70, 86–87, 111, 129, 148
  relationship with Gough, 80–81, 83, 87–88
  testimony during the Red Book Case, 51
  theological college in South Africa, 174
  views on the episcopy, 196
Knox, David James
  influence on Loane, 112
  response to news of Mowll's death, 76
  support for Li's ordination, 43
Knox, EA, mentorship of Mowll, 37
Kokoda Trail, 113
Kolini, Emmanuel, 223
Korean War, 64
Kuan, Jonathan Wei-Han, 261–62

laity, empowerment of, 4, 10, 51–52, 184, 200. *See also* Lay and Diaconal Administration; parish churches
Lamb, R. E., 157n43
Lambeth Conferences, 1968–2008, 120, 47–49, 132, 172, 154, 222, 257–58
Lambeth Quadrilateral, 1888, 56–57, 267
Lane, Adrian, 139
Lane, Peter, 133
Lang, Cosmo Gordon, 37
Langford-Smith, Neville, 61n26
Langshaw, Reg, 104n102
Law of the Church of England Clarification Canon 1992, 168
The Laws of Ecclesiastical Polity (Hooker), 54–55
Lay and Diaconal Administration. *See also* Holy Communion, Lord's Supper
  activities associated with, 170–71, 171n93
  authorization of by the Sydney Synod, 246
  debates about, 43, 170–71, 179, 202–3, 219–20, 245–46
  legal issues, 220–21
  Peter Jensen on, 245–46
  and professionalizing of the laity, 200
  support for in the Sydney Diocese, 4, 219–20
  supporting principles, 171–72n95
Lee, Dorothy, 151–52
Le Fanu, Henry, 38
Lethbridge-King, Robert, 17

Index

Li, Florence Tim Oi, 42, 72, 151
liberal theology, Modernism, 8, 26–27, 27n49, 39, 64, 133
Little, Jimmy, 100
Liturgical Commission, proposed *Prayer Book* revision, 135
liturgy, Anglican, 199, 219, 230–31. *See also Book of Common Prayer*; *Thirty-Nine Articles*
Loane, Marcus, influences on, 110
Loane, Marcus Lawrence, 109f
   and the *AAPB*, 135
   background and education, 110
   biography of Mowll, 36
   contributions to *ACR*, 84
   on Davies' homilies, 27
   election as Archbishop of Sydney, 78, 111
   emphasis on church unity, 109–10, 132
   Evangelical theology, 136–37
   experiences, emphasis on pastoral care, 30–31, 110–11, 131
   and Foord's consecration, 173
   influences on, 112–13
   on inner-city ministry, 139–40
   knighthood honors, 131–32
   legacy, 108–10
   letter praising Wood, 130
   Mark These Men, 80
   at the Melbourne NEAC, 136–37
   outside events during episcopate of, 114
   parting words, 141
   personality, leadership style, 113, 140–41
   as Primate, enlarged focus, 130–32
   as Principal of Moore College, 70, 86, 111
   relationship with Gough, 83, 105
   relationship with Hammond, 113, 113n20
   relationship with Robinson, 112, 148
   relationship with Stott, 92
   relationship with Strong, 110
   response to the Vietnam War, 113–14
   views on Anglicanism, 23n35
   views on homosexuality, 116–17
   views on women's ministry, 119
   on "vogue theology," 101–2
Loane, Patricia Knox, 112
Lombard, Peter, 211
London Bible College, 40
London Diocesan Conference, 42
Long, George Merrick, 57–58
Lord's Supper. *See* Holy Communion, Lord's Supper
Lucas, Dick, 194, 232
Luther, Martin, 100, 132, 171
Lux Mundi, 8
"Lyndhurst" theological college, 15, 20

MacArthur, John, 46, 46n44
MacCulloch, Diarmaid, 54–56
Machen, J. Gresham, 28n52
MacKay, George, 112–13
male headship. *See* headship of the male
Mann, William J.G., 61n25
Mao Tse Tung, 71
Maple, Grant, 17–18
Mark These Men (Loane), 80
marriage, church-sanctioned, 225. *See also* adultery; divorce
Marriage of Divorced Persons Ordinance 1985, 170
Marsden, George, 271–72
Marsden, Samuel, 14
Marshall, Barry, 133
Mascord, Keith (*A Restless Faith*), 254
Mason, J.G., 157n43
Mason, Keith, 161–62, 165–66, 203
Matthew 6:28, 106
Matthew 28:19, 7
Matthew 28:19–20, 263n4
Matthias Media, 193–94, 254
McGillion, Chris (*The Chosen Ones*), 4, 183, 254
McIntosh, John, 7–8, 23–24, 27
McKerihan, Steve, 255
McPherson, James, on women's ministry, 204–5
Memorialists, 31–33
Menzies, Robert, 64
Merriman v Williams (1880), 33

Methodist Church, 56, 113n22, 132, 151
migrant populations, ministry to, 44–45, 64, 68, 114, 139, 236
The Ministry of Women (General Synod Commission on Doctrine), 120, 156, 156n38
missionary work, Mission strategy. *See also* Church Missionary Society (CMS); church planting; Lay and Diaconal Administration; parish churches
  assessing effectiveness of, 239–40, 240n52
  and church planting, 216, 244
  as focus of Jensen's episcopate, 234–36, 245
  as focus of Mowll's episcopate, 70–71
  and the Sydney Diocese focus on parishes, 239, 263
Modernism. *See* liberal theology, Modernism
Moore College
  accreditation, 248
  curriculum, faculty, 27, 175
  clergy trained at, 9, 31, 32–33, 41–42, 243
  Davies as Principal of, 24, 26–30
  enrollment of women, 86
  External Studies Department, 249, 249f
  focus on biblical scholarship, 40, 41
  founding, 13, 16–18
  during Goodhew's episcopate, 190–91
  growth during the 1970s, 129
  growth under Woodhouse, 248
  Hammond as Principal of, 31–32
  Hill as Principal of, 21
  importance within the Sydney Diocese, 181, 231
  increasing enrollments during the 1990s, 223
  Independent Evangelical Church, 242
  Jensen as Principal of, 35
  Jones as Principal of, 23
  Knox as Principal of, 70, 83, 86–87
  Loane as Principal of, 111
  move to Newtown, 17, 20
  during Mowll's episcopate, 30–32, 38, 69–70
  Preliminary Theological Course, 127, 175
  Reformation Rallies, 22–23
  Robinson as lecturer at, 144, 146
  during Robinson's episcopate, 175
  students from St. Matthias parish, 192
  Tooher's lectures, 250
Moorehouse, Geoffrey, 127
Moorehouse Lectures, 39
Morris, George Frederick ("Fred"), 48–49, 75–76
Morris, Leon, 40n20, 120n48, 156–59, 156n39
Move in for Action report, 138
Movement for the Ordination of Women, 119, 205
Movement for the Ordination of Women (MOW), 153, 202–3
Mowll, Dorothy, 37, 74
Mowll, Howard West Kilvinton, 30f
  addresses/letters to the Diocese, 44–45
  background, education, 36, 36n2
  candidates for successor, 78
  death, responses, 76–77
  destruction of papers and correspondence, 26, 36n1
  early focus and activities, 38–39
  election as Archbishop, 30, 36
  election as Primate, 129
  emphasis on evangelical mission, 39, 46, 66–71
  evangelical scholarship, 39–40
  Every Member Congress, 69
  external events during episcopate, 70
  final years, 75
  influence on the Diocese of Sydney, 31–32
  influences, mentors, 37, 39
  legacy, 75–76
  Loane biography, 35
  marriage, 37

and the Memorialists, 33
and Moore College, 23, 30–31, 38
and move for Australian Anglican Constitution, 99
and parish growth, 46, 68
personality, leadership style, 38
policies related to Aborigines, 45
as Primate, 39, 70
Red Book Case, 49–50
Reformation Rallies, 71
relationship with Davies, 31, 31n60
relationship with Fisher, 47–49, 59, 75
relationship with Loane, 110, 112
Stott's visit with, 92
support for the *Australian Church Record*, 47
support for World Council of Churches, 45–46
theology, 37
work during the Second World War, 34
youth ministry, 38, 66
Muggeridge, Malcolm, 138
Mulready, David, 232
Murphy, Chuck, 223
Myles, Jacinth, 206–8, 208n78, 253

National Evangelical Anglican Conference (NEAC), 135–37
National Register for the ACA, 215, 215n104
New Capital Project, 244
Newman, P.J., 228–29
The New Puritans: The Rise of Fundamentalism in the Anglican Church (Porter), 4, 106
New South Wales
 Independent Evangelical Churches in, 242
 Independent Evangelical Church in, 242
 New South Wales Corps., 14
 Supreme Court, 166–67
New Zealand, ordination of Anglican women in, 152
the Nexus, 53–54, 57

Nicolios, Di, 117n118, 193n43, 200–202, 201f
Nightingale, Florence, 103–4
Noll, Stephen, 259
"non-jurors," 56n10
Northcott, John, 89
Norton, Thomas, 98n77

O'Brien, Anne, 43
O'Brien, Peter T., 157n43, 167–68
Olson, Warwick, 99–100
"Open Letter to the Diocese of Sydney" (Mascord), 254
Order of Deaconesses, 72
ordination, selection process for, 190–91
ordination of women. *See also* General Synod
 approaches to thinking about, 42–43, 150–51, 176–77, 202–3
 Cameron's views, 157
 C. Knox's views, 122–24
 debates about, Evangelical perspectives, 4, 10, 72–74
 debates during Goodhew's episcopate, 179
 and departures of clergy from the Sydney Diocese, 177, 177n117
 and the "Equal but Different" group, 205
 as legal issue, 51, 124, 162, 162n64, 164–65
 Loane's views, 119
 Myles' views, 208
 Nicolios' views, 202
 numbers of female priests, 1992, 168
 Phillip Jensen's views, 197–99
 Robinson's views, 143, 148–50, 163
 Scriptural/theological arguments, 103–4, 117–20, 156–62, 156n40
 Smith's views, 203–4
 support for in Anglican Communion, 168
The Ordination of Women as Presbyters (Phillip Jensen), 198
Oxford University, Oxford Movement, 15n13

Paddison, Evonne, 117n118, 177f

parish churches. *See also* Lay and
Diaconal Administration
  Anglicare focus on, 239
  country/rural dioceses, 243
  and the Every Member Congress, 69
  Goodhew's focus on, 180, 186–87
  growth of during the 1950s, 68
  and in-home Bible studies, 126–27
  importance and empowerment of,
    9–10, 196, 227
  independence of practice, 195–96
  and the Inner City Committee,
    139–40
  Loane's visits to, 131
  Mowll's attentions to, 38, 46
  Myles' service to, 207
  parish Sunday Schools, 127
  and "Vision for Growth" initiative,
    174
Parish Disputes Ordinance, 189
Parker, Joy, 103
Parkes, Henry, 18
Paul the apostle, 72–73, 119n42
Payne, Tony, 193, 254
penal substitutionary view, 8
Pentecostal/Charismatic movement,
  100–102
Perini, Paul, 190–91
Permanent Diaconate, and team
  approach to ministry, 246
Perry, Charles, as Bishop of Melbourne,
  15, 19
I Peter 2, 171
I Peter 2:9, 171–72n95, 219n116
Petrov Affair, 64
Pidgeon, Rosie, 253
Piggin, Stuart (*Evangelical Christianity
  in Australia*), 18
Piggin, Stuart (*Evangelical Christianity
  in Autralia*), 37–38, 90, 154, 181
Pitt, E.A., 71, 81–82
Pitt, William, 13–14
The Place of Anglicanism in Australia
  (Fletcher), 136n107
Polding, John Bede, 13
Pope, David, 133
Porter, Brian, 129–31, 133
Porter, Muriel, 4, 106, 235

Prayer Book, absence of mention in the
  Lambeth Quadrilateral, 57
Prayer Book Commission, establishment
  and purpose, 99
*A Prayer Book for Australia (APBA). See
  also* Red Book Case
  liturgy in, 144
  publication of, controversies
    surrounding, 218–19
Preliminary Theological Course (PTC),
  175
Preliminary Theological Course (PTC),
  Moore College, 127
Presbyterian Church, 151
Presbyterian Church of Australia, 193
Priddle, Charles, 13
Primate of Australia, redefining role of,
  129–30
Primates' Council (GAFCON), 259
Priscilla and Aquila Center, 250–51
"progressive revelation," 27, 27n49
Prophets, Preachers and Heretics, 119
Protestant Church of England Union
  (PCEU), 22
Public Schools Acts, 18
Purgatory doctrine, 22
purgatory prayers, 16, 22
Puritans
  Church of England efforts to
    discredit, 55
  linkages of Evangelicalism with, 6,
    35
  support for Reformed tradition, 55
Pusey, Edward Bouverie, "Puseyites,"
  7–8, 15, 15n13
Pymble Matter, 188–89
Pymble matter, 179

The Quest for Power (Barnett and
  Jensen), 101

Racial Discrimination Act of 1975, 115
Raffel, Kanishka, 232–33
Ramsey, Michael, 84–85, 113n22, 114
"Rathane," purchase of, 66
Raven, Charles, 145
Rayner, Keith

on Lay and Diaconal
    Administration, 221–22
on the ordination of women,
    156n38, 168–69
on role of the Primate, 129
on Woods, 131
Recognised Churches Ordinance, 215–16, 218, 244
recovered memories of sexual abuse, 213–14
Red Book Case, 49–52, 59
Reformation Rallies, 71–72
Reformation Settlement principles, 83
Reformed Evangelical Protestant Association (REPA), 181–82, 190
Reid, George, 115–16
Reid, John R.
    arguments for Sydney remaining within the ACA, 185–86, 253
    candidacy for Archbishop of Sydney, 148n19, 182
    concept of "extreme congregationalism," 196–97
    at NEAC conferences, 136
    relationship with Myles, 207
    relationship with Phillip Jensen, 193, 196
    on the unique ethos of Sydney Diocese, 184–85
Relators, case against Wylde, 50–51
remarriage of divorced people, 170
Report on Discrimination and Homosexuality (NSW Anti-Discrimination Board), 172
"reserved sacrament," 171
Restless Faith. Leaving Fundamentalism in a Quest for God (Mascord), 254
revelation. *See also* subordinist views on the Trinity; the Bible, Holy Scripture, Evangelical understandings, 7–8, 211
Revised Prayer Book (1928), 99
Richardson, Athol, 80
Rivers, Charlotte, 127, 231
Robert Menzies College, 175
Robinson, David, 142–43
Robinson, Donald William Bradley, 147f
    and Biblical Theology, 87n33, 176
    birth and early education, 143
    and the Constitution Act, 61–64, 81
    contributions to the *Australian Church Record*, 47, 84
    criticisms of, 162
    on Dodd, 146
    education, military service, 144, 145, 145n11
    efforts to subdivide the Sydney Diocese, 174–75
    election as Archbishop, 148
    focus of episcopate, 143, 145
    on the General Synod, Appellate Tribunal, 166
    on homosexual practice, 172
    influences on, 145–47
    on Lay and Diaconal Presidency, 220
    legacy, 175–76
    legalistic perspective, 149, 166
    marriage, 148
    on marriage of divorced persons, 170
    on Mowll, 37
    on the ordination of women, 149–50, 154–55, 157, 162–64, 166–67, 169
    personality, leadership style, 146, 148–49
    and relationship with other Anglican dioceses, 143
    retirement, 181
    and revision of the *Book of Prayer*, 99, 135
    term of office, 173
    as Vice-Principal of Moore College, 148
    "Vision for Growth" initiative, 174
Robinson, Gene, 223, 257
Robinson, John A.T. (*Honest to God*), 101, 133
Robinson, Marie Taubmann, 148
Robinson, Richard Bradley, 38–39, 112, 143
Rodgers, John, 223

Rodgers, Margaret, 103, 122, 157n43, 267–68
Roman Catholic Church, dialogue with Anglicans, limitations, 172–73
Rosner, Brian, 248
Ross, Gertrude Marsden, 143
Runcie, Robert, 114
rural areas, and the future of Australian Anglicanism, 243
Ryle, John Charles, 141

Salvation Army, 151, 238
same-sex marriage/partnerships, 105, 117, 223, 257, 260. *See also* homosexual practice
Scandrett, Laurie, *Scandrett v Dowling* 1.01.1992, 166–67n81, 166–68
Scarfe, Janet, 168
Schleicher, Bernard, 17
Schleicher, Thelma, 43n34
School for Christian Studies (SOCS), 175
Scott, Thomas Hobbes, 14
Scottish Episcopal Church, 202
Scripture. *See* the Bible, Holy Scripture
Scripture Union (SU), 67–68
Second World War, 34, 144–45
Secretariat, Diocese of Sydney, 128
secular courts, resolution of intra-Christian conflicts, responses to, 167–68
secularization, impacts on societal behaviors, 8–9
sexual abuse, predation, 213–15, 215n104
sexual behavior, rigorous standards for in the Sydney Diocese, 106
Sharwood, Robin, 133
Shaw, F., 38
Shelley, K.N., 81
Shirriff, Phil, 255
Shore (Sydney Church of England Grammar School at North Sydney), 143–44
Short, Augustus, 56
Short, David, 233, 260
Short, Ken, 174

"Sinless Perfectionism" movement, 34, 148
Smith, Bruce, 138
Smith, Claire, 198, 203–6, 254
Smith, Thomas, 124
Smith, William Saumarez, 21–22
social justice, social welfare activities, 10, 14, 184, 196–97. *See also* Anglicare; Home Mission Society
Society for the Propagation of the Gospel (SPG), 16
Society of the Sacred Mission (SSM), 146
South Africa, Anglican churches in, 33–34, 47–49
Southern Cross
  articles about ordination of women, 160
  Gough's farewell letter, 105
  review of *A Woman's Place*, 158
  survey on church music, 99–100
  "Sydney sure to take issue with new Primate Comment" (Rogers), 267–68
  Tong letter on ordination of women, 252
  Totterdell article about computers in, 114
  "Why I am going to Israel" (Peter Jensen), 257
Sowada, Karin, 253
spiritual birth, mission, importance to the ethos of the Sydney Diocese, 184
Standing Committee (Diocese of Sydney)
  Anglican Counseling Center inquiry, 179
  and authority of parish churches, 187
  Blue Ticket election, 188
  censuring of by the General Synod, 214
  election of Rodgers to, 122
  election of women to, 122
  funds for struggling parishes, 131

INDEX   307

Goodhew's relationship with, 187, 190
and Gough's resignation, 105–6
investigation of the Anglican Counseling Center, 213–14
and Lay and Diaconal Administration, 171
meetings of, 105n107
role in Diocese administration, 128, 131
Standing Committee (General Synod), Primate's role, 129
St. Andrew's Cathedral, 21, 24, 246–47
St. Andrew's College, United Theological Faculty, 26
St. Andrew's House, 127
St. Barnabas' Broadway parish, 124–26
St. Catherine's School, Waverly, 18, 21
Stephens, Tony, 105n105
Stewart, Al, 247, 247n78
Stewart, Colleen, 164
St. John's Darlinghurst, 139–140
St. John's Parramatta, 174
St John's Shaughnessy, Vancouver, Canada, 233
St. Matthias parish, 185, 185n15, 192–93
St. Michael's Wollongong, 174
Stott, John
   Basic Christianity, 93
   candidacy for Archbishop of Sydney, 78
   at the CMS Summer Schools, 102
   on "DJ" Johnson, 40
   influence, 92n52, 228
   relationship with Loane, 92
   relationship with Phillip Jensen, 196
   Sydney University mission, 67, 92–93
   on women's ordination, 159
St Paul's College, 20
Strings, The Joy, 100
Strong, Philip, 110, 129, 148–49
St Swithun's Pymble, 42
St Thomas' Shekkipmei, Kowloon, 102
Studd, Charles T., 40
Student Christian Movement (SCM), 36

Subordination of the Son
   and Arianism, 210
   and debate about the ordination of women, 208–9
   and Loane's theology, 119
   and the role of women in the church, 158
Sugden, Chris, 258–260
Sydney Anglicanism. An Apology (Jensen), 121
Sydney Anglicanism. An Apology (Michael Jensen), 254
Sydney Anglicans (Judd and Cable), 32, 33, 128
Sydney Anglicans and the Threat to World Anglicanism (Porter), 4
Sydney Church of England Girls' Grammar School (SCEGGS), 128
Sydney Church of England Girls' Grammar School Darlinghurst (SCEGGS), 21
Sydney Church Society, 18–19
Sydney City Mission, 19
Sydney Clerical Prayer Union, 22–23
Sydney Diocesan Magazine
   articles about Mowll's travels in, 46
   on early, 72
   Mowll's monthly letter in, 44
   tribute to Dorothy Mowll, 74
Sydney Diocesan Ministry Training and Development (MT&D), Jensen's role, 194
Sydney Heresy, 209
Sydney Morning Herald
   erroneous assumptions about Christine Jensen's leadership role, 247
   publication of sermons in, 226
   regular coverage of Peter Jensen's activities, 237
Sydney Property Trust, 96n71
Sydney School of Preaching, 207
"Sydney sure to take issue with new Primate Comment" (Rogers), 267–68

Synod of the Diocese of Sydney. *See also* ordination of women
   Anglican Counseling Center inquiry, 214
   and the Australian Anglican Constitution, 64, 164–65
   cartoon criticizing, 150f
   Doctrine Commission, 163
   "The Doctrine of the Trinity and its bearing on the relationship of Men and Women," 209
   endorsement of Lay and Diaconal Administration, 171, 221, 246
   Goodhew's stand against the *APBA*, 219
   impact of the Pymble Matter, 189
   inclusion of women on, 104
   Inner City Committee, 139
   as law-making body, 153
   Marriage of Divorced Persons Ordinance 1985, 170
   Mowll's address to, 44–45
   nonfinancial support for Independent Evangelical Churches in, 243
   and the ordination of women, 156n40, 157n53, 162, 162n63, 169, 201
   and Peter Jensen's Mission, 237
   report of the Archbishop's Commission, 96
   Report on Clerical Tenure, 189
   report to on state of Evangelism in the Diocese, 138
   and retirement age for archbishops, 182n10
   Standing Committee, 105–6, 105n107, 187–88

Talbot, Edward Albert, 23–24, 26, 29–30
Tanner, Lindsay, 114–15
Tasker, Peter, 224, 231, 237, 256
Tay, Moses, 223
Taylor, H. Minton, 50, 58
I Thessalonians 5:12–13, 203
Thiering, Barbara (*A Woman's Place*), 120n48, 158

Thirty-Nine Articles of Religion, 3, 5, 9, 57–58, 85
Thomas, Griffith (*The Principles of Theology*), 24, 171–72n95
Thomas, Mesac, 22
Time magazine, on Stott, 92
I Timothy 2, 250
I Timothy 2:11–14, 159
I Timothy 2:11–15, 161, 203
I Timothy 2:12, 73, 198–99, 253–54
I Timothy 3:5, 203
Titus 2:5, 158n50
Tong, Robert, 218, 252–53, 274–75
Tooher, Jane, 250–51, 251f
Toowoon Bay Beach Mission, 67
Torrey, R.A., 37
Tractarian movement. *See* Anglo-Catholic movement, Pusey, Edward Bouverie
transubstantiation, defined, 49n55
Tress, Nora, 73–74
tribal law, 200
"Tridentine," defined, 16n15
the Trinity, doctrine of, 208–12. *See also* male headship; Subordination of the Son
The Trinity and Subordinationism: The Doctrine of God and the Contemporary Gender Debate (Giles), 208–9
Trinity College, Melbourne, 17, 151
Tyndale House, Cambridge, 40–41, 40n20

In Understanding Be Men (Hammond), 32, 209
university missions, 124–26, 139, 234
University of New South Wales, Phillip Jensen's work at, 192
University of Sydney, 20, 34

Van Culin, Sam, 142
Vietnam War, 113–14
"Vision for Growth," "Vision 2001" initiatives, 174
voluntary society principle, 184

Wade, Graham, 150f

Walker, Ronald S., 69
Wand, John William Charles, 58
Ward, Kevin (*History of Global Anglicanism*), 4
Warren, Riley, 18, 20–21
Watson, Peter, 6–7, 7f, 195–96
Weatherhead, Leslie Dixon, 93, 93n58
Wentworth, William C., 20
Wentworth-Shields, W. Francis, 24
West, J., 31
Whitgift, John, 55
Whitlam, E. Gough, 105n105, 114–15
Who's Tampering with the Trinity? An Assessment of the Subordination Debate (Erickson), 208
"Why I am going to Israel" (Peter Jensen), 257
Wilberforce, William, 13
Williams, Lukyn, 17
Williams, Rowan, 211, 257
Williamson, Paul, 248
Winter, Bruce, 40n20
A Woman's Place (Gaden, Morris, Thiering), 120n48, 158
women, lay women/women's ministry. *See also* deaconesses; Lay and Diaconal Administration; ordination of women
  and changing leadership positions, 102–4, 122
  exclusion from public ministry, 42
  and the Priscilla and Aquila Center, 250–51
  Phillip Jensen's views on, 199
  role and activities, 44, 205–6, 253
  subordination to men, 121, 209
Women, Sermons and the Bible (eds. Payne and Bolt), 254
Women and their Ministry (Giles), 122
Women's Ministry Report, 202
"Women's Witnessing Community," 154
Woodhouse, John

  and the Anglican Counseling Center investigation, 213–14
  on Moore College, 181, 248–49
  on the ordination of women, 160–62, 160n58
  Priscilla and Aquila Center, 250–51
  resignation from the Standing Committee, 214
Wood Royal Commission, 213, 215
Woods, Frank, 129–133
Woolley, John, 12–13
Word of God. *See* the Bible, Holy Scripture
World Council of Churches (WCC)
  Commission on the Life and Work of Women in the Church, 72
  establishment and purpose, 133
  Mowll as delegate to, 70
  Mowll's support for, 45–46
  roll of Evangelicals in, 134
World War I. *See* First World War
Wright, John Charles
  and the Australian Anglican Constitution, 57
  background and beliefs, 23–24
  and the chasuble controversy, 25–26
  death, succession controversy, 29
  influences and mentors, 37
  personality, leadership style, 24, 29
Wycliffe College, Toronto, 36, 40
Wylde, Thomas Lomas, 49–52

Yates, John III, 262–63
Yong Chen Fah, 232
Young, Ann, 229, 229n15
Young, Peter, 162n64
Youth Leaders' Training Course, 66
youth work. *See also* education; Katoomba CMS Summer School; Moore College
  Phillip Jensen's influence, 194
  as Sydney Diocese focus, 10
Youthworks, 223–24

www.ingramcontent.com/pod-product-compliance
Lightning Source LLC
Chambersburg PA
CBHW050621300426
44112CB00012B/1597